W. K. Kellogg Foundation Grant

# POPULATION
## QUANTITY vs. QUALITY

**a sociological examination of the causes and consequences of the population explosion**

*Shirley Foster Hartley*

PRENTICE-HALL, INC., Englewood Cliffs, New Jersey

PRENTICE-HALL SOCIOLOGY SERIES
NEIL J. SMELSER, EDITOR



ISBN: P-0-13-686600-X
C-0-13-686618-2

Library of Congress Card Catalog Number: 76-39060

10 9 8 7 6 5 4 3 2 1

PRINTED IN THE UNITED STATES OF AMERICA

*Prentice-Hall International, Inc., London*
*Prentice-Hall of Australia, Pty. Ltd., Sydney*
*Prentice-Hall of Canada, Ltd., Toronto*
*Prentice-Hall of India Private Limited, New Delhi*
*Prentice-Hall of Japan, Inc., Tokyo*

# Contents



 

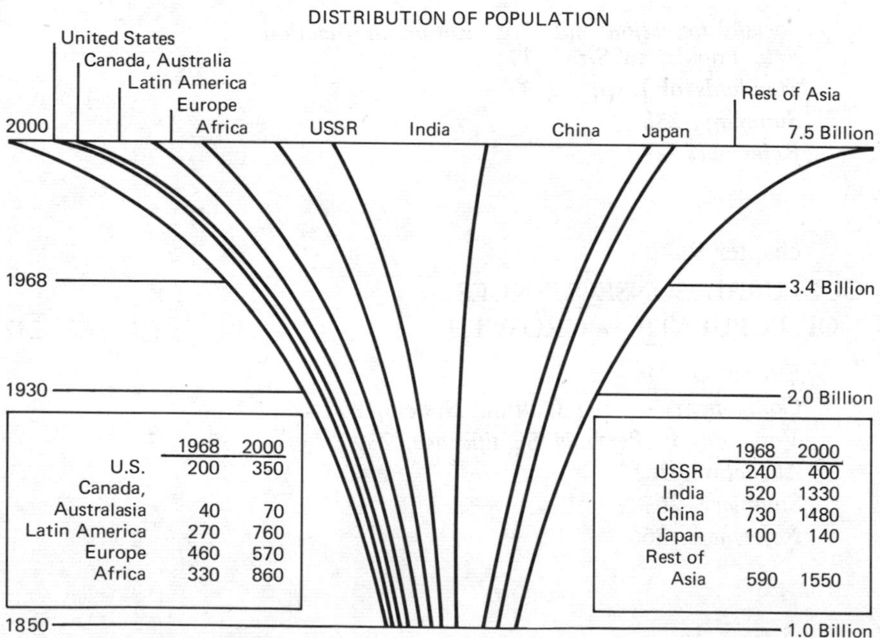


| | 1968 | 2000 |
|---|---|---|
| U.S. | 200 | 350 |
| Canada, Australasia | 40 | 70 |
| Latin America | 270 | 760 |
| Europe | 460 | 570 |
| Africa | 330 | 860 |

| | 1968 | 2000 |
|---|---|---|
| USSR | 240 | 400 |
| India | 520 | 1330 |
| China | 730 | 1480 |
| Japan | 100 | 140 |
| Rest of Asia | 590 | 1550 |

*Source:* United Nations Association of the United States of America, *World Population*. New York: UNA-USA National Policy Panel, 1969, p. 12.

*United Nations Projection with Assumption of Constant Fertility and Declining Mortality*

# Preface

An understanding of the historical causes and contemporary consequences of population growth is necessary to an understanding of most of the great world problems of the late twentieth century. This volume examines the population explosion from a sociological perspective. Two themes are simultaneously developed: one is the contrast in both the causes and the consequences of population growth for the advanced, industrialized countries versus those for the less developed nations; a second theme is that the increasing numbers of persons and the rate of population growth have been retarding worldwide efforts to improve the quality of life for all. Our inability to maximize both the quantity and the quality of human life is not merely something to worry about as we look toward the future; trade-offs have already been occurring as a result of the recent population explosion. The so-called "Development Decade" of the 1960s would have been declared a great success if population growth had not reduced or nullified the advances made in many fields.

I have emphasized the international aspects of population growth with nation by nation records of numerical increase since 1920 and projections to the year 2000. The historical growth of population in European nations was different in origin and in speed from that experienced by the less developed countries since World War II. Those initial differences lead to vastly different consequences for the two groups of nations. The multi-dimensionality of both causes and consequences will be examined in a straightforward and factual manner.

My purpose is to simplify the basic data related to population growth so that anyone, whatever his or her area of specialization, may understand the contribution of population variables to environmental, economic, social and political problems. An underlying assumption is that people everywhere share the humane goal of improving the many different aspects of life—health and vitality, housing, education, and social relationships—that make up our standard of living. A concern for the quality of human life requires an interest in the quantity of human beings.

I am hopeful that readers will be stimulated to follow this presentation with a more detailed study of population characteristics and measurements in general or specific to a nation in which an interest has been aroused. The references following each chapter provide some source materials for continued exploration. In addition, *Population Index* provides a complete and continuing bibliographic source.

Because the coverage is broad, no one claims to be an expert in all of the areas discussed. I have tried to cite some of the major contributors to each subject area and to indicate some central points of controversy. My attempt to bring a wide variety of materials together has meant that many of the particulars which fascinate those of us who continue research on population are not included.

The book begins with a brief examination of the pace of recent growth in population, and an international overview of past, present, and projected future populations for major nations and the world as a whole. Subsequent discussion of both the causes and consequences of population growth frequently separates nations into the categories "developed" and "less developed." Although differences *within* each of these two categories are great, for our purposes there are far more similarities within each category than across the division. A review of the different causes of population growth is followed by the consequences: for population density and urban-rural settlement, for food and natural resources, for economic development, for social and cultural advance, and for political relationships within and among nations. Finally, the potential impact of population theories and ideology on national policy is examined, with a detailed look at the controversy between those who would rely on family planning to halt the growth of population and those who are convinced that population control must move beyond family planning.

My intellectual debt to Kingsley Davis will be apparent throughout the manuscript. A more general debt of gratitude is owed the graduate faculty at Berkeley who have offered a model of hard work and clear exposition of their own detailed analyses and creative syntheses. In addition I want to thank those colleagues and friends who made constructive comments on an early draft of this manuscript. I remain responsible for the final product.

S. Hartley

## chapter I

# AN INTRODUCTION TO THE POPULATION EXPLOSION

*We are facing one of the great crises in the history of man. There are, almost everywhere, too many people.*

Margaret Mead (1969)

Many people in different professions have begun to recognize that there may well be too many human beings in the world. Is it possible that the dominant species has been too successful for its own good? What are the reasons for the recent explosion in human numbers, and what are the consequences for the present and future of mankind? If we value human life, it is important that we recognize the trade-offs now occurring between the quantity and the quality of life.

Population has come to be a controversial subject, with some people predicting doom and others arguing that there is nothing to worry about. Although the experts themselves often disagree, one aspect of the population explosion is noncontroversial: the world cannot support an infinite number of persons. Opinions differ as to what the upper limit on human numbers ought to be. With some knowledge of the causes and consequences of population growth, we may discuss the problem in relation to desired standards of health, nutrition, education, etc. Yet we must keep in mind that population decisions involve not just a few, but billions of persons with more or less understanding of the implications of their behavior for the future of us all.

Even if there were no population explosion, the study of population would be important for its own sake. Each country, community, school district and so forth, must be concerned with the numbers of its people and changes in population size and composition. The rapid growth of population since World War II affects every person, whether or not he recognizes the causes of increasing human numbers. According to the World Health Organization, 3.7 human beings are born every second. This works out to 221 per minute, 318,575 per day, or more than 2.2 million per week. With an average of only one death for every two and a half births, the world population, now about 3.6 billion, will number between 6 and 7 billion persons by the year 2000.

The more interested we are in planning for the future and in improving human life on earth, the more concerned we must become with population questions. One aim of this book is to describe what is known about the causes and consequences of increasing numbers of various age distributions, and of the movement (especially the urbanization) of the human population.

## *WORLD PROBLEMS*

Our world is complicated by many far-reaching problems. For many individuals and many world leaders the most important of these is the establishment and maintenance of national and international peace. On the other hand, the great mass of people around the world may be most immediately concerned with improving their own living standards and providing more adequately for the food, medical, and housing needs of their families. In many parts of the world people are demanding the extension of political freedom. An increase in political democracy and a rise in standards of living, however, require not merely literate populations, but the continued advance of education for rational action in even the most developed nations. In the less developed nations, in spite of recent increases in the *proportions* of literate persons, there is simultaneously, a *rise* in the *number* of illiterates. The population explosion, a problem in its own right, underlies and exaggerates all other problems. The relationship between uncontrolled birth rates and the possibility of setting off the nuclear weapons already on hand is of widespread concern, as Figure 1-1 implies. Nations have long used the press of population as an excuse for war. Both the press of people and the destructive capacity of our weapons are greater now than during any previous period. The recent and unprecedented population explosion forces us to consider how mankind may prevent the

*Source:* LePelley, in *The Christian Science Monitor,* June 10, 1969. Reprinted by permission from The Christian Science Monitor, © 1969 by The Christian Science Publishing Society. All rights reserved.

FIG. 1–1

*quantity* of human beings from diminishing the *quality* of human life.

The theme of quantity versus quality will be carried throughout this text. I do not want to suggest that limiting population growth will automatically raise standards of living. We must still work at improving health, nutrition, housing, education, and reducing environmental pollution. The increasing numbers of persons make the job of improving the quality of life in general, and human potential in particular, more difficult. Moreover, increasing numbers automatically reduce per capita resources and physical space. Even the most affluent countries have limited means with which to meet a proliferation of goals. With rising expectations and with rapidly increasing populations the less developed countries cannot accomplish all they would like to.

## GROWTH RATE VS. NUMBERS OVER TIME

The problem is excess population growth. The enemy is not a number, however, but a rate. According to the latest United Nations figures, the population of the world is now growing at just over 2 percent per year. Although it may seem difficult to get excited over a growth rate as small as 2 percent, let's examine that rate in the perspective of time.

### *Growth Rates*

Throughout most of human history, the population grew very slowly —that is, there were about as many deaths as births. Despite the lack of accurate census data, population experts believe that up to about 1750, population growth averaged considerably less than 0.1 percent per year. Between 1750 and 1900, population grew at about 0.5 percent per year. From 1900 to 1950 population grew at about 1.0 percent per year; from 1950 to 1960, at about 1.7 percent per year; and in the most recent decade, growth has increased to about 2 percent per year. At 2 percent per year, a number doubles every 35 years, so that by the year 2000, *if* the present rate of growth continues, the world population will be almost seven billion. Actually, the *rate* of growth has not stopped increasing. It is only by making assumptions unrelated to significant evidence that a lower rate of population growth may be projected into the future.

The 2 percent growth rate is so great that if the human race had begun with a single couple at the time of Christ, and had grown steadily at 2 percent per year since then, there would now be 20 million people for every person alive on the earth today! That would be the equivalent of 100 people per square foot of the earth's surface (Population Council, 1965). Of course, these figures are absurd—purely mathematical calculations. Yet, the computations dramatize that the world cannot sustain such a growth rate for very long. Over the long run, *either the birth rate of the world must go down, or the death rate will go up.* There are no other choices. Those who suggest that the problem might be solved by interplanetary colonization or earth satellites or ocean cities had better examine the problem in numerical terms.[1]

[1] Even the high estimate of 100,000 people living on the moon 100 years from now would equal only half of one day's population increase.

## *Numerical Growth*

On the average, about 130,000 persons were added to the world population each year for about 1500 years from the birth of Christ to the discovery of America by Columbus. But from about 1492 to 1850, approximately one million persons were added each year (see Figure 1-2). Under

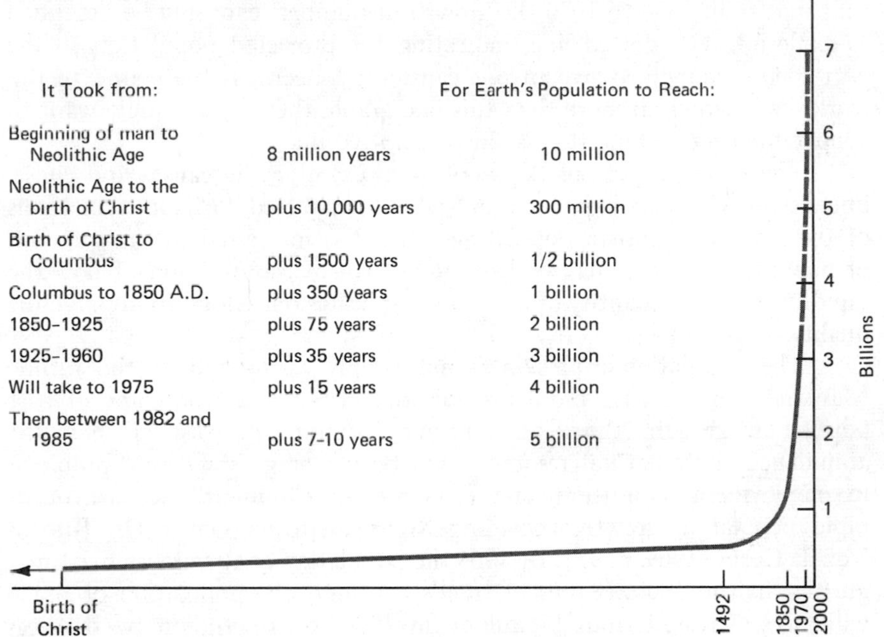


FIG. 1–2 *A Time Line of Population Increase*

those conditions, it would have taken 1000 years to add a billion persons. However, at our present rate of growth it will take less than 13 years to add a billion people to the world total.

The yearly addition in numbers continues to increase very rapidly. In 1965 an estimated 65 million persons were added; in 1970 there were about 72 million added. That means that a number equal to the total populations of England and Wales, Scotland, Ireland, Sweden, and Norway is being added to the world's population each year! In only three years the world total has increased by the number of persons alive in the United States in 1970. (The present population of the United States was actually born over an 80- to 90-year period.)

If the data are simplified to show world population in the billions (as in Figure 1-2), it is clear that it took all of human history up to about 1850 to produce a world population of one billion. It took 75 years to add the second billion and 35 years for the third billion. It is now taking about 15 years to add the fourth billion. How can one hope for the general improvement of the human condition with such staggering population increases? The time line of Figure 1-2 illustrates that from the birth of Christ to Columbus's discovery of America, population grew very slowly. From 1492 to 1850 the increase in numbers of people begins to be significant, but from 1850 to 1970 the growth in numbers can only be described as explosive. The dotted line, indicating the projected population to the year 2000 is enough to give anyone cause for concern. If the people of the world understood no more than this one graph, they would surely want to cooperate in forestalling the rise in that dotted line.

The main purpose of this book is to examine the causes and consequences of what has happened and what is expected to happen in terms of the growth of human population. I am less interested in the question of how many persons may be kept alive than in the question of how the rapidly increasing quantity of persons complicates our efforts to improve the quality of human life.

The population explosion is not simply a problem of the future. Mankind is living with problems now that are a direct outcome of past population growth. Brazil, for instance, despite its vastness and the abundance of its natural resources, has been facing "staggering problems in employment, education, and economic development" because of its rapid population growth, according to Brazilian economist Dr. Rubens Vaz da Costa (1969, p. 93). By 1965 the population of Brazil was five times greater than in 1900. If present trends continue, the population of Brazil will have increased from 17 million in 1900 to 219 million by the year 2000. Whatever problems that nation and the world face are surely multiplied by such prospects.

## *Predictions vs. Projections*

When demographers speak of future populations, they do not refer to these as "predictions" or forecasts of what will be. Instead, they "project" the population on the basis of a variety of very specific assumptions, such as (1) a continuation of present birth and death rates or (2) a 50 percent decline in birth rates between 1970 and 1990 with constant age-specific mortality. Demographers do not necessarily pretend to know which set of assumptions will be achieved. It is interesting to note that population estimates have often been far too low. During the 1940s Notestein estimated a world population of 3.3 billion by the year 2000, Clark estimated 3.5 billion by 1990, and the United Nations demographers' projection to 1980 was 3.6 billion (United Nations, 1953). However, by mid-1970 the world had already reached 3.6 billion. Clearly, variations from the assumptions underlying current projections must be anticipated as well. The United Nations demographers now compute high, medium, and low projections under three different sets of assumptions regarding births (fertility) and deaths (mortality). Six of the most recent projections of world population to the year 2000 are reproduced in Figure 1-3. Each line on the graph represents somewhat different assumptions regarding the future trends in births and deaths.

Donald Bogue (1969, p. 880) is convinced that by the 1980–1981 censuses "there should be unmistakable signs of fertility decline and slackening growth rates almost everywhere." His optimistic projection to 4.5 billion is based upon his thesis that "growth rates could well be zero almost everywhere by the year 2000" (p. 883). Details of his reasoning will be reviewed in Chapter 11. It should be noted at the start, however, that even if each couple were to have only 2 children, growth rates of the heavily "young" population of the world would continue well above zero for 70 more years.

The United Nations' low, medium, and high projections all assume some decline in mortality and fertility rates, although at different speeds of decline and at different starting dates.

A continuation of the current 2 percent rate of natural increase would lead to a world population of approximately 6.5 billion by the year 2000. The estimate with fertility kept constant and a continuing but slowing decline in mortality would produce a natural increase in excess of 2 percent per year, and a population of 7.5 billion by the year 2000. This "dismal prospect is not impossible, since fertility actually does increase as one immediate effect of industrialization under some circumstances, and one does not know how to weigh the weakening of such traditional controls as the non-remarriage of widows in India against the introduction of birth control" (Keyfitz, 1969, p. 55).

Which of these six projections is most likely to be realized? Most of us will live long enough to find out. While population specialists would overwhelmingly like to believe the Bogue projection, there are few who consider it probable. Since 37 percent of the population of the world is now under 15 years of age and less than 10 percent is over 60 years of age, the potential for births, even if controlled, remains very high.

## *CONTRASTING "DEVELOPED" AND "DEVELOPING" COUNTRIES*

Since the world's population growth is measured by the excess of births over deaths, the growth could be due to a higher birth rate, a lower

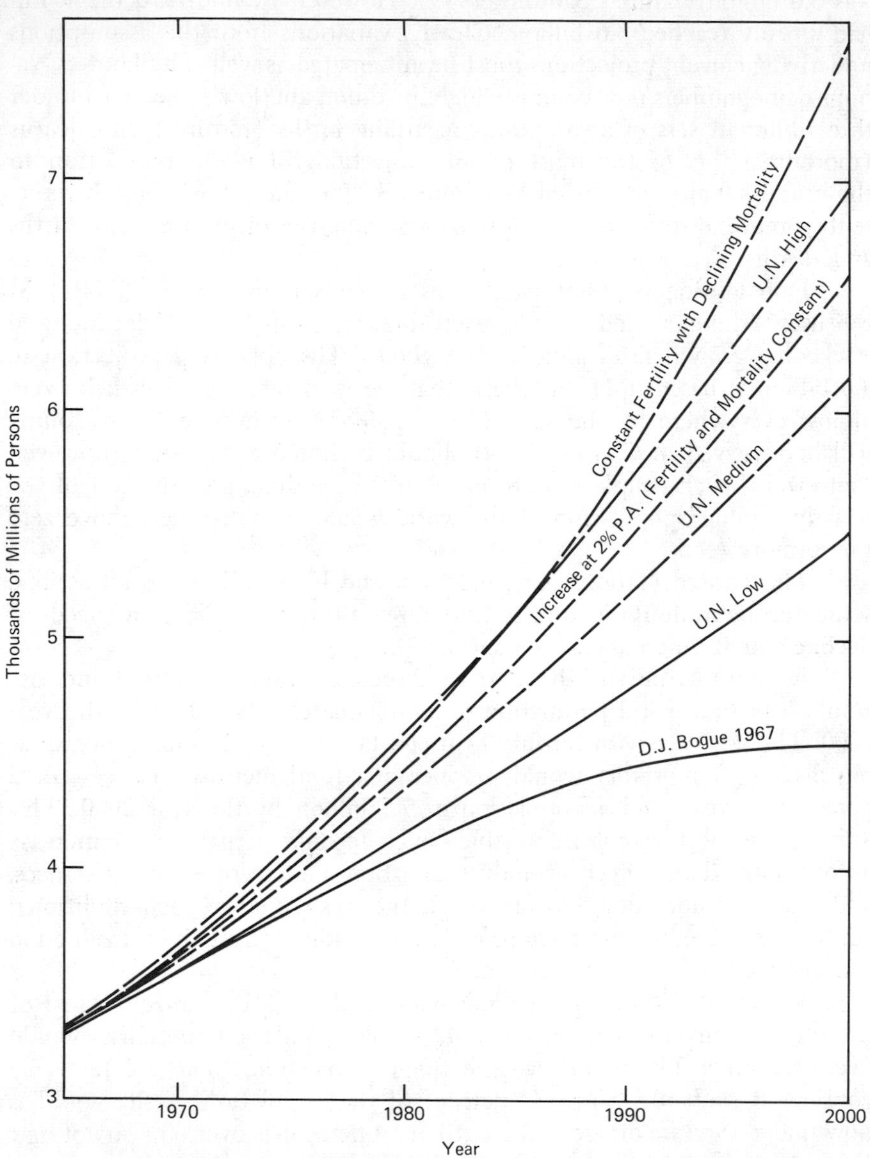


*Source:* Nathan Keyfitz, "United States and World Populations," in *Resources and Man: A Study and Recommendations,* by the Committee on Resources and Man of the Division of Earth Sciences, National Academy of Sciences, National Research Council, with the cooperation of the Division of Biology and Agriculture. San Francisco: W. H. Freeman and Company, © 1969, p. 55.

FIG. 1–3 *Six Estimates of World Population, 1965–2000*

death rate, or both. The term "population explosion" may suggest that an increase in the birth rate is at fault, but that is not the case for the world as a whole. An unprecedented decline in the death rate, especially since World War II, is the main cause of the recent rapid rise in the world's population. The recent decline in mortality is especially apparent in what are referred to as "undeveloped," "underdeveloped," "less developed," or "developing" countries. These are nations with low per capita income whose economies are based largely upon subsistence agriculture. The death rate has responded much more rapidly than the birth rate to the development and use of science and technology in such areas as improved food distribution, a more effective social organization, and the mass application of modern public health measures; vaccines, antibiotics, sulfa drugs, and especially the use of new insecticides that brought malaria under control.

Comparing both causes and consequences of population growth for the advanced and underdeveloped countries shows two distinct types of growth. Although the population growth rate for the world is about 2 percent per year, more advanced nations are growing moderately fast at 0.5 to 1 percent per year, and the less developed nations are growing very rapidly at 2.5 to 3.5 percent per year. Unfortunately, the nations growing most rapidly are those least able to afford the increase in people. Fundamentally, then, there are two types of countries in the world: (1) those with a high standard of living and low fertility and (2) those with a low standard of living and high fertility. Since death rates for both groups have been reduced, fertility becomes the main differentiating variable. Moreover, as the next chapter will demonstrate, because further reduction in the death rates in many of the underdeveloped countries can be expected, it is quite possible that rates of natural increase for these countries will continue to rise.

## *WHO CARES?*

The population of the world is growing very rapidly. One of the questions that arises in reviewing this growth is: does anybody care?

Although national political leaders have been slow to recognize—much less do anything about—the increasing numbers of their people, population specialists have long been concerned with the causes and consequences of population changes. Recently, specialists in other fields have been concerned with how population growth may influence and interfere with attempts at improving the quality of human life. The December 1968 meetings of the American Association for the Advancement of Science were devoted to examining the problems associated with population growth. Economics and nutrition specialists, brought together by the

World Affairs Council of Northern California and the American Assembly of Columbia University, meeting in the latter part of the same year, passed a resolution that recommended making use of all effective instruments of birth control, including all known methods of contraception, voluntary sterilization and abortion under proper medical controls (*Oakland Tribune,* November 25, 1968).

In his initial speech as president of the World Bank (International Bank for Reconstruction and Development), Robert McNamara (1968, p. 74) proposed that the bank "take new initiative" in a new area, "the control of population growth." Recognizing that this is a "thorny subject" which it would be "very much more convenient to leave alone," Mr. McNamara noted that rapid population increase is "one of the greatest barriers to the economic growth and social well-being of our member states."

At the International Industrial Conference in San Francisco, seven hundred of the world's leading industrialists representing 70 countries stressed rapidly increasing populations, lack of education, and a shortage of management personnel as obstacles that must be overcome if all nations are to be prosperous.

In January 1969, U Thant, Secretary General of the United Nations said:

> Population growth, particularly in the developing countries, continues rapidly—so much so that by the late 1970s the peoples of the developing world will total a third more than in the early 1960s. Due to the heavy pressures thereby exerted on the economic and social structures of the developing countries, both great and small, there exists today growing interest among the governments of the world in moderating the increase, not only in the cause of economic advancement, but for reasons of humanity: the enrichment of human life, the happiness of the peoples, and their right to decide on the number and spacing of their children. There is everincreasing realization that too rapid population growth constitutes a major obstacle to education and the promotion of the welfare of the young in general, the attainment of adequate standards of health, the chance of earning a decent living, and in many cases, even the availability of food at subsistence level. We must conclude from the demographic projections that the task of providing opportunities for the world's as yet unborn children and developing their talents and their capabilities to the full appears in a number of countries well-nigh insuperable, unless action is taken to moderate the population growth rate.

More and more professionals—zoologists, agriculturalists, economists, nutritionists, educators, as well as biologists, demographers, and sociologists—are recognizing that there can be no significant rise in the standard of living when an increase of 3 or 4 percent in gross national product is wiped out by a like increase in population. How have we reached our present state? What are the direct and implied consequences of population growth?

Can anything be done to lighten the world's population problem? These broad questions underlie the presentation in succeeding chapters.

## *PLAN OF THE BOOK*

Following a broad overview of the international data and the components of population in the various individual nations and areas of the world, a more detailed examination of the causes of the population explosion will be made. It is especially important to recognize that population growth in the industrialized countries during their period of early industrialization was of a different kind as well as far lower in quantity than the growth taking place in the underdeveloped countries of today. In the first case population growth accompanied a general rise in living standards, while the present decline in death rates has preceded and limits general improvements in living conditions for people in the less developed nations. The contrast between industrialized and underdeveloped countries will be carried throughout our inquiry into the causes and consequences of population growth.

There are a great many direct and indirect effects of rapid population growth. A review of the density studies of subhuman species may suggest a need to study how humans behave in crowded conditions. In fact, patterns of urban and rural density have different meanings for specific nations of the world and even for particular cities. Population pressures on food supplies and natural resources, as well as problems of pollution will be examined in Chapters 5 and 6.

Although population control cannot guarantee economic development, population growth is retarding economic improvement, full employment, and attempts at increasing the standards of living in many countries of the world. A variety of the social and cultural consequences of population growth will be explored in Chapters 8 and 9. Providing adequate health services, housing, recreation, and transportation, as well as basic education, is much more difficult wherever the population is increasing rapidly. As we study these factors in detail, the various political effects of population growth within countries and the tensions among the nations of the world will become more understandable.

Finally, the impact of theories and ideologies of population on national planning will be reviewed. I will want to draw a sharp distinction between the "family planning" and "population control" approaches to resolving rapid population growth. As Kingsley Davis pointed out some twenty years ago: "Even if the whole world becomes industrialized, the countries with excessive numbers will still be penalized" (Davis, 1951, p. 231). The sooner population control is widespread, the better. Since people may "plan" to have many as well as few children, the question of how to motivate couples to want fewer children must eventually be faced.

## REFERENCES

BOGUE, DONALD J. 1969. *Principles of demography*. New York: John Wiley.

DAVIS, KINGSLEY. 1951. *The population of India and Pakistan*. Princeton, New Jersey: Princeton University Press.

KEYFITZ, NATHAN. 1969. United States and world populations. In *Resources and man: A study and recommendations by the Committee on Resources And Man of the Division of Earth Sciences, National Academy of Sciences, National Research Council with the cooperation of the Division of Biology and Agriculture*, pp. 43–63. San Francisco: W. H. Freeman.

MCNAMARA, ROBERT S. 1968. "Address to the board of governors, World Bank." *Population Bulletin* 24 no. 3 (November), 69–80.

*Oakland Tribune*. 1968. All-out population curbs demanded. (November 25.)

THE POPULATION COUNCIL. 1965. *The Population Council 1952–1964: A report*. New York: The Population Council (July).

UNITED NATIONS, Department of Economic and Social Affairs. 1953. *Determinants and consequences of population trends*. New York: United Nations Population Studies no. 17, ST/SOA/Series A/17.

U THANT. 1969. An address by the Secretary General of the United Nations. (January 14.)

VAZ DA COSTA, RUBENS. 1969. "Population and Development: The Brazilian Case." *Population Bulletin* 25, no. 4 (September), 91–115.

## chapter 2

# THE INTERNATIONAL OVERVIEW

*Have you noticed meanwhile the population explosion*
*Of man on earth, the torrents of new-born babies, the*
*bursting schools? Astonishing. It saps man's dignity.*

Robinson Jeffers, poet,
in "Birth and Death" (1954)*

*Growth for growth's sake is the philosophy of*
*the cancer cell.*

Zero Population Growth

The recent rapid growth in world population has led to a present total of over 3.6 billion persons. Just as the rates of increase have recently been very different for the advanced and less developed countries, so too is the proportional share of the total world population different for the two groups. The total population of all the industrialized countries is about 1.0 billion, while the underdeveloped countries have populations totaling 2.5 billions. Since the latter group is increasing its population at a more rapid rate than the former, it becomes clear that the problems for the world in improving living standards, health, and education are increasing at the same time that there is a worldwide effort to reduce those problems.

Let us use food production as an example to dramatize the point. With tremendous effort on their own and help from the more advanced countries and the United Nations agencies, the developing nations have increased their general index (see Chapter 5) of food production from 87 to 147 in the last twenty years. (United Nations, 1969). Despite wide variation from one country to another, let's assume that continued effort from within the less developed countries and outside help will produce an

* Reprinted by permission from Robinson Jeffers, "The Beginning and The End and Other Poems," New York: Random House, Inc., © 1954.

overall additional 50 percent increase in the next twenty years. There would then be a per capita decrease in food production, unless a drastic curtailment in population growth occurs. At present rates of increase, 41 underdeveloped countries (see Table 2-1) will double their populations in the next 20 to 25 years. These are countries whose populations are presently just above the subsistence level. A 100 percent increase in the numbers of persons, coupled with an increase of only 50 percent in food production in approximately the same time period, can only worsen an already pitiful situation.

As Nathan Keyfitz (1964) suggests, objections may be made to comparisons of past food increase with expected future population increase. The possibilities and probabilities of more rapid increase in future food production will be considered in detail in Chapter 5. However, even if it were possible to increase food production to meet population increases, the problem, as Keyfitz points out, remains "unchanged except in one respect: its *scale* is increased. And in the matter of population, scale is everything. *Anything that leaves the problem unchanged except for increasing its scale is making it worse.*" (p. 158; italics mine). Twice as many persons in need of help make any resolution of their problems more difficult.

Following an attempt to conceptualize a "billion," the numerical size and proportions of world population in specific nations will be discussed. A decennial listing of national populations, back to 1920 with projections to the year 2000, allows a perspective over time. The numbers are given added meaning if one understands the population equation and its conversion to rates of growth. Birth and death rates and resulting rates of natural increase facilitate comparisons across nations and over time. This chapter will conclude by reviewing the implications of present and future age distributions of national groups and of the proportion of young dependents within different types of societies.

## *WHAT IS A BILLION?*

One difficulty in explaining the many problems associated with world population is the human inability to conceptualize billions of persons. What does the word "billion" mean? It is not easy to imagine a million anything, much less people, and a billion is a thousand million! The Population Reference Bureau has suggested that one way to visualize a billion is by the use of dots, as shown in Figure 2-1. At present population trends, shortly after the year 2000 it would take almost 20 Manhattan telephone books to carry seven billion dots. Reminding ourselves that each tiny dot represents one human being, and that the number of human beings on this finite earth is being increased by some 72 million each year,

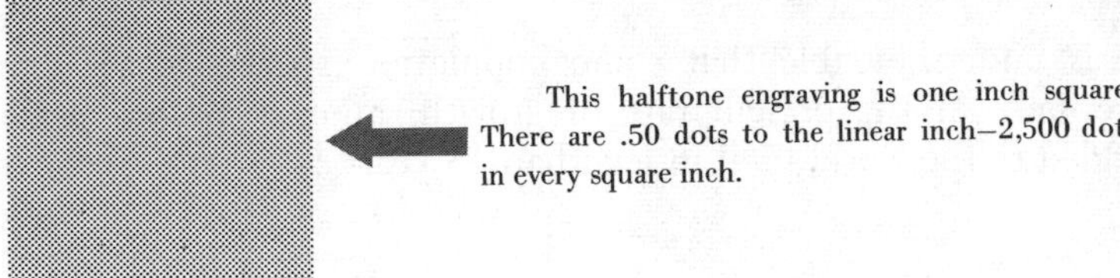

This halftone engraving is one inch square. There are .50 dots to the linear inch–2,500 dots in every square inch.

2,500 dots

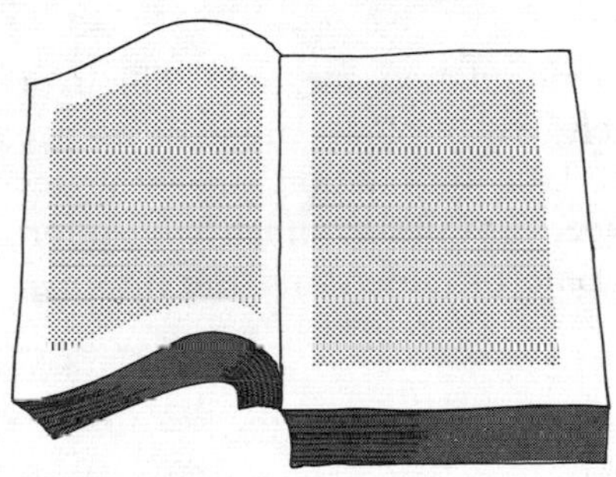

The printed area of a single page of a metropolitan telephone book is eight inches by ten inches–or 80 square inches. If the dot pattern shown above were increased to 8 X 10 inches, it would contain 200,000 dots (80 X 2,500). There would be a million dots on five such pages (5 X 200,000). A billion dots would cover 5,000 pages of 8 X 10 inch size (5 X 1,000).

200,000 dots per page

The Manhattan telephone directory has just over 1,800 pages in the 1967 edition. Thus, a billion dots would fill nearly three Manhattan telephone books.

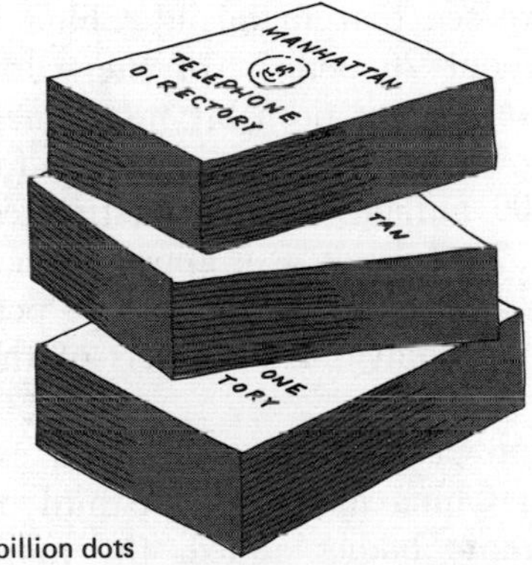


The population of the world today is 3 1/2 billion. If we allow one dot per person, this would require almost ten Manhattan telephone books.

The population of the world increased about 72 million a year–adding 360 pages of dots. At this rate, still allowing one dot per person, world population will expand to fill a dozen Manhattan telephone books by 1975.

1 billion dots

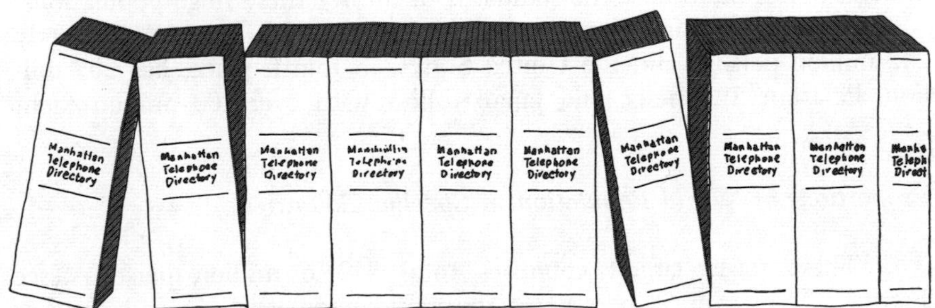


One dot for each human being on earth today.

*Source:* Population Reference Bureau, Washington, D. C.: September 1967.

FIG. 2–1 *What Is a Billion?*

it is understandable that some population specialists are crying "catastrophe." At the present rate of growth, another billion persons will be added to the world total in less than 13 years.

## *NATIONAL AND REGIONAL POPULATION ESTIMATES: 1970*

The 111 nations of the world with populations of two million or more are listed by region in Table 2-1. Each year the Population Reference Bureau produces a data sheet utilizing the best information and estimates of the United Nations. The 1970 data sheet provides so much vital information that it is worthwhile to take the time to understand the information presented.

### *The Largest Countries in Numerical Size*

Scanning column 1 of Table 2-1, we see that mainland China is the most populous country, containing about 20 percent of the world population. The 760 millions estimated moreover, is probably more *questionable* than for any other major country. The population estimates for mainland China vary between 700 and 900 million. With an estimated per capita gross national product of about $90 per year, it is apparent that large numbers alone do not contribute to, and may even retard, the possibility of an adequate standard of living for individual members of the population.

India, with an estimated 554.6 million persons, also reports an extremely low per capita income. India and China make up one-third of the population of the world. And the more bodies added, the more difficult it will be to raise the standards of life for these huge populations.

Russia, the third largest country of the world, has approximately 242 million persons and the United States, in fourth place, has 205 million. Pakistan, Indonesia, and Japan follow with over 100 million each.

### *Proportions of World Population in Specific Countries*

These seven largest countries total 2123.6 million persons (see Figure 2-2) or over 58 percent of the world population. Over 130 other countries (some of which are smaller than the 2 million required for inclusion in Table 2-1) hold the remaining 42 percent of the peoples of the earth. Only three of the most populous seven nations are relatively

TABLE 2-1 1970 World Population Data Sheet

| Region or Country | Population Estimates Mid-1970 (Millions) [a] | Births per 1,000 Population [b] | Deaths per 1,000 Population [b] | Current Rate of Population Growth | Number of Years to Double Population [e] | Infant Mortality Rate (Deaths under one year per 1000 live births) [b] | Population Under 15 Years (Percent) [c] | Population Projections to 1985 (Millions) [a] | Per Capita Gross National Product (U.S. $) [d] | Population Increase 1965–1970 (Millions) [a] |
|---|---|---|---|---|---|---|---|---|---|---|
| WORLD | 3,632 [1] | 34 | 14 | 2.0 | 35 | | 37 | 4,933 | | 343 |
| AFRICA | 344 [2] | 47 | 20 | 2.6 | 27 | | 44 | 530 | | 41 |
| Northern Africa | 87 | 47 | 16 | 3.1 | 23 | | 45 | 140 | | 12.1 |
| Algeria | 14.0 | 44 | 14 | 3.2 | 22 | | 47 | 23.9 | 250 | 2.1 |
| Morocco | 15.7 | 46 | 15 | 3.3 | 21 | 149 | 46 | 26.2 | 190 | 2.4 |
| Sudan | 15.8 | 52 | 18 | 3.2 | 22 | | 47 | 26.0 | 90 | 2.2 |
| Tunisia | 5.1 | 45 | 16 | 3.0 | 24 | | 44 | 8.3 | 210 | 0.7 |
| UAR | 33.9 | 43 | 15 | 2.8 | 25 | 117 | 43 | 52.3 | 160 | 4.4 |
| Western Africa | 101 | 49 | 23 | 2.5 | 28 | | 44 | 155 | | 11.7 |
| Dahomey | 2.7 | 54 | 26 | 2.6 | 27 | 110 | 46 | 4.1 | 80 | 0.3 |
| Ghana | 9.0 | 47 | 20 | 2.9 | 24 | 156 | 45 | 14.9 | 200 | 1.3 |
| Guinea | 3.9 | 49 | 26 | 2.3 | 31 | 216 | 44 | 5.7 | 90 | 0.4 |
| Ivory Coast | 4.3 | 50 | 25 | 2.4 | 29 | 138 | 43 | 6.4 | 230 | 0.5 |
| Mali | 5.1 | 50 | 25 | 2.4 | 29 | 120 | 46 | 7.6 | 80 | 0.6 |
| Niger | 3.8 | 52 | 25 | 2.9 | 24 | 200 | 46 | 6.2 | 70 | 0.5 |
| Nigeria | 55.1 | 50 | 25 | 2.6 | 27 | | 43 | 84.7 | 80 | 6.4 |
| Senegal | 3.9 | 46 | 22 | 2.4 | 29 | | 42 | 5.8 | 190 | 0.4 |
| Sierra Leone | 2.6 | 44 | 22 | 2.3 | 31 | 136 | | 3.9 | 140 | 0.3 |
| Upper Volta | 5.4 | 49 | 28 | 2.1 | 33 | 182 | 42 | 7.7 | 50 | 0.5 |
| Eastern Africa | 98 | 47 | 21 | 2.6 | 27 | | 44 | 149 | | 11.4 |
| Burundi | 3.6 | 46 | 26 | 2.3 | 31 | 150 | 47 | 5.3 | 50 | 0.4 |
| Ethiopia | 25.0 | | | 2.1 | 33 | | | 35.7 | 60 | 2.4 |

TABLE 2-1 (cont.)

| Region or Country | Population Estimates Mid-1970 (Millions) [a] | Births per 1,000 Population [b] | Deaths per 1,000 Population [b] | Current Rate of Population Growth | Number of Years to Double Population [e] | Infant Mortality Rate (Deaths under one year per 1,000 live births) [b] | Population Under 15 Years (Percent) [c] | Population Projections to 1985 (Millions) [a] | Per Capita Gross National Product (U.S. $) [d] | Population Increase 1965–1970 (Millions) [a] |
|---|---|---|---|---|---|---|---|---|---|---|
| Kenya | 10.9 | 50 | 20 | 3.1 | 23 | | 46 | 17.9 | 120 | 1.5 |
| Madagascar | 6.9 | 46 | 22 | 2.7 | 26 | 102 | 46 | 10.8 | 100 | 0.9 |
| Malawi | 4.4 | | | 2.5 | 28 | 148 | 45 | 6.8 | 60 | 0.5 |
| Mozambique * | 7.7 | 47 | | 2.1 | 33 | | | 11.1 | 180 | 0.7 |
| Rwanda | 3.6 | 52 | 22 | 2.9 | 24 | 137 | | 5.7 | 60 | 0.5 |
| Somalia | 2.8 | | | 2.4 | 29 | | | 4.2 | 50 | 0.3 |
| Southern Rhodesia * | 5.0 | 48 | 14 | 3.4 | 21 | 122 | 47 | 8.6 | 230 | 0.8 |
| Tanzania | 13.2 | 47 | 22 | 2.6 | 27 | 163 | 42 | 20.3 | 80 | 1.6 |
| Uganda | 8.6 | 43 | 18 | 2.6 | 27 | 160 | 41 | 13.1 | 100 | 1.0 |
| Zambia | 4.3 | 51 | 20 | 3.0 | 24 | 259 | 45 | 7.0 | 180 | 0.6 |
| Middle Africa | 36 | 46 | 23 | 2.2 | 32 | | 42 | 52 | | 3.6 |
| Angola * | 5.7 | | | 2.1 | 33 | | 42 | 8.1 | 190 | 0.5 |
| Cameroon (West) | 5.8 | 50 | 26 | 2.2 | 32 | 137 | 39 | 8.4 | 130 | 0.6 |
| Chad | 3.7 | 45 | 23 | 2.4 | 29 | 160 | 46 | 5.5 | 70 | 0.4 |
| Congo (Democratic Republic) | 17.4 | 43 | 20 | 2.2 | 32 | 104 | 42 | 25.8 | 90 | 1.8 |
| Southern Africa | 23 | 41 | 17 | 2.4 | 29 | | 40 | 34 | | 2.5 |
| South Africa | 20.1 | 40 | 16 | 2.4 | 29 | | 40 | 29.7 | 590 | 2.2 |
| ASIA | 2,056 [2] | 38 | 15 | 2.3 | 31 | | 40 | 2,874 | | 223 |
| Southwest Asia | 77 | 44 | 15 | 2.9 | 24 | | 43 | 121 | | 10.3 |
| Iraq | 9.7 | 48 | 15 | 3.4 | 21 | | 45 | 16.7 | 230 | 1.5 |
| Israel | 2.9 | 26 | 7 | 2.4 | 29 | 26 | 33 | 4.0 | 1,200 | 0.3 |
| Jordan | 2.3 | 47 | 16 | 3.3 | 21 | | 46 | 3.9 | 250 | 0.3 |
| Lebanon | 2.8 | | | 3.0 | 24 | | | 4.3 | 520 | 0.4 |

| | | | | | | | | | | |
|---|---|---|---|---|---|---|---|---|---|---|
| Saudi Arabia | 7.7 | | | 2.8 | 25 | | | 12.2 | 350 | 1.0 |
| Syria | 6.2 | 47 | 15 | 3.3 | 21 | | 46 | 10.5 | 180 | 0.9 |
| Turkey | 35.6 | 43 | 16 | 2.7 | 26 | 155 | 44 | 52.8 | 290 | 4.4 |
| Yemen | 5.7 | | | 2.8 | 25 | | | 9.1 | 70 | 0.7 |
| Middle South Asia | 762 | 44 | 16 | 2.7 | 26 | | 43 | 1,137 | | 96.9 |
| Afghanistan | 17.0 | | | 2.5 | 28 | | | 25.0 | 70 | 1.9 |
| Ceylon | 12.6 | 32 | 8 | 2.4 | 29 | 53 | 41 | 17.7 | 160 | 1.4 |
| India | 554.6 | 42 | 17 | 2.6 | 27 | 139 | 41 | 807.6 | 90 | 67.9 |
| Iran | 28.4 | 48 | 18 | 3.0 | 24 | | 46 | 45.0 | 280 | 3.8 |
| Nepal | 11.2 | 41 | 21 | 2.2 | 32 | | 40 | 15.8 | 70 | 1.2 |
| Pakistan | 136.9 | 50 | 18 | 3.3 | 21 | 142 | 45 | 224.2 | 90 | 20.6 |
| Southeast Asia | 287 | 43 | 15 | 2.8 | 25 | | 44 | 434 | | 37.6 |
| Burma | 27.7 | | | 2.3 | 31 | | 40 | 39.2 | 70 | 3.0 |
| Cambodia | 7.1 | 50 | 20 | 3.0 | 24 | 127 | 44 | 11.3 | 130 | 1.0 |
| Indonesia | 121.2 | 49 | 21 | 2.9 | 24 | 125 | 42 | 183.8 | 100 | 16.3 |
| Laos | 3.0 | 42 | 17 | 2.5 | 28 | | | 4.4 | 90 | 0.4 |
| Malaysia (East and West) | 10.8 | 35 | 8 | 2.8 | 25 | 48 | 44 | 16.4 | 290 | 1.4 |
| Philippines | 38.1 | 50 | | 3.4 | 21 | 72 | 47 | 64.0 | 180 | 5.8 |
| Singapore | 2.1 | 25 | 6 | 2.4 | 29 | 25 | 43 | 3.0 | 600 | 0.2 |
| Thailand | 36.2 | 46 | 13 | 3.3 | 21 | | 43 | 57.7 | 130 | 5.4 |
| North Vietnam | 21.2 | | | 2.1 | 33 | | | 28.2 | 100 | 2.2 |
| South Vietnam | 18.0 | | | 2.1 | 33 | | | 23.9 | 120 | 1.8 |
| East Asia | 930 | 30 | 13 | 1.8 | 39 | | 36 | 1,182 | | 78.1 |
| China (Mainland) | 759.6 | 34 | 15 | 1.8 | 39 | | | 964.6 | 90 | 64.6 |
| China (Taiwan) | 14.0 | 29 | 6 | 2.3 | 31 | 21 | 44 | 19.4 | 250 | 1.6 |
| Hong Kong * | 4.2 | 21 | 5 | 2.5 | 28 | 23 | 40 | 6.0 | 620 | 0.5 |
| Japan | 103.5 | 19 | 7 | 1.1 | 63 | 15 | 25 | 121.3 | 1,000 | 5.5 |
| Korea (North) | 13.9 | 39 | 11 | 2.8 | 25 | | | 20.7 | 230 | 1.8 |
| Korea (South) | 32.1 | 36 | 11 | 2.5 | 28 | | 42 | 45.9 | 160 | 3.7 |
| NORTHERN AMERICA | 282 [2] | 18 | 9 | 1.1 | 63 | | 30 | 280 | | 13.2 |
| Canada | 21.4 | 17.7 | 7.4 | 1.7 | 41 | 22.0 | 33 | 27.3 | 2,380 | 1.8 |
| United States [3] | 205.2 | 17.6 | 9.6 | 1.0 | 70 | 21.2 | 30 | 241.7 | 3,670 | 11.4 |

TABLE 2-1 (cont.)

| Region or Country | Population Estimates Mid-1970 (Millions) [a] | Births per 1,000 Population [b] | Deaths per 1,000 Population [b] | Current Rate of Population Growth | Number of Years to Double Population [e] | Infant Mortality Rate (Deaths under one year per 1,000 live births) [b] | Population Under 15 Years (Percent) [c] | Population Projections to 1985 (Millions) [a] | Per Capita Gross National Product (U.S. $) [d] | Population Increase 1965–1970 (Millions) [a] |
|---|---|---|---|---|---|---|---|---|---|---|
| LATIN AMERICA | 283 [2] | 38 | 9 | 2.9 | 24 | | 42 | 435 | | 37 |
| Middle America | 67 | 43 | 9 | 3.4 | 21 | | 46 | 112 | | 10.5 |
| El Salvador | 3.4 | 48 | 13 | 3.4 | 21 | | 45 | 5.9 | 270 | 0.5 |
| Guatemala | 5.1 | 46 | 16 | 2.9 | 24 | 89 | 46 | 7.9 | 310 | 0.7 |
| Honduras | 2.7 | 49 | 16 | 3.4 | 21 | | 51 | 4.6 | 240 | 0.4 |
| Mexico | 50.7 | 44 | 10 | 3.4 | 21 | 64 | 46 | 84.4 | 490 | 8.0 |
| Nicaragua | 2.0 | 47 | 16 | 3.0 | 24 | | 48 | 3.3 | 360 | 0.3 |
| Caribbean | 26 | 35 | 11 | 2.2 | 32 | | 40 | 36 | | 2.7 |
| Cuba | 8.4 | 28 | 8 | 1.9 | 37 | 38 | 37 | 11.0 | 330 | 0.8 |
| Dominican Republic | 4.3 | 48 | 15 | 3.4 | 21 | 73 | 47 | 7.3 | 260 | 0.7 |
| Haiti | 5.2 | 45 | 20 | 2.5 | 28 | | 42 | 7.9 | 70 | 0.6 |
| Jamaica | 2.0 | 39 | 8 | 2.1 | 33 | 30 | 41 | 2.6 | 460 | 0.2 |
| Puerto Rico * | 2.8 | 25 | 6 | 1.4 | 50 | 28 | 39 | 3.4 | 1,210 | 0.2 |
| Tropical South America | 151 | 39 | 9 | 3.0 | 24 | | 43 | 236 | | 20.8 |
| Bolivia | 4.6 | 44 | 20 | 2.4 | 29 | | 44 | 6.8 | 170 | 0.5 |
| Brazil | 93.0 | 39 | 11 | 2.8 | 25 | 170 | 43 | 142.6 | 250 | 12.3 |
| Colombia | 21.4 | 44 | 11 | 3.4 | 21 | 78 | 47 | 35.6 | 300 | 3.3 |
| Ecuador | 6.1 | 47 | 13 | 3.4 | 21 | 90 | 48 | 10.1 | 210 | 1.0 |
| Peru | 13.6 | 44 | 12 | 3.1 | 23 | 62 | 45 | 21.6 | 350 | 1.9 |
| Venezuela | 10.8 | 46 | 10 | 3.4 | 21 | 46 | 46 | 17.4 | 880 | 1.6 |
| Temperate South America | 39 | 26 | 9 | 1.8 | 39 | | 33 | 51 | | 3.4 |
| Argentina | 24.3 | 22 | 8 | 1.5 | 47 | 58 | 29 | 29.6 | 800 | 1.7 |
| Chile | 9.8 | 34 | 11 | 2.3 | 31 | 100 | 40 | 13.6 | 470 | 1.1 |
| Paraguay | 2.4 | 45 | 12 | 3.4 | 21 | 52 | 45 | 4.1 | 220 | 0.4 |
| Uruguay | 2.9 | 24 | 9 | 1.2 | 58 | 43 | 28 | 3.4 | 550 | 0.2 |

| | | | | | | | | | | |
|---|---|---|---|---|---|---|---|---|---|---|
| EUROPE | 462 [2] | 18 | 10 | 0.8 | 88 | | 25 | 515 | | 18 |
| Northern Europe | 81 | 18 | 11 | 0.6 | 117 | | 24 | 90 | | 2.3 |
| Denmark | 4.9 | 16.8 | 9.7 | 0.8 | 88 | 15.8 | 24 | 5.5 | 1,950 | 0.2 |
| Finland | 4.7 | 16.0 | 9.6 | 0.4 | 175 | 14.0 | 27 | 5.0 | 1,660 | 0.1 |
| Ireland | 3.0 | 20.9 | 11.3 | 0.7 | 100 | 24.4 | 31 | 3.5 | 910 | 0.1 |
| Norway | 3.9 | 17.6 | 9.7 | 0.9 | 78 | 12.8 | 25 | 4.5 | 1,860 | 0.2 |
| Sweden | 8.0 | 14.3 | 10.4 | 0.8 | 88 | 12.9 | 21 | 8.8 | 2,500 | 0.3 |
| United Kingdom | 56.0 | 17.1 | 11.9 | 0.5 | 140 | 18.8 | 23 | 61.8 | 1,700 | 1.4 |
| Western Europe | 149 | 17 | 11 | 0.8 | 88 | | 24 | 163 | | 5.5 |
| Austria | 7.4 | 17.2 | 13.1 | 0.4 | 175 | 25.5 | 24 | 8.0 | 1,210 | 0.2 |
| Belguim | 9.7 | 14.8 | 12.8 | 0.4 | 175 | 22.9 | 24 | 10.4 | 1,740 | 0.2 |
| France | 51.1 | 16.8 | 11.0 | 0.8 | 88 | 20.4 | 25 | 57.6 | 1,950 | 2.4 |
| West Germany | 58.6 | 19.7 | 11.9 | 0.6 | 117 | 22.8 | 23 | 62.3 | 1,750 | 1.7 |
| Netherlands | 13.0 | 13.6 | 8.2 | 1.1 | 63 | 13.6 | 28 | 15.3 | 1,520 | 0.7 |
| Switzerland | 6.3 | 17.1 | 9.3 | 1.1 | 63 | 16.1 | 23 | 7.4 | 2,310 | 0.3 |
| Eastern Europe | 104 | 17 | 10 | 0.8 | 88 | | 25 | 116 | | 4.0 |
| Bulgaria | 8.5 | 15.9 | 8.6 | 0.8 | 88 | 28.3 | 24 | 9.4 | 690 | 0.3 |
| Czechoslovakia | 14.7 | 14.9 | 10.7 | 0.7 | 100 | 22.1 | 25 | 16.2 | 1,110 | 0.5 |
| East Germany | 16.2 | 14.3 | 14.3 | 0.3 | 233 | 20.4 | 22 | 16.9 | 1,300 | 0.2 |
| Hungary | 10.3 | 15.1 | 11.2 | 0.4 | 175 | 35.8 | 23 | 11.0 | 900 | 0.1 |
| Poland | 33.0 | 16.2 | 7.6 | 0.9 | 78 | 33.4 | 30 | 38.2 | 780 | 1.5 |
| Romania | 20.3 | 26.3 | 9.6 | 1.3 | 54 | 59.5 | 26 | 23.3 | 720 | 1.3 |
| Southern Europe | 128 | 19 | 9 | 0.9 | 78 | | 27 | 146 | | 5.7 |
| Albania | 2.2 | 35.6 | 8.0 | 2.7 | 26 | 86.8 | | 3.3 | 320 | 0.3 |
| Greece | 8.9 | 18.2 | 8.3 | 0.8 | 88 | 34.4 | 25 | 9.7 | 700 | 0.3 |
| Italy | 53.7 | 17.6 | 10.1 | 0.8 | 88 | 32.8 | 24 | 60.0 | 1,120 | 2.1 |
| Portugal | 9.6 | 20.5 | 10.0 | 0.7 | 100 | 59.2 | 29 | 10.7 | 420 | 0.3 |
| Spain | 33.2 | 20.5 | 8.7 | 1.0 | 70 | 32.0 | 27 | 38.1 | 680 | 1.6 |
| Yugoslavia | 20.6 | 18.9 | 8.6 | 1.1 | 63 | 61.4 | 30 | 23.8 | 530 | 1.1 |
| U.S.S.R. | 242.6 | 17.9 | 7.7 | 1.0 | 70 | 26.5 | 28 | 286.9 | 970 | 12.1 |
| Oceania | 19 [2] | 25 | 10 | 2.0 | 35 | | 32 | 27 | | 2.0 |
| Australia | 12.5 | 20.0 | 9.1 | 1.9 | 37 | 18.3 | 29 | 17.0 | 1,970 | 1.1 |
| New Zealand | 2.9 | 22.6 | 8.9 | 1.7 | 41 | 18.7 | 33 | 3.8 | 1,890 | 0.2 |

TABLE 2-1 (*cont.*)

WORLD AND REGIONAL POPULATION (*Millions*)

| | *World* | *Africa* | *Asia* | *North America* | *Latin America* | *Europe* | *Oceania* | USSR |
|---|---|---|---|---|---|---|---|---|
| Mid-1970 | 3,632 | 344 | 2,056 | 228 | 283 | 462 | 19 | 243 |
| 2000 Projections, U.N. Constant Fertility | 7,522 | 860 | 4,513 | 388 | 756 | 571 | 33 | 402 |
| 2000 Projections, U.N. Medium Estimate | 6,130 | 768 | 3,458 | 354 | 638 | 527 | 32 | 353 |

[a] Estimates from United Nations. *World Population Prospects, 1965–85, As Assessed in 1968,* United Nations Population Division Working Paper No. 30, December 1969.

[b] Latest available year. Except for North American rates computed by PRB, world and regional estimates are derived from *World Population Prospects* (see footnote [a]). The country estimates are essentially those available as of October 1969 in United Nations *Population and Vital Statistics Report*, Series A, Vol. XXI, No. 4, with some adjustments which were necessary in view of the deficiency of registration in some countries.

[c] Latest available year. Derived from *World Population Prospects* (see footnote [a]) and United Nations *Demographic Yearbook, 1967.*

[d] 1967 data supplied by the International Bank for Reconstruction and Development.

[e] Assuming continued growth at current annual rate.

* Non-sovereign country.

[1] Total reflects United Nations adjustments of discrepancies in international migration data.

[2] Regional population totals take into account small areas not listed on the Data Sheet.

[3] U.S. figures are based on data from the U.S. Bureau of the Census and the National Center for Health Statistics. The total mid-year population has not been adjusted to accommodate the estimated 5.7 million "undercount" of the U.S. population in the 1960 census.

*Note:* In general, for many of the developing countries, the demographic data including total population, age reporting and vital rates are subject to deficiencies of varying degrees. In some cases, the data are estimates of the United Nations Secretariat.

*Source:* Population Reference Bureau, Washington, D.C., April 1970.

developed and, of these, only the United States reports per capita gross national product of well over $1000 per person.

As is shown in Figure 2-2, the 23 countries with populations of over 25 million altogether contain 2.83 billion persons or 78 percent of the world's people. The remaining 88 countries listed in Table 2-1, with populations between 2 million and 25 million, make up only 21 percent

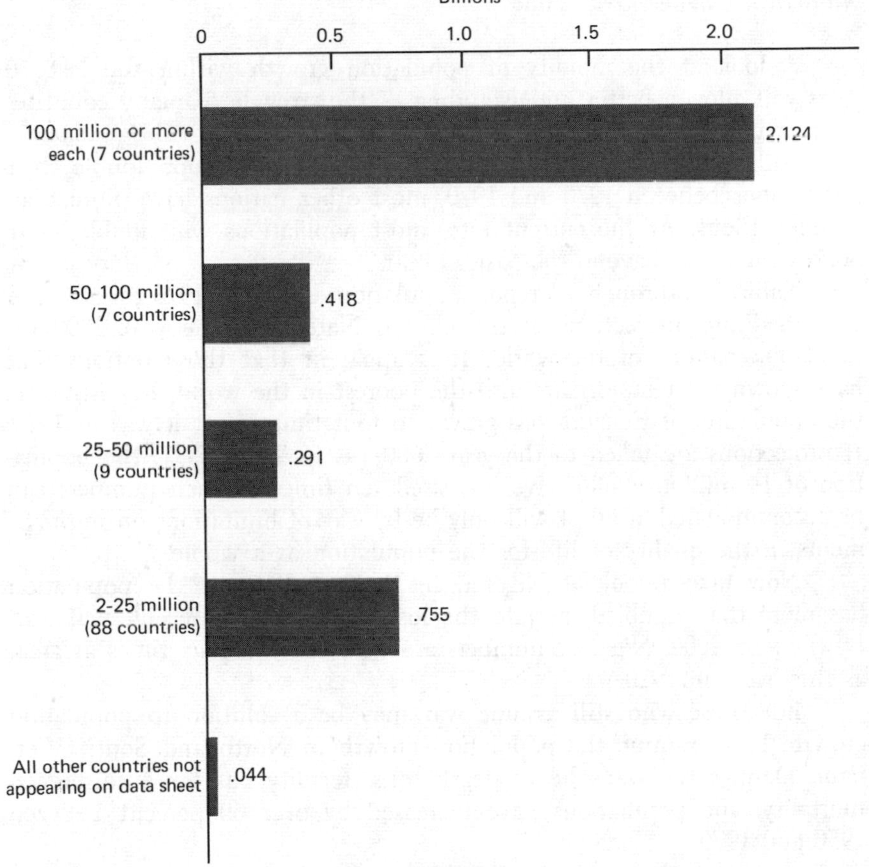


FIG. 2–2 *Distribution of World Population—1970 (Computations from Table 2–1)*

of the world's population. Over 30 other countries not listed, which have populations of less than two million, comprise about one percent of the world's total.

Because so many nations have small populations, one might assume that population problems are limited to a relatively few countries of the world. This is not true, since rates of population growth are more significant measures than are absolute numbers. In fact, most of the smaller countries face the same population problems as the larger ones, especially in having difficulty providing food, housing, and an improved standard of life for their ever-increasing inhabitants.

*Numerical Change Over Time*

A look at the rapidity of population growth within the last 50 years will allow a better understanding of the struggle so many countries are currently undergoing.

Although China and the European countries did not double their populations between 1920 and 1970, most other nations have more than doubled theirs. At the current rate, most populations will double more rapidly than they have in the past 50 years.

Tables 2-2 through 2-5 report population data from 1920 to 1970 and the "medium" projections of the United Nations to the year 2000 for the larger nations of the world. It is apparent that those nations that have grown most rapidly are also the poorest in the world. For instance, the population of Ecuador has grown to four times what it was in 1920. If projections are taken to the year 2000 (as in Table 2-3), the population of 14 million would have increased ten times. If such numbers can be accommodated at all, it will only be by way of limitations on improvements in the quality of life for the population as a whole.

Now take a look at Nigeria. In the last 50 years the population has more than doubled, despite the loss of life in the recent civil war. By the year 2000, Nigeria's numbers are expected to be six times as great as they were in 1920.

For those who still assume war may be a solution to population growth, let's examine the population growth in North and South Vietnam. Despite the war's heavy death tolls, fertility has far outdistanced mortality, and populations have increased by over 60 percent between 1950 and 1970.

Even though atomic war would dramatically increase the mortality of persons in the nations involved, war is not an acceptable solution to population growth. It would be far less painful in the long run to concentrate on reducing fertility than to wait for, or promote, an increase in mortality.

Nations trying to industrialize, democratize, educate and otherwise improve the lives of their people are strangling themselves with the rising scale of the problems they hope to solve. Egypt provides a case in point. In 1960, eight years after the ouster of the old monarchy, the Egyptians numbered barely twice as many as in 1920. Recent growth has been more

*TABLE 2-2 Decennial Changes in the Populations of Major African Countries from 1920 to 2000*

| *Regions and Countries* | *1920* | *1930* | *1940* | *1950* | *1960* | *1970* | *1980* | *1990* | *2000* |
|---|---|---|---|---|---|---|---|---|---|
| Western Africa | | | | | millions | | | | |
| Nigeria | 23.2 | 27.9 | 33.7 | 39.2 | 50.0 | 55.1 | 73.1 | 98.5 | 135.2 |
| Ghana | | | | | 6.7 | 9.0 | 11.9 | 16.1 | 22.1 |
| Upper Volta | | | | | 4.3 | 5.4 | 7.2 | 9.7 | 13.3 |
| Mali | | | | | 4.1 | 5.1 | 6.8 | 9.1 | 12.5 |
| Eastern Africa | | | | | | | | | |
| Ethiopia | 10.7 | 12.3 | 14.4 | 16.7 | 20.0 | 25.0 | 31.1 | 39.4 | 50.7 |
| Tanganyika [a] | | | | | 9.2 | 13.2 | 16.4 | 20.8 | 26.7 |
| Kenya | | | | | 8.1 | 10.9 | 13.6 | 17.2 | 22.1 |
| Uganda | | | | | 6.7 | 8.6 | 10.7 | 13.6 | 17.4 |
| Mozambique | | | | | 6.5 | 7.7 | 9.6 | 12.2 | 15.6 |
| Madagascar | | | | | 5.4 | 6.7 | 8.6 | 10.9 | 14.0 |
| Rhodesia | | | | | 3.6 | 5.0 | 6.2 | 7.9 | 10.1 |
| Nyasaland (now Malawi) | | | | | 3.5 | 4.4 | 5.5 | 7.0 | 8.9 |
| Northern Rhodesia (now Zambia) | | | | | 3.2 | 4.3 | 5.4 | 6.8 | 8.7 |
| Middle Africa | | | | | | | | | |
| Dem. Rep. of Congo | 10.0 | 10.5 | 11.5 | 12.5 | 14.1 | 17.4 | 21.2 | 26.5 | 33.7 |
| Angola | | | | | 4.6 | 5.7 | 7.0 | 8.7 | 11.1 |
| Cameroon (W) | | | | | 4.1 | 5.8 | 7.1 | 8.8 | 11.2 |
| Northern Africa | | | | | | | | | |
| UAR (Egypt) | 13.3 | 14.8 | 16.9 | 20.4 | 26.0 | 33.9 | 45.5 | 59.6 | 75.1 |
| Sudan | 6.8 | 7.5 | 8.5 | 9.8 | 11.8 | 15.8 | 20.2 | 26.5 | 33.4 |
| Morocco | 6.3 | 7.0 | 7.8 | 8.9 | 11.6 | 15.2 | 20.1 | 26.3 | 33.1 |
| Algeria | 5.8 | 6.5 | 7.6 | 8.8 | 11.0 | 14.0 | 18.8 | 24.6 | 31.0 |
| Tunisia | 2.1 | 2.4 | 2.9 | 3.6 | 4.2 | 5.1 | 6.8 | 9.0 | 11.3 |
| Southern Africa | | | | | | | | | |
| South Africa | 6.8 | 8.5 | 10.4 | 12.4 | 15.8 | 20.1 | 26.2 | 34.7 | 45.0 |

[a] Merged with Zanzibar to form the United Republic of Tanzania.

*Sources:* Data for 1920–1960: United Nations, Bureau of Social Affairs, (1966), *World Population Prospects, as Assessed in 1963*, United Nations Documents ST/SOA/ Series A/41, New York, Table A3.8. Data for 1970: Table 2-1. Data for 1980–2000: Projections on the basis of "medium" estimates of decennial rates of increase for major areas and regions of the world as reported in United Nations (1966), Table A3.6.

rapid. In fact, during the time required for construction of the Aswan Dam, population increase had already nullified any per capita advantage derived from the additional irrigated acreage. This is true even though the new acreage is counted at two crops per year. Furthermore, although increasing the tilled acreage, the Aswan Dam will hold back the flooding and eventually fill its lake with silt. For thousands of years, with each flooding of the Nile, the silt deposited by the floodwaters enriched the land and kept productivity high. Now the new Aswan Dam, in which so much of the hope of the people has lain, is finished, but the population has not ceased growing. By the year 2000 it is expected that there will be about three times as many Egyptians as in 1960, almost six times as

FIG. 2–3 *World Map, 1971*

U. S. S. R.
MONGOLIA
TURKEY
SYR.
LEB.
IRAQ
ISRAEL
JORDAN
AFGHANISTAN
IRAN
PAKISTAN
SIKKIM
CHINA
NEPAL
BHUTAN
N.
KOREA
S.
JAPAN
Pacific Ocean
U.A.R. (EGYPT)
KUWAIT
TRUCIAL OMAN
SAUDI ARABIA
MUSCAT OMAN
DHOFAR
INDIA
BANGLADESH
BURMA
LAOS
N. VIET NAM
THAILAND
S. VIETNAM
CAMBODIA
PHILIPPINES
YEMEN
SOUTH YEMEN
SUDAN
FR. T. OF A.& I.
ETHIOPIA
SOMALIA
CEYLON
MALAYSIA
UGANDA
KENYA
RW.
BU.
SINGAPORE
INDONESIA
NEW GUINEA
PAPUA
TIMOR
TANZANIA
ZAMBIA
MALAWI
Indian Ocean
RHOD.
MOZAMB.
MALAGASY REP.
AUSTRALIA
SWAZILD.
LESOTHO
North Sea
SWEDEN
DENMARK
IRELAND
UNITED KINGDOM
NETHERLANDS
Baltic Sea
U.S.S.R.
NEW ZEALAND
Atlantic Ocean
BELGIUM
LUXEMBOURG
EAST G.
WEST GERMANY
POLAND
FRANCE
CZECHOSLOVAKIA
SWITZERLAND
AUSTRIA
HUNGARY
YUGOSLAVIA
ROMANIA
Adriatic Sea
Black Sea
PORTUGAL
SPAIN
BULGARIA
ALBANIA
ITALY
TURKEY
GREECE
Mediterranean Sea
MOROCCO
ALGERIA
TUNISIA
MALTA
CYPRUS

*TABLE 2-3 Decennial Changes in the Populations of Major American Countries and Oceania from 1920 to 2000*

| *Regions and Countries* | *1920* | *1930* | *1940* | *1950* | *1960* | *1970* | *1980* | *1990* | *2000* |
|---|---|---|---|---|---|---|---|---|---|
| North America | | | | | millions | | | | |
| United States | 106.8 | 123.6 | 132.6 | 152.3 | 180.7 | 205.2 | 236.8 | 276.8 | 320.3 |
| Canada | 8.8 | 10.5 | 11.7 | 13.7 | 17.9 | 21.4 | 24.7 | 28.9 | 33.4 |
| Tropical S. America | | | | | | | | | |
| Brazil | 27.6 | 33.7 | 41.5 | 52.3 | 70.5 | 93.0 | 126.7 | 169.1 | 219.0 |
| Colombia | 6.1 | 7.3 | 9.1 | 11.7 | 15.5 | 21.4 | 29.1 | 38.9 | 50.4 |
| Peru | 5.3 | 5.8 | 6.8 | 8.1 | 10.2 | 13.6 | 18.5 | 24.7 | 32.0 |
| Venezuela | 2.4 | 3.0 | 3.7 | 5.0 | 7.4 | 10.8 | 14.7 | 19.6 | 25.4 |
| Ecuador | 1.4 | 2.1 | 2.5 | 3.3 | 4.4 | 6.1 | 8.3 | 11.1 | 14.1 |
| Bolivia | 1.9 | 2.2 | 2.5 | 3.0 | 3.7 | 4.6 | 6.3 | 8.4 | 10.9 |
| Middle America | | | | | | | | | |
| Mexico | 14.5 | 16.6 | 19.8 | 25.8 | 35.0 | 50.7 | 71.0 | 97.8 | 130.2 |
| Guatemala | 1.5 | 1.8 | 2.2 | 2.8 | 3.8 | 5.1 | 7.1 | 9.8 | 13.1 |
| Temperate S. America | | | | | | | | | |
| Argentina | 8.9 | 11.9 | 14.2 | 17.2 | 21.0 | 24.3 | 28.6 | 32.9 | 37.4 |
| Chile | 3.8 | 4.4 | 5.1 | 6.1 | 7.6 | 9.8 | 11.5 | 13.3 | 15.1 |
| Carribbean | | | | | | | | | |
| Cuba | 3.0 | 3.8 | 4.6 | 5.5 | 6.8 | 8.4 | 10.6 | 13.3 | 16.4 |
| Haiti | 2.1 | 2.4 | 2.8 | 3.4 | 4.1 | 5.2 | 6.6 | 8.2 | 10.1 |
| Dominican Repub. | 1.1 | 1.4 | 1.8 | 2.2 | 3.0 | 4.3 | 5.4 | 6.8 | 8.4 |
| Oceania | | | | | | | | | |
| Australia | 5.4 | 6.5 | 7.1 | 8.2 | 10.3 | 12.5 | 14.8 | 17.6 | 20.4 |
| New Zealand | 1.2 | 1.5 | 1.6 | 1.9 | 2.4 | 2.9 | 3.7 | 4.4 | 5.1 |

*Sources:* See Table 2-2.

many as in 1920. Technology cannot be expected to overcome all of the problems associated with the rapid growth of population.

Each reader may follow for himself the past and projected growth of those countries in which he is most interested. The U.N. "medium" projections to the year 2000 may turn out to be too low, since they assume long-term fertility declines that have hardly begun in the less developed nations.

Since recent "high" projections of the United Nations have been consistently too low as their projected dates were reached, there is reason to suppose that the medium projections of Tables 2-2 to 2-5 may also be lower than actual populations in the future.[1]

[1] The United Nations medium projections are based upon continued, though slowing, declines in death rates and considerable declines in fertility which have not yet begun in most countries. The extent and timing of assumed declines vary for specific geographical regions of the world.

*TABLE 2-4 Decennial Changes in the Populations of Major Asian Countries from 1920 to 2000*

| *Regions and Countries* | *1920* | *1930* | *1940* | *1950* | *1960* | *1970* | *1980* | *1990* | *2000* |
|---|---|---|---|---|---|---|---|---|---|
| East Asia | | | | | millions | | | | |
| China (mainland) | 475.0 | 500.0 | 530.0 | 560.0 | 650.0 | 759.6 | 862.9 | 963.7 | 1,059.1 |
| Japan | 55.4 | 63.9 | 71.4 | 82.9 | 93.2 | 103.5 | 113.3 | 120.7 | 124.9 |
| Korea | 17.3 | 20.4 | 25.5 | 29.9 | 34.7 | 46.0 | 60.3 | 75.1 | 90.3 |
| China (Taiwan) | 3.7 | 4.6 | 6.0 | 7.6 | 10.6 | 14.0 | 18.4 | 22.9 | 27.5 |
| South Asia | | | | | | | | | |
| India | 250.5 | 278.0 | 317.0 | 359.3 | 432.8 | 554.6 | 708.2 | 873.9 | 1,038.2 |
| Pakistan | 54.0 | 60.0 | 67.5 | 75.0 | 92.6 | 136.9 | 174.8 | 215.7 | 256.3 |
| Iran | 11.0 | 12.4 | 14.0 | 16.3 | 20.2 | 28.5 | 36.4 | 44.9 | 53.4 |
| Afghanistan | 7.0 | 8.4 | 10.0 | 12.0 | 14.4 | 17.0 | 21.7 | 26.8 | 31.8 |
| Ceylon | 4.5 | 5.3 | 6.0 | 7.7 | 10.0 | 12.6 | 16.1 | 19.9 | 23.6 |
| Nepal | 5.6 | 6.3 | 7.0 | 8.0 | 9.2 | 11.2 | 14.3 | 17.7 | 21.0 |
| South East Asia | | | | | | | | | |
| Indonesia | 52.3 | 60.8 | 70.5 | 76.7 | 94.3 | 121.2 | 156.0 | 202.2 | 258.4 |
| Vietnam | 15.0 | 17.5 | 21.0 | 24.5 | 30.5 | 39.2 | 50.5 | 65.4 | 83.6 |
| Philippines | 10.6 | 13.1 | 16.5 | 20.3 | 27.4 | 38.1 | 49.0 | 63.5 | 81.2 |
| Thailand | 9.5 | 11.8 | 15.3 | 19.5 | 26.4 | 36.2 | 46.6 | 60.4 | 77.2 |
| Burma | 13.1 | 14.3 | 16.1 | 18.5 | 22.3 | 27.7 | 35.7 | 46.2 | 59.1 |
| Malaysia | 3.9 | 5.0 | 6.0 | 7.1 | 8.4 | 10.8 | 13.9 | 18.0 | 23.0 |
| Cambodia | 2.4 | 2.8 | 3.4 | 4.1 | 5.6 | 7.1 | 9.1 | 11.8 | 15.1 |
| South West Asia | | | | | | | | | |
| Turkey | 13.0 | 15.1 | 17.8 | 20.9 | 27.8 | 35.6 | 47.3 | 61.7 | 77.9 |
| Iraq | | | | | 7.0 | 9.7 | 12.9 | 16.8 | 21.2 |
| Saudi Arabia | | | | | 6.2 | 7.7 | 10.2 | 13.4 | 16.9 |
| Syria | | | | | 4.7 | 6.2 | 8.2 | 10.7 | 13.6 |
| Yemen | | | | | 4.5 | 5.7 | 7.6 | 9.9 | 12.5 |

*Sources:* See Table 2-2.

We don't know yet if the world will be able to feed the populations that are projected. We do know that the present rates of increase cannot continue indefinitely, for these would produce 56 billion persons by the year 3010. The world is probably not capable of holding that many people, but whatever the maximum holding capacity at minimum subsistence, it is limited. In the relatively near future either birth rates must come down or death rates will go up. Presently, the human species is playing a waiting game to see which will happen first.

Human beings have the means to put an end to the game and to lighten the load of life for the billions now alive. But so far there is little evidence of the understanding and commitment necessary to put an end to this greatest of all survival tests.

*TABLE 2-5 Decennial Changes in the Populations of the Larger European Countries from 1920 to 2000*

| *Regions and Countries* | *1920* | *1930* | *1940* | *1950* | *1960* | *1970* | *1980* | *1990* | *2000* |
|---|---|---|---|---|---|---|---|---|---|
| Western Europe | | | | | millions | | | | |
| Fed. Rep. of Germany | 35.0 | 37.5 | 40.6 | 47.8 | 53.2 | 58.6 | 61.9 | 65.1 | 68.4 |
| France | 38.8 | 41.2 | 41.3 | 41.7 | 45.7 | 51.1 | 54.0 | 56.8 | 59.6 |
| The Netherlands | 6.8 | 7.4 | 8.9 | 10.1 | 11.5 | 13.0 | 13.7 | 14.4 | 15.2 |
| Belguim | 7.6 | 8.1 | 8.3 | 8.6 | 9.2 | 9.7 | 10.2 | 10.8 | 11.3 |
| Austria | 6.5 | 6.7 | 6.7 | 6.9 | 7.1 | 7.4 | 7.8 | 8.2 | 8.6 |
| Switzerland | 3.9 | 4.1 | 4.2 | 4.7 | 5.4 | 6.3 | 6.7 | 7.0 | 7.4 |
| Southern Europe | | | | | | | | | |
| Italy | 37.0 | 40.3 | 43.8 | 46.6 | 49.6 | 53.7 | 56.4 | 59.2 | 61.8 |
| Spain | 21.2 | 23.4 | 25.8 | 27.9 | 30.3 | 33.2 | 35.0 | 36.8 | 38.4 |
| Yugoslavia | 12.5 | 14.4 | 16.4 | 16.3 | 18.4 | 20.6 | 21.7 | 21.8 | 22.8 |
| Portugal | 6.0 | 6.8 | 7.7 | 8.4 | 8.8 | 9.6 | 9.8 | 10.3 | 10.8 |
| Greece | 5.1 | 6.5 | 7.4 | 7.6 | 8.3 | 8.9 | 9.5 | 10.0 | 10.4 |
| Eastern Europe | | | | | | | | | |
| Poland | 27.8 | 30.5 | 32.4 | 25.0 | 29.7 | 33.0 | 35.6 | 38.1 | 40.2 |
| Romania | 12.4 | 14.2 | 15.9 | 16.1 | 18.4 | 20.3 | 21.9 | 23.4 | 25.7 |
| Dem. Rep. of Germany | 14.3 | 15.4 | 16.8 | 18.4 | 17.2 | 16.2 | 17.5 | 18.8 | 19.8 |
| Czechoslovakia | 13.0 | 14.0 | 14.7 | 12.4 | 13.7 | 14.7 | 15.9 | 17.0 | 17.9 |
| Hungary | 8.0 | 8.6 | 9.3 | 9.3 | 10.0 | 10.3 | 11.1 | 11.9 | 12.6 |
| Bulgaria | 5.1 | 6.0 | 6.7 | 7.3 | 7.9 | 8.5 | 9.3 | 10.0 | 10.6 |
| Northern Europe | | | | | | | | | |
| United Kingdom | 43.7 | 45.9 | 48.2 | 50.6 | 52.5 | 56.0 | 57.6 | 58.9 | 60.5 |
| Sweden | 5.9 | 6.1 | 6.4 | 7.0 | 7.5 | 8.0 | 8.4 | 8.6 | 8.8 |
| Denmark | 3.2 | 3.5 | 3.8 | 4.3 | 4.6 | 4.9 | 5.0 | 5.2 | 5.3 |
| Finland | 3.1 | 3.5 | 3.7 | 4.0 | 4.4 | 4.7 | 4.8 | 4.9 | 5.1 |
| Norway | 2.6 | 2.8 | 3.0 | 3.3 | 3.6 | 3.9 | 4.0 | 4.1 | 4.2 |
| USSR | 155.3 | 179.0 | 195.0 | 180.0 | 214.4 | 242.6 | 274.4 | 312.3 | 348.8 |

*Sources:* See Table 2-2.

## *THE POPULATION EQUATION*

The understanding of population change requires a review of its basic components: births, deaths, and migration.

### *In Absolute Numbers*

The decennial populations of individual nations for 1920 to the year 2000 may be examined in terms of the population equation. The data of Tables 2-2 through 2-5 are the result of what has occurred and is expected to occur with respect to births, deaths, and migration in the countries listed. For instance, the numbers of persons in any country in 1930 may be viewed as a result of the numbers in 1920 plus births during the ten-year period, minus deaths, and plus or minus migration. The process may be described as follows:

$$P_2 = P_1 + B - D \pm M$$

The population at any point in time ($P_2$) is equal to the population at an earlier time ($P_1$), plus the births (B) occurring between the two points in time, minus the deaths (D) occurring in the same period of time, plus and/or minus the external migration (M), which then becomes the net migration, that has taken place. When the formula is used to compute the population of the world as a whole, the migration factor, of course, drops off. Furthermore, because international migration has declined very greatly in recent years, it is an insignificant figure for most nations of the world.

In some of the more advanced countries, vital statistics are collected so that the governments have current monthly or yearly data on the total population. In other nations, the vital statistics on births and deaths are not uniformly registered and, therefore, the estimates of current population may be found to be inaccurate at census time. Most national governments now take a census at five or ten-year intervals. A relatively accurate census provides a corrective to incomplete vital registrations.

### *Relative Growth: Rates* [2]

To compare the population growth of various nations, the proportional change in relation to a specific beginning time is more useful than the absolute numbers of the increase. For instance, referring back to Table 2-3, notice that between 1940 and 1950 the population of Brazil increased by 10.8 million persons, while the number of residents in Colombia increased by only 2.6 million. The increased numbers were four times greater in Brazil than in Colombia. However, the relative growth in Colombia (29 percent for the decade) was greater than in Brazil (26 percent). Although it may be of some interest to know absolute numbers, it is more valuable to find the growth in relation to the size of the beginning population. The growth rate gives a better idea of the population problems encountered by a country in relation to its earlier size and facilitates population comparisons among nations.

Using Tables 2-2 to 2-5 one may compute the growth rate for any country and for any period of time by simply subtracting the numbers at

[2] These are all "crude" rates, relative to an entire population. There are many refinements on these. See Barclay (1959) or any standard population text for a review of the various types of rates and ratios and their utility in comparison to crude measures.

the earlier from those at the later date and then dividing by the numbers at the earlier date. For any single year, the rate of natural increase is found very simply by subtracting the death rate from the birth rate.[3]

Because birth and death rates provide information on the composition of current rates of natural increase in any country, referring to the data in Table 2-1 will be helpful in examining the variations in these rates.

BIRTH RATES. Births per thousand persons in each country are given in column 2 of Table 2-1. These range from a low of 14.3 in East Germany and Sweden to a high of 50 and above in many African countries, Pakistan, Cambodia, and the Philippines. That means that there are at least three times as many births per thousand people of all ages in most of Africa, Pakistan, or Cambodia as in Sweden, East Germany, or Belgium. Because of differences in age structure, the births per thousand women in the childbearing years would have an even greater differential than is exhibited in these crude birth rates.

Throughout most of history, birth rates have had to remain high because death rates were equally high. In recent years, however, death rates have been brought down even in the less developed countries.

DEATH RATES. In fact, the lowest crude death rates (see column 3 of Table 2-1) are currently reported by some of the less developed countries of the world. Because of outside help in death reduction and because of a young population, deaths of only six or seven per thousand population per year are reported by Puerto Rico, Israel, Singapore, Taiwan, Hong Kong, and Japan. The highest crude death rates are reported for African countries, but even these have been lowered, and will continue to be lowered, to a level which allows for a very rapid increase in human numbers.

RATES OF NATURAL INCREASE. Subtracting the crude death rate from the crude birth rate determines the rate of natural increase. Converting the "per thousand" population to "per hundred" determines the yearly percentage increases. For example, subtracting the crude death rate of the world (14) from the crude birth rate (34) one obtains a rate of natural increase of 20 per thousand, more commonly expressed as 2 percent increase per year. The "current rate of population growth" listed in column 4 of Table 2-1 has used the rate of natural increase adjusted for net migration for the individual countries.

For Algeria, then, the birth rate of 44 minus the death rate of 14 would produce a rate of natural increase of 3 percent. Yet the table shows a current rate of population growth of 3.2 percent, indicating that 0.2 percent of the population was added by immigration. For Jamaica, in

[3] In case the death rate should be higher than the birth rate, one would find the rate of natural *decrease*. There is no country reporting a natural decrease in recent years.

contrast, the natural increase would have been 3.1 percent but emigration has reduced the overall rate of population growth to 2.1 percent for 1970. Natural increase for the United States was 0.8 percent, but immigration brought population increase up to 1.0 percent for 1970. Few nations have such large migration effects.

### *Doubling Times*

The number of years to double a population (column 5 of Table 2-1) is computed directly from the current rate of population growth, assuming a continuance of that rate for the years involved. The assumption itself is fallacious, since no country is likely to maintain the same growth rate over any considerable period of time. Fluctuations on both sides of the given rate of growth might produce a doubled population in a similar period of time as is given. The computations show that if present trends continue, the number of persons in country X will have doubled in *x* years. At present trends, the world population will double to seven billion persons in just thirty-five years. A child born today, living 70 years, would experience a quadrupling of world population in his lifetime. Again, there is great variation from one country to another. Yet a clear distinction exists between two groups of countries: those whose populations are likely to double in less than thirty years (many of which will double in 21–25 years) and those whose populations will take more than fifty years to double at present rates. This latter group consists mainly of industrialized nations.

In other words, the least developed nations of the world—those less capable of taking care of the individuals already born—are adding human beings at a more rapid rate than are the more developed countries. One may suggest that the difference in growth rates might be due to the educational differences of the persons within the two groups of countries. But how are the less developed nations to educate a population that is increasing more rapidly than schools can be built and teachers trained? The human race has bound itself in a vicious circle from which extrication is difficult. Patterns of human reproduction, intimately linked to all other aspects of human group life, will have to be radically altered to prevent the disastrous effects of overpopulation on this planet.

## *AGE AND SEX STRUCTURE*

### *Youth Dependency*

The problem is not merely that populations will be doubled in a specific period of time under the stated assumptions, but that the added numbers of people will be helpless, dependent beings. These children require many years of care, including investments of resources that cannot be used elsewhere, before they are ready to contribute to their own support and the support of others. One indication of the current weight of youth dependency may be seen in column 7 of Table 2-1, where the proportions of national populations 14 years and under are given for those countries that report such information. In most underdeveloped countries 40 to 51 percent of the populations are in the early dependent years. The less productive the work force, the more mouths there are to be fed.

While it is true that in some agricultural nations, children provide additional labor on the farm, many of the agricultural areas of the world could be farmed more efficiently with fewer people, as will be discussed in Chapter 5.

Furthermore, not only is youth dependency greater in the less developed countries than ever before in history, but by continuous childbearing and childrearing, women are kept out of the labor force. Although women performed necessary services throughout human history to improve the life of the population, it is increasingly important that women as well as men become skilled workers, trained educators, nurses, doctors, and engineers. In order to do this they must be freed from constant childbearing. In the very nations most in need of the productive potential of each individual one finds that women's reproductive performance prevents their making other contributions.

In contrast to the 40 to 50 percent of the populations of the less developed countries in the age group under 15, the European nations report only 21 to 25 percent of their populations in the same age group. This leaves a much larger proportion of the people, including mothers, to support and educate the young. One reason that rich nations are rich, is that they remain able to develop the capacities of most of the individuals of their populations. That human development, whether through formal or informal education, occurs when other individuals are available to use their talents, training, and commitment to raising the quality of human life. The dependency ratios of youth and of the aged (in relation to the population of working age) have been computed for 22 nations (Table 8-2) and are discussed in Chapter 8.

## *Population Pyramids*

One shorthand means of dramatizing the differences in age and sex structures of populations is by use of the population pyramid (Figure 2-4). For any given nation or group, the pyramid is typically constructed as a bar graph, with males plotted to the left and females to the right of the center vertical line. (For purposes of the typology explained below,

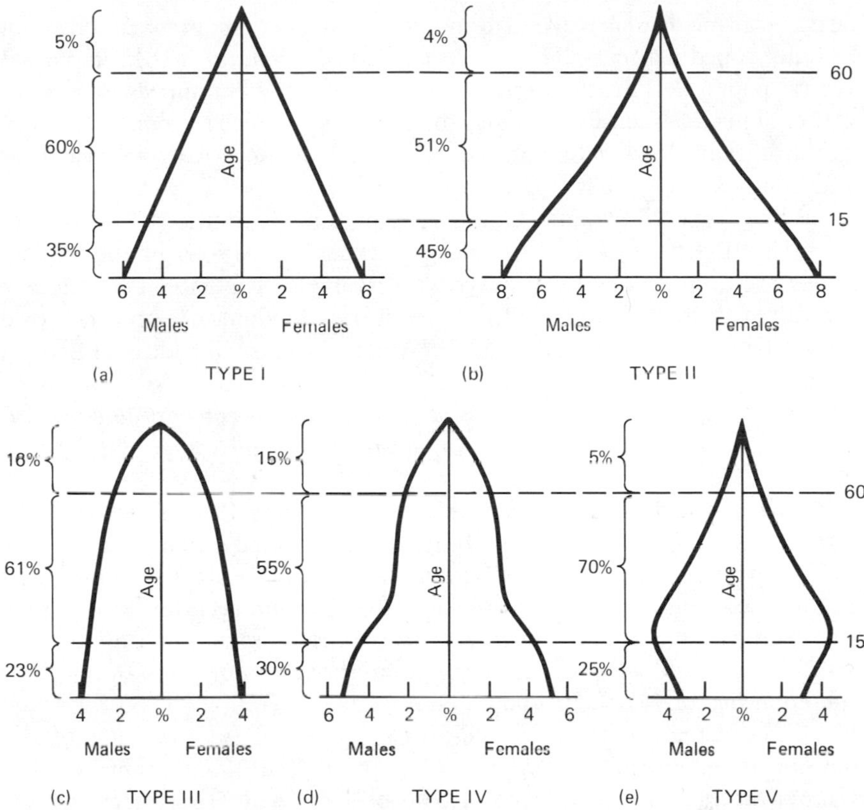


*Source:* Warren S. Thompson and David T. Lewis, *Population Problems*. New York: McGraw-Hill, 1965. Reprinted by permission.

FIG. 2–4A-E *A Typology of Population Pyramids*

the sides of the bar graph have been smoothed.) The graph may be constructed for single-year age intervals, but for simplicity is usually constructed for five-year age intervals. For comparisons between nations the *proportions* of the total population for each age group and sex are necessary. Although specific national examples are fascinating to those specifically interested, to introduce the subject of age and sex composition of population, I will point out five types of distributions that characterize nations.[4]

The first type of pyramid represents nations with very high birth and death rates. It shows the typical age and sex structure of all nations prior to the control of either deaths or births. This pattern, however, no longer represents the actual structure of any contemporary nation, since

[4] For greater detail on this subject see Thompson and Lewis (1969), Chap. 5.

death control has prevailed to a significant extent even among the less developed nations. This perfectly-shaped pyramid would represent typical population distributions of the less developed countries in 1950 or earlier. The 1951 census of India, for example, reported a population distribution that would be graphed as a Type I pyramid with a broad base and gently sloping sides.

The Type II pyramid typifies population distributions in all those countries that have 40 to 50 percent of their populations in the 14-and-under age groups. These nations have very high birth rates and recently a reduced death rate. The Type II countries predominate in the world today. They include almost all of the African, Asian, and Latin American countries. Not only is the median age of these populations low and youth dependency high, but *there is also a huge potential for continued population increase as the young population moves into the childbearing years.*

The Type III pyramid represents populations that have low birth rates as well as low death rates. Its shape is more like that of a beehive than a pyramid, with a narrow base and almost vertical sides. The graph begins to come to a point about the age-60 line when, even in the advanced countries, the age-specific death rates rise. This approximation of the beehive shape would be produced by graphing the populations of most of the countries of Northern and Western Europe (although World Wars I and II created some idiosyncrasies in the age and sex structures of the nations most directly involved). The population distributions of the United States and Canada were of the beehive variety until the postwar baby boom increased the proportion of youth, leading to a new shape.

The Type IV, or bell-shaped pyramid, is representative of the populations of the United States and Canada. Low birth and death rates were followed in the post-World War II period by relatively high fertility. Of all of the advanced countries these have the highest proportion (about 30 percent) of persons aged 14 and below. Although they have less of a youth dependency problem than the underdeveloped nations have, these countries, like those of Type II, have a potential for continued high fertility as their young people move into the childbearing ages.

Type V, another new variety, is exemplary only of Japan. The shape represents a population that, at one time, had been growing very rapidly, with high birth rates and lowered death rates as in Type II, but that later experienced a powerful and continued reduction in the birth rate. Both Types IV and V are temporary and will change as these populations move through the age structure.

Those concerned with population growth are hoping that other nations will follow the Japanese pattern; yet Japan's example remains unique in this century. Why haven't more countries followed the Japanese example of "demographic transition" from high birth and death rates to low birth and death rates? An attempt to explain and compare the different rates and causes of population change in the developed as contrasted to the less developed nations will be pursued in the next chapter.

## *SUMMARY*

Although a very few nations contain great numbers of people and therefore a large proportion of the world population, the rapid rates of growth make it difficult for even very small nations to provide for their increasing human burden.

Growth in population depends on the difference between births and deaths, with international migration a relatively insignificant consideration. When the numbers of births and/or deaths are compared with the initial population, one may obtain rates of births and deaths and the rate of natural increase. These rates facilitate comparisons over time and between geographical and political units. Although the growth rate of 2 percent per year for the world as a whole would lead to a doubling of population in 35 years, the nations of the world are actually divided into two groups: (1) the advanced industrialized countries whose growth rates are less than one percent per year, and (2) the majority of underdeveloped, impoverished nations whose populations are growing at 2½ to 3½ percent per year.

Those countries whose people are doubling their numbers in 20 to 25 years are struggling to double everything needed to support the new numbers. Their efforts to meet the minimal needs of the young and dependent additions reduces the possibility of raising standards of education, health, food, and housing for those previously in need.

The very high proportions of young people and children in the less developed nations means that: (1) the proportion of dependent persons is very high in relation to the number of productive persons; and (2) there is greater potential for continued population growth as these youth move into the childbearing ages.

The more concerned we are with raising the quality of human life, the more we must consider how the rapidly increasing quantity of persons impedes our efforts to improve living standards. We must consider how to provide adequate food and housing, clean air and water, and the education needed to develop the potentialities of each of the world's billions of persons.

## *REFERENCES*

BARCLAY, GEORGE W. 1958. *Techniques of population analysis.* New York: John Wiley.

KEYFITZ, NATHAN. 1964. Population trends in newly developing countries. *Population: The vital revolution,* ed. R. R. Freedman, pp. 149–65. Garden City, N. Y.: Doubleday; Anchor Books.

POPULATION REFERENCE BUREAU. 1970. *1970 world population data sheet.* Washington, D.C.: Population Reference Bureau.

THOMPSON, WARREN S. AND DAVID T. LEWIS. 1965. *Population problems.* New York: McGraw-Hill.

UNITED NATIONS, FOOD AND AGRICULTURE ORGANIZATION. 1969. *The state of food and agriculture, 1969.* Rome: FAO.

## chapter 3

# THE CAUSES OF THE POPULATION EXPLOSION

*Unlike plagues of the dark ages or contemporary diseases we do not understand, the modern plague of over-population is soluble by means we have discovered and with resources we possess. What is lacking is not sufficient knowledge of the solution but universal consciousness of the gravity of the problem and education of the billions who are its victims.*

Martin Luther King (1966)

In analyzing the causes of any complex social phenomenon, we must keep in mind the interdependence of various contributing factors. There are three general levels of causation relevant to population: the biological, the social-structural, and the cultural. All three interact to produce variations in population. These factors may lead to change or they may prevent change. The task then, is to look at the relative contribution of the many different factors involved in population growth.

After considering some of the biological, social-structural, and cultural aspects of differences and changes in births and deaths, we will compare the historical population growth of Europe as a whole with that of the less developed countries in recent years. In both cases mortality decline initiated the increase in population. The factors contributing to the decline in death rates will be reviewed. Finally, we will ask what factors influenced fertility change in the westernized countries and to what extent these may be at work within the less developed nations.

First, however, let us examine some general determinants of population measures.

## *LEVELS OF CAUSATION*

### *The Biological*

The most obvious biological factors relating to population are those affecting fecundity, fertility, and mortality. The capacity to reproduce is called *fecundity* while actual reproduction is called *fertility*.

Now, there is no known society in the world that maximizes fertility, or actual reproduction. The upper limits on human fecundity are, therefore, unknown. Some demographers have estimated that maximum birth rates might be 70 per 1000 population, or about twice the present crude birth rate of the world. The highest crude birth rates reported currently (for some African and Asian countries) are about 55 per 1000 population. During their entire reproductive span, healthy women may give birth to as many as 25 children. This may sound incredible to young people in the advanced countries who often assume that two to four children indicate normal human reproduction. But historically women have been known to give birth to twenty or more living children. Since it takes nine months from conception to birth, and since a woman has about 30 reproductive years, it is theoretically possible for a healthy, fecund female to average about a birth every year during that time. In fact, however, such levels of reproduction are unusual and never an average for all women in any social group.

Since no known society reproduces at these maximums, one may conclude that all societies have some means of reducing fertility from the biological maximum. In many societies, the means for limiting or increasing fertility have been ineffectual. In many less knowledgeable societies some of these methods are connected with superstition and magic and are unrelated to the biological processes of conception and birth. On the other hand, some cultural beliefs and related behaviors may reduce conception without specifically intending to do so. For instance, taboos on sexual intercourse for specified time periods (sometimes up to two or three years after the birth of a child) are an important example of such systematic, if unintentional, limitation on births (see Nag, 1962).

In some countries where significant proportions of the population in the childbearing years had been incapable of reproduction because of a high incidence of venereal disease, the sterility itself has been reduced by prompt medical attention to the disease at an early stage. In Jamaica, where there is nearly a "free sex" society and births out of wedlock average over 70 percent of all live births each year (Hartley, 1969), about one-fifth of the women over 35 reported in 1943 that they had never had a child. By the census of 1960, the proportion of childless women had declined sharply for each age group under 35. The increase in fertility is associated with the medical control of venereal disease.

Although fecundity and therefore fertility has some biological maximum, the range of variation from one society to another and from one period in time to another is largely dependent upon the social structure and the culture (see Davis and Blake, 1956; Freedman, 1961).

An increase in the body of knowledge developed by any social group is dependent upon its cultural orientation towards the scientific and rational. A discovery once made, however, may be disseminated to other populations that do not share the same level of technical knowledge. New knowledge may be used in whole, in part, or not at all. The less developed countries, for example, have been more willing to utilize biological knowledge for death control than for birth control.

BIOLOGICAL CONTROL OF DEATHS. The lowering of mortality is the major cause of the population explosion. Many factors contributed to this reduction of death rates. Prominent among these was the increased biological knowledge which permitted the use of relatively inexpensive, lifesaving public health measures. The more expensive medical techniques are very recent and in widespread use only in the most advanced countries.

As the average age of death has risen more parental units have survived through the child-producing years. Medical science has therefore improved fecundity (the biological capacity to reproduce) by lengthening life spans, improving general health, and decreasing sterility. But also, better nutrition and health (at least in the more advanced countries) have lowered the age of puberty, thereby increasing fecundity. The result has been a slight rise in fertility (or the actual production of offspring) together with a dramatic reduction of mortality in the less developed nations.

LIMITATIONS SET BY THE BIOSPHERE. Human beings exist not only within a cultural but also within a physical environment, the earth's biosphere: that relatively thin layer surrounding our global mass, capable of contributing to the support of various forms of life. The biosphere simply cannot be controlled or expanded as desired; it must be taken into consideration for the sake of the survival of the species.

Our finite world is in a delicate balance. As there is some limit to the carrying capacity of the earth, the human population cannot continue increasing indefinitely. "Open spaces" on the landscape are no longer open. They are, for the most part, used for: (1) growing food, or (2) grazing cattle, or (3) lying fallow, as in soil bank programs, to maintain the productivity of the soil, or (4) they are habitable or arable only with great difficulty. Furthermore, human beings have been polluting the environment so rapidly that there is danger of upsetting the ecological balance to such an extent that many species, including our own, may not be able to survive. (These problems will be discussed in Chapter 6.) The possibility of achieving any economy of scale either in biological advantage to the species or by increasing social organization has already passed. Further increase of the human population increases the danger of upsetting the entire ecology upon which man depends. While our capacity to manipulate environment has increased, altering the balance of nature is a danger that cannot be ignored.

### *Social Structure*

A search for the social-structural causes of human behavior is a result of the recognition that most human behavior is patterned in time and space. People relate to one another as individuals and members of groups in typically nonrandom ways. It is important to recognize how patterns of social relationships vary from one society to another. Social structure affects fertility by influencing the exposure to sexual intercouse, the exposure to conception, and the probable outcome in abortion or childbirth (Davis and Blake, 1956). While the economic and political influences on fertility will be examined in later chapters, the more direct influence of the social group comes through its organization of family relationships. The various styles of family life must surely be included among the causes of the levels and changes in population over time and for different societies. Although the basic functions of the family are much the same all over the world (Murdock, 1949), various societies differ in the many ways these family matters are handled. Who controls marriage and to what purpose? What are the economic advantages of many children or few children? How and by whom are the very young and the very old cared for? The answers to such questions have myriad implications for the population levels and changes within societies.

Kingsley Davis (1955) has suggested that in agrarian societies the nuclear family (husband, wife, and offspring) is controlled by the parents of the married couple. The young couple, whose marriage was probably arranged for by their elders, typically live with one set of parents, usually the young man's. The new couple normally live in a subservient position, dependent upon the elders for decision making and economic support.

The consequences of this joint household structure are conducive to a high rate of reproduction. The inconvenience, cost, and effort of childbearing, rather than falling directly on the parents, is shared by the members of the large household. That a newly-married couple need not establish a new residence allows marriage at an early age. These factors, together with an emphasis on kin relationships and solidarity, make the compulsion to marry a very strong one. The young wife, moving into the home of her husband, is motivated to prove her worth by producing offspring early and frequently. The man is motivated to demand offspring so that he may head a large household himself and be taken care of in his old age. Furthermore, the strict segregation of male and female roles does not allow a choice of alternatives to the normal structuring of relationships in most agrarian societies.

Even transitional societies, moving from an agricultural to an industrial economy, carry on for some time the tradition of frequent childbearing. In the extreme, these practices may prohibit or postpone per capita improvements in living standards.

Unlike the family structure in an agrarian society, the pattern of relationships in the more developed countries discourages large families. In a more industrialized society, there are fewer advantages in producing many offspring. Not only does the child no longer contribute any economic advantage or labor to the family unit, but he becomes an economic liability. It has been estimated that the average American child costs his family $17,000 to $23,000 from his birth to his eighteenth birthday. Childbirth itself has gone up in costs each year. Families are now reporting that medical and hospital fees for a single birth may cost a thousand dollars! Having many children, therefore, will multiply the problems of families who have to bear the dollar cost of childbearing and childrearing. The "advantages" of life that parents usually desire for their children often cost a great deal. The more children, the more difficult it becomes to provide some of the niceties that increase the quality of their lives.

Nevertheless, most families do not think in terms of dollar cost when they are planning the number and spacing of children. Many couples reproduce because the social definition of a "family" includes children. Hopefully, as people recognize that overpopulation is a problem, young couples will be able to choose not to have children and will be respected for their decision. People unwilling to make the emotional as well as economic commitment to childrearing would be doing their community a service to refrain from childbearing. Others may recognize that the best thing they can do for children in general is not to add any more to their number.[1]

Childrearing in advanced societies is more complex than ever before in the history of the world. The education of children no longer simply consists of having them observe mother and father at work and imitate those patterns of behavior. Rather, children are trained to be adaptive

[1] Headlines were made across the United States when Stephanie Mills, the young, attractive valedictorian of Mills College in 1969, announced in her address that the most humane thing she could do for the world was not to add to the numbers of children.

and flexible. It is increasingly rare for a child to enter the same occupation as his father. The young have a long and increasingly complex period of education to which the parents contribute interest and emotional involvement in order to maximize the interests of the child.[2]

In advanced societies, relationships between aging parents and their adult offspring differ markedly from those in agrarian societies. In the more advanced societies, the elderly have little hold on their grown children. They have already given the young whatever advantages they needed to become self-sufficient adults, and the dependency of children on their parents is over at this point in life. Nor are the grown children expected to be financially responsible for their parents. Most of the advanced societies have systems of social security and welfare that allow the elderly to maintain at least a minimum standard of living. People no longer depend on many children to care for them in their advanced years. Although many older persons live with their offspring at some time during their advancing years, it is most often a temporary arrangement, and separate living quarters are both the ideal and the statistical norm. Reciprocal visiting relationships are typically maintained between adult couples and both their sets of parents, becoming more active in time of sickness or crisis. Nevertheless, dependency in adulthood is not an institutionalized pattern in the industrialized nations as it is in the less affluent countries.

Patterns of interaction among family members, then, affect the desire to reproduce many or only a few offspring. Patterns of relationships for whole societies are reflected in statistics, such as the average age at marriage, proportion of women and men marrying, proportion of women bearing children, and average number of children per mother or family.

Actually, the establishment of a family unit is not a necessary precondition to entry into a sexual union. In some countries a large proportion of all conceptions and births occur prior to or outside of legal marital units (Hartley, 1966, 1970, 1971). Age-old patterns of family organization have often been broken by slavery, foreign domination, or free migration. In many Latin American and Caribbean nations a large proportion of all births occur outside of socially or legally sanctioned unions. In Jamaica, for instance, all measures of fertility are very high in spite of a high average age at marriage and a low proportion of women ever marrying. In some years the probability of an unmarried woman giving birth has been about equal to the probability of childbirth for a married woman. Although some writers suggest that "consensual unions" are the "functional equivalent" of marriage, for Jamaica, at least, the assumption that consensual unions

[2] The intensive Head Start program for preschoolers in the 1960s in the United States has convinced those who did not recognize it before that parents must be involved in order for children to be encouraged to take advantage of whatever educational opportunities exist.

are an accompaniment to out-of-wedlock births is unwarranted. First births for the overwhelming majority of unmarried women occurred *prior to* (if ever) entry into consensual unions (Hartley, 1969). In spite of these data, family stability seems to remain the ideal even where people have difficulty exercising control over their lives.

Just as forced migration under slavery changes traditional patterns of human relationships, many other changes in social structure—the movement of people from rural to urban areas, from agricultural to industrial or service occupations, the participation of women in the nonagricultural labor force, and the expansion of formal education—tend to alter patterns of human interaction. These structural changes working through changed family relationships influence fertility, though often only after an extended time lag.

## *The Culture*

The cultural system of any society includes all of the shared beliefs and knowledge, the norms, or expectations of the way people are likely to behave, and the values or ideas of what is most desirable, as well as the evaluations of actual behavior in light of the shared beliefs, expectations and values.

Although many people make a sharp distinction between *beliefs* and *knowledge*, I would like to suggest that these are not two separate categories, but rather, two aspects of the same phenomenon. Those ideas that are not capable of being proved or disproved or are based on little reliable evidence may be called *beliefs*. Those ideas that are supported by reliable evidence may be called *knowledge*. All cultures have ideas that range from beliefs, on one hand, to knowledge, on the other (see Figure 3-1).

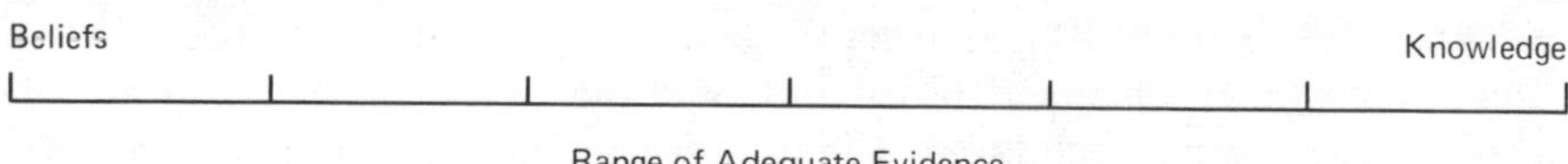


FIG. 3-1

Some of our "knowledge" today will be viewed as beliefs in the future. Most knowledge should be viewed as tentative and capable of further proof or disproof. Perhaps the best example of the movement from knowledge to belief to knowledge (or the tentativeness of our definition of knowledge) is found in the field of medicine. Often through the last hundred years, what was defined as "medical knowledge" at one point in time, was superceded by new knowledge. When the knowledge of one period is found to be in error, it is subsequently defined as "belief." Furthermore, an idea defined as knowledge by one group may be defined as a belief by another cultural unit. The important thing to remember is that each group acts upon its own definition of the situation.

In what ways may various beliefs and knowledge independently affect social change? The belief in the sacredness of the cow, as one instance, limits the supply of scarce protein for the Hindu people of India. This works in three ways: first, the cows are not defined as food for a hungry population; second, their great numbers (estimates run from 225 to 280 million cows in India alone) consume the food grains that the human population desperately needs; and third, the cows are undernourished due to cattle overpopulation, resulting in very low quantity and quality of milk output per cow.

As students of the population situation, we must recognize both the knowledge and beliefs that societies hold about (1) the advantages and disadvantages of raising large or small families, (2) conception, and (3) contraception. Although the findings of national surveys will be reviewed in detail in Chapter 9, these general points must be made in the beginning.

Throughout most of history social groups have had to focus on the advantages of having many children. Death rates were historically so high that there would not now exist on earth the remnants of any society that did not have high fertility values. The desire for many children has been modified in some countries as death rates (especially infant mortality) have been reduced. Although humans universally desire death control, they do not all desire birth control. Nevertheless, as more children are surviving, people are recognizing that providing for many offspring is a difficult task. Families may want to limit the number of children they have since the probability of their offspring's survival has increased (see Heer and Smith, 1968).

The desire for birth control, however, may be combined with continuing high fertility. It has recently been reported, for instance, that of the many women clients at birth control clinics in India, half had already produced six or more children! Eighty percent had had four or more and only 1.8 percent had two or fewer children. It is not just a desire for birth control but rather a control of births beyond replacement of the two parents that is needed to eventually limit population growth. The populations of less developed countries are so heavily concentrated in the young ages that even if these young people limit themselves to two children each, there will be continued population growth.

The ideas (beliefs and knowledge) about how babies are conceived vary greatly from one society to another. Knowledge of conception need not be complete and specific as long as conception is recognized as a possible result of sexual intercourse. Women in varying proportions for various societies report that they did not know how babies were made prior to their own pregnancy (Blake, 1961). Incorrect knowledge may be dangerous, as well. For instance, a recent text published in the United States, that is used in many college courses on marriage and the family, estimates that a girl having sexual intercourse only once every two months without contraceptives runs only one chance in 1850 of becoming pregnant during a year. The correct probability is one chance in five (see the critique by Rodman, 1965). With those published odds the reproduction of the human species would be highly questionable, but imagine the behavior of individuals who believe everything they read!

Knowledge about contraception also varies from one society to another, and also varies in accuracy and efficacy of application. Primitive social groups may "know" that unseen spirits cause conception and, therefore, devise rituals and taboos to avoid it, or more likely, to encourage the powers of procreation. Contemporary scientists, on the other hand, recognize that they do not know as much about conception and, therefore, contraception as they would like. While the primitive may think he knows about conception, he is unlikely to be able to control that phase of life as adequately as the scientist, who, recognizing that more detailed knowledge is desireable, may nevertheless be able to control conception very well with the knowledge which is already available. Although the search for the ideal contraceptive still goes on, there seem to be enough means at present for the widespread control of conception (see Chapter 11) where it is desired. If rational behavior on the part of individuals is to be encouraged, it would seem advantageous for social systems to disseminate specific and detailed information regarding birth control. In many countries, however, leaders work in the opposite direction to suppress contraceptive information and supplies.

Suppression of the knowledge about contraception indicates that several types of beliefs and goals may be in conflict. Political leaders have been ready to see increasing numbers of citizens as increasing national strength or military might (see Chapter 10). Religious leaders may believe contraception to be contrary to divine plan or enlargement of their particular religious group. Politicians and priests, for different reasons, may attempt to restrict the availability of knowledge about, and means of, preventing births. While national governments have not been noticeably successful in their attempts to either increase or decrease fertility, family planning programs have at least demonstrated that some fertility reductions may be facilitated by distributing information and the tools of contraception.

Many components of culture have implications for the study of population composition and changes; and these interact with each other and with the various aspects of the biological and social-structural levels of population causation to influence particular outcomes. These components of demographic change are both reflexive and behavioral. As Kingsley Davis states it: "They are reflexive in that a change in one acts upon and produces a change in other variables and these in turn reflect back upon and change the initial variables under examination" (Davis, 1963, p. 345). Yet human populations change only as the biological, social-structural, and cultural systems work through the actual behavior of human beings motivated in certain directions within specific situations. A reversal of current population trends, therefore, represents one of mankind's greatest challenges.

## *THE DIRECT CAUSES OF POPULATION GROWTH IN THE "DEVELOPED" AS CONTRASTED WITH THE "UNDERDEVELOPED" COUNTRIES*

Let us now examine the changes that occurred among the now developed countries of Europe during their period of industrialization and compare those changes with what has been occurring most recently among the less developed countries. Not only are the timing and severity of the population growth vastly different for the two sets of nations, but the causes of the changes are also different.

A schematic graph of the transformation in birth and death rates will aid our understanding of the differences in the two types of nations. Figure 3-2a shows approximate declines in birth and death rates as these occurred in Western Europe after 1800. Until that time birth and death rates everywhere in the world were high. Death rates had always fluctuated somewhat as famines, wars, and epidemics of various types came and went. Only in the nineteenth century did death rates begin a steady decline. This decline occurred gradually in Europe over a period ranging from 75 to 150 years for specific countries. The birth rate began to decline shortly after the drop in the death rate had begun, and a rate of natural increase of 0.5 to 1.5 percent per year resulted.

However, the birth rates had not been as high in Europe as in the presently less developed countries, and their growth rate was never as high as now evidenced in the less developed nations. The shaded portions of Figure 3-2 indicate the growth rates experienced by the two sets of countries and dramatize the differences between them. European countries often had 70 or more years to accommodate a doubling of their population. Many of the less developed countries currently have populations doubling in 23 years or less. The difference in 140 years at these rates would be a 4-fold increase in the one case and a (calculable but improbable) 64-fold increase in the other, the underdeveloped nations.

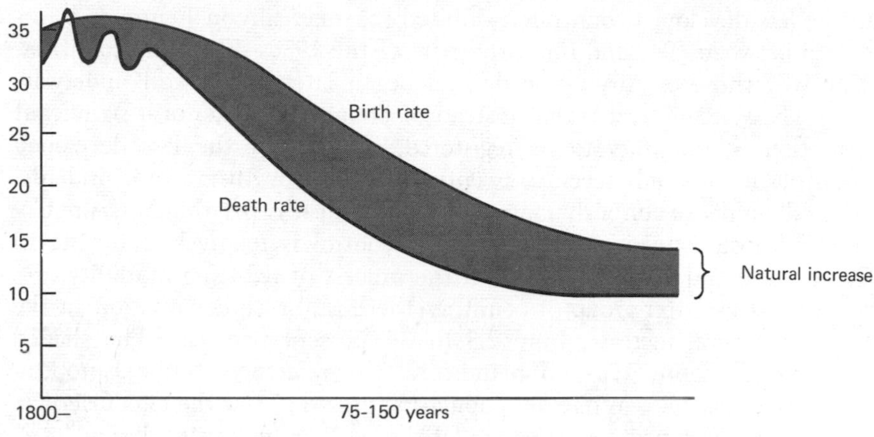

(a) Western Europe after 1800

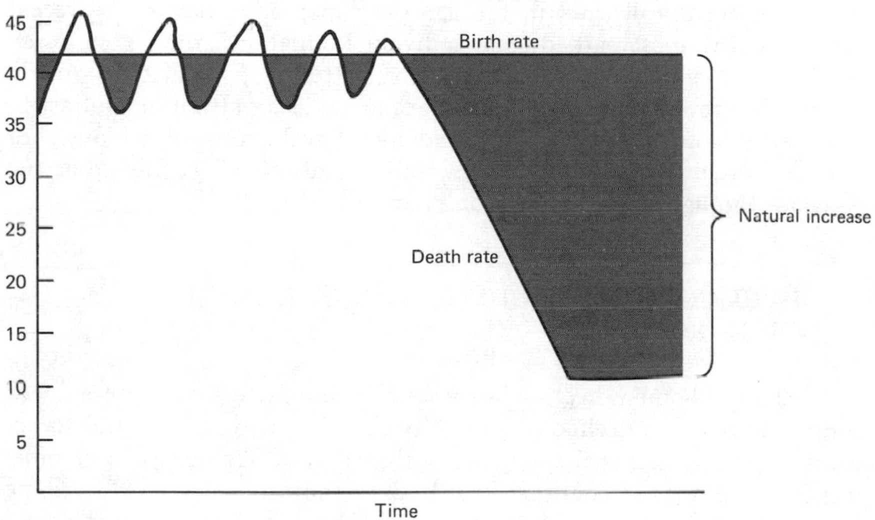


(b) Less Developed Countries, Mid-20th Century
(The sharp drop in the death rate began between 1940 and 1960, depending upon the specific country)

FIG. 3–2 *Approximation of the Birth and Death Rates for Two Different Groups of Nations Over Time*

Birth rates and death rates for the underdeveloped countries are believed to have been somewhat higher than those of the developed countries prior to their industrialization. But again, the death rates fluctuated rather wildly until approximately the 1940s. The decline in the death rates in the less developed countries, exhibited schematically in Figure 3-2b, occurred between 1940 and the early years of the 1950s. For some countries, especially those of Africa, the decline began later and is still underway.

The startling fact is that instead of taking 100 years for a significant reduction in mortality to be registered, in most of the less developed countries it took only seven to twenty years. The death rates for underdeveloped countries currently range from 5 or 6 deaths per thousand population in those countries where mortality control is relatively complete to 20 per thousand in countries still in the process of reducing mortality.

For this latter group of countries there is also some variation in the rates of natural increase, from 2.5 to 3.5 percent per year. The shaded portions of Figure 3-2a and b indicate why reference to the European historical situation is as one of "population growth," and the circumstances in the less developed countries are labelled a "population explosion."

We need to examine the different reasons for population changes in Europe historically and in the less developed countries during recent years. For the most part, despite individual variations, the Westernized nations were more alike than different in patterns of population growth. Their slow growth may, therefore, be examined as a pattern in contrast to the very explosive growth of the underdeveloped group of nations. For both sets of countries, deaths, births, and migration will be viewed as the variables through which population changes occur.

## *PATTERNS OF POPULATION IN THE HISTORY OF EUROPE*

Ralph Thomlinson (1965) suggests that ten factors were "prominent contributors to the decline of mortality that began weakly in the seventeenth century, gathered momentum through the eighteenth and nineteenth centuries and continue unabated to the present" (p. 91). These factors were relatively slow-moving and closely related to a general rise in the overall standards of living that occurred in Europe during its industrialization.

### *Mortality Decline in Europe*

1. Improvements in agricultural techniques increased the quantity of food produced. Although farming methods had been virtually unchanged for centuries, several innovations were put into practice near the end of the seventeenth century. These included crop rotation, the use of better fertilizers, and improved machinery and implements. Increasing

food production meant that more persons could be spared for nonagricultural labor. A larger proportion of populations could live in urban areas. Higher density living, together with a commitment to rational organization and the scientific method, facilitated specialization and the division of labor, which further promoted increased invention and discovery.

2. The change from a home handicraft to a machine factory system increased the amount and variety of products available for use by the public. Although Thomlinson suggests that the unhealthy living and working conditions of the factories and factory towns probably increased mortality prior to the eventual lowering of the death rate, population growth estimates imply that death rates may have been declining all through the period of early industrialization (Petersen, 1969). In the long run, more people were able to buy more goods, at least some of which helped the population resist death. People could now have enough clothing so that clean changes could be more frequent. For the first time, warm clothing could be distributed on a wide scale. The advent of the factory system also made feasible the production of large quantities of the commodities required for improved agriculture (i.e., the iron plowshare), transportation (the steam engine), and most of the other factors in the list.

3. Improvements in transportation facilitated distribution of the agricultural and industrial products to a wider populace than was formerly possible. Thus, the well-being of residents in an area was no longer strictly tied to its local productivity. For example, famines had always been local. If one area had a crop failure, it meant that the people in that area starved, for there were no means to quickly transport adequate food supplies from another area. Now, not only is it possible to move agricultural goods within a country, but international trade in agricultural produce is taken for granted. Furthermore, foods may be rushed to hungry people by airplane to prevent the starvation that in the past would have taken many lives.

4. The social reforms of the nineteenth and twentieth centuries alleviated many of the hardships of early factory life. Maximum working hours, minimum working ages, and various safety devices eventually improved working conditions. Life had not been much easier, if different in organization, prior to the factory system. The subordination and long working hours of the family and servants under cottage industry simply continued in the factory itself (Laslett, 1965). An indication of the earlier conditions is found in the legislation of 1802, limiting the hours children were permitted to work to a maximum of 12 per day. Child labor laws were opposed most vehemently by the parents of the children involved. The 1833 education act, requiring children who worked in a factory to attend a certain amount of school, was again fought by parents (Smelser,

1959, Chaps. 9–11). Gradually, as child labor reforms were instituted and compulsory education laws were passed, children became less of an economic asset and more of a liability.

With the early factory system, it became easier than it had been under agriculture or cottage industry for the government to legislate and enforce protections on the hours and conditions of work for children (and others as well). Resistance to disease and survival through the high mortality period of youth was thus facilitated.

5. The ability to control temperature and humidity in homes and places of work probably contributed to decline of respiratory infections in winter months, and certainly provided more comfort and presumably stimulated more productivity in extreme heat and cold. Although tuberculosis had been a major cause of death, its contribution to the death rates of advanced countries is now very minor.

6. The general improvement in public sanitation, especially in cities, has cut down the deaths due to water-borne diseases, such as cholera, typhoid, and dysentery. In the nineteenth century, public utilities were introduced in many cities of Europe, providing a water supply, water purification, and sewage disposal, (Thomlinson, 1965). Historically, urban areas have had higher death rates than rural areas. In the countryside, where people lived some distance apart, contamination from sewage was limited. But in cities, raw sewage from the denser population usually flowed in open trenches along the streets. Not only did flies and other insects transmit disease germs from the sewage to food, but most of the sewage flowed into the urban water supply and contaminated it. (Petersen, 1969). In modern countries, sanitary engineering, applying bacteriological knowledge, has practically wiped out cholera, typhoid fever, and other water-borne infections.

7. Changes in habits of personal hygiene, such as the wearing (and more frequent washing) of cheap cotton clothing facilitated cleanliness. Soap, once a luxury, became available to almost everyone. (It is still not widely available throughout the less developed countries.) Europeans gradually stopped thinking of baths as unnatural and men came to understand that the body is not kept clean by perspiration. Cleanliness, or the absence of dirt, is not merely aestheticly attractive but, more important, a sanitary safeguard, since one of the most effective vehicles of disease is dirt (Sedgwick, 1901, quoted in Thomlinson, 1965).

8. Medical improvements occurring late in the nineteenth century —especially the development of asepsis (the exclusion of pathogenic microorganisms) and antisepsis (the killing of microorganisms already present)—helped reduce mortality. Thomlinson (1965) suggests that aseptic and antiseptic surgery, founded by Joseph Lister, who introduced the sterilization of instruments, the use of masks, and disinfection of the

operating theater by carbolic acid, probably saved more lives than all the wars of the nineteenth century had sacrificed. As the germ theory of disease became widely accepted, not only were hospital deaths reduced, but methods were developed to safeguard food through pasteurization and sterilization.

9. The development of immunology also contributed to the decline of mortality. Despite the discovery of the smallpox vaccine, it was a long time before Koch and Pasteur found the key to immunization. Once they discovered that innoculation with an attenuated virus from microbe cultures produces a mild case of the disease, preventing serious recurrence later, vaccines were developed for chicken cholera, sheep anthrax, hydrophobia, diphtheria, and syphilis. Now there are prophylactic antitoxins against tetanus, typhoid, scarlet fever, poliomyelitis, influenza, and many other previously dangerous diseases (Thomlinson, 1965).

10. Virulent diseases tend to become relatively benign through changes in the disease-producing organism itself, mutual adaptation between man and the disease, and increased resistance from antibodies (possible from selective survival of the medically fit). Bubonic plague, pneumonic plague, leprosy, and syphilis were once far more acute and lethal than they are today. Measles, diphtheria, and smallpox, when introduced into a society with no natural immunity, strike with much greater violence than in societies where they have long been endemic. These changes began before modern preventive and curative methods exerted any noticeable influence (Thomlinson, 1965).

### *Fertility Declines in Europe*

Because the decline of mortality in Europe in the nineteenth century was slow and related to a general rise in the standards of living, people had time to adjust their desired family size to the changing patterns of life. These motivated the gradual utilization of methods of birth control. The birth rates of Western Europe are supposed never to have been as high as in most of the less developed countries of the present. Fertility trends, as well as mortality trends, were quite different for European countries historically than in recent years in the underdeveloped countries. Figure 3-2 shows that, for Europe in general, the birth rates followed the death rates in their long-run decline, although for some of the European countries there is evidence of a slight initial rise in fertility prior to its long slow decline (Petersen, 1969).

Thus far, there has been no significant decline in birth rates in the less developed countries as a whole (although there are a few cases of decline, others of increase in individual countries). The historical example of Europe had led population specialists and national governmental leaders to conclude that an improvement in the general standards of living by economic development was all that was needed to reduce births. Many persons felt that what had happened in Europe was predictive of what would happen in the less developed countries.

The change from high birth and death rates to low birth and death rates has been called "the demographic transition" (discussed in Chapter 11). It has been used both as a description of what happened in Europe and as a theory to predict what would happen in the less developed countries. It must be clear from Figure 3-2a and b, that the theory of the demographic transition can no longer be accepted as a predictor of demographic behavior. Births in the less developed countries have not declined following a reduction in death rates, and it appears equally probable for birth rates to rise as for them to decline. The real problem of the theory of demographic transition as a predictor has been that it led to a concentration on economic development as the way to automatically lower birth rates. High birth rates, however, have used up much of the potential for economic advance in the less developed countries (for details, see Chapter 7).

Why was the situation in Europe so different from that of the less developed countries in recent years? In the first place, preindustrial Europe apparently had a lower birth rate prior to its mortality decline than do countries presently industrializing. Available data indicate a range of from 5 to 10 per thousand lower birth rates in preindustrial Europe than in underdeveloped countries today. In part this reflects a difference in age at marriage or age at entry into sexual unions.

Estimates of average ages at first marriage (Wrigley, 1966, p. 86) in Colyton, England, for males and females are:

| | *Male* | *Female* |
|---|---|---|
| 1560–1646 | 27.2 | 27.0 |
| 1647–1719 | 27.7 | 29.6 |
| 1720–1769 | 25.7 | 26.8 |
| 1770–1837 | 26.5 | 25.1 |

As averages, these ages are quite high. They may be contrasted with many underdeveloped countries, where the young traditionally marry at or near the age of puberty. In Europe the late age of marriage was due in part to the necessity of establishing a new home. If a young man typically moves his wife in with his own family, he doesn't need to be concerned about providing a separate residence. The European pattern of neolocal residence sometimes made it necessary for a man to work many years before he could afford to marry.

Peter Laslett (1967) concludes that, although many of the literary novels set in historical Europe imply that early age at marriage was the pattern, in fact, the average age at marriage was late. Fictional writings cannot be used as indicators of what was happening over a large population, just as television, movies, and plays typically portray the unusual and not average lives. How, then, is age at marriage related to childbearing? Research has demonstrated that the later people marry and the later childbearing begins, the fewer the number of children born, on the average (Lorimer, 1954). Only recently have we gained the capacity to change this pattern. Now, by using effective birth control methods, it is *possible* to marry young and still have few children. Yet, even today, within countries where there are relatively low birth rates, those who marry at an early age tend to have more children than those marrying later. The relationship has been very close over large groups and over time. The variation, historically, in the average number of children according to age at marriage has been computed for Colyton, England, for the years from 1560 to 1837. At each of the time periods for which data are available, women married before their twenty-fifth birthday averaged 1.6 to 2.8 children more than those married between the ages 25–29. The difference was much greater for those married after age 30 (Wrigley, 1966).

It would also appear that relatively large proportions of the populations of Europe, in the early years of the industrial revolution, never married. Of course, there were variations from one country to another in the timing and significance of these factors in reducing the birth rates.

Another factor to be considered is that during the industrial revolution there was a steady migration from rural to urban areas. The movement itself meant that people were changing their ways of life and in Europe, at least, it meant new opportunities. The move from rural to urban areas also meant doing some planning with regard to physically changing one's life situation. We know that when one is able to plan some aspect of one's life, the *idea of planning* is liable to carry over into other areas of life as well. If the individual's life situation can be changed by moving from rural to urban centers or can be changed by continuing education, the relationship between establishing goals and proceeding toward those goals becomes obvious. When people find that they can plan and organize their lives on one level it is more likely that they will plan the number of children they will produce. One of the most significant correlations found in early studies of family size was the correlation between planning in general and family planning in particular (Kiser and Whelpton, 1958).

Furthermore, as industrialization drew people to the cities, children became economic liabilities to their parents. With the passage of child labor laws and compulsory educational laws, which prevented children from contributing to the family income, parents were motivated to limit the numbers of children they produced.

Coinciding with increased motivation to limit family size was an increase in the level of knowledge about various means of contraception. Coitus interruptus is thought to have been the most commonly used contraceptive method contributing to the steady decline in French fertility in the eighteenth and early nineteenth centuries (Wrigley, 1969). By the late nineteenth century the birth control movement was highly publicized in England through the Bradlaugh-Besant trials, an attempt at suppression. Books justifying and describing birth control had been published some 50 years earlier, beginning in 1822 (Petersen, 1969). In the late nineteenth and early twentieth centuries, abortion also played a role in reducing birth rates in Europe. A summary of data by Glass in 1940 for eight northwest European countries gives the impression that the attitude toward abortion was more tolerant between 1900 and 1935 than it is today (Davis, 1963).

### *European Emigration*

While birth rates were declining, rates of natural growth were further neutralized by the great migrations from Europe. Many nations of Europe encouraged the rapid colonization of Africa, Asia, North and South America, and even Oceania. As a result, over 50 million people—more than one-third of whom came from the British Isles—emigrated between 1846 and 1932 to colonize these lands, (Woytinsky, 1968). Not only did the emigration lighten population pressures in the home countries, but the flow of raw materials and produce to the mother countries stimulated a rise in living standards and facilitated the industrial revolution. Unfortunately, migration on a significant world scale is no longer possible. Only a few nations are willing to accept sizeable numbers of "qualified" immigrants, usually those most similar to the native population in color, language, and customs.

## *RAPID POPULATION INCREASE IN LESS DEVELOPED COUNTRIES*

Having reviewed the factors contributing to the gradual population increase in the past 150 years in the westernized countries, let us examine the direct causes of recent population changes in the underdeveloped countries. The multiplicity of factors that produce particular levels and/or changes in population are reflected in the available data on mortality and fertility.

## *Changes in Mortality in the Less Developed Countries*

The most dramatic difference between the population changes for Europe and for the less developed nations has been the rapid reduction in mortality in the underdeveloped countries in recent years in contrast to the more gradual declines over time for Europe. (See Figure 3-2.) As late as the 1930s, mortality was so high in most Latin American countries that a newborn baby had less than a 50 percent chance of being alive at age 30. Life expectancy is now about 60 years for Latin Americans (Arriaga, 1970).

An indication of the declines in mortality for a few representative countries may be seen by examining Figure 3-3. A comparison of crude death rates for the years 1910–1911 and 1960–1961 show a reduction of at least 50 percent in Mexico, India, Thailand, Japan, Venezuela, USSR, and Puerto Rico, among others. For the most part these declines began after World War II and were concentrated into approximately a ten-year period.

In contrast, the decline over these years for the United States was only ten percent. The death rates in the industrial countries had reached an approximate "floor" before 1940 so that recent declines have been very slight. In fact, crude death rates are currently lower in many of the less developed than in the more advanced countries that have higher proportions of old people. Continued mortality reductions in advanced countries are difficult and expensive because the prevailing causes of death such as cancer and heart diseases which affect mostly older people are not easily controlled.

The reductions in death rates already accomplished in the less developed countries have been produced by relatively cheap means. Unlike the decline in mortality in Europe, the reasons for the reduction are *external* to the underdeveloped countries and unrelated to any significant rise in their living standards. The massive application of DDT for instance which all but eradicated the mosquito, a carrier of malaria, was accomplished through the efforts of the United Nations (United Nations, 1953). Relatively inexpensive public health measures and purification of water supplies were also largely financed by outside help. The World Health Organization (WHO) carried out immunization campaigns in the less developed countries, undoubtedly saving the lives of millions of children.

The increase in the average person's lifespan in the less developed countries has taken much less time than in the industrialized nations. It took over 100 years, from 1840 to 1940, for Denmark, England and Wales,

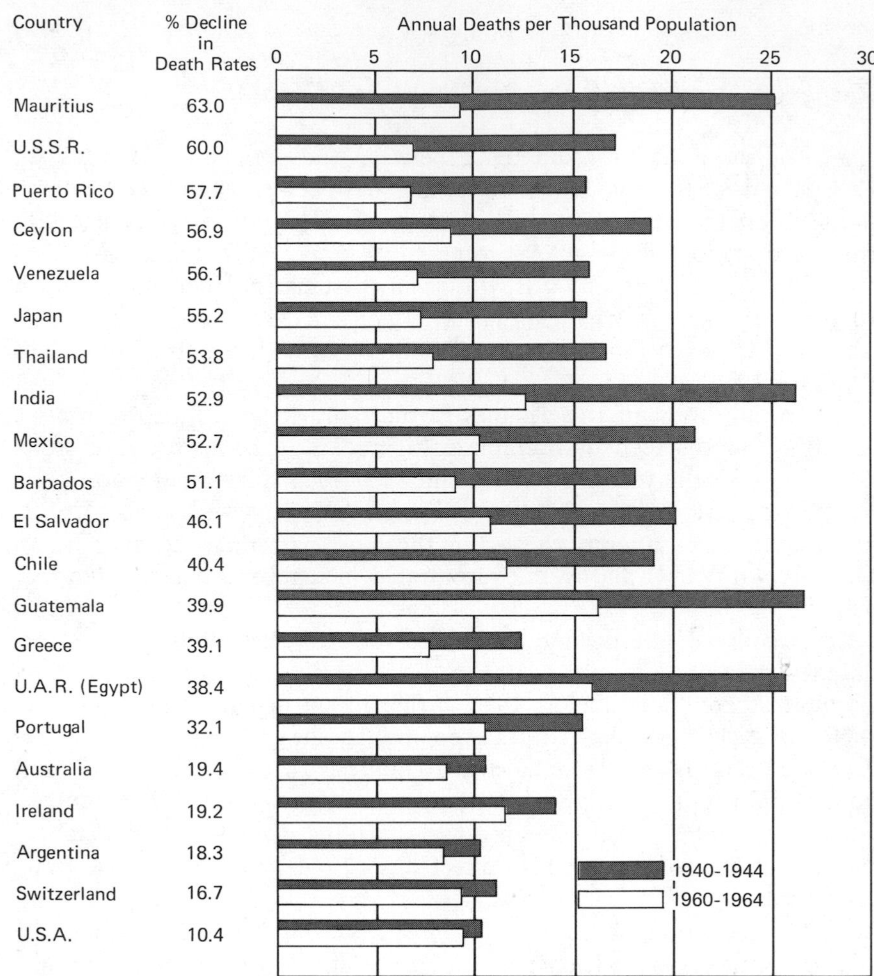


*Source:* Population Reference Bureau, "Spaceship Earth in Peril," *Population Bulletin,* Vol. 25 (March 1969), 1.

FIG. 3–3 *Percent Decline in Death Rates, 1940–1944 to 1960–1964*

France, the Netherlands, Norway, and Sweden to raise their life expectancy from 41 to 64 years. In some of the less developed countries the same increase in life expectancy took only 20 years.

> We can expect that the later in historical time a massive public health program is applied in an underdeveloped country previously lacking public health programs, the higher the rate of mortality decline will be. (Arriaga, 1970, p. 31).

Jean Bourgeois-Pichat (1966) has suggested that for the less developed countries:

> The discoveries of sulfa drugs and especially of antibiotics, as well as of insecticides and other means of combating disease-carrying parasites, radically altered the situation. It became possible to lower mortality irrespective of economic development. This was man's first major victory over death. Within a few years, this victory was to be responsible for the rapid population growth that jeopardized the economic growth of the developing areas. The decline in mortality thus became not only independent of economic development but a positive obstacle to it (p. 61).

Although dramatic declines in death rates have already occurred in every country of the world, a continued decline for most countries is anticipated. Figure 3-4 shows the United Nations medium variant population projections of crude death rates up to the year 2000. The higher the death rates, the more rapidly they are expected to drop. By the year 2000 the less developed regions of the world are expected to add between 11 and 20 years to the life expectancy of the average individual. Without a comparable decline in births, however, these countries would face an even more rapid natural increase in their populations than is already the case. The probable future decline in mortality frustrates any hope for the reduction of rates of natural increase.

Not only do birth rates need to be lowered to reduce the present rates of natural increase, but if death rates continue to fall, then birth rates must decline even more in order to cancel out their effect on the rates of natural increase. Thus, if the birth rates of Nigeria should decline from 50 to 40 per thousand by the year 2000, one might expect a lowering of the rate of natural increase from 2.5 percent to 1.5 percent per year. However, if the death rate also declines by 10 per thousand population, there would be no reduction in the rate of natural increase.

One would assume that increasing length of life might be an indicator of improvement in the quality of life. However, in many countries it has simply meant that more persons are kept alive, though malnourished, illiterate, and impoverished. The increasing number of bodies to provide for has, in many cases, reduced the possibility of (1) providing adequate nourishment, (2) increasing educational standards, and even (3) raising health standards in general. These and other complications of increasing populations will be discussed in the chapters to follow.

Since we expect further reduction in death rates, with little opportunity for emigration from the underdeveloped countries, birth control remains the only possibility of reducing population growth. Although some limits on births have always been present in underdeveloped socie-

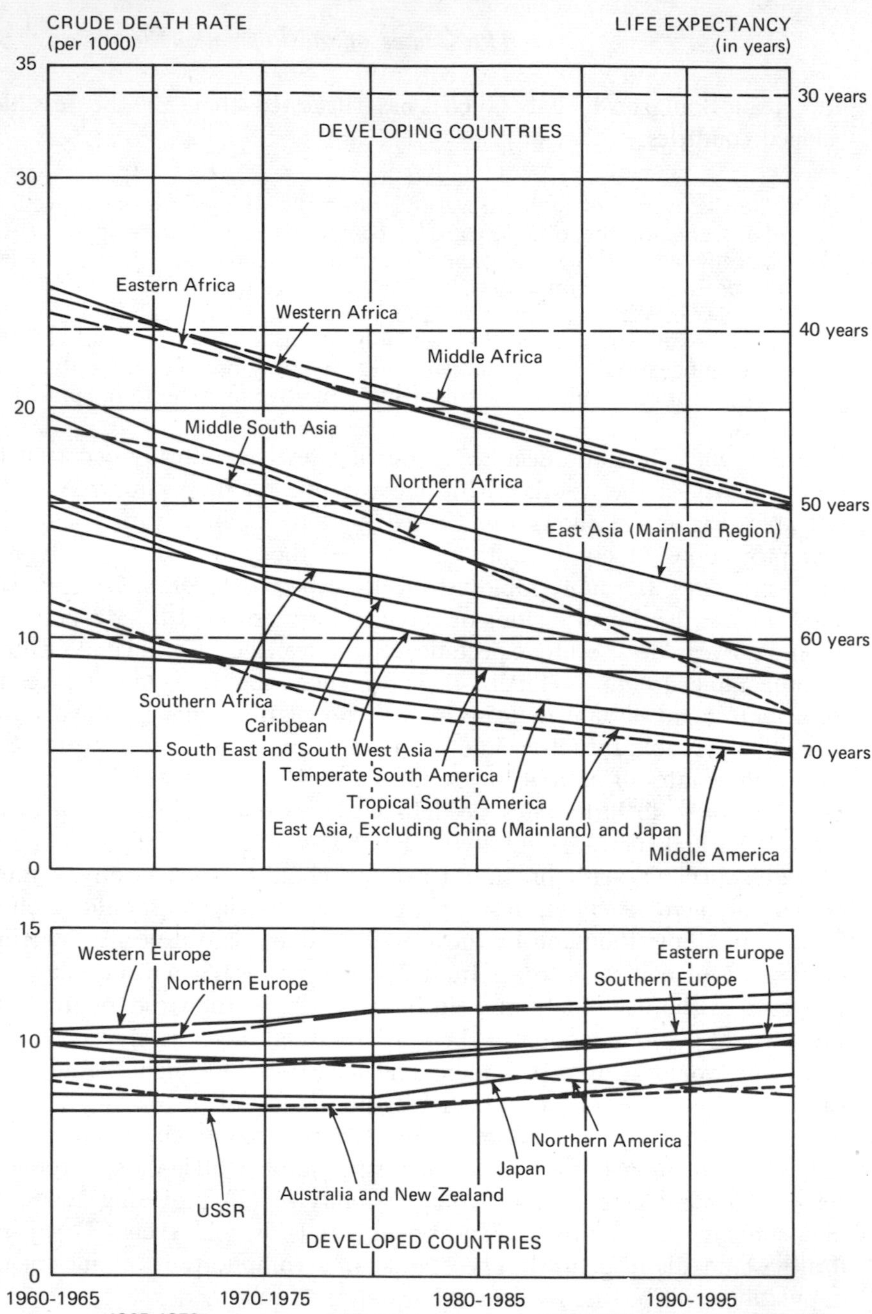


*Source:* Jean Bourgeois-Pichat, *Population Growth and Development*. New York: Carnegie Endowment for International Peace, 1966, p. 64, Graph 10.

FIG. 3–4 *Crude Death Rates of the Major Regions of the World According to the Medium Variant Population Projections of the United Nations*

ties, there are a number of problems encountered in introducing effective means of birth control on a large scale.

### *Birth Control in the Less Developed Countries*

While introducing death control into a traditional society entails some planning and effort, introducing birth control is much more difficult. Human beings everywhere, regardless of culture, prefer health to sickness, life to death. Once the means to better health are available, people will use them with increasing effectiveness. But changing the birth rate of a society may involve long-term social patterns, cultural beliefs, family traditions, economic arrangements, religious customs, and psychological conditions (Population Council, 1965).

High birth rates were necessary for the survival of the human species when death rates were equally high. No society could have survived under conditions of high mortality without maintaining high rates of fertility. Now, in the less developed countries, the whole system of traditional beliefs and practices lends the weight of historical legitimacy to high rates of reproduction. The complexity of the problems encountered in attempting to introduce birth control are suggested by the Population Council (1965) and elaborated as follows:

1. In most of the less developed countries marriage takes place at an early age so that virtually all of the woman's reproductive years are available for childbearing.

2. Because of their subordinate status in most underdeveloped countries, women must legitimate their very existence by having offspring.

3. The desire for sons, an important part of many cultures, complicates the spread of birth control. In some cultures, sons are supposed to take care of the parents in their old age; in others a son is needed to perform specific rituals at the death of the father. For whatever reasons, the desire for sons does not necessarily mean that one or two sons will be adequate. Rather, the traditional high rate of mortality has required that families raise several sons to insure that at least one will be alive in the father's old age. This necessity for sons, of course, means large families. To keep families small and still have sons, female infanticide was traditionally a means of population limitation in many countries. Now that societies no longer accept that means of limiting population, and child mortality has been drastically reduced, the proportion of all births which survive is increasing. In Latin America, at least, the number of births per female has increased since 1935 (Collver, 1965).

4. Because there had been an absence of family planning in the less developed countries, there is an expectation that social support for family

planning is lacking. In many countries there had not been much thought or discussion about family planning until very recently, so that people who are interested in limiting their births may expect to be condemned by family and friends if they indicate an interest in family limitation.

5. The delicacy and intimacy of the subject may be an obstacle to communication and the development of a new concensus on family size. Not only sex, but family goals in general have been presumed to be private matters. In many countries a male doctor would be prohibited from discussing family planning with female patients.

6. The low literacy rates in many less developed nations prevent wide distribution of printed birth control information. In Taiwan, where literacy is relatively high, research teams found printed brochures an efficient means of communicating family planning information. Attempts to reduce illiteracy are, unfortunately, retarded by rapid population increase in most of the underdeveloped countries.

7. Prior to the large-scale use of the pill and intrauterine devices, there has been some reluctance to use the diaphragm and douche (which were less effective anyway) mostly because of lack of privacy in housing for so many people in the less developed countries. The new means of birth control, however, require less physical privacy and present less limitations on their use.

8. The general absence of organization within the less developed societies has prevented large-scale education in, and application of, birth control. The less organized a society, the more difficult it is to initiate an organized program in family planning. Wherever organizations already exist, a new program may be assimilated or spun off the old.

9. Closely tied to the general absence of organization is the lack of distributional facilities in most of the less developed countries. In India, where mobile clinics are used, the lack of an adequate system of roads hampers the distribution of birth control information and devices.

10. Although the economic costs of a family planning program seem small per person, the total required funds for an adequate nationwide program are often considered prohibitive by legislators or financial planners. It has been established that for less developed nations on the whole, appropriate funding would require about 30 cents per capita per year, or an equivalent of two dollars per woman in the childbearing ages per year, or approximately ten dollars per birth prevented. When one contrasts that sum to the amount required year after year for each birth produced, the money would seem an investment in an ultimate saving. Yet, an active birth control program would require funding by the national government. These funds then compete with other budget needs. The costs of preventing births might not seem quite so problematic, if viewed in light of the long run savings to both family and nation (to be explored in Chapter 7).

11. One reason families have not recognized a need to limit births is the delay in perceiving a lowered infant and child mortality. Because so many children used to die before reaching maturity, families needed to produce many offspring. It takes almost a generation to realize that one's children are surviving, and by then, it's too late to practice birth control! Heer (1966) found that fertility is still strongly associated with infant mortality in many underdeveloped countries.

12. Birth control in less developed countries is not necessarily prohibited by religious or ideological objections. Although one of the most common reasons cited for high birth rates in Latin America is the Catholic religion, Catholicism in Europe does not prevent low crude birth rates (see Figure 11-1). Therefore, other than religious factors must influence the high birth rate in the less developed countries.

13. More important than religion in influencing birth rates is the general inertia, apathy, and resistance to change prevalent in the less developed areas of the world. While there may be religious and ideological factors influencing behavior, in many cases populations are simply carrying out the behavior patterns of previous generations without questioning why. A general resistance to change also involves a resistance to rethinking and family planning.

In spite of all these factors working against birth control in underdeveloped nations, following are a few favorable factors.

1. The pressures of overpopulation and undernourishment are felt by the people in their daily lives. Yet, poverty and hunger have been experienced by most people throughout history without their forcing an examination of behaviors that might reduce the problems of existence. In most of the underdeveloped countries of the world today, there is a growing recognition that something better is possible. If that recognition can be tied to individual motivation to improve the conditions of life, the control of population increase may be accepted as an aid to human betterment.

2. Because of reductions in child mortality, families are larger. This makes extended family units larger, too, and people are beginning to recognize the inconveniences that result. Birth control may then be recognized as a means of limiting family strains.

3. Innovations in the technology of birth prevention have already increased the number of methods of family planning. An increase in the number of techniques of birth control should lead to an increased probability of finding an acceptable means for individuals according to cultural requirements.

4. Some governing groups, informed by demographic and economic analysis, as well as surveys of popular sentiment, have determined to respond to the need for controlling the growth of their populations.

A verbal commitment to the need for a lowering of births, however, is not necessarily translated into programs for family planning or population control. Even where family planning clinics have been initiated, they have not been sufficient to make any measurable change in birth rates. National costs and ultimate savings of birth control programs will be discussed in Chapter 7. Even though average costs are very low, the total amount of funds required for a government-sponsored birth control program are significant, and few government leaders have been willing to divert scarce government income to a widespread, aggressive birth control program.

Only as leaders begin to recognize the negative consequences of rapid population growth, will birth control become a top-priority issue in governmental programs.

### *Migration*

Even if we assumed some lowering of costs, interplanetary migration is clearly too expensive to involve significant numbers of human beings, *if* they could be supported indefinitely on another planet or on space stations. Therefore, migration has not had, and is unlikely ever to have, any impact on the total population of the earth.

*International migration* has historically had a profound effect on many nations of the world. We know that emigration helped relieve and slow the population growth of Europe from 1850 to 1950, with the heaviest migration occurring between 1880 and 1930. The United States was largely populated by these migrants, absorbing 70 percent of all intercontinental migrants from 1851 to 1890 and 60 percent of those migrating during 1890 and 1910 (Woytinsky, 1968). The United States probably has more citizens of Irish and Swedish extraction than presently reside in Ireland or Sweden, respectively.

Historic migrations of various types (see Petersen, 1969) have been more important than they are today. Not only were the numbers involved generally larger, depending upon the specific country, but all nations had much smaller populations to begin with so that the migrants had a very much greater proportional effect on both the countries of emigration and those of immigration.

Revised immigration laws and/or conditional clauses now essentially nullify former open door policies for migrants. Few advanced nations are willing to accept large numbers of immigrants. The United States, Canada, and Australia are the only countries which have been and are presently willing to take in as many as 100,000 or more permanent immigrants yearly.[3] Not just anyone is welcome, however, since there are numerous restrictions and regulations established for immigration to these three. Altogether between one-half and two-thirds of a million persons are able to move to these "developed" countries yearly (U. N., 1966, Table 29). In light of the 72 millions added yearly to world population, mainly in the less developed nations, these migration levels are insignificant.

Emigration from India has been relatively high, both numerically and proportionally, for an underdeveloped country. How might it have affected the total population of the country? Excluding the mass migration during partition of India and Pakistan, an estimate of 250,000 intercontinental emigrants for 1951 to 1960 would seem high according to historical reports (Woytinsky, 1968, p. 308). Using that figure to place migration in national perspective, it would mean that in ten years only one-third of 1 percent of the *additions* to population had emigrated. If emigration had been double, triple, or even ten times larger than our estimate it would have had little effect on total population or its increase. Migration cannot solve the problems associated with rapid population growth.

The recent impelled migration of East Pakistani refugees into India has added more people than have emigrated in this century. Yet they represent only a fraction of the yearly natural increase of the Indian population. This new flood of immigrants is not really wanted by the people of eastern India. It increases the hardships of the residents in that area. Yet, the government of India together with international relief agencies is doing its best to care for the minimal food and health needs of these new dependents.

Numbers of migrants which have little effect on large nations may have a significant proportional impact on small nations. The emigration from Jamaica has reduced their current population increase to about 70 percent of the natural increase of the population. For Israel, migration both in and out, during the last 25 years, has significantly altered the Jewish/Arab proportions of residents. Moreover, because migrants tend to concentrate in the early adult ages, their movement is an important subject of study, affecting the age-structure and thus the crude birth and death rates both of the country (or area) of emigration and that of immigration. A crowded nation or area, therefore, may promote emigration or internal migration to reduce both current population and fertility levels of dense aggregations.

*Internal migration* has found expression mainly through urbanization. As increasing proportions of people live in cities, fertility is expected

[3] West Germany, France, and the United Kingdom have such numbers moving in and out on work permits, visitor status, etc.

to decline, though one or two generations may be required before the decrease is evident. In the meantime rapid urbanization creates many problems. The extent of recent and projected urbanization together with some of the connected problems will be explored in detail in Chapter 4.

Rather than, or in addition to, rural-urban movement, some nations have encouraged the internal migration from more to less densely populated agricultural areas. Indonesia is a classic case in point. The government has been promoting movement from crowded Java to the more sparsely populated islands of that country. Yet, in its peak year (far above the overall average) the recorded out-migration from Java was only three percent of the yearly increase in numbers on Java alone. Even when the

**Tight little isle**

*Source:* LePelley in *The Christian Science Monitor,* Feb. 27, 1971. Reprinted by permission from *The Christian Science Monitor,* © 1971 by The Christian Science Publishing Society. All rights reserved.

FIG. 3–5

advantages of lower birth rates over time are computed and added to the population reductions due to migration, the conclusion reached is that "Neither internal movement within a country nor movement to foreign countries is a substitute for contraception as a means of population control" (Keyfitz, 1971, p. 3).

Many countries would like to promote emigration to relieve the pressure of rapid population growth. Yet, few nations are willing to accept large numbers of immigrants. Nor would the costs of moving significant numbers allow us to hope that migration could relieve the distribution problems which accompany the very rapid increase in human numbers.

## *SUMMARY*

Biological, social structural, and cultural factors influence birth and death rates.

Improved health measures may increase the ability to reproduce (fecundity) as well as reducing deaths. Without a corresponding increase in birth control, populations of the underdeveloped countries have been growing very rapidly. The biological control of deaths has been easier for populations to accept than the biological control of births. In part this is due to social patterns that dictate early and frequent childbearing, in which children are economic assets to the family and in which many children are born so that a few will still be alive when the parents are old.

Cultural beliefs, knowledge, expectations, and ideals affect the behavior of persons. The expectations that humans share both reflect and carry on cultural traditions. High reproductive values have been necessary to the survival of the human species as long as death rates were also very high. Societies universally share the desire to control deaths but they differ widely on the desirability of birth control. Not only are there conflicting beliefs and values regarding birth control among societies, but knowledge about the means of birth control may be restricted in some societies and promoted in others.

Although our current focus is on birth control to limit population, the direct cause of the population explosion has been a decline in mortality.

In Europe the reduction of death rates was gradual over a 75 to 150-year period. It was followed by a slow decline in birth rates. Emigration further eased the gradual increase in numbers of people.

In the less developed countries in recent years, however, relatively cheap death control was introduced from the outside, without any corresponding improvements in other aspects of life. Not only did the decline in death rates occur over a very short period of time, but in most cases there has been no evidence that birth rates are also going to decrease.

There are two very distinct patterns of population increase: the sudden rapid one of the underdeveloped nations (due to death control) and the gradual decline of the both death and birth rates during the past 150 years in Europe. Because the people of the underdeveloped countries make up two-thirds of the world population, their explosive growth becomes a concern for the entire world. And because their numbers are so great, international migration is no longer a possible solution.

As populations continue to grow, internal migration to cities increases the existing problems. Food experts argue about whether, or for how long, such increasing populations can be kept from starvation. Natural resources are everywhere abused and polluted. Economic development, supposed to solve the population problem, is reduced or nullified by the need to support increasing numbers of people. Attempts to improve the social and cultural standards of the less advantaged peoples are made increasingly difficult by the rising tide of human numbers.

## *REFERENCES*

Arriaga, Eduardo E. 1970. *Mortality decline and its demographic effects in Latin America*. Berkeley: University of California, Institute of International Studies.

Blake, Judith. 1961. *Family structure in Jamaica; The social context of reproduction*. Glencoe, Ill.: The Free Press.

Bourgeois-Pichat, Jean. 1966. *Population growth and development*. New York: Carnegie Endowment for International Peace.

Collver, O. Andrew. 1965. *Birth rates in Latin America: New estimates of historical trends and fluctuations*. Research Series no. 7. Berkeley; University of California, Institute of International Studies.

Davis, Kingsley. 1955. Institutional patterns favoring high fertility in underdeveloped areas. *Eugenics quarterly* 2 (March): 33–39.

———. 1963. The theory of change and response in modern demographic history. *Population index* 29, no. 4 (October), 345–66.

Davis, Kingsley and Judith Blake. 1956. Social structure and fertility: An analytic framework. *Economic Development and Cultural Change* 4 (April), 211–35.

Freedman, Ronald. 1961–1962. The sociology of human fertility. *Current Sociology* 10–11, no. 2. 35–68.

Hartley, Shirley Foster. 1966. The amazing rise of illegitimacy in Great Britain. *Social Forces* 44, no. 4 (June), 533–45.

———. 1970. Standardization procedures in the analysis of cross-national variations in illegitimacy measures. *Journal of Biosocial Science* 2 (April): 95–109.

———. 1971. The contributions of illegitimate and pre-maritally conceived legitimate births to total fertility. *Social Biology* 18, no. 2 (June), 178–87.

Heer, David. 1966. Economic development and fertility. *Demography* 3 no. 2, 423–44.

Heer, David and Dean O. Smith. 1968. Mortality level, desired family size, and population increase. *Demography* 5, no. 1, 104–21.

Keyfitz, Nathan. 1971. "Migration as a means of Population Control." *Population Studies,* 25, no. 1 (March), 63–72.

Kiser, Clyde V. and Pascal K. Whelpton. 1958. Summary of chief findings and implications for future studies. *Social and Psychological Factors Affecting Fertility* 5 (July), 1325–69.

Laslett, Peter. 1965. *The world we have lost.* London: Methuen & Co.

———. 1967. The extent of bastardy in restoration England. A mimeographed paper from Stanford University, December 1967. Presented by Prof. Laslett at a colloquium of the Department of Demography, University of California at Berkeley.

Lorimer, Frank. 1954, General Theory. Part One, *Culture and human fertility,* ed. UNESCO, pp. 13–247.

Murdock, George. 1949. *Social structure.* New York: Macmillan.

Nag, Moni. 1962. *Factors affecting human fertility in nonindustrial societies: A cross-cultural study.* Yale University Publication in Anthropology no. 66. New Haven: Yale University Press.

Petersen, William. 1969. *Population.* New York: Macmillan.

The Population Council. 1965. *The Population Council 1952–1964: A report,* New York: The Population Council (July).

Rele, J. R. 1963. Fertility differentials in India. *Milbank Memorial Fund Quarterly* 41, 183–99.

Rodman, Hyman. 1965. Essay review: The textbook world of family sociology. *Social Problems* 12 (Spring), 445–57.

Smelser, Neil J. 1959. *Social change in the industrial revolution: An application of theory to the British cotton industry.* Chicago: Univeristy of Chicago Press.

Thomlinson, Ralph. 1965. *Population dynamics: Causes and consequences of world demographic change.* New York: Random House.

United Nations, Department of Economic and Social Affairs. 1953. *Determinants and consequences of population trends.* New York: United Nations Population Studies no. 17, ST/SOA/Series A/17.

United Nations, Economic and Social Council. 1967. *Demographic Yearbook 1966.* New York: United Nations.

Woytinsky, W. S. & E. S. Woytinsky. 1968. World immigration patterns. In *Population and society,* ed. Charles B. Nam, pp. 298–313. Boston: Houghton Mifflin.

Wrigley, E. A. 1966. Family limitation in pre-industrial England. *Economic History Review* (April), 82–109.

———. 1969. *Population and history.* New York: McGraw-Hill.

chapter 4

# CONSEQUENCES OF THE POPULATION EXPLOSION: DENSITY

*Maximum welfare, not maximum population, is our human objective.*

Arnold Toynbee, historian (1963)

*It is important that we understand what recent research has revealed: that the whole urban system of our society, from the beginning of the nineteenth century on, has been in a state of decline. This phenomenon is international: for example, we still build systems of highways leading to the central city, but the central cities are (already) overloaded. Therefore, to say the population of the United States will double over a certain number of years, without saying that the urban population and area will grow even more, is misleading. We may well have to face the problem of serving urban areas which will be ten to twenty times larger than at present by the year 2000.*

Constantinos A. Doxiadis, architect (1969)

Population densities for the human species are determined to a great extent by the interaction of the environment, the level of technology, and the type of social organization. Among subhuman species densities are more directly dependent upon the environment alone. But, while we have been congratulating ourselves on the ways in which our technology and our social organizations have enabled ever more human beings to live, it has become more and more apparent that human beings are also bound by their environments. The emphasis on Earth Week in the spring of 1970 brought home to many persons for the first time the fact that we are limited in what can be done on our "spaceship earth." Human beings may indeed be gradually destroying the limited environment within which they must exist.

Because mankind is living under space restrictions and because man shares some of the physiological characteristics of subhuman species, we will want to consider the studies of density among the lower species. It is, of course, not acceptable to experiment with human subjects in the same ways as with rats. But some "natural" human situations can be likened to experimental density studies with animals to help us answer the question of how human subjects react to high-density conditions.

Human groups can support *various* population densities, depending on the types of technologies, social organizations, and environments. The relative importance of these factors will also be investigated in this chapter. The capacity of human beings to organize, innovate, and plan ahead has led to an evolution of societal types, but the urban-industrial type of society has in many ways become a chaotic society. Therefore, as we shall see later in this chapter, the most advantaged societies may also have the greatest potential for disorder.

Elements of contemporary chaos—the population explosion, urbanization, diversification, and technological change—are increasingly evident in the less developed as well as the more developed countries of the world. How does population density compound our other problems? An examination of distinct urban and rural densities and some of the difficulties these present for specific countries will conclude the present chapter.

## *IMPLICATIONS OF ANIMAL STUDIES*

Nature deals with overcrowding in animal societies in a number of ways, few of which are pleasant. Because many of these mechanisms appear to be automatic or self-steering, they are often called the "cybernetics of population control."

### *S-Shaped Population Growth Curves*

Hudson Hoagland (1963) describes the growth rate of multiplying cultures of microorganisms as an S-shaped curve. Initially, the growth rate accelerates exponentially; the curve rises slowly at first, then more rapidly.

However, at a certain density, a build-up of toxic metabolic products, such as acids or alcohol, occurs, causing the growth rate to decline and the curve to flatten out.

Studies on population regulation among insects, such as the fruit fly Drosophila, find a decrease in egg laying above a certain population density. The decrease is proportional to the group's density. Many studies of flour beetles show that, below a fixed number of grams of flour per beetle, cannibalism and decreased egg production occurs. In one species crowding results in the females puncturing and destroying some of the eggs they have produced. Frequency of copulation also declines as crowding increases.

## *Cyclical Growth*

Several species of mammals, both in the laboratory and in natural settings, have been found to increase and decrease numerically in a cyclical pattern.

In his "Cautionary Tale," Edward Deevey (1960) reviews three major theories of the cyclical growth of mammal populations. The first and oldest theory suggests that as a species' prey begin to increase, so do their slower-breeding predators. At peak abundance the predators nearly exterminate the prey and then starve to death, thereby clearing the way for the prey to start the cycle over again. However, the theory does not explain the fact that on islands *without* their natural predators, populations of rats and snowshoe hares (rabbits) still vary numerically in a cyclic pattern.

The second theory, the disease theory, proposes that any infection is small when an animal is scarce, but that as the hosts become more numerous, infections spread faster and become epidemic in proportion. Those who survive will increase in numbers again until some new disease decimates the ranks of the species. When pathologists began to seriously test the theory, however, they found that the abundance of microbes had *no* connection with the abundance of their hosts. Worse, animals harboring the microbes seemed to enjoy their ill health even when their numbers were greatest. When they died, there was no sign of an epidemic, at least not of an infectious disease. There was only one malady that caused large numbers of the animals to die: *shock disease*. The symptoms were similar to those of apoplexy or insulin shock. The diagnosis amounted to saying that the animals were scared to death by each other.

The third theory of cyclical population growth, therefore, suggests that populations of mammals increase in number until, in the words of John Christian, head of the animal laboratories of the Naval Medical Research Institute, "exhaustion of the adreno-pituitary system resulting from increased stresses inherent in a high population, especially in winter, plus the late winter demands of the reproductive system precipitate population-wide death with the symptoms of adrenal insufficiency and hypoglycemic convulsions (see Deevey, 1960: p. 176). The state of endocrine strain, stress, is a physical embodiment of a mental state, anxiety. Both are fed by a whole array of built-in mechanisms. Under conditions of crowding and stress, a tiny added stress can activate the adrenal medulla into sending a jolt of adrenalin to the muscles; the blood is thereby drained of sugar and the brain is suddenly starved.

Animals in dense populations show an increase in the adrenal stress syndrome. Hypertension, more fighting among males, sex drives at a low or unpredictable ebb, the eating of young, adrenal insufficiency, and convulsions have all been observed. The killing of the young and cannibalism are known to occur quite widely in rodents, lions, and primitive man. In *all* cases experimentally investigated, these reactions are found to be density-dependent and to cease below certain critical population densities (Hoagland, 1963, p. 17).

Studies of crowding within communities of subhuman species are important because, although human beings have other distinctive characteristics, there is overall agreement among scientists that *the pituitary-adrenal system of the human responds under stress in a way similar to that of other animals.*

Recent studies have led John B. Calhoun (1970) to hypothesize that "the larger the number of colonizing [initial group of] individuals the larger the ultimate size of the population before stress from increased density leads mortality and natality to come into balance" (p. 113). The implication is that space requirements are relative and that change or the rate of change may be more upsetting than absolute density. Studies of human beings (Sommer, 1969) indicate that "personal space" is culturally determined; although the boundaries of personal space may be relative, infringement of the person's invisible space will bring about behavioral indications of stress.

A well-known experiment relating density and stress in higher animals involved cutting out and weighing the adrenal glands of deer. A few deer released on uninhabited James Island in Chesapeake Bay bred through the years until at maximum density there were about 280–300, or approximately one deer per acre. In 1955 John Christian, who had been interested in density studies across various species began periodic sampling of the deer for the detailed study and weighing of the organs. In 1958 maximum density was achieved, there was a mass die-off, even while food was adequate; 161 carcasses were recovered. Following another die-off in 1959, population stabilized at about 80 deer. Christian found that during the high-density period the adrenal glands of deer were an average of 46 percent larger than in the lower-density periods. The adrenal glands had been overworked in the stressful period of crowding. Christian concluded that "mortality evidently resulted from shock. There was no evidence of infection, starvation, or other obvious cause to explain the mass mortality" (see Hall, 1966, p. 19).

In an investigation of the cyclical die-off of lemmings, Collett said, "life quickly leaves them, and they die from the slightest injury. It is constantly stated by eyewitnesses that they can die from their great excitment" (quoted in Deevey, 1960, p. 167). As early as 1939 an inquest on the Minnesota snowshoe hares reported: "This syndrome was characterized primarily by fatty degeneration and atrophy of the liver. The hares characteristically die in convulsive seizures with a sudden onset, running movements, hindleg extension, retraction of the head and neck, and sudden leaps with clonic seizures. Other animals were typically lethargic or comatose" (quoted in Deevey, 1960, p. 167). To one who has read anything of life and, especially, death in concentration camps, these descriptions do not sound unlike the behavior of humans.

## *Studies of Human Crowding*

Many experiments on rats and mice cannot be replicated with human subjects. Yet some examples of unplanned, "natural experiments" have been recorded. These include examples from war, from prisoner-of-war and concentration camps, and from urban slums.

Biderman et al. (1963) conclude in *Historical Incidents of Extreme Overcrowding* that "physical density, *per se*, is not regarded as a fruitful unitary concept for use in scientific study. For all but those extreme values approaching the physical displacement of the human body, density of occupancy has significance only in interdependent relationship with many other variables of the situation: environmental, structural, temporal, psychological and social" (p. 40). Their findings suggest, however, that it is only in very rare instances when morale is high and crowding temporary, as in the Jewish Exodus to Israel, that behavioral pathology is minimized. For the most part the historical examples of the social and psychological aspects of overcrowding are evidence of the ugly and undesirable potentialities of human behavior. "Just as has been observed in subhuman populations under conditions of crowding, human populations tend toward aberrant sexual behavior under conditions of extreme overcrowding. There may be a decrease of sexual motivation, or general stress of a short-term nature may increase sexuality" (p. 33).

Much of the research on shock disease has apparently been classified

Photo courtesy Grant Heilman.

FIG. 4–1 *It is possible to increase density almost indefinitely, and competition may be eliminated by separating individuals, but to what purpose?*

as military secrets. "Armies are not supposed to react like frightened rabbits, but the simple truth is that civilians in uniform can suffer and die from shock disease" (Deevey, 1960, p. 168). Studies conducted during the Korean War were more sophisticated than ever before. As was made horrifyingly evident after the war, "hundreds of American captives, life-trapped while away from home and families, had turned lethargic or comatose, or died in convulsive seizures with sudden onset. The crowding of anxious but idle seamen in submarines has apparently also had some effects unbefitting servicemen" (Deevey, 1960, p. 168).

Reports by Bruno Bettleheim and Victor Frankl (1963) on their experiences and observations in the German concentration camps describe some of the bizarre behaviors of the human inmates. However, they also emphasize the life-saving effect they felt, even while interred, when they focussed their mental abilities on what was going on around them.

The major objection to comparisons of human with subhuman species revolves around our very *different mental abilities*. Even in the most horrible circumstances, those abilities which are peculiarly human may be used in more ways than one to preserve life. If human beings decline to use their mental capacities, they are little different from subhuman species. Man is the only animal that can *purposefully direct* its own evolution. In the area of population growth only birth rates and death rates can be manipulated. Overcrowding may be solved by a decrease in birth rates or by increasing death rates; by way of famine, wars, or nuclear extermination. The control of births and of nuclear power are linked. Both challenge man's thinking and his ability to organize for the survival of the species.

In accepting the Nobel Peace Prize for his contribution to the "Green Revolution," Norman Borlaug (1971) noted that "man could not have forseen the disturbing and destructive physical consequences of the grotesque concentration of human beings into the poisoned and clangorous environment of pathologically hypertrophied megapoles. Can human beings endure the strain? Abnormal stresses and strains tend to accentuate man's animal instincts and provoke irrational and socially disruptive behavior among the less stable individuals in the maddening crowd."

Recent research by Omer Galle (1971) and his associates detailed the ecological correlations between five different measures of population density and five indicators of social pathology for 1960 data from 75 community areas of Chicago. Although persons per acre and structures per acre were not related to indicators of social problems, the number of persons per room, a measure of "interpersonal press," was found to have a very strong relationship with measures of mortality, juvenile delinquency, fertility, and public assistance. Most importantly, the correlations were *not* erased when ethnicity and social class were held constant. Although we must be cautious with ecological data, it is clear by now that the influence of density on human behavior is worth further study and, in the meantime, obligates us to concern ourselves with the ways we organize human living arrangements.

The implications of animal and human studies are clear-cut. Just as the offspring of frustrated mother rats, part of whose pregnancy was spent trapped in problem boxes with no exits, carried an emotional disturbance throughout their own lives, so too may the children of frustrated human mothers, trapped in urban slums, show behavioral manifestations of emotional disturbances.

Ecologist V. C. Wynne-Edwards (1965) suggests that social rivalry in both subhuman and human species is inherently density-dependent—the more competitors seeking limited rewards, the keener the contest. The impact of such stress on the pituitary-adrenal system has already been established. Members of any society would be wise to organize the least harmful and most beneficial staging of conventional competition. Yet, the intensification of competition occurs on many levels in urban areas. People compete for living space, for jobs, for transportation, and even for privacy—a quiet place in the country or a home in the suburbs becomes the ideal of the urban man. "If the city is, on the one hand, a jungle of potentially infinite and destroying competition, on the other hand, it shows the nearly infinite capacity of its members to differentiate themselves, to become useful to one another, to become needed" (Keyfitz, 1966, p. 869).

Hebb and Thompson (1968), in comparing studies of various mammalian species, have found that emotional susceptibility *increases* with intellectual capacity. Man, they conclude, is the most emotional as well as the most rational species. "Man is a rational, unemotional animal so long as there is nothing to disturb his emotions" (p. 769). Civilized society and social organization are part of man's attempt to create an environment in which overly disruptive, strong emotion is least likely to occur.

A second objection to comparisons of human with subhuman populations may be based upon the far greater rapidity of reproduction of many nonhuman species. It is true that the potentialities for rapid proliferation are much lower for humans than for many other species. Nevertheless, the possibilities for human population growth may be illustrated by an unusual, but true, story of "One Man's Family." Following reports of a Swedish family with 265 members and a Mormon couple claiming 334 living descendants, Glenn D. Everett (1961) found John Miller, who at age 94, had a grand total of 410 *living* descendants.

> John Miller actually had seen with his own eyes a population explosion in his own lifetime. His data were not statistics on a graph or chart, but the scores of children at every family gathering who ran up to kiss Grandpa, so many that it confused a poor old man. His confusion can be forgiven for there were among them no less than 15 John Millers, all named in his honor. And what young man, much less an old one, could remember the names of 61 grandchildren and 338 great-grandchildren and keep straight just who their parents were?
>
> The remarkable thing about this great clan of his was that it started with a family of just seven children. This was actually a little *smaller* than the typical family among the Amish, who have been found by one researcher to average 8.4 children per completed family. . . . During most of his long life, therefore, John Miller's family was not unusually large. It is just that he lived long enough to find out what simple multiplication can do. . . .
>
> What did John Miller think about his family? Did it worry him to see it growing so large? Significantly, *his concerns were the very ones that the demographers, the economists, the sociologists, the other serious students of world population problems have been voicing.* He is not an educated man, for the Amish still believe eight grades of education in a one-room country school is sufficient, but John Miller summarized it in one simple question he constantly repeated, "Where will they all find farms?" Some day, at some point, John Miller's plaintive question, "where will they all find farms?" will have to be answered in the bleak negative. They can continue now only by buying farms others will sell

them. Some day no more farms anywhere will be for sale. A finite world is of limited size. So, ultimately at some point, is the population it can hold" (pp. 42–44; italics added).

## *THE INCREASING DENSITY OF HUMAN SOCIETIES*

Studies on density of nonhuman populations, as we have seen, report an S-shaped, or wavelike, growth curve. Within a limited space, with a control on a species' predators, and a plentiful food supply, a particular species seems to increase in numbers only slowly to begin with, but with increasing rapidity until a slowdown and leveling-off occurs with no subsequent increase in numbers. In some cases a decrease in the birth rate contributes to the leveling-off, but the major factor seems to be an increase in deaths, with a related pathology that implies a physically unhealthy and socially disorganized system of relationships.

> From students of bacteria, trees, insects or any of the sundry groups of vertebrate animals, fish, fowl, or mammal we get the same story. No known form of life has been observed to multiply indefinitely without bumping up against the limitation imposed by the space it occupies. *The limitations involve not only quantity but quality.* And quality rests upon the pattern of the complex of factors, whether known or unknown, that are necessary to sustain the species in question (Sears, 1958, p. 11; italics added).[1]

The whole process appears to be self-steering for the lower species. An examination of human populations, however, must take into consideration the capacity of human beings to alter the automatic aspects of population control.

Homo sapiens appear to be the only species which are capable of reorganizing their spatial environment and their food supply, as well as controlling their predators and the reproduction and mortality of their own kind. The totally unique aspects of these human capacities cannot be overemphasized. *Man alone has the ability to improve the quality of existence within the natural environment.* Man has already used his mental abilities to reduce death rates from their "natural" levels. Many population specialists are now suggesting that the period of rapid human population growth will level off as a result of a rise in death rates, accompanied by an increase in hunger and misery.

Intelligence requires that we examine what has been occurring. What do present trends and future possibilities and probabilities tell us about the advisability of different patterns of human behavior? Is man really

[1] See also Ardrey (1966).

interested in increasing the quality of human life on this finite earth, rather than arguing about and waiting to see how many human bodies the earth can support at minimum levels of existence? If so, there is every advantage to be gained from learning about population limitation *now,* not years and billions of bodies in the future. It is difficult to imagine that as individuals become aware of the complexity and implications of population growth they will not want to put their knowledge to work for the survival and betterment of the human species.

## *Types of Societies and Population Density*

Man's ability to exist in varying population densities results from technological and organizational changes within and among societies. A typology of the evolution of societies has been proposed by Walter Goldschmidt (1959, pp. 185–217). He suggests that the earliest type of society was one in which the primary supportive activity was *nomadic hunting and food gathering.* About one square mile per person was required for the survival of small bands, which probably averaged no more than 20 to 50 persons per unit. For perhaps 98 percent of his time on earth, man has lived from gathering food (Petersen, 1969, p. 345). The maximum world population possible during that period of human history has been computed by Petersen to have been on the order of 30 million. Restricting the area to that known by archeologists to have actually been inhabited at the time, however, it could hardly have been more than 5 million (p. 347).

The improvement of hunting tools, the use of the spear instead of the club, and then the development of the bow and arrow, which was more efficient than the spear, allowed tribes to settle down in one or more settlements within tribal boundaries. In the *sedentary hunting and food-gathering societies,* groups would go out on forays and return to their small settlements with their game. The permanent villages may have averaged about 100 persons, divided into separate family units.

The settling down of nomadic tribes facilitated the emergence of the cultivation of land and/or the herding of animals. The invention of the hoe and the development of horticulture (the planting of seeds, roots, or tubers) allowed a significant increase in subsistence and, therefore, had a major role in the rise in human numbers in this third type of society. Densities between 26 and 64 persons per square mile may have been supported by the early *horticultural societies.*

A fourth type of society is characterized by a fully developed agriculture and the accumulation of a sufficient agricultural surplus to allow for the settlement of a portion of the population in cities. This type began to emerge around 4000 B.C. in the Nile delta of Egypt, the Tigris-

Euphrates valley in Iraq, the Indus valley in Pakistan, and the Yellow and Yangtze valleys in China. The *agricultural-stage society* is characterized by the presence of domesticated animals, and the irrigation of agricultural land wherever possible. In addition, other technological developments such as terracing, fertilizing, the regular rotation of crops, the use of wheeled vehicles, sailboats, metallurgy, and the alphabet date from around this period and contributed to increased productivity and/or distribution. In addition, more highly organized and unified political systems eventuated in the "elimination of constant warfare and feuding" and helped to "support large and stable populations" (Goldschmidt, 1959, p. 196).

These developments combined to facilitate the rise of cities in many parts of the world. For a city to exist, farmers must produce a surplus and city-dwellers must have something to offer in exchange for the agricultural goods *or* the power to simply confiscate a portion of the agricultural produce. In the preindustrial period there were limits on the proportion of a population which might be supported in cities and in the products that city-dwellers could offer in exchange for food. Estimates are that prior to the industrial revolution no more than 2 percent of the world's population lived in urban areas.

In the fifth, or *urban-industrial* type of society, "the division of labor becomes very complex, subsistence is obtained largely through the application of inanimate sources of energy (such as coal and petroleum), and much or most of the population lives in cities. Each of these types of society progressively allows population of given size to procure a greater supply of goods and services from a given territory. Therefore, each societal type progressively allows for a higher density of population. In fact, as actual societies have progressed upward along this typology, *all* of them have experienced increased population density" (Heer, 1968, p. 5).

Such diverse writers as Plato and Durkheim have discussed the necessity of specific population distributions for the development of a division of labor. Durkheim (1933) spoke of the importance of an increase in both the "physical and moral density" of population, or social contact and social interaction (Book II, Chapter 2).

Certainly there are advantages to be had in the economies of scale, when sparsely settled populations are able to grow and reorganize into social groups capable of developing and sharing special skills. It is becoming more and more obvious, however, that almost every country in the world has moved beyond these advantages to a situation where there are diminishing returns from the addition of units to the labor force or to the population as a whole. For instance, as city size increases, there is an increase in the per capita, as well as total costs of many city services, such as government, education, and protective agencies. Large cities in the U.S. spend, on the average, 2½ times as much per inhabitant for police protection as do small

TABLE 4-1 *Municipal Police Department Expenditures*

| | *Population Size—Group of Cities* | | | | | |
|---|---|---|---|---|---|---|
| | *10,001–25,000* | *25,001–50,000* | *50,001–100,000* | *100,001–250,000* | *250,000–500,000* | *Over 500,000* |
| Per capita expended | $15.23 | $18.56 | $16.61 | $17.75 | $20.19 | $38.65 |
| Total in million dollars | $158 | $197 | $167 | $187 | $142 | $1,049 |
| Number cities reporting | 683 | 307 | 148 | 73 | 21 | 20 |

*Source:* United States, Bureau of the Census (1970), Table 231, p. 151.

cities (see Table 4-1). Although increased educational costs may be related to improved education, increased protective services are required by crime rates five to seven times higher in large than in small cities (see Table 4-3).

## THE CHAOTIC SOCIETY

In his presidential address to the American Sociological Association, Philip Hauser (1969) suggested that contemporary society has become a "chaotic society." His analysis of the type of society that has evolved with increasing population densities is worth a detailed summary.

### *Unique Factors in Contemporary Chaos*

Although societies have had periods of disorder throughout human history, there are several unique aspects of contemporary chaos.

First of all, our contemporary society is faced with the greatest number of cultural layers ever known. The more layers [2] there are, the more differences in living patterns and the greater the potential confusion. Societies are usually defined by a *shared* culture encompassing such aspects as language, legal statutes, and governmental supervision. But at the same time that societies communicate by way of a single language, they may tolerate great diversity in the ways of living or subcultural patterns. The number of different "designs for living" has received tremendous impetus from international mobility and from enlarged freedom of choice allowed to individuals in many advanced societies.

Second, in addition to the fact that the number of cultural layers

[2] In the United States, in particular, each new group of immigrants brought with it an established style of life and added to, but rarely completely assimilated with, a general "American" pattern. Each group added a distinctive flavor to the whole and yet maintained some differences, making the whole more analogous to a fruitcake than to a melting pot.

has increased, the patterns themselves are much more diverse than in previous societies. Rather than striving for assimilation or accomodation, social groups within the same basic society may strive to maintain or even increase their distinctiveness, and this striving for diversity may be interpreted by other groups as rejection. In that case, group antagonism, competition, and/or conflict is likely to result. The increase in the mass media and transportation facilities also increases the *awareness* of differences between "in-groups" and "out-groups," both within and among societies.

Third, contemporary society contains the means of its own destruction. Annihilation of whole societies and even of the human race itself becomes possible with nuclear weapons. The old suspicions and antagonisms between social groups have assumed a magnitude of fear unknown to our forefathers.

Fortunately, however, contemporary society has the knowledge (and the capacity to increase that knowledge through sociological research) to reduce the confusion and to reorganize to restore order. But first it is necessary to understand the complex reasons for society's present plight. Hauser's thesis is that "contemporary society, the chaotic and anachronistic society, is experiencing unprecedented tensions and strains by reasons of the social morphological revolution" (p. 2).

The "social morphological revolution" refers to the changes in the size, density, and heterogeneity of population and also to the influence of these changes on man and society. There are four factors, then, involved in the "social morphological revolution": (1) the population explosion; (2) the population "implosion"—the increasing proportion of populations living in cities; (3) population diversification—differentiation in the way of life and/or occupational specialization; and, finally, (4) the related technological and social changes following from the first three factors.

### *The Size-Density Model*

To demonstrate what happens when the size and density of a population are increased, Hauser has computed the "multiplier effect" on *potential* human interaction with different population densities in a fixed land area. Table 4-2 compares the potential contacts, or number of persons in a circle of ten-mile radius, under various densities.

Hauser suggests that the Indian population of the United States prior to European settlement (about 1500 A.D.) approximated one person per square mile, leading to a potential 314 human contacts in a circular area with a 10-mile radius. Other estimates place the density of the United States' Indian population about 1500 at about one-third of this level (Petersen, 1969, pp. 359–60). By 1960, however, the population

*TABLE 4-2 The Multiplier Effect on Potential Human Interaction with Increased Population Density in a Fixed Land Area*

| *Assumed Population Density—Persons per Square Mile* | *Area with the Approximate Density Assumed* | *Number of Persons in a Circle of 10-Mile Radius* |
|---|---|---|
| 1 | U.S. in 1500 | 314 |
| 50 | U.S. and world in 1960 | 15,700 |
| 8,000 | Average central city, metropolitan U.S.—1960 | 2,512,000 |
| 17,000 | Chicago | 5,338,000 |
| 25,000 | New York City | 7,850,000 |
| 75,000 | Manhattan | 23,550,000 |

*Source:* Philip M. Hauser, "The Chaotic Society: Product of the Social Morphological Revolution," in *American Sociological Review*, 34 (February, 1969), 3.

density of the United States and of the world as a whole was about 50 persons per square mile. That density would produce a potential of 15,700 human contacts within a circle of 10-mile radius.

However, human beings are not spread evenly over the United States or the face of the earth. More and more people are living in high-density urban areas. Table 4-2 indicates a tremendous leap in density to 8,000 persons per square mile in the average central portion of metropolitan cities in the United States by 1960. The potential for human interaction in the given circle increases to 2.5 million! Even that staggering figure does not exhaust the possibilities, however. The average central city densities in Chicago, New York City, and Manhattan Island allow potential contacts within a circle of 10-mile radius to rise to 23,550,000.

Nor does Manhattan Island with 75,000 persons per square mile, *maximize* human population density. The densely settled areas of Hong Kong average about 250,000 persons per square mile, over three times the density of Manhattan. For areas smaller than a square mile, the 1961 census of Hong Kong reported two divisions with over 2,800 persons per acre and eleven more divisions averaging over 2,000 persons per acre.

While it may be possible for human beings to survive in population densities of up to a quarter of a million persons per square mile when food is imported, no one *recommends* that such densities are helpful to the full development of human potentialities.

Sociological and psychological evidence indicates that human beings at birth are merely bundles of potentialities. The development of human capacities is totally dependent upon the social and physical environment. When additional babies added to the social environment seriously reduce the developmental chances of those already born, it can only be wise to curtail reproduction. And if a child born in the United States will use up 25 times as much of the world's natural resources as a child born in India, his birth can lead to increased suffering *anywhere* in the world. Even parents who are economically affluent themselves must be willing to consider how their childbearing, if unlimited, would affect other human beings around the world. It is difficult for people in the advanced nations to believe that an estimated 10,000 persons, most of them children, die from malnutrition *every day* in the less developed nations. There is no way to count those who die from other immediate causes because they were physically weakened from malnutrition.

People are just beginning to recognize the psychological results of crowding in cities. The question of whether or not human beings may be increasingly mentally isolated within crowds is frequently raised. If we cannot socially interact with millions of persons in the city, isn't it likely that we will build a psychological wall to keep out the floods of "others" who threaten to invade our personal worlds? Why, in the midst of our togetherness, has alienation become such a popular contemporary theme?

"In overcrowded living social and psychological devices for maintaining privacy partially substitute for the lack of physical ones. . . . Psychological withdrawal and psychic insulation, as noted in various prisoner groups, provide sources of protection" (Biderman *et al.*, 1963, p. 35). It is no longer uncommon to hear or read of people watching from sidewalks or apartment windows as other human beings are brutally beaten or stabbed on the city streets. Without a minimal phone call to alert protective agencies, these passive observers demonstrate that social isolation has become pathological in urban areas.

### *Heterogeneity*

The cultural and occupational diversification of the population gives us a greater range of choices, but also makes it easier for individuals to pull apart from the human group, to socially isolate themselves even while superficially interacting with others. It is possible that the family, as a "primary group," becomes more important as the superficiality of contacts outside of the family increases. Biderman *et al.* (1963) observed that "in stress situations, despite continuous close physical contact with many others, people tend to restrict their intimate, reciprocal social contacts to just one or two others" (p. 35). Human beings need authentic relationships and family members may provide one another with satisfying human interchanges. However, the family cannot separate itself from the larger human group called society. Although one may remove himself psychologically, human beings are actually becoming more interdependent both within and among the nations of the world.

A high degree of occupational specialization, by itself, makes man dependent upon others for the necessities and niceties of life. The division of labor found in contemporary society makes for greater interdependence and, therefore, more vulnerability to disruptions in the network of relationships. Hauser (1969) suggests that both the employee's right to strike *and* the employer's right to a lockout are attempts to impose solutions through force or violence and are, therefore, no better than the laws of the jungle. With thousands of occupational specializations, it must be increasingly clear that a situation in which each one attempts to maximize group goals will evolve into a war of all against all, in which everyone may suffer. Interdependence would seem to require compromise or, in the case of labor disputes, compulsory arbitration. Competition which is advantageous to the whole society must be promoted, while that which is destructive must be held within strict limits. The problem for every society over time is how to take advantage of a human striving for excellence and at the same time limit the divisive tendencies which may also result from competition.

Hauser suggests that our vulnerability requires a commitment to the "brotherhood of man" and a "social-engineering approach" to the organization of human group life:

> The practical purpose of social data is to permit social accounting . . . (which becomes) possible only after goals are decided. . . . Social scientists may participate in goal formation by (1) the examination of choices, and (2) the examination of possible and probable consequences.
>
> Man is the only significant culture-building animal on earth. He not only adapts to environment, he creates it as well. He has created a world in which mankind itself is the crucial environment—a mankind characterized by large numbers, high densities, and great heterogeneity. He is still learning how to live in this new world he has created. The product of the chief components of the social morphological revolution—the population explosion, the population implosion, and population diversification—together with rapid technological and social change—is contemporary society, a chaotic society, an anachronistic society. It is a society characterized by dissonant cultural strata—by confusion and disorder. It is also a society which for the first time in human history possesses the capacity to destroy itself—globally as well as nation by nation (p. 16).

The major purpose of this book is to present the choices before us and the probable consequences of our behavior in relation to population. Not only is the number of people in the world increasing, but human beings are also flocking to the already overcrowded cities so that the populations of the most densely crowded areas are growing even more rapidly than that of the world or of any single nation. "Pathological togetherness" has been observed in many species. Calhoun (1964) describes the pathological behavior of male and female rats. Deranged patterns of behavior ranging from frenetic overactivity to pathological withdrawal, occurred at a density that was only *twice* that of a healthy community.

Inhabitants of congested urban slums are more frequently exposed to, and more likely to engage in, forms of social pathology. It is difficult for slum dwellers to avoid street gangs, criminals, and con men of all varieties. "Urban slums have been the subject of study for hundreds of years in connection with the dangers to health and morality arising from chronic conditions of overcrowding. Yet, the literature does not advance us much beyond a general statement that crowded housing is demonstrably unhealthy, physically, psychologically, and socially" (Biderman *et al.*, 1963, p. F-2). Several studies have indicated a higher incidence of schizophrenia and other psychotic and neurotic behavior in congested urban areas than in more spacious surroundings (Hoagland, 1963). Although pathological behaviors are more numerous in high density areas of Chicago even when social class is neutralized as a causal factor (see Galle, 1971), discussion tends to center on poverty areas because the congestion problem is most noticeable there. The social pathology of the slum is probably a result of the interaction of two factors: (1) persons with behavior problems gravitate toward the slum areas, and (2) the congestion itself produces aberrant behavior. The number of crimes in a city is not only related arithmetically to the number of persons. Rather, crime rates *per 100,000 people* increase dramatically as city size increases (see Table 4-3). Either the actual or imagined advantages of urban living outweigh the disadvantages or we are indeed

TABLE 4-3 *Crime Rates, by City Size and Type: 1968 (Offenses known to the police per 100,000 population)*

| *Population Group* | | | |
|---|---|---|---|
| *City Size* | *No. of Cities* | *Violent Crime* | *Property Crime* |
| 250,000 or more | 57 | 779 | 5,283 |
| 100,000–249,999 | 97 | 331 | 4,401 |
| 50,000–99,999 | 257 | 224 | 3,630 |
| 25,000–49,999 | 464 | 153 | 3,003 |
| 10,000–24,999 | 1,176 | 128 | 2,596 |
| Less than 10,000 | 2,224 | 113 | 2,044 |
| Suburbs | 2,235 agencies * | 149 | 2,507 |
| Rural areas | 1,598 agencies * | 104 | 1,073 |

* Law-enforcement agencies reporting.
*Source:* United States, Bureau of the Census (1970), Table 216, p. 144.

propelled toward "pathological togetherness," since both the numbers *and* the proportions of persons living in urban areas are increasing even more rapidly than is the population as a whole.

## *URBAN GROWTH COMPARED TO RURAL GROWTH*

The relationship between the population explosion, the population implosion, and population diversification has been highlighted. Let us now turn to an investigation of the growth of population and the rise in density for the world as a whole and for the various areas of the world. Urban-rural differences and densities will then be specified.

### *Density for the World as a Whole and for Areas of the World*

In Table 4-4 are the data on population growth between 1920 and 1960 and medium variant estimates to 2000. Since the land area of the world is fixed, the density of population for the world and regions of the world

TABLE 4-4 *Total Population and Density (per square kilometer) of the World and Major Areas, as Estimated for 1920, 1960, and 2000*

| *Major Area* | *Area (thous. of sq. km.)* | *Population (millions)* 1920 | 1960 | 2000 | *Density per Square Kilometer* 1920 | 1960 | 2000 |
|---|---|---|---|---|---|---|---|
| World total | 135,129 | 1,860 | 2,991 | 6,112 | 13.8 | 22.1 | 45.2 |
| More developed areas | 57,495 | 604 | 854 | 1,266 | 10.5 | 14.9 | 22.1 |
| Europe | 4,931 | 325 | 425 | 527 | 15.9 | 86.2 | 106.9 |
| North America | 21,515 | 116 | 199 | 354 | 5.4 | 9.3 | 16.5 |
| Soviet Union | 22,402 | 155 | 214 | 353 | 6.9 | 9.6 | 15.8 |
| Oceania | 8,557 | 8 | 16 | 32 | .9 | 1.9 | 3.7 |
| Less developed areas | 77,724 | 1,256 | 2,137 | 4,846 | 16.2 | 27.5 | 62.4 |
| East Asia | 11,726 | 553 | 794 | 1,287 | 47.2 | 67.7 | 109.7 |
| South Asia | 15,234 | 470 | 858 | 2,153 | 30.9 | 56.3 | 141.3 |
| Latin America | 20,537 | 90 | 212 | 638 | 4.4 | 10.3 | 31.1 |
| Africa | 30,227 | 143 | 273 | 768 | 4.7 | 9.0 | 25.4 |

*Source:* Computations from United Nations, Bureau of Social Affairs, "Growth of the World's Urban and Rural Population, 1920–2000." New York: United Nations, 1969.

varies directly with the numerical population itself. At the present rate of growth, it would appear that the medium estimate of the United Nations will be too low. Even with this conservative projection, however, population density for the world would double between 1960 and 2000. For the "developing" countries (those least capable of adjusting to the increase) the increase would be greater than for the "developed" countries.

Latin America, the most rapidly growing area of the world, is likely to triple in numbers and density between 1960 and 2000. Medium estimates of growth indicate that by the year 2000 both East and South Asia will have surpassed Europe in overall population densities. Yet the ability to support such densities by the nations of Asia is highly questionable. An *average* of 141 persons per square kilometer, or about 400 persons per square mile,[3] in agricultural South Asia is difficult to imagine.

Moreover, some portions of each region of the world are unsuitable for human habitation. Average densities, therefore, are not necessarily the same as the actual population density of the inhabited land mass. Although man may, through invention and perseverance, expand usable land, there are limits on the feasibility of doing so. For numerous reasons, then, historical as well as geographic and climatic, it is not always the largest country geographically that has the biggest population (Bourgeois-Pichat, 1966, p. 42). A study of the food problem (see Chapter 5) suggests that in order to grow more food for expanding populations more land might be put under cultivation. However, while some limited areas might be developed, almost all of the world's usable land is presently in use, either for crop production or for grazing. Furthermore, the expansion of urban areas is presently reducing agricultural lands (by one million acres per year in the United States alone).

Although the densities of the major areas of the world vary greatly, the underdeveloped, agricultural countries, as a group, already have higher average densities than the developed countries. Yet they have not reached the urban-industrial stage of societal evolution. Some are not yet fully developed agricultural societies, others have overworked and ruined once fertile lands. Population density has increased in spite of low levels of technology, not in response to the improved organization and technology suggested by theories of societal evolution. In the chapters to follow we will see repeatedly that the so-called agricultural societies are barely able to feed rapidly increasing and dense populations. In fact, the more developed countries, regardless of levels of density, evidence higher quality in the overall level of support in food, housing, education, and so forth.

### *Urban-rural Differences*

Differences in population densities between urban and rural areas within countries vary more greatly than do differences among countries (the United States, for example, averages 50 persons per square mile over-

[3] It should be noted that a lineal kilometer is equal to six-tenths of a square mile. A square kilometer is, therefore, only a little over one-third of a square mile. Densities per square kilometer have to be multiplied by three in order to approximate densities per square mile.

all, but 8,000 persons per square mile in average central cities). What are the levels of urbanization that is, the proportions of populations living in urban areas and how have these changed over time? Moreover, what do these differences mean under various circumstances, and what are the possibilities for the continuing urbanization of the world?

Historically, for the world as a whole, the proportion of the total population living in urban areas (communities of 20,000 or more persons) has risen only slowly. Nevertheless, the proportion has approximately doubled within each of the last three half-centuries (see Table 4-5).

*TABLE 4-5 Percentage of World's Population Living in Cities*

| | *Cities of 20,000 or More* | *Cities of 100,000 or More* |
|---|---|---|
| 1800 | 2.4 | 1.7 |
| 1850 | 4.3 | 2.3 |
| 1900 | 9.2 | 5.5 |
| 1950 | 20.9 | 13.1 |

*Source:* Kingsley Davis, *The Modern Urban Revolution.* New York: Random House, 1967.

By 1950 the percentage of the world's population living in cities of 20,000 and over was greater than for *any* country in 1800 (Davis, 1955, p. 433). It is estimated that the proportion of world population living in cities of 20,000 persons or more will almost double again by the year 2000. Although cities themselves are not a result of industrialization, a high proportion of human populations dwelling in urban areas *is.*

## *Developed vs. Less Developed Countries*

In the now developed countries, gradual increases in the proportion of urban population seem to have accompanied industrial development. In the nonindustrial countries, urbanization seems to be occurring in response to overcrowding in rural areas. Contemporary urbanization in less developed countries is more often the result of a "push" from rural areas than a "pull" or attraction toward opportunities in urban places.

Currently, an average of one-fourth of the population of 170 underdeveloped countries is living in urban places, while almost 70 percent of the population of developed countries live in cities (United Nations, 1969, p. 73). There is a theoretical limit of 100 percent of populations living in urban areas, and a practical limit somewhat lower, because some rural inhabitants are needed to produce food. Since the advanced countries are nearer to both the theoretical and practical limits, the less developed countries have a greater capacity for continued urbanization. In fact, projections to the year 2000 indicate an expected 81 percent urban in the developed regions as a whole and 41 percent urban for the less developed regions (see Table 4-6). The 40 year increase from 20 to 41 percent urban estimated for the less developed regions represents a 105 percent increase in the initial *proportion* urban.

*TABLE 4-6 Estimated Percentages of Urban Population, as Nationally Defined, in the Total Population of the World and Major Areas: 1920, 1940, 1960, 1980, and 2000*

| *Major Area* | *1920* | *1940* | *1960* | *1980* | *2000* |
|---|---|---|---|---|---|
| World Total | 19 | 25 | 33 | 46 | 51 |
| More developed major areas | 40 | 48 | 59 | 70 | 80 |
| Europe | 46 | 53 | 58 | 65 | 71 |
| Northern America | 52 | 59 | 70 | 81 | 87 |
| Soviet Union | 15 | 32 | 49 | 68 | 85 |
| Oceania | 47 | 53 | 64 | 75 | 80 |
| Less developed major areas | 10 | 14 | 23 | 32 | 43 |
| East Asia | 9 | 13 | 23 | 31 | 40 |
| South Asia | 9 | 12 | 18 | 25 | 35 |
| Latin America | 22 | 31 | 49 | 60 | 80 |
| Africa | 7 | 11 | 18 | 28 | 39 |
| More developed regions | 39 | 47 | 60 | 71 | 81 |
| Less developed regions | 8 | 12 | 20 | 30 | 41 |

*Source:* United Nations, Bureau of Social Affairs, *Growth of the World's Urban and Rural Population, 1920–2000*. Population Studies, No. 44. ST/SOA/Series A/44. New York, 1969, p. 73.

Projections of numerical increases in urban population in the less developed countries are far more astounding. If India's population increases as United Nations' projections indicate it will, the rapidity of growth interacting with increasing proportions urban lead to projections of 36 to 66 million persons for the city of Calcutta by the year 2000 (Davis, 1965, p. 22). That city, as we will see in some detail, cannot now provide adequately for 7 million; how will it manage with five to nine times as many? Surely the trends underlying such projections must be altered to forestall these numerical concentrations.

An indication of the problems ahead may be gathered from a careful look at Figure 4-2, which allows simultaneous comparison of numerical differences between more and less developed areas and urban-rural growth over time. The numerical growth of the developed areas of the world on the left-hand side of the graph, is shown to be much smaller than growth in the less developed regions of the world (on the right-hand

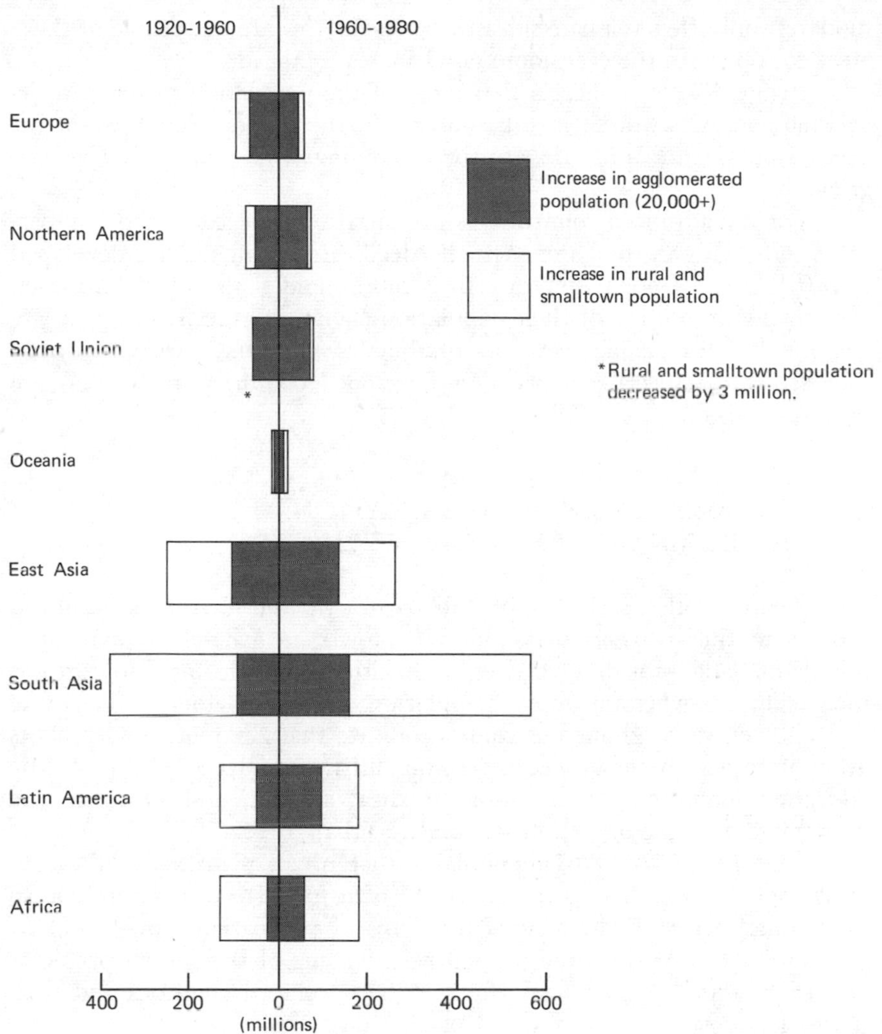


*Source:* United Nations, Bureau of Social Affairs, *Growth of the World's Urban and Rural Population, 1920–2000.* Population Studies, No. 44. ST/SOA/Series A/44. New York, 1969, p. 62.

FIG. 4–2 *Increases in Agglomerated and Rural and Smalltown Population in Eight Major Areas, 1920–1960 and 1960–1980*

side of the graph). The growth pattern between 1920 and 1960 is displayed below the horizontal and the growth expected from 1960 to 1980 above the horizontal. It is clear that the growth expected during the current 20 years is greater than that of the previous 40 years, except in Europe and North America. The growth of the last forty years has been accommodated, but often at a bare subsistence level. How are the people of these areas to cope with the even more rapid increases ahead?

Figure 4-2 also indicates that most of the population increase in developed countries will be in urban areas. In the less developed countries, even while urban areas are greatly expanding, the rural areas will be growing.

For the advanced countries, as urbanization proceeded, the numbers of persons living in rural areas actually declined. Yet in the less developed countries because population growth is more rapid than ever before, even though the proportion of their populations living in cities is rising, so are the numbers of people living in rural areas. Not only are cities overcrowded, but, especially in the less developed countries, rural areas are overcrowded, too.

## *THE MEANING OF URBANIZATION: PROBLEMS OF URBAN GROWTH*

Many of the problems of urban growth and density are related directly to the problems of population growth in general. Supporting a population and providing services in health, education, and so forth is more difficult wherever rapid population growth is found. To make matters even worse, numerous studies indicate that the more governments attempt to accommodate the increasing urban populations by providing education, housing, transportation, medical services, and so forth, the more rapidly people migrate from rural to urban areas.

Kingsley Davis (1965) complains that urban planners continue to treat population growth as something *to plan for* instead of something *to be planned.* Most of the general problems of population growth will be examined later. At this time we will review some of the special problems created by rapid urban growth, first in the developed countries and then in the less developed nations.

### *Urban Problems in Developed Countries*

All of the major cities in the developed countries of the world are now encountering problems with pollution in its many forms. The more affluent the society, the more potentiality for spoiling our communal resources—air, water, and the natural environment. The average American uses up 25 times as much of the world's resources as the average person in India; he also puts back into the environment an average of four pounds of garbage per day (United States, Bureau of the Census, 1970, p. 172).

Although each would like to blame "others," everyone contributes in many ways. The larger the city, the more difficult the disposal problem. San Francisco has had so much difficulty finding another community willing to take its refuse that it had considered shipping its garbage by rail to Lassen County, 200 miles away. Despite their enormity, it may be less difficult to solve the pollution problems that accompany high population densities than to reduce the human strains.

Although civil disturbances have occurred in many large cities, city size alone does not cause riots. Most of the disturbances have occurred in black ghetto areas. (A ghetto involves a geographical area which is limited in size even if its population is expanding.) Using data from the Kerner Commission (National Advisory Commission, 1968, pp. 158–159), I found that one could clearly separate riot from nonriot cities on the basis of the rate of increase of the black population in the 30 largest cities in the United States from 1950 to 1965. The more serious the riot, the higher the rate of increase was likely to have been. The addition of more persons to a relatively contained ghetto area undoubtedly further increased the already stressful physical and human environments.

Obviously, the more rapidly the population grows within a confined area, the more dense it becomes. Just as the subhuman animals in dense conditions described above found a slight added stress intolerable, so too the incidents precipitating mob action in ghettos are often relatively unimportant in themselves. The arrest or insult which might otherwise be ignored lights the spark which incites human beings to mob action. Reduced urban density will not cure discrimination, but increased ghetto density will surely make difficult situations worse.

In 1900 the Lower East Side of New York City was so packed with human beings that at the same density[4] the entire population of the United States up to 1938 could have been crammed into the five boroughs of New York City! The prospect is not a pleasant one, but even without an increase in its proportion of the total population, merely in response to the growth of the United States population, Kinsley Davis (1965) projects a New York urban area population of 30 million by the year 2010. Will there be increases in civil disturbances too?

With the exception of concentration camps, ghetto areas are the human environment most similar to the contained space of the subhuman species whose reactions we discussed. It is frightening to make the analogy explicit, but everyone has heard and read about the high incidence of crime and delinquency, the high and random sexual activity, and the hyperactivity versus apathy and withdrawal in ghetto areas. While many ghetto residents want to "get out," others merely want to improve the

[4] 350,000 persons per square mile (see Thomlinson, 1965).

situation within which they find themselves. Meanwhile, still others are migrating from areas that they feel are worse. To improve ghetto conditions we must not only improve the physical and social situation within, but must raise the quality of life and opportunities outside of these concentrated areas.

Within the framework of the general population explosion and implosion in the entire nation, there has occurred an even more dramatic population explosion and implosion among Afro-Americans (Hauser, 1969, p. 7). Whenever rural persons with skills appropriate to rural communities move to urban areas, they encounter problems in adjusting to the new way of life. When the move is from the relatively backward rural areas of the southern United States to central urban districts of the most advanced nation in the world, and when discrimination on the basis of race is added to discrimination on the basis of rural background, the problems of adjustment are heightened.

From 1910, before the heavy out-migration of the Negro from the South began, to 1960, just fifty years later, the black population of the United States was transformed from 73 percent rural to 73 percent urban. The urbanization of black Americans has continued throughout the sixties and a higher proportion of blacks than of whites now live in urban areas in the United States.

One cannot leave the exploration of urban problems in developed countries with the idea that poverty and slums prevail. The largest cities of the advanced countries also contain the most affluent populations of the world. One reason for the rapid migration into these areas is the desire of outsiders to share in the higher standards of living and in the opportunities for better schooling and jobs. These things do not come automatically, however, and in both developed and underdeveloped countries planners are beginning to recognize that the more provision is made for decent educational facilities, housing, and health care in the urban areas, the more persons move in to take advantage of the improvements, and the more difficult it becomes to meet the ever-increasing needs of the ever-increasing population.

The wealthiest population in the world, residing in the "megalopolis" that stretches from Washington, D.C., to Boston, Massachusetts, has been having increasing difficulty meeting its needs for pure water, fresh air, and electricity as well as housing. People have long taken the "natural environment" for granted, but clean air, uncontaminated water, and open spaces are rapidly increasing in cost as urbanization continues to advance. When Manhattan Island, surrounded by water, must ration its supply available for drinking, washing and so forth, the group is forced to recognize the need to reorganize its system of priorities. The declining quality of our urban environment and the rush to surburbia are becoming more evident yearly. Pressures are rising to put livability back into city living. Paul and Anne Ehrlich (1970) have suggested that if smog had reached its present level in Los Angeles overnight, the residents would have fled the city. Since it increased gradually, however, people came to accept it and live with it. So, too, with commuter traffic tie-ups: we have learned to tolerate transportation problems, to build more freeways to accomodate more cars so that more persons working shorter hours are able to devote more time to commuting longer distances so that they don't have to live in the same crowded city in which they work. A recent Rand study (Dyckman, 1965) concluded that additional accommodation to the automobile creates additional traffic. Continued population increases, together with rising standards of living (including more cars per family), will continue to aggravate traffic problems in the major cities of the world.

Although the results of the 1970 United States census show a decline in population for 22 of the 50 largest cities since 1960, there was an increase in the proportion of the total population living in urban areas. We should recognize that as suburban areas and transportation facilities increase, more people are able to live outside the city and add themselves only to the daytime population of the central city. Meanwhile, we know that a decrease in numbers of residents does not necessarily mean a reduction in central city residential density. Urban renewal and central city building in general have often meant the replacement of residential units by office buildings, hotels, stores, freeways, or high-rise, high-density residential units, none of which alleviate the problems of high density in living areas.

### *Urban Problems in Underdeveloped Countries*

Urban problems in the less developed countries are similar in some ways to those faced by the advanced countries. Yet there are some major differences relating to the timing and magnitude of population increases and urbanization. In addition, the resources for coping with resultant problems are far fewer in the less developed than in the advanced countries.

Very rapid human multiplication, together with increasing proportions of the populations living in urban areas, have forced fantastic population growth on some cities in the less developed areas of the world. Between 1941 and 1963 the population of Caracas, Venezuela quadrupled. More than half of the large cities of the world are in underdeveloped countries. These cities have appeared in traditional agricultural economics in *advance* of the industrial revolution that is supposed to beget urbanization.

In Calcutta over seven million persons live in an area of 490 square miles. Three-quarters of these people live in overcrowded tenement and slum quarters. Over 50 percent have only 30 square feet, *or less,* of living space per person (Bose, 1965), barely over the 18 square feet which

FIG. 4–3 *In Calcutta high density is maintained even though single-storied shacks prevail. Wide World Photo*

would be needed for a single bed. Observers have indicated that although the dwellings are clean inside, garbage is dumped everywhere outside, implying a lack of concern for neighbors who share the living space. Population projections for Calcutta, as mentioned above, range from a low of 36 million to a high of 66 million by the year 2000. The migration of males has already been so great that there are almost twice as many males as females in the city. Such an unbalanced "sex ratio" contributes to instability of family life and to other problems (for instance, homelessness and political riots). Bose claims that migrations to Calcutta are *not* prompted by the "dual spur of specialization and cooperation of labor" but rather by the hope of an easier life. Although there is the advantage of some caste breakdown in the city, new jobs have not kept pace with the rapid population increase. Simple occupational specialization and even voluntary organizations to expand education and mutual aid are ethnically separated. Tensions, therefore, are likely to continue for a long time to come (p. 73).

Central Calcutta in 1961 averaged 102,010 persons per square mile (in contrast to 75,000 in central Manhattan). That high density is made up mainly of one and two-story structures, rather than high-rise apartments interspersed with parks. The Calcutta Metropolitan Planning Organization (1966) reports that:

> Calcutta is a city in crisis. All who live in this huge metropolitan complex have daily experience of its characteristic problems: chronic deficits in basic utilities such as water supply, sewerage and drainage; and in community facilities such as schools, hospitals, parks and recreation spaces; severe unemployment and under-employment, congested and inadequate transportation; vast housing shortages and proliferating slum areas; soaring land prices and rents; administrative delays and confusion of responsibility for corrective action; absence of clear development objectives over a longer perspective than the next 5 year plan; limited state and municipal financial resources to cope with the situation.
>
> Over the past two hundred years many boards and committees and commissions have met and deliberated on the problems of the city and issued reports calling for remedial action. The improvements that were made, if indeed any action was taken, were invariably piecemeal, sporadic, and inadequate to meet the needs of the rapidly increasing population of Calcutta (p. 3).

As a city-state, Hong Kong is a unique case, but its heavy population density warrants our attention. Refugees from mainland China have swelled the population from 1,600,000 in 1946 to 1,950,000 in 1950 to over 3 million in 1960; estimates for 1970 are 4,105,000 (Davis, 1969). The government has been trying to keep up with the flow of refugees to Hong Kong from mainland China as well as the natural increase in population, and about 1,000 new residential buildings have been constructed *every year* since the end of World War II. The housing shortage is such, however, that five adult persons have been the minimum number required to obtain a single unit. Alternately, two children may be substituted for one adult, so that combinations of four adults and two children or three adults and four children or two adults and six children may apply for and eventually be granted residence in units measuring, in total, *ten by twelve feet,* without a private bath or a separate room for cooking. Each unit is said to have a balcony to expand the space for sleeping, but extreme crowding cannot be avoided. Nevertheless, residents and foreigners alike have agreed that these were "middle-class" housing units.

When my husband and I visited the Hong Kong Kowloon area in 1954, I attempted to estimate the residential density in the government-built, H-shaped block housing. It would appear that about a quarter of a million persons are housed in a square mile of such units. Since there are only about 12 square miles of built-up area altogether, such density may be a bit conservative, unless one assumes that approximately one-fourth of the 4 million people reside in the surrounding rural areas leased from Communist China.

In spite of police surveillance in both the Communist and British sectors, refugees continue to accentuate the housing problems of Hong Kong. Many thousands live in temporary roof-top and squatters' shacks, as well as on small boats in the harbor. A housing survey conducted by the University of Hong Kong in 1957 and 1958 showed that 75 percent of all households were sharing their accommodation with others. Less than 10 percent of the 267,000 households surveyed had a living room not used for sleeping. New government units have been apportioned by lottery, since the demand has always exceeded the supply (Schmitt, 1963, p. 211). The pressures of crowding under these circumstances can hardly be imagined by those of us more fortunate.

A recent large-scale study of residents of Hong Kong found that

FIG. 4–4 *Density in Hong Kong is maximized by the multistoried resettlement blocks built by the government. Census figures report up to 2,800 persons per gross acre. Wide World Photo*

unhappiness and worry, measures of "superficial strain," increased with density of living space only among the lower-income respondents (Mitchell, 1971, p. 23). Perhaps higher incomes allowed people to use space outside of their living unit to a greater extent. Findings did indicate that the higher the density, the higher the proportion of parents who said that they generally didn't know where their children (18 years of age and under) were playing. Mitchell concluded that this may "facilitate the development of many of the social problems of youth assumed to be characteristic of high-density slum communities around the world" (p. 26). Density was also related to a lack of exchange of friendly visits; 49 percent of the married Hong Kong subjects said they *never* invited people into their homes (p. 27).

Although human beings may organize living quarters that multiply the square footage of land area by building very tall buildings, one must question the quality of life under these circumstances. Most people would prefer to maximize the quality of human life rather than to maximize the number of bodies the earth is capable of carrying.

## *RURAL DENSITIES*

In the developed countries urbanization was related to a decline in the absolute numbers of rural persons. In the underdeveloped countries, however, this has not been the case.

A report on rural overpopulation by the United Nations Asian Population Conference of 1963 claims that "many studies have shown that agricultural incomes would be increased by a *reduction* in the number of farmers" (p. 41). The question then is; why don't all the excess farmers migrate to the cities? In part it is because there is a high rate of natural increase in the cities. Reproduction, overcrowding, and unemployment are already high in the urban areas of less developed nations. In spite of rapid urbanization, young women in the underdeveloped countries desire about the same number of children as the actual reproduction of older women: 6.6 per mother in Lebanon, 6.0 in Ghana, and 5.1 in Latin America. Young families have not changed their goals in congruence with the societal changes that accompany increased urbanization and some industrialization. *The overall problem is the increase of population.* Both urban and rural densities of the underdeveloped countries are growing.

Kingsley Davis has computed approximate rural densities for the nations of the world. Table 4-7 lists the nonurban persons per square kilometer in specified nations (multiply by three in order to approximate persons per square mile). Since subtractions for useless lands (such as mountains or deserts) were *not* made, these densities are much lower in many cases than they would be for *usable* agricultural land areas. Nevertheless, a few examples will highlight some of the problems of rural density.

Between 1950 and 1970 the rural density of El Salvador almost

*TABLE 4-7 Approximate Rural Density, Specified Nations, 1950, 1960, 1970*

| | (Nonurban persons per square kilometer) 1950 | 1960 | 1970 |
|---|---|---|---|
| Belguim | 104 | 101 | 100 |
| Canada | 1 | 1 | 1 |
| Ceylon | 100 | 128 | 161 |
| China (Mainland) | 52 | 58 | 60 |
| China (Taiwan) | 101 | 122 | 143 |
| El Salvador | 55 | 71 | 98 |
| France | 35 | 32 | 30 |
| Honduras | 11 | 14 | 18 |
| India | 97 | 116 | 145 |
| Indonesia | 45 | 53 | 65 |
| Japan | 141 | 92 | 47 |
| Nigeria | 29 | 41 | 56 |
| Pakistan | 71 | 85 | 101 |
| Philippines | 54 | 71 | 98 |
| Puerto Rico | 148 | 148 | 168 |
| The Netherlands | 89 | 111 | 109 |
| U.A.R. (Egypt) | 14 | 16 | 19 |
| United Kingdom | 47 | 47 | 48 |
| U.S.A. | 6 | 6 | 5 |
| U.S.S.R. | 5 | 5 | 4 |
| Vietnam | | | |
| North | 70 | 87 | 106 |
| South | 52 | 65 | 80 |

*Source:* Kingsley Davis, *World Urbanization 1950–70*, Table H, in Vol. 1: Basic Data for Cities, Counties and Regions, Population Monograph Series. IIS: University of California, Berkeley, 1969.

doubled, from 55 to 98 persons per square kilometer. In neighboring Honduras rural density averages only 18 persons per square kilometer. Is it any surprise that some of the excess population of El Salvador spilled over into Honduras, provoking a short war between the two countries? Hondurans had enough problems trying to meet the demands created by their own population increase without welcoming migrating competitors for jobs and farm lands.

Even *within* the underdeveloped countries, migration is not often a solution to high rural density. Indonesia has experienced extremely rapid population growth, but most of the increase has occurred on the single island of Java. Millions of people would have to be transported to the sparsely populated islands of Indonesia in order to significantly alter the density of Java itself. That island is now so densely populated and growing so rapidly that there is no way to finance the physical movement of the numbers involved. The more rapidly these populations grow, the more difficult it becomes to alleviate the uneven distribution. Sukarno used to claim that there was no population problem in Indonesia, but just because one does not recognize the "label" a social problem, does not mean it doesn't exist.

Returning to rural densities (see Table 4-7), India stands out among the large underdeveloped countries as having the highest overall rural density. On the average, there were 145 rural persons per square kilometer of land, good and bad, in 1970. The nation's agricultural production would be more efficient with fewer people living on the land. In fact, agriculturalists are now suggesting that India should not be referred to as an underdeveloped land. Rather, the land is poor because it has been *overdeveloped* by many years of trying to support a heavy population which has recently grown even larger (Paddock and Paddock, 1964).

High rural densities may be a problem in the more advanced countries as in the less developed. The Netherlands and Belgium have 109 and 100 rural inhabitants, respectively, for each square kilometer of land. The efforts and heavy spending of the Dutch in reclaiming farm lands from the sea have been well publicized. These nations have nevertheless had less difficulty supporting their populations because they have, in the past, had other lands to colonize. Now they have industrial and artistic products that are in high demand in international trade. Not all countries are so fortunate.

## *SUMMARY*

The study of subhuman species seems to imply that certain drastic automatic control mechanisms limit the numbers of these species within any given environment.

Human beings, while sharing some of the physiological characteristics of the subhuman species, also have the unique abilities to organize themselves and manipulate their environment, to invent tools to make life easier, and to plan ahead to achieve desired goals. Recent population increases have made it more difficult to take advantage of these capacities. The increasing quantity of persons presents a barrier to improving the quality of life for all.

Over time, however, human beings have evolved societies that are capable of supporting, at least minimally, ever greater numbers of persons. The urban-industrial society may have so increased its population numbers, density, and diversity that chaos is the result. The use of man's capacity to plan ahead will be required if increasing atomization is to be avoided.

The world as a whole is a finite mass. There is *nowhere* else for human beings to migrate. The more people there are, the more densely crowded the world will become. Furthermore, a great deal of the land mass is uninhabitable. A great proportion of land must be given to agricultural pursuits. Yet, some agricultural areas are already so densely settled that agriculturalists claim that more food could be produced with fewer farm hands.

Urban areas, too, typically have more persons than can be adequately housed, fed, and clothed. The less developed the country, the more likely that urban workers will be underemployed or unemployed, that they will not be drawn to the city by actual opportunities, but rather will be pushed from overcrowded rural areas.

Developed nations also face problems of urban crowding. Slums become increasingly difficult to rehabilitate, traffic problems increase, and the costs of limiting or treating air and water pollution climb as the number of residents increases.

Urban areas in both developed and underdeveloped nations are growing even more rapidly in population than the world as a whole. It would appear that attempts to improve life in the city become ineffective as more and more people move in to take advantage of the increased efforts to solve recurrent problems.

## *REFERENCES*

ARDREY, ROBERT. 1966. *The territorial imperative.* New York: Dell.

BIDERMAN, A. D., M. LOURIA, AND J. BACCHUS. 1963. *Historical incidents of extreme overcrowding.* Washington, D.C.: Bureau of Social Science Research.

BORLAUG, NORMAN E. 1971. The Green Revolution, peace and humanity. Nobel Peace Prize acceptance speech, December 10, 1970. Reprinted: Washington, D.C.: Population Reference Bureau no. 35 (January).

BOSE, NIRMAL KUMAR. 1965. Calcutta: A premature metropolis. In *Cities,* ed. Scientific American, pp. 59–74. New York: Alfred A. Knopf.

BOURGEOIS-PICHAT, JEAN. 1966. *Population growth and development.* New York: Carnegie Endowment for International Peace.

CALCUTTA METROPOLITAN PLANNING ORGANIZATION. 1966. *Basic development plan for the Calcutta metropolitan district 1966–1986.* Calcutta, India: Development and Planning Department of Government of West Bengal.

CALHOUN, JOHN. 1964. Population density and social pathology. *Population, evolution, and birth control,* ed. Garrett Hardin, pp. 101–5. San Francisco: W. H. Freeman.

———. 1970. Population. In *Population control,* ed. Anthony Allison, pp. 110–30. Middlesex, England: Penguin Books.

DAVIS, KINGSLEY. 1955. The origin and growth of urbanization in the world. *The American Journal of Sociology,* 60, no. 4 (January), 429–37.

———. 1965. The urbanization of the human population. In *Cities,* ed. Scientific American, pp. 3–24. New York: Alfred A. Knopf.

———. 1967. *The modern urban revolution.* New York: Random House.

DEEVEY, EDWARD S. 1960. The hare and the haruspex: A cautionary tale. *The Yale Review* 49, no. 2 (Winter): 161–79.

DURKHEIM, EMILE. 1933. *On the division of labor in society,* trans. George Simpson. New York: Free Press, 1960. (Originally published in France in 1893.)

DYCKMAN, JOHN W. 1965. Transportation in cities. In *Cities,* ed. Scientific American, pp. 133–55. New York: Alfred A. Knopf.

EHRLICH, PAUL R., AND ANNE H. EHRLICH. 1970. *Population-resources-environment: Issues in human ecology.* San Francisco: W. H. Freeman.

EVERETT, GLENN D. 1961. One man's family. In *Population, evolution, and birth control,* ed. Garrett Hardin, pp. 41–44. San Francisco: W.H. Freeman.

FRANKL, VIKTOR E. 1963. *Man's search for meaning: An introduction to logotherapy.* New York: Washington Square Press, Inc.

GALLE, OMER R., WALTER R. GOVE, AND J. MILLER MCPHERSON. 1971. Population density and pathology: What are the relationships for man? A paper delivered at the 1971 meetings of the American Sociological Association, Denver, Colo.

GOLDSCHMIDT, WALTER. 1959. *Man's way.* New York: Holt.

HALL, EDWARD T. 1966. *The hidden dimension.* Garden City, N.Y.: Doubleday.

HAUSER, PHILIP M. 1969. The chaotic society: Product of the social morphological revolution. *American Sociological Review,* 34 (February), 1–19.

HEBB, D. O., AND W. R. THOMPSON. 1968. The social significance of animal studies. In *The handbook of social psychology,* ed. G. Lindzey & E. Aronson, Vol. 2, 729–74. Reading, Mass.: Addison-Wesley.

HEER, DAVID M. 1968. *Society and population.* Englewood Cliffs, N.J.: Prentice-Hall.

HOAGLAND, HUDSON. 1963. Cybernetics of population control. In *Human fertility and population problems,* ed. Roy O. Greep, pp. 1–20. Cambridge, Mass.: Schenkman Publishing Co.

KEYFITZ, NATHAN. 1966. Population density and the style of social life. *Bioscience* 16, no. 12 (December), 868–73.

MITCHELL, ROBERT EDWARD. 1971. Some social implications of high density housing. *American Sociological Review* 36 (February), 18–29.

NATIONAL ADVISORY COMMISSION ON CIVIL DISORDERS. 1968. *Report of the national advisory commission on civil disorders.* New York: Bantam Books.

PADDOCK, WILLIAM, AND PAUL PADDOCK. 1964. Hungry nations. In *Population, evolution, and birth control,* ed. Garrett Hardin, pp. 84–87. San Francisco: W.H. Freeman.

PETERSEN, WILLIAM. 1969. *Population.* New York: Macmillan.

SCHMITT, ROBERT C. 1963. Implications of density in Hong Kong. *American Institute of Planners Journal,* 29, 3 (August), 210–16.

SEARS, PAUL B. 1958. The inexorable problem of space. *Science* 127, 9–16.

SOMMER, ROBERT. 1969. *Personal space.* Englewood Cliffs, N.J.: Prentice-Hall.

THOMLINSON, RALPH. 1965. *Population Dynamics: Causes and consequences of world demographic change.* New York: Random House.

United Nations, Bureau of Social Affairs. 1969. *Growth of the world's urban and rural population, 1920–2000*. Population Studies no. 44, St/SOA/ Series A/44.

United Nations, Economic Commission for Asia and the Far East. 1964. Report of the Asian Population Conference, 1963. New York: United Nations.

United States, Bureau of the Census. 1966. Characteristics of the south and east Los Angeles areas, November 1965. *Current Population Reports* Series p-23, no. 18 (June 28). Washington, D.C.: U.S. Department of Commerce.

———. 1970. *Statistical abstract of the United States, 1970*. Washington, D.C.: U.S. Department of Commerce.

Wynne-Edwards, V.C. 1969. Self-regulating systems in populations of animals. In *The subversive science, essays toward an ecology of man*, eds. Paul Shephard and Daniel McKinley, pp. 99–111. Boston: Houghton Mifflin.

chapter 5

# CONSEQUENCES IN QUANTITY AND QUALITY OF FOOD

*Many millions of people in the poor countries are going to starve to death before our eyes . . . upon the television sets. . . . To avoid the catastrophe . . . is going to mean sacrifices such as the rich countries have never contemplated, except in major war. . . . It is the duty of all the rest of us to keep before the world its long-term fate. Peace. Food. No more people than the earth can take.*

Sir C.P. Snow, British
scientist and novelist (1968)

*Hunger and overpopulation: What is involved is prognosticated deterioration of the average food balance in which localized food crises merge into a sea of hunger, intolerable suffering and desperation, the grief and fury of millions of people. This is a tragic threat to all mankind.*

Andrei D. Sakharov, Soviet
physicist and "father" of the
Russian hydrogen bomb (1968)

Those who, for political or ideological reasons, do not want to recognize the problems of rapid population growth talk at great length about the possibilities of increasing food supplies. All we need to do, they say, is to put our present knowledge to work. But that is easier said than done. Too few people share in the knowledge or the job would already have been done.

In this chapter I will survey the world production and supply of food in recent years and at present. Comparisons between the developed and less developed nations will focus on the increases in total production and also on the way in which these are diluted by population increases.

Recent optimism over the "green revolution" must be qualified.

Many complications must still be overcome before we can assume that the world's food problem has been solved.

There are so many proposals for increasing the supply of food for the billions of people on earth that our inquiry into what can be done might lead one to conclude that the problem is strictly temporary. This review of the possibilities, therefore, will include attention to the difficulties of implementation. At the same time, the reader should keep in mind that whatever advances might be made may still be nullified if population growth continues at its present rate.

Sripati Chandrasekhar, well-known Indian demographer (1967), calls attention to the fact that:

> All the Asian countries from Arab Western Asia to Indonesia, with the single possible exception of Japan, are dependent on traditional and near-primitive agriculture for the meagre livelihood of a majority—70 to 80 percent—of their population. The man-land ratio is so adverse and the pressure of population on the soil so great that agriculture is by and large more a pathetic and sentimental way of life than a successful business or commercial proposition. Despite some sprawling, unplanned urbanization in almost every Asian country, between 70 and 80 percent of the population is dependent on the soil for a livelihood. Hunger, particularly in Communist China, and to a steadily lessening extent in India, is almost endemic (p. 19).

## *WHAT IS THE FOOD SITUATION?*

The "ifs" of the future may become more understandable if we look at the record of the recent past. Since World War II, there has been a worldwide effort of unprecedented intensity to increase food production.

### *Production*

THE WORLD AS A WHOLE. The increases which have actually been brought about by the tremendous efforts put into agricultural development are reported in Table 5-1. If we take the average production for the years 1952–1956 as a standard, the yearly changes may be viewed independent of inflationary prices. From the standard years (assumed to be equal to 100) to 1968 there was a 47 percent increase in the total agricultural production of the world. Such rapid increases in agricultural production had never before been recorded. Whether such increases can continue or not or whether production can increase even more rapidly begs the question. When the agricultural increase is measured against the population, which increased 32 percent during the same period of time, the per capita gain in agricultural production is only 12 percent. So small a gain over a period

TABLE 5-1 *Indices of World*[1] *Production of Agricultural, Fishery and Forestry Products*

| | *Average 1948–52* | 1957 | 1958 | 1959 | 1960 | 1961 | 1962 | 1963 | 1964 | 1965 | 1966 | 1967 | 1968 | *Change 1967 to 1968* | *Annual Rate of Growth 1955–57—1965–67* |
|---|---|---|---|---|---|---|---|---|---|---|---|---|---|---|---|
| | | | | | | *1952–56 average = 100* | | | | | | | | *Percent* | |
| Total production | | 107 | 113 | 116 | 119 | 121 | 125 | 128 | 131 | 133 | 137 | 143 | 146 | 3 | 2.7 |
| Agriculture | 87 | 107 | 114 | 116 | 120 | 121 | 126 | 129 | 132 | 133 | 138 | 143 | 147 | 3 | 2.7 |
| Fisheries | 85 | 110 | 112 | 116 | 121 | 127 | 135 | 139 | 146 | 154 | 162 | 169 | 176 | 4 | 4.2 |
| Forestry | | 105 | 106 | 111 | 112 | 111 | 113 | 115 | 121 | 122 | 124 | 125 | 128 | 2 | 1.6 |
| Population | 93 | 106 | 108 | 110 | 112 | 114 | 117 | 119 | 122 | 124 | 127 | 129 | 132 | 2 | 2.0 |
| Per capita production | | 101 | 105 | 106 | 106 | 106 | 107 | 107 | 108 | 107 | 109 | 110 | 111 | 1 | 0.6 |
| Agriculture | 93 | 101 | 105 | 106 | 107 | 106 | 108 | 108 | 108 | 107 | 109 | 111 | 112 | 1 | 0.7 |
| Fisheries | 92 | 104 | 104 | 105 | 108 | 111 | 116 | 117 | 120 | 124 | 128 | 131 | 133 | 2 | 2.1 |
| Forestry | | 100 | 98 | 101 | 100 | 97 | 97 | 97 | 99 | 99 | 98 | 97 | 97 | | 0.4 |

[1] Excluding China (Mainland).

*Source:* United Nations, Food and Agricultural Organization, The State of Food and Agriculture, 1969. Rome: FAO, 1969, p. 5.

of approximately 15 years can hardly be noticed by the peoples of the world. And, as will be seen, the gains are even smaller in the less developed countries than in the already advanced regions of the world.

The point to be made is that *if population had remained constant, the world's people would already have an adequate food supply* to maintain minimal health standards. They would have increased energy to fight diseases and to further increase agricultural production and the general standard of living. It should be clear that in a fifteen-year period those who were added to the population, all of whom are still in the dependent ages, have contributed little or nothing to the added food production.

REGIONS OF THE WORLD. When food production [1] is reported according to the regions of the world for the same time period (see Table 5-2), it becomes clear that the proportional improvement is not much different for the developed and less developed countries. The data for food products (in contrast to all agricultural production) show that the developed nations as a whole recorded a 51 percent increase during the period from 1952–1956 through 1968, while the less developed countries recorded a 47 percent increase during the same period of time.

However, the lower half of the table uses an index of per capita production. On this scale, the developing countries show an increase of only 4 percent over the fifteen-year period. Most of these countries have made tremendous efforts just to break even on a per capita basis. Because population growth has been greater in North America than in any other developed region, the per capita increase in food production has also been negligible there. However, since population growth has been lower in the Eastern European countries and the USSR, their large increase in total production is translated into the highest increase of any region on a per capita basis. Trends in food production and population in the four developing regions are charted in Figure 5-1. The increases in food production and population parallel one another for the years from 1960 through 1968. The production of food has kept up with population, but the very significant gains in food production cannot be translated into a noticeable advantage for the individual people of these areas. Most peoples of the developing countries have "rising expectations," stimulated by the recent political independence of many of these nations. Political leaders, moreover, are always anxious to tell the populace about increases in production. The natives, who do not often recognize the population growth, may well be getting restless to appropriate for themselves some of the increased production. It will be surprising if political turmoil does not continue and even increase.

[1] Food production differs from total agricultural production in excluding production of non-edibles—cotton, hemp, etc.

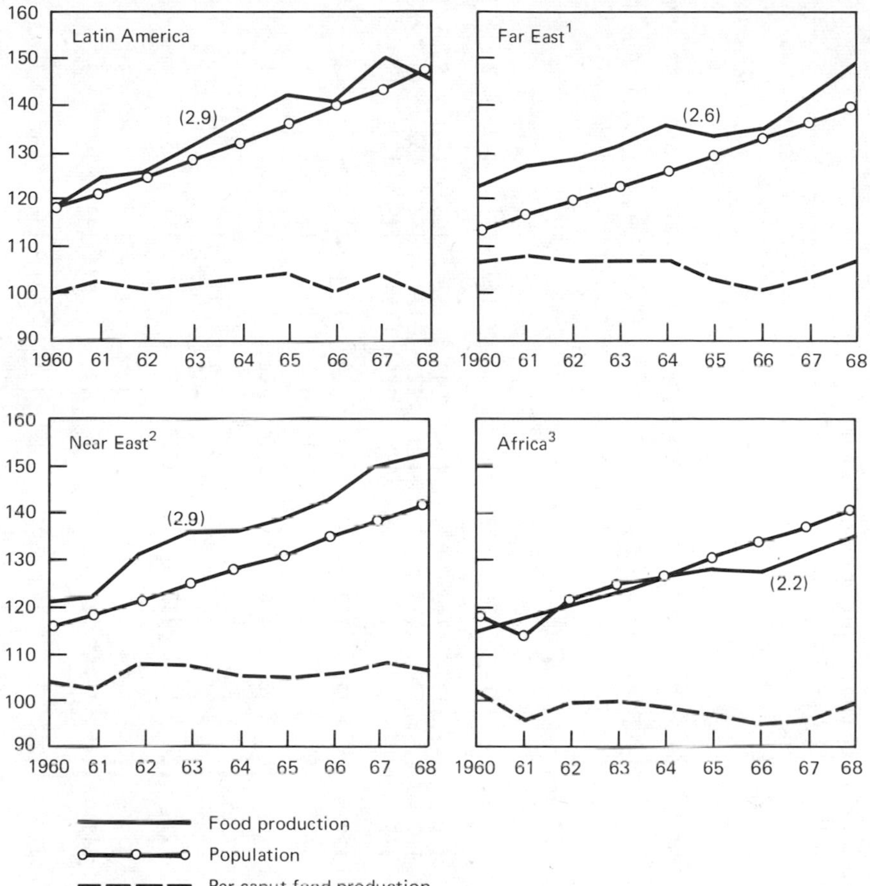


Note: The figures in brackets show the food production annual rate of growth in the decade 1955-57 to 1965-67.

[1] Excluding Japan and China (Mainland).

[2] Excluding Israel.

[3] Excluding South Africa.

*Source*: United Nations, Food and Agriculture Organization, *The State of Food and Agriculture, 1969*, FAO, Rome, 1969, p. 7.

FIG. 5–1 *Trends in Food Production and Population in the Developing Regions*

The four areas of the world graphed in Figure 5-1 are living examples of the Malthusian theory that the human population multiplies up to the amount of food available for its subsistence. Even though food produc-

TABLE 5-2 *Indices of World*[1] *and Regional Food Production in Relation to Population*

| | 1948–52 Average | 1957 | 1958 | 1959 | 1960 | 1961 | 1962 | 1963 | 1964 | 1965 | 1966 | 1967 | 1968[2] | Change 1967 to 1968[2] | Annual Rate of Growth 1955–57—1965–67 |
|---|---|---|---|---|---|---|---|---|---|---|---|---|---|---|---|
| | 1952–56 average = 100 | | | | | | | | | | | | | Percent | |
| Total production | | | | | | | | | | | | | | | |
| FOOD PRODUCTS ONLY | | | | | | | | | | | | | | | |
| Western Europe | 84 | 106 | 109 | 113 | 119 | 118 | 126 | 128 | 130 | 130 | 134 | 144 | 147 | 2 | 2.7 |
| Eastern Europe and U.S.S.R. | 83 | 118 | 129 | 131 | 133 | 137 | 140 | 134 | 146 | 149 | 167 | 168 | 177 | 5 | 3.7 |
| North America | 92 | 101 | 109 | 110 | 111 | 110 | 114 | 121 | 119 | 122 | 127 | 132 | 132 | — | 2.2 |
| Oceania | 92 | 97 | 118 | 115 | 121 | 124 | 135 | 138 | 144 | 136 | 158 | 145 | 173 | 19 | 3.8 |
| Other developed countries[3] | 82 | 115 | 117 | 120 | 123 | 127 | 137 | 137 | 139 | 139 | 147 | 170 | 167 | –2 | 3.1 |
| Developed countries | 87 | 108 | 115 | 117 | 120 | 121 | 126 | 128 | 131 | 133 | 142 | 147 | 151 | 3 | 2.9 |
| Latin America | 86 | 111 | 117 | 116 | 118 | 124 | 126 | 132 | 137 | 142 | 141 | 151 | 148 | –1 | 3.0 |
| Far East[1] (excl. Japan) | 87 | 107 | 112 | 118 | 123 | 127 | 129 | 132 | 136 | 134 | 135 | 142 | 149 | 5 | 2.6 |
| Near East (excl. Israel) | 84 | 115 | 118 | 121 | 121 | 123 | 132 | 136 | 136 | 139 | 144 | 151 | 152 | 1 | 2.9 |
| Africa (excl. South Africa) | 88 | 106 | 109 | 112 | 119 | 115 | 122 | 125 | 127 | 129 | 128 | 132 | 136 | 3 | 2.2 |
| Developing countries | 87 | 109 | 114 | 117 | 121 | 124 | 128 | 131 | 135 | 136 | 136 | 144 | 147 | 3 | 2.7 |
| World[1] | 87 | 108 | 115 | 117 | 120 | 122 | 126 | 129 | 132 | 134 | 140 | 146 | 150 | 3 | 2.8 |

Per capita production

FOOD PRODUCTS ONLY

| | | | | | | | | | | | | | | |
|---|---|---|---|---|---|---|---|---|---|---|---|---|---|---|
| Western Europe | 86 | 104 | 106 | 108 | 114 | 112 | 118 | 118 | 119 | 118 | 120 | 129 | 130 | 1 | 1.8 |
| Eastern Europe and U.S.S.R. | 88 | 113 | 122 | 122 | 122 | 123 | 124 | 118 | 127 | 128 | 143 | 142 | 148 | 4 | 2.4 |
| North America | 99 | 96 | 101 | 100 | 100 | 98 | 99 | 104 | 101 | 102 | 104 | 107 | 106 | —1 | 0.6 |
| Oceania | 102 | 91 | 107 | 102 | 106 | 105 | 113 | 113 | 116 | 107 | 122 | 109 | 128 | 17 | 1.6 |
| Other developed countries [3] | 87 | 110 | 111 | 113 | 114 | 117 | 124 | 122 | 123 | 121 | 127 | 145 | 140 | —3 | 1.9 |
| Developed countries | 92 | 103 | 109 | 110 | 111 | 110 | 113 | 114 | 115 | 116 | 122 | 126 | 128 | 2 | 1.6 |
| Latin America | 96 | 103 | 105 | 101 | 100 | 103 | 101 | 102 | 104 | 104 | 101 | 104 | 100 | —4 | 0.1 |
| Far East (excl. Japan) | 94 | 101 | 103 | 106 | 107 | 108 | 107 | 107 | 108 | 103 | 101 | 104 | 107 | 3 | 0.1 |
| Near East (excl. Israel) | 92 | 107 | 107 | 107 | 105 | 103 | 108 | 108 | 106 | 105 | 106 | 108 | 107 | —1 | 0.3 |
| Africa (excl. South Africa) | 97 | 99 | 99 | 100 | 103 | 97 | 101 | 101 | 100 | 98 | 96 | 96 | 97 | 1 | —0.3 |
| Developing countries | 94 | 102 | 104 | 104 | 105 | 105 | 105 | 106 | 106 | 104 | 101 | 104 | 104 | — | 0.1 |
| World [1] | 93 | 102 | 106 | 106 | 107 | 106 | 108 | 108 | 109 | 108 | 111 | 113 | 114 | 1 | 0.8 |

[1] Excluding China (Mainland).
[2] Preliminary.
[3] Japan, South Africa and Israel.

*Source:* United Nations, Food and Agriculture Organization, The State of Food and Agriculture, 1969 Rome: FAO, 1969, p. 6.

tion increased rapidly in Latin America, the Near and Far East, and Africa, population growth nullified any gain on a per capita basis. One could conclude along with Kenneth Boulding (1964) "that any technological improvement will have the ultimate effect of increasing the sum of human misery, as it permits a larger population to live in precisely the same state of misery and starvation as before the change" (p. 81).

However, the phenomenon described by the Malthusian theory has not been operative in those now industrialized countries where population growth has been slow enough to allow human beings to reorganize their attitudes and behavior in relation to the numbers of offspring produced.

Furthermore, the world now has the capacity to transport foods and to share the technologies of the advanced countries with those that are less developed. The food *supplies* of a country, therefore, may be quite different than the food *production* within the nation itself. Although international trade in manufactures is greater than in agricultural products, there have been increasing exchanges of food between countries. Before World War II, Asia, Africa, and Latin America altogether exported 11 million metric tons of grains per year. By 1964 the same areas were *importing* 25 million metric tons of grains per year. Only a few countries produce more food than they consume, and they are most likely to be the advanced industrial countries, not the so-called "agricultural" nations of the world.

Recognizing, then, that the supply of food in a country is not limited to its own production, let us look at the supply in terms of quantity versus quality and then in terms of the sharing by developed countries with underdeveloped countries.

## *Supply*

Because an imbalance is apparent in the food production of various countries and regions of the world, the question of a more equitable distribution may be raised. Since a minority of the world's people are well fed, however, taking from that group and equally distributing the world's supply of food would mean that *all* the people of the world would be malnourished, assuming that transportation and equal distribution were possible. On the other hand, if the world's supply of food were parceled out *at the average dietary level of the population of the United States, only one-third of the human race could be fed.* If India were to distribute food according to United States dietary standards, its food production could support only 90 million people, or about one-sixth of its present population (Borgstrom, 1965).

QUANTITY. People in the developed countries consume on the average about 50 percent more calories than people in the underdeveloped nations. There has been little change over time in the relative caloric intake of the peoples of these two groups of countries. In the less developed countries, improvements in production have been absorbed by an increase in the populations. Therefore, even though the already industrialized nations have made gains in the average nutritional levels of their populations and have shared some of their overproduction with the less developed nations, those latter nations have had little noticeable improvement and have not bettered their relative position on caloric intake. The gap between the rich and poor nations has been growing greater because, on the one hand, wealthy nations are increasing production faster and, on the other hand, the more rapid population increases in the less developed countries decrease the improvements actually made when these are considered in per capita terms.

Of course calorie requirements vary for specific ages, occupations, body types, and so forth. The lighter body weight of people in most of the less developed countries means that calorie requirements may be scaled down. However, one reason body weight is light is poor diet. With improved nutrition since 1950, Japanese youth have significantly increased in average weight and height in a single generation.

The range in average daily caloric intake for the nations within each region may be reviewed in Table 5-3. The range is very wide for some of the regions, however, because one or two countries may have unusually high average caloric supplies. (This is true of South Africa in the African region, Israel in the Near Eastern nations, and Uruguay, Argentina, and Chile in the Latin American countries.) Therefore, I have indicated the average daily caloric supply of the country in the median position for each region as a more adequate indicator of the regional average. Even these data may be somewhat misleading, since the most populous country of the Far Eastern group, India, has the lowest average calorie supply, 1810 calories per person per day. Nevertheless, it is clear that the least developed, most populous regions of the world, even those which are importing millions of tons of grains, are not able to supply their growing populations with adequate calories. The situation becomes even worse when we examine the quality as well as the quantity of food.

QUALITY. Although the food supply is usually discussed in terms of a caloric measure, the difference between sickness and health is most often determined by the quality, not merely the quantity, of intake. The quality of food is determined by the protein and vitamin sufficiency, as well as the general balance of the diet. As Borgstrom (1965) suggests in *The Hungry Planet:*

*TABLE 5-3 The Range and Median of National Estimates within Regions: Calorie and Protein Content of Average per Capita Food Supply—Latest Date*

| | | *Average Number of Calories per Person per Day* | | *Average Grams of Protein per Person per Day* | | | |
|---|---|---|---|---|---|---|---|
| | | | | *Total* | | *Animal* | |
| *Regions* | *Date* | *Range* | *Median* | *Range* | *Median* | *Range* | *Median* |
| Western Europe | 1966–67 | 2860–3400 | 2900 | 75–100 | 86.4 | 29.8–61.0 | 49.4 |
| Eastern Europe (only Hungary, Poland, Romania) | 1960–62 | 3030–3350 | 3160 | 91.7–97.3 | 92.9 | 27.9–37.6 | 37.2 |
| North America | 1967–68 | 3180–3200 | 3200 | 95.4–95.6 | 95.6 | 64.1–68.6 | 68.6 |
| Oceania | 1966–67 | 3120–3470 | | 90.0–109 | | 60.0–75.0 | |
| Africa | 1962–63 | 1800–2820 | 2120 | 35.9–80.2 | 52.3 | 3.1–31.5 | 10.3 |
| Far East | 1966 | 1810–2400 | 2230 | 44.0–77.0 | 51.5 | 5.4–24.6 | 11.5 |
| Latin America | 1966 | 1840–3170 | 2350 | 41.0–101 | 57.9 | 8.3–67.1 | 18.3 |
| Near East | 1966 | 1850–2920 | 2190 | 54.9–89.2 | 63.9 | 7.7–41.3 | 12.1 |

*Source:* United Nations, Food and Agriculture Organization, *The State of Food and Agriculture 1969*. Rome: FAO, 1969, pp. 151, 156, 162, 167, 174, 181, 189, and 196.

> In his food man needs protein—the living substrate of the cell's protoplasm—and in addition his protein intake has to satisfy very narrow specifications as to molecular structure. Man, furthermore, requires a number of vitamins, also special fats and, it would appear, certain specified carbohydrates. The proteins, however, are key compounds. It is more than a coincidence that, during recent decades, protein deficiency diseases have come to prevail in most continents and must be regarded as the chief nutritional deficiency of the world (p. 27).

The quality of food in terms of protein intake must be examined separately from the quantity of calories available to the peoples of the world. Whereas malnutrition is caused by a lack of quality in their food, undernutrition is caused by an insufficient quantity of food. Malnutrition is even more common than undernourishment, but malnutrition is most prevalent among those peoples who also suffer undernourishment.

Nutritionists point out that even affluent segments of the world's population may not make the best choices in the quality or balance of the foods they eat.

> A large group of Americans are malnourished because many of them: (1) know too little about nutrition to prepare well-balanced meals, even when they have the money to do so; (2) resist altering long-established preferences for nutritionally deficient foods; (3) have far more children than their resources enable them to care for. On July 11, 1967, six witnesses appeared at the Senate hearing to testify regarding their difficulties in getting food for their families. Between them, these six individuals had a total of 53 children! (Fisher, 1968, p. 99.)

The range of protein intake for the countries within the various regions of the world can be found on the right-hand side of Table 5-3. Data for all sources of protein are contrasted with those for animal sources of protein. Although about two-thirds of world protein consumption comes from such plant products as grain, beans, and potatoes, the one-third represented by milk, meat, eggs, and fish is qualitatively more important. Animal protein is better qualified to provide building stones for man's body protein. The so-called amino-gram (the relative amount of amino acids) of animal protein lies closer to man's specifications than do those of most plant proteins. Animal protein is also readily digestible in the human gastric system, while plant protein is encased within an impenetrable cell wall, the breakdown of which requires elaborate processing (Borgstrom, 1965, pp. 40–43).

The most important animal sources of protein are found in great disproportion among the diets of peoples in various countries. The average citizen of North America, Australia, or New Zealand consumes five to six times as much animal protein as the peoples of Africa or the Far or Near East. North Americans' intake of animal proteins has, by United Nations figures, increased by more than one-third since before World War II, while the per capita intake for people in the less developed countries is as likely to have decreased as increased (United Nations, Food and Agriculture Organization, 1969).

A look at a *price-weighted* index of per capita food supplies over time highlights the differences between developed and less developed countries (see Figure 5-2). If the world average per capita price for all food for the years 1948 to 1952 is taken as 100, the per capita values of the average food supply for the peoples of the regions of the world have changed very little. Yet the people of Africa and the Far East have been consuming food valued at only one-sixth that of the average North American. This price-weighted index varies even more than calorie intake between the developed and underdeveloped countries and it gives an indication of the much greater cost (and price) of livestock products. Because animal protein requires between five and eight primary calories to produce one calorie of protein, the investment in animal protein is high.

Not only are animal proteins expensive to produce, but the increasing numbers of malnourished human beings make it more difficult to raise their food quality in the future. And the lack of both quantity and quality of food impairs the capacity of human beings to produce the increased food supply they so badly need. Some observers may describe slow-moving poor persons as "lazy," but nutritionists know that human beings need food "fuel" in order to work energetically.

Thus, a global protein shortage remains a major problem. It may be that protein-deficiency diseases have been aggravated instead of alleviated.

> A series of disease symptoms, described in reports from several continents and latitudes, have become more and more amalgamated and interrelated as evidence has accumulated that they all belong to the protein deficiency syndrome. Peculiar words such as marasmus, kwashiorkor, infantile dystrophy, weaning damages, sugar babies, and Annam obesity are a few of the many terms which gradually have found their way into the news media. They are all designations for various symptoms of protein deficiency (Borgstrom, 1965, p. 49).

Furthermore, scientists now agree that a lack of protein in the early years of life produces *permanent* brain damage. The brain of a human infant grows to 80 percent of its adult size in the first three years of the child's life. If adequate proteins are not available to the child during this critical period, the brain stops growing. Nothing can reverse the

Price-Weighted Indices, World[1] Average for All Food,
1948-52 = 100

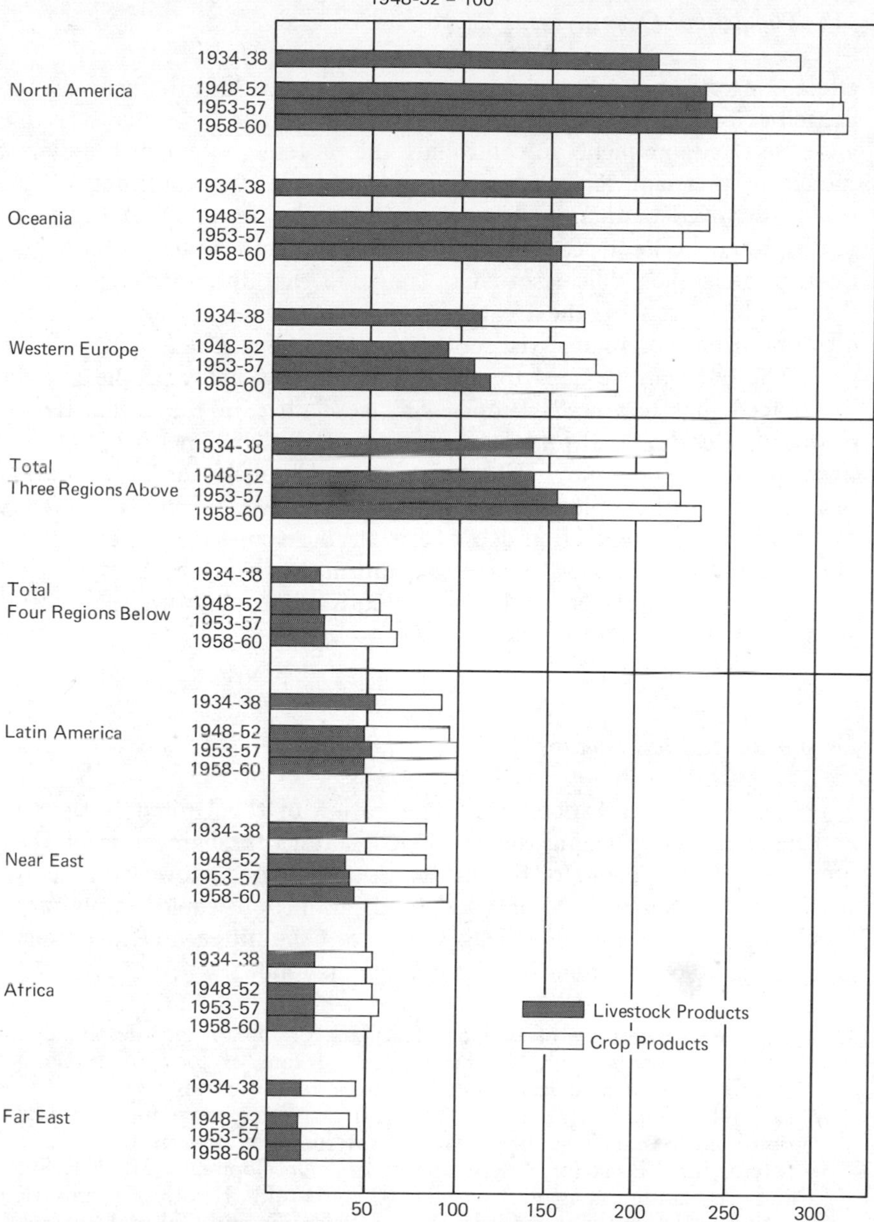


[1] Excluding USSR, Eastern Europe and Mainland China. [2] Excluding Mainland China.

*Source:* United Nations, Food and Agricultural Organization, *State of Food and Agriculture, 1961*; reported by Joseph L. Fisher and Neal Potter, "Resources in the United States and the World," in Philip M. Hauser, ed., *The Population Dilemma*, 1963, by the American Assembly, Columbia University. By permission of Prentice-Hall, Inc.

FIG. 5–2 *Estimate of Per Capita Food Supplies, by World Regions, Prewar to 1958–1960*

effect. No one knows how many persons now alive have reduced mental capacities because of a deficiency of protein.

Recent experiments in controlling the protein content in the diet of groups of pregnant rats offer significant evidence that offspring of the protein-deprived mothers had lower brain weight, fewer DNA cells, and lower protein content per cell than offspring of mothers with a more adequate protein diet. The researchers conclude that these differences may "constitute a basis for the frequently reported impaired behavior of the offspring from protein-deprived mothers" (Zamenhof *et al.*, 1968, p. 322).

The question we need to consider is not how *many* people can the world feed, but how *well?* People were kept alive in the concentration camps of World War II on less than a thousand calories per day, but they lived in misery and agony. Who can claim as his goal the maximization of the number of people alive regardless of their level of human development? Limiting reproduction does not in itself guarantee a better life, but allowing the present growth rate to continue reduces the possibility of improving the quality of life for the billions of people already alive and yet to be born.

### *Developed Nations Sharing with Less Developed*

The Food and Agricultural Organization of the United Nations is, and has been, encouraging the developed nations to share more of their produce with the peoples of the less developed nations. However, an equal sharing at the present state of world food production would simply mean equalizing malnutrition. The U.S. Congress Committee on Government Operations (1968) summarized the problem as follows:

> Despite expenditures of billions of dollars for foreign aid; despite donations and concessional sales of millions of tons of food to developing nations; despite herculean efforts by numerous voluntary groups; despite examples of highly productive technical assistance programs by foundations; and despite years of activity by international organizations such as International Bank for Reconstruction and Development (IBRD), Food and Agriculture Organization (FAO), World Health Organization (WHO), United Nations Educational, Scientific and Cultural Organization (UNESCO), and United Nations International Children's Emergency Fund (UNICEF), there are more hungry mouths in the world today than ever before in history (pp. 324–25).

In 1954, the U.S. Congress enacted Public Law 480, called "Food for Peace," which provided for the free distribution of surplus foods to charitable institutions willing to pay the costs of shipping it to the needy around the world. During the first ten years of the program, over $12 billion worth of basic foods were shipped. At its peak in 1966, nearly half of the entire grain crop of the United States was being exported. This provoked the animosity of other nations, who claimed that their grain sales were lowered by these free shipments, and ultimately even the people of India, who had come to rely on peak shipments to supplement indigenous production. A fifth of the total U.S. wheat crop was shipped to India alone in both 1966 and 1967 (Brown, 1970, p. 169). We cannot expect this high level of export to be continued indefinitely, however. As will be detailed in the next chapter, the productivity of the soils and the available irrigation water have been reduced in much of the United States.

Surplus stocks of wheat, grains, butter, and dried skim milk in the United States were rapidly depleted in the early 1960s, in both tonnage and in proportion of the world's surplus foods (United Nations, Food and Agriculture Organization, 1969, p. 12). Prudent national planning requires that some reserves be retained in case of poor harvests due to bad weather or other uncontrollable conditions.

Two of the less developed countries have recently joined the list of nations that hold surplus agricultural stocks. Kenya, with maize, and Mexico, with wheat, have just encountered the problem of disposal. Newly developed seeds have initiated what some are calling a "green revolution." The new seeds increase yield, but production is only a part of the problem. Farmers do not want to give away their produce (they need a return on their investment if they are to buy more seeds, fertilizer, and so forth). Nor can these countries afford to distribute their surpluses free, but the other less developed, hungry nations have little to exchange for food imports. The keen competition for customers may result in price declines and thus discourage other farmers from increasing investments and thus production.

### *The "Green Revolution"*

In the last few years there have been spectacular increases in grain production in some areas of Africa, Asia, and Latin America. Much of the new agricultural technology has been developed during the past 25 years by the Rockefeller Foundation at the International Maize and Wheat Improvement Center in Mexico. The use of improved seed lines, water control, more fertilizer, and disease and pest controls have together brought about a stepwise increase (i.e., a series of sharp rather than gradual increases) in production.

However, a great deal of caution should be used in evaluating whether these successes can solve the food problems of the world.

First, it has taken approximately 25 years to develop high-yield varieties (HYV) for specific geographical locations. The same seeds are not necessarily as successful in other locales.

Second, even within the geographical areas for which the seeds have been designed, the Food and Agriculture Organization (1970) warns:

> Because the potential of high-yielding seeds is realized only if they are used in effective combination with fertilizer, pesticides, well-prepared soil, adequate water, and greater skill in cultivation, a package of locally adapted inputs and services must be available for the rapid adoption of high-yield varieties. A pilot programme can be started with limited supplies of fertilizer and other inputs and services, but the widespread adoption of HYV by producers requires adequate supplies of the essential physical inputs, cash or credit to buy them, trained manpower to teach the new skills, and assurance of remunerative prices for the crop. Governments will need to take the action necessary to ensure availability of essential inputs and services. *This requires men and money and materials.* . . . In most countries, the scarcest resource is trained manpower (p. 3).

Farmers must have some minimum training and investment capital if they are to feed the increasing billions of world peoples. Seeds do not grow themselves, not in the quantity necessary to feed even current, much less projected, populations.

Third, as the new seeds are used in the less developed countries, it is becoming evident that the protein content of some of the new strains of corn and wheat have fallen by 20–25 percent from that of grains grown at the end of World War II. The lessening of quality may continue, despite increases in the quantity of foods.

Small battles will not win this war. An increase in food production, while worthy of celebration, will only postpone the inevitable unless people recognize the population problem. Norman E. Borlaug was awarded the 1970 Nobel Peace Prize for his achievements in bringing about the "green revolution." In his acceptance speech (1971) he said:

> Recalling that 50 percent of the present world population is undernourished and that an even larger percentage, perhaps 65 percent is malnourished, no room is left for complacency. It is not enough to prevent the currently bad situation from getting worse as population increases. Our aim must be to produce enough food to eradicate all present hunger while at the same time striving to correct malnutrition. . . .
>
> I am convinced that if all policy-makers would take sufficient interest in population control and in aggressively employing and exploiting agricultural development as a potent instrument of agrarian prosperity and economic advancement, many of the social ills of the present day could soon become problems of the past. . . .
>
> The green revolution has won a temporary success in man's war against

hunger and deprivation; it has given man a breathing space. If fully implemented, the revolution can provide sufficient food for sustenance during the next three decades. But the frightening power of human reproduction must also be curbed; otherwise, the success of the green revolution will be ephemeral only.

## *OUTLOOK FOR THE FUTURE*

There are so many proposals to increase the world's food supply by applying present knowledge and research potential that I would like to survey these *possibilities* in light of the *probabilities* involved.

Imaginative thinking is certainly necessary, but suggestions that purport to solve the problems of the world without evaluating the practicality of implementing the proposed solution are irresponsible. Such schemes as layered farming in skyscrapers with special lighting systems need not be taken seriously, because the costs of construction and maintenance, on the scale necessary to provide added billions of persons with food, would be prohibitive.

We will attempt to determine the possibilities for agricultural improvements from expanding the acreage cultivated and/or increasing the yields per acre. There are problems in obtaining the necessary fertilizers, water, and improved seeds, and trained manpower to facilitate such expansion and whether or not these can all be coordinated is an open question. Suggestions for increasing the food yields from the oceans and the possibilities of producing synthetic proteins and vitamins or making new combinations of these will also be explored.

### *Agricultural Improvement*

An increase in the production of food from the land may be accomplished either by expanding the land area being used, by increasing the amount of food obtained from the land already cultivated, or by a combination of these two strategies.

EXPANSION OF AGRICULTURAL ACREAGE. In the past, population growth was accommodated by the colonization of new land areas—North and South America, Australia, New Zealand, and even Siberia. The irrigation of arid regions as a means of expanding agricultural acreage has also been practiced over the centuries, but only recently has it found widespread use.

Population growth and the resultant need for land have increased so rapidly in recent years that most of the land which is readily cultivatable is already being used. Continued expansion of the land area on the scale of the past is, therefore, unlikely. Although the presently cultivated acreage is only about half of that classified as "potentially arable" (see Table 5-4), the unused portion lies idle for good reasons. In most cases

*TABLE 5-4 "Cultivated" Land on Each Continent, Compared with Potentially Arable Land*

| | *Area in Billions of Acres* | | |
|---|---|---|---|
| *Continent* | *Total* | *Potentially Arable* | *"Cultivated"* |
| Africa | 7.40 | 1.81 | 0.39 |
| Asia | 6.76 | 1.55 | 1.28 |
| Australia and New Zealand | 2.03 | 0.38 | 0.04 |
| Europe | 1.18 | 0.43 | 0.38 |
| North America | 5.21 | 1.15 | 0.59 |
| South America | 4.33 | 1.68 | 0.19 |
| USSR | 5.52 | 0.88 | 0.56 |
| Totals | 32.49 | 7.88 | 3.43 |

*Source:* United States Congress, Senate, Committee on Government Operations, Hearing, *Population Crisis,* Part 2, January 31, 1968, p. 302.

the necessary inputs of energy and investment are greater than anticipated yields. For instance, it is often suggested that the tropical rain forests of northern South America, Africa, and Indonesia could be used for agriculture. Indeed, the present heavy foliage would imply a fertile soil. There is also adequate water and plenty of sunlight. Yet wherever the overgrowth has been cut down and the soil cultivated, the returns have been disappointing. The soils are apparently extremely poor in quality and the areas are infested with insects and fungi. Crops may be harvested for only one, two, or sometimes three years before soil becomes "leached out," dried, and cracked—useless to man or beast. The work necessary to clear the land, therefore, has hardly been worth the short-term returns. The land is uncultivated now for good reasons.

Table 5-4 also indicates that virtually all of the potentially arable land of Asia is presently under cultivation. This is why many agricultural specialists refer to the region as "overdeveloped" rather than "underdeveloped." They suggest that, over time, the soils have been overworked and exhausted. In India, so many forests have been cleared that the land suffers from an inability to hold moisture. Thus the area alternates between extremes of parched soils and flooding. The recommendation that soils not be used every year lest they become exhausted apparently has some merit, but population pressure in many areas of the world will not allow the land an occasional recuperative year.

INCREASING THE YIELD PER ACRE. There are many possibilities for raising the yields per acre of land, but most of them require the same high investments that would be necessary to expand the acreage in use.

First, yields can be improved simply by changing the particular crops grown. Sugar beets, if grown under the kind of intensive farming practices found in Northern Europe would seem to maximize the caloric yield per acre per year. Under these conditions, sugar beets could contribute three times the calories of wheat or twice the calories of rice per acre (Brown *et al.*, 1957, p. 72). If energy intake constituted the only nutritional requirement of human beings, the average person could live adequately by consuming 1.5 pounds of sugar a day. However, a person who consumes a diet consisting only of carbohydrates (sugar and starches) or fats will soon die. For proper functioning the body also needs proteins and amino acids, vitamins, and minerals, such as calcium, phosphorus, salt, iron, and iodine (Brown, 1954, p. 108). Maximizing the yield per acre in either calories or protein content does not solve the world problem of how to feed the multiplying numbers of human beings.

Harrison Brown points out that although alfalfa is presently grown to supply protein in animal diets (and thus *indirectly* in the human diet), it could be used to supply protein *directly* in the human diet (see Table 5-5). Clearly, the returns would be multiplied if alfalfa were consumed

*TABLE 5-5 Production of Protein per Acre by Different Methods of Land Management* [1]

| *Method of Land Management* | *Method of Recovering Protein* | *Edible Protein (lbs/acre/year)* |
|---|---|---|
| Planted to forage, grain fed to steers | as beef | 43 |
| Planted to forage, silage fed to cows | as milk | 77 |
| Planted to soybeans | as soybeans | 450 |
| Planted to alfalfa, U.S. average crop | as extracted protein | 600 |
| Planted to alfalfa, Western U.S., irrigated | as extracted protein | 1500 |

[1] All values for cultivated crops on arable land.

*Source:* Harrison Brown, James Bonner, and John Weir, *The Next Hundred Years*. New York: Viking Press, 1957, p. 71.

directly by human beings. One of the difficulties noted by Brown *et al.* (1957) is that:

> In order to use plant protein on a large scale as food for people, however, it would be necessary to devise methods by which the plant may be ground and the protein thus extracted into materials resembling meat, milk, eggs, and so forth. But these are merely technological problems and are certainly soluable. This modification of our food technology would permit us to supplement human diets with the needed amino acids

> at a fraction of the cost in acres that characterizes our present system (p. 72).

It would also be necessary to convince people that reconstituted alfalfa is something they *want* to eat. Not much is known about how to motivate people to eat what is good for them—whether they be poor or affluent.

The yield per acre varies in different geographic and climatic areas and under different types of cultivation the caloric and protein value per acre also varies according to the crops grown and the uses to which they are put. Increasing the yield of particular crops on particular acreage, in any geographic area is dependent upon maximizing the advantages of additional inputs of fertilizers, irrigation, improved seeds or animal breeds, and pest control. Adequate utilization of these inputs, furthermore, requires intelligent labor, trained in the technical skills necessary for quantity production. Perhaps in no other area is the Marxian theory of labor shown to be so clearly in error as in agriculture: additional output will not result from adding additional labor; rather increased production will come from added capital investment, including investment in improving the technological skills of human beings.

Land reform, the division of large landholdings (often with absentee landowners) into small, family-owned plots, may provide a greater incentive to farm workers to put more effort into improving yields. Sharecropping often reduces the incentives of both the landowner and the worker to invest in improved seeds, fertilizer, tools, and so forth. Subdivision of large land holdings is necessary in many parts of the world for a variety of reasons. By itself, it may provide increased motivation for the farm worker to increase productivity. If, at the same time, training in new methods, lending for the purchase of new seeds, fertilizer, and tools, or even cooperatively owned equipment are made available stepwise increases in yields may be expected. Land reform alone, however, cannot guarantee improvement. If population continues its rapid climb, small plots(such as five-acre parcels) might be subdivided among sons until the size of an individual unit will not even support a farm family at the subsistence level, much less allow for marketable produce.

### *Adding Necessary Inputs to Increase Agricultural Output*

If the potentially arable land of the earth is indeed twice as great as that presently cultivated and if yields per acre vary greatly from crop to crop, then the possibility of increasing the world's food supply must be great. What inputs are required to effect the necessary increases and how may they be obtained?

FERTILIZERS. These are made from nonrenewable materials. The manufacturing technology involved is not complex, but does depend heavily on energy sources for nitrogen fixation and, eventually, for phosphate treatment. Mining and transport are important; the tonnages distributed are large and involve global trade. Supplies of raw materials—potassium compounds, sulfur and sulfates, phosphate rock, limestone, natural gas or coal, and air (for nitrogen)—are adequate at present and for moderately increased rates of use. Increased fertilizer costs, however, would occur quickly if the needs of the less developed countries were to be met (Hendricks, 1969, p. 73). The production of fertilizer must increase more rapidly than in the past to meet the food crisis.

TABLE 5-6 *Fertilizer Needed to Increase Agricultural Production on Acreage Now under Cultivation in Asia,[1] Africa, and Latin America by the Percentages Indicated*

| *Percent Increase in Agricultural Production* | *Tonnage of Plant Nutrients Needed (millions of metric tons)* | *Percent Increase in Fertilizer Usage* | *Capital Needed* (million dollars) | *Total Annual Cost to Farmers* (million dollars) |
|---|---|---|---|---|
| ... | 6[2] | ... | ... | $ 1,300 |
| 10 | 11 | 80 | $ 2,500 | 2,400 |
| 26 | 19 | 220 | 6,500 | 4,200 |
| 43 | 28 | 370 | 11,000 | 6,200 |
| 63 | 40 | 570 | 17,000 | 8,800 |
| 100 | 67 | 1,000 | 30,500 | 14,800 |

[1] Except Mainland China and Japan.
[2] Actual consumption in 1966.
*Source:* United States Congress, Committee on Government Operations (1968), p. 303.

The phenomenal increase in food production in the United States since the first World War has actually occurred simultaneously with a reduction in acreage farmed and increased use of fertilizers. The Japanese and Western Europeans use fertilizers even more intensively than U.S. farmers (Mayer, 1969, p. 468).

The less developed countries together used 6.9 million metric tons of fertilizer—almost three times their own production of fertilizer—in 1968 (United Nations, Food and Agriculture Organization, p. 28). One of the world's largest plants for manufacturing fertilizers is located in Sindri in India. Its annual production is approximately 350,000 metric tons, but this quantity is barely enough to grow food for the *annual* population *increment* of India! In other words, India would need an additional factory of this size every year simply to keep pace with the population increase. Yet it would require at least three to five years to build such a plant and to get it into final operation (Borgstrom, 1965, p. 130). Table 5-6 indicates the amount of fertilizer needed to increase agricultural production on acreage now under cultivation in Asia, Africa, and Latin America. In order to increase the agricultural production of these areas by 43 percent (which might give the *present* populations an adequate diet), an initial capital investment of $11 billion would be needed. The total annual cost to farmers would then approximate $6 billion. However, by the time the

FIG. 5–3 *Members of the Tungchia commune in China use the same method employed by their ancestors as they apply manure to a field. UPI Photo*

plants were built, fertilizer produced and distributed, and additional crops grown, population increases would be significant. The less developed regions of the world are, in fact, doubling their population in about 20 years. In order to increase food production during that time by 100 percent, which would allow the same per capita rations as presently exist, would require a $30 billion investment in fertilizer alone, with an annual cost to the farmers of $14.8 billion.

Borgstrom (1965) claims that by the end of this century the weight of the fertilizer that will require distribution around the world will exceed the total weight of the human race. Even so, that fertilizer would replace only about three or four key substances that crop lands require and not the whole range of nutrients that will have to be taken into account by then.

IRRIGATION. Irrigation will become even more important as the use of fertilizers increases. Sometimes irrigation alone can add an additional crop per year in warm climates. Water for irrigation may be drawn from three basic sources: underground supplies, fresh water rivers and lakes, and desalination of sea waters. All have limited applicability.

Wells are used around the world to retrieve water from underground. The capacity to pump water from below ground gives the illusion of an inexhaustible supply. When the amount of water pumped exceeds the amount replaced, however, the supply is reduced, the water level falls, and wells must be dug deeper. The process may be repeated until the water supply is exhausted or until the costs of pumping are prohibitive. The underground water table that has been tapped to irrigate the desert areas of Texas, Arizona, and southern California has dropped 100 feet since the irrigation began. The United States Geological Survey estimates that it would take 104 years to restore the groundwater to its natural level through natural replenishment, *if* it were not being pumped out in the meantime. Furthermore, saltwater is seeping into the continent from the ocean and filling the space evacuated by pumping out fresh water (Borgstrom, 1965, p. 418).

The supply of river water can fluctuate widely; thus, for purposes of irrigation (and power), great dams have been built to hold back an adequate supply of water for the times at which it is needed. Again, the possibilities are not limitless: some rivers in the United States are already so "dammed" that salmon cannot get upstream to spawn; on some there are no more locations where new dams could be built. Furthermore, the estimated lifetime of a dam is from 30 to 100 years; it then fills with silt and becomes useless. Few people know that there was a little Aswan Dam, which was rendered useless in this way. The new, billion-dollar Aswan Dam will hold back the silt which used to be spread over the adjacent

FIG. 5–4 *One form of irrigation still used on Indian farms near Delhi is the Persian waterwheel. Wide World Photo*

land each time the Nile River flooded and one of the richest river valleys in the world will lose its main source of fertility.

At present about 11 percent of the world's cultivated acres are irrigated by conventional methods. If the river waters of the world were conserved and distributed, it is estimated that it would ultimately be possible to irrigate 14 percent of the acreage now under cultivation (at current prices of water and of farm products). By building more expensive conventional irrigation projects, a maximum of 20 percent of the world's cultivated acreage could be served (Brown, *et al.* 1957, p. 74). Thus fresh water is not available in sufficient quantity to supply more than one-fifth of the presently cultivated land, much less to supply the deserts and other "potentially arable" acreage.

The desalination of sea water is another possibility in the quest for increasing sources of fresh water. There are already a number of techniques or processes for removing the salt from sea water—all of them expensive. The problems of desalination are infinitely more complex than one would gather from reading a typical newspaper account. Cost, plant size, transportation, and salt disposal difficulties are among the problems that would need to be resolved before any widespread use of desalination would be feasible.

The cost of the reclamation of ocean water has been estimated at between $100 and $200 per acre-foot. To this must be added the cost of building canals and pipelines to distribute the water. Irrigation water in the United States presently costs approximately $10 per acre-foot delivered (Brown, *et al.*, 1957, p. 75). The cost of desalinated water for irrigation would be far more than the value of crops which could be produced.

Recently, Governor Rockefeller proposed a desalination plant for New York City, which would produce a million gallons of fresh water daily. The city of New York needs 1.2 billion gallons per day, however, so that 1,200 such plants would be needed to supply the city with water (Paddock and Paddock, 1967, pp. 65f).

Plans were recently drawn up for the irrigation of southern Texas, whose groundwater reserves will have been so reduced by the year 2000 that desalting the waters of the Gulf of Mexico will be the only recourse. The construction of no less than 15,000 plants would be required, each equal in size to the largest chemical plants in the present-day United States (Borgstrom, 1965). Moreover, the water required to eventually produce one ton of milk would produce 35 tons of salt!

The water needs of the world are inflated further by population growth.

NEW SEEDS AND BREEDS. The selective breeding of both plants and animals has allowed us to make giant leaps in the quantities of food produced.

> Remarkable productive new seeds [have] made possible the development of cereals and other plant species that are more tolerant to cold, more resistant to drought, less susceptible to disease, more responsive to fertilizer, higher in yield and richer in protein. . . .
> The results of man's efforts to increase the productivity of domestic animals are equally impressive. When the ancestors of our present chickens were domesticated, they laid a clutch of about 15 eggs per year. Hens in the U.S. today average 220 eggs per year and the figure is rising steadily as a result of continuing advances in breeding and feeding. When cattle were originally domesticated, they probably did not produce more than 600 pounds of milk per year, barely enough for a calf. (It is roughly the average amount produced by cows in India today.) The 13 million dairy cows in the U.S. today average 9,000 pounds of milk yearly, outproducing their ancestors 15 to one (Brown, 1970, pp. 162–63).

New seeds, techniques, and knowledge are far from being utilized on a world-wide scale, however. The time lag between development and acceptance has been very long. It took nearly 25 years for hybrid corn to be accepted by farmers in the United States, where high incentives and technical manpower existed. The new high-yield varieties (HYV) have yet to be promoted and accepted among farmers on a wide scale. Furthermore, the seeds, fertilizers, pesticides, and agricultural techniques which produce stepwise increase in production in one geographical area cannot be simply transferred; they must be adapted to new locations.

PEST CONTROL. There is no way to adequately assess the amount of farm produce lost to pests. Between 10 and 25 percent of the total grain crops of India are estimated to be lost to insects, rodents, birds, monkeys, and cattle. Billions of rats, millions of monkeys, and between 225 and 280 million cows compete with human beings for rice and wheat. Yet when a proposal to reduce the numbers of sacred cows came before the Indian Parliament, 100,000 Hindus turned out to protest. The only war ever sanctioned by the pacifist Gandhi was for the reduction of the monkey population. The death of 10 million monkeys make little difference, however, since millions of new monkeys quickly replaced those that were killed. Tigers, leopards, and other natural predators of the monkeys had previously been eliminated as the forests were cleared in order to cultivate all available land (Borgstrom, 1965, pp. 121ff).

Other national groups that do not share the Hindu reverence for all forms of life have fewer problems with mammalian pests, but continuing problems with insects. Table 5-7 indicates the amounts of pesticides

*TABLE 5-7 Pesticides Needed to Increase Agricultural Production on Acreage Now under Cultivation in Asia,[1] Africa, and Latin America by the Percentages Indicated*

| Percent Increase in Agricultural Production | Tonnage Needed (metric tons) | Capital: Manufacturing (in millions) | Capital: Formulation and Distribution (in millions) | Total Annual Cost to Farmers |
|---|---|---|---|---|
| | 120,000 | $ | $ | $ 580 |
| 10 | 150,000 | 70 | 40 | 730 |
| 26 | 220,000 | 200 | 110 | 1,060 |
| 43 | 300,000 | 380 | 200 | 1,460 |
| 63 | 420,000 | 630 | 340 | 2,040 |
| 100 | 720,000 | 1,240 | 670 | 3,500 |

[1] Except Mainland China and Japan.

*Source:* United States Congress, Senate, Committees on Government Operations, *Population Crisis,* Vol. 2. Washington, D.C.: Government Printing Office, 1968, p. 304.

that would be needed to increase the agricultural production on acreage now under cultivation in Asia (except China and Japan), Africa, and Latin America. To double the agricultural production would require a six-fold increase in the tonnage of pesticides and an annual cost to farmers of $3.5 billion. In the next chapter we will discuss some of the problems caused by the use of certain pesticides.

TRAINED MANPOWER. Many people assume that because almost anyone can grow flowers, fruits, or vegetables in a backyard garden, there is little technical training required for farming. Indeed, farmers are often classified as unskilled laborers. Yet, it is the scientific approach and the application of its techniques that have made some farms productive while others stagnate.

Land ownership patterns have little effect on productivity, without technical leadership. In Latin America and many parts of Asia, rich landlords with extensive holdings maintain a feudal system and collect rent, services, or shares of the harvest from peasant farmers. The landlords have little motive or desire to help the peasants. However, if governments seize large estates and divide them among peasants, the result is often *decreased* production. The new peasant owners lack the knowledge, money, and equipment to make the most of what they have acquired. Furthermore, these small bits of land become divided into inheritance or marriage dowry parcels to the point that the individual plots are so reduced in size that subsistence is about all that can be had from them (Fisher, 1968, p. 95). Land reform is desirable for social progress, but some authors assume it is the whole solution.

AGRICULTURAL EDUCATION. Agricultural education has a long history in the United States. The Land Grant College Act was passed in 1862. Prior to World War II, one-third of all research money funded by the United States government went to agriculture.

In the countries which need them most, however, agricultural research specialists and technicians are not being trained in the numbers needed. University students majoring in agriculture declined from 3 to 1 percent of all university students in South America. Of 10,541 students in Central American universities, only 187 were studying agriculture in 1960 (Paddock & Paddock, 1967, pp. 73–78).

The number of agricultural research workers per 100,000 persons active in agriculture in specific countries in 1960 is given in Table 5-8. One reason for the shortage of trained manpower is that young people in food-deficit nations tend to decline an agricultural education; farming represents a lowly occupation to them. Students fortunate enough to obtain an education abroad hold the same prejudice. In 1967–1968, 42 percent of the foreign students in the United States were studying engineering or humanities. Only 3 percent had chosen agriculture (Fisher, 1968, p. 94). Some nations (Egypt, the Philippines) now have an excess and underemployed group of university-trained persons, while lacking adequate trained manpower in agriculture. It is clear from Table 5-8 that even if we could double or triple the number of research workers in India and the Philippines, it would still be difficult for individualized help to reach the millions of farmers.

*TABLE 5-8 Agricultural Research Workers per 100,000 People Active in Agriculture, 1960*

| | |
|---|---|
| India | 1.2 |
| Philippines | 1.6 |
| Mexico | 3.8 |
| Pakistan | 4.5 |
| Thailand | 4.7 |
| Colombia | 9.0 |
| Iran | 10.0 |
| Argentina | 14.0 |
| Japan | 60.0 |
| Taiwan | 79.0 |
| Netherlands | 133.0 |

*Source:* United States Department of Agriculture, *Changes in Agriculture in 26 Developing Nations,* 1948–1963. Washington: Government Printing Office, 1965, Table 46.

MACHINERY. The tools in use by farmers range from the primitive digging stick and the hoe to very complex, sophisticated machinery. In the United States, according to Lenski (1966).

> As Edward Higbee so dramatically describes in *Farms And Farmers In An Urban Age,* agriculture is rapidly losing its distinctiveness and more and more coming to resemble other forms of industrial activity. Mechanization has proceeded to the point where a single lettuce packing machine costs over $20,000 and a single diesel tractor as much as $32,000. In fact, the average capital investment for workers in agriculture exceeds by one-third the average capital investment for workers in all other industries. (In 1960 the figures were $21,300 and $15,900.) In addition, those farmers who are surviving and prospering in the increased intense competition find themselves caught up in a network of business relationship, government controls, and financial transactions no less complex than those of their urban counterparts in the business world (p. 383).

By 1969 the total value of farm implements and machinery in the United States had reached over $32 billion. Farmers were spending $5 billion yearly for additions and replacements of machinery and equipment, and for motor vehicles for farm use (United States Bureau of the Census, 1970, p. 590). There is little possibility that the less developed nations will be able to meet these kinds of costs for advanced machinery.

## *Food From the Oceans*

PRESENT CATCH. In the search for means of increasing the world's supply of food, man has turned to the seas. The 1968 worldwide catch of fish, crustaceans, and mollusks was 58 million metric tons. The yield

TABLE 5-9 *Estimated World*[1] *Catch of Fish, Crustacea, and Molluscs*

| | *Average 1948–52* | *1957* | *1960* | *1962* | *1965* | *1967* | *1968*[2] | *Change 1967 to 1968*[2] | *Annual Rate of Growth 1955–57 1965–67* |
|---|---|---|---|---|---|---|---|---|---|
| | | | | *Million metric tons* | | | | *Percent* | |
| Western Europe | 6.31 | 7.59 | 7.71 | 8.21 | 10.24 | 11.26 | 10.97 | −3 | 3.4 |
| Eastern Europe and USSR | 1.94 | 2.82 | 3.40 | 4.02 | 5.73 | 6.43 | 6.93 | 8 | 8.0 |
| North America | 3.50 | 3.80 | 3.79 | 4.15 | 4.04 | 3.78 | 3.97 | 5 | — |
| Oceania | 0.09 | 0.11 | 0.13 | 0.15 | 0.18 | 0.20 | 0.21 | 5 | 6.3 |
| Latin America | 0.63 | 1.36 | 4.73 | 8.62 | 9.43 | 12.71 | 13.48 | 6 | 26.0 |
| Far East[1] | 6.85 | 10.30 | 11.81 | 13.04 | 14.52 | 16.41 | 18.04 | 10 | 4.8 |
| Near East | 0.35 | 0.39 | 0.40 | 0.44 | 0.52 | 0.49 | 0.53 | 8 | 2.5 |
| Africa | 1.20 | 1.98 | 2.20 | 2.52 | 3.04 | 3.62 | 4.10 | 13 | 5.8 |
| World[1] | 20.90 | 28.40 | 34.20 | 41.20 | 47.70 | 54.90 | 58.20 | 6 | 6.4 |

[1] Excluding China (Mainland).
[2] Preliminary.

*Source:* United Nations, Food and Agriculture Organization, *The State of Food and Agriculture, 1969.* Rome: FAO, 1969, p. 13.

from the seas has been increasing at a faster rate than any other source of food. The annual rate of growth from the 1955–1957 average to the 1965–1967 average was 6.4 percent per year (see Table 5-9). In fifteen years the total world catch almost tripled.

Even with the rapid increase in fishery products, the present totals contribute only about two percent of the caloric consumption of the world. At the same time, however, fish supplies valuable protein, equal to about 20 percent of the animal protein consumption of the world. The relatively minor role of fish protein in comparison to other animal and vegetable protein consumption is indicated in Figure 5-5. But, although the supply is small, it has been growing more rapidly than world population.

A large part of the total catch, which has increased most rapidly in the Latin American nations, is being sold to the developed nations. And, a significant portion of that is fed to hogs and chickens rather than going directly (and more efficiently) to human consumption. Some of the fish meal so used is defined as inedible by humans, but could be used as a protein additive in other foods.

Fish products are consumed unevenly around the world. They make up a far larger proportion of both calorie and protein consumption in Norway and Japan than in many other parts of the world. India recently advanced to sixth place among the world's fishing nations. Most of the catch of the Asian countries is destined for local consumption. Yet, even if the total world catch could be used for India alone, it would not provide each individual inhabitant with more protein than the equivalent of one average herring a day (Borgstrom, 1965, pp. 121ff.). The 1969 improved catch of two million metric tons for India yields about the equivalent of one herring per person per month.

FUTURE POSSIBILITIES. Oceanographers estimate that, with a massive investment in ships, by the year 2000 a maximum of 100 million metric tons of fish could be harvested from the oceans yearly without damaging future supplies. However, with the anticipated population increase, the per capita harvest in the year 2000 could average 8 *percent less* than at present.

Two problems threaten to reduce the maximum possible catches of the future. One is overexploitation: man has become such an efficient fisherman that numerous species are now in danger of becoming extinct. Another problem is oceanic pollution: the areas close to shorelines, where fish are in greatest abundance, are being polluted at an increasing rate.

Most of the ocean, approximately 90.7 percent of the surface, is a biological desert. It is only close to the shorelines and in a few areas where powerful upwellings bring nutrients to the surface that fish are abundant enough to be caught in quantity.

*Source:* S. J. Holt, "The Food Resources of the Ocean," in *Scientific American*, 223:3 (September 1969), 188. 

FIG. 5–5 *Average Daily Fish Consumption in Comparison to Consumption of Other Animal Protein and Vegetable Protein*

Although marine farming has a long history, the world has hardly begun to tap the potential of farming fish and shellfish. Man has the knowledge and experience to move beyond the primitive hunting and gathering of food in the sea. Especially as some of the high-demand species are in danger of overexploitation, we may expect and encourage the stocking and the farming of portions of the ocean. The numerous complications are for the most part known and resolvable with investments that are reasonable in relation to the expected returns (Pinchot, 1970).

However, the fish is a relatively inefficient converter of ocean plants to human food. It is estimated that 100,000 pounds of algae are necessary to produce about one pound of codfish (Brown, *et al.* 1957, p. 76). There are numerous suggestions, therefore, that we might increase the ocean's yield of human food by moving down the food chain and harvesting smaller fish. Algae could even be strained from the ocean water directly by some mechanical means. However, a lot of straining would have to be done, since one cubic meter of sea water contains on the average only about one cubic centimeter of plant material (Brown, *et al.* 1957, p. 76). Suggestions that algae cultivation (hydroponics) in huge tanks could produce 40 tons of algae per acre per year have not been implemented because of the high investment required (from 10 to 100 times the investment in conventional agriculture) and because of the small likelihood that human beings would be interested in eating the "nasty little green vegetable." An attempt to sell algae tablets and candy is currently being made in Japan.

Although there are possibilities for continuing to increase the harvest from the oceans, there are limits to what is possible. And those limits may be reached before population growth comes to a halt.

## *Synthetic Proteins and Vitamins*

SYNTHETIC FOOD. The chemical synthesis of food would seem to be a remote possibility. The human body requires chemical compounds that are complex and exceedingly various. Although scientists know how to use simple compounds as the starting materials for the chemical synthesis of the sugars, fats, amino acids, and vitamins necessary in the human diet, it is still a complicated chemical operation (Brown *et al.* 1957, p. 77).

During World War II the Germans manufactured synthetic fats from both coal and petroleum to feed to forced laborers. These fats did not conform to desirable standards of taste or safety. The petroleum-based fats retained a petroleum-like odor and were probably not fully metabolized by the human body. Although there has been a recent renewal of interest in the low-cost production of food from petroleum sources, some of the old problems remain. Furthermore, the world supplies of petroleum and coal are exhaustable and are in demand as energy supplies. Reserves will be driven far lower before atomic power comes into such widespread use as to reduce the demand for coal and oil. Further, chemical plants are themselves expensive and even if people would accept these sources of food, bulk distribution would remain a problem.

It would be possible to supplement diets with synthetically produced amino acids, which typically are lacking in the cereal diets of persons in underdeveloped areas. But the plan is not economically feasible. The cost is estimated at $40.00 per person, and would thus require half of the entire national income in many of the nations whose people need it most. Foreign aid is an unlikely source of funds for such a program, since the yearly cost of supplying this single food supplement to India alone would be about $22 billion.

Borgstrom (1965, p. 401) points out that even if it were economically, physically, and aesthetically possible to use synthetic foods, man cannot withdraw from a fundamental cooperation with nature. Man is dependent upon the green plant to pull carbon dioxide from the air and return it to the great carbon cycle of nature. Too many men destroying our green acres and poisoning the green plants of the ocean will destroy the air they breathe. The interrelationships of nature must be respected, which is one reason why the population problem is not merely a food problem.

VITAMINS. Although the chemical synthesis and the widespread production and distribution of bulky foods remains impractical, vitamin production and supply is a different story. Harrison Brown *et al.* (1957, p. 78) claim that it is possible to supply a human being with his required rations of vitamins, all synthetically produced, at a cost of between 25 cents and one dollar per year. Vitamins, although complex and expensive to manufacture, are required by human beings only in minute amounts. The mass distribution of vitamins would be a reasonable minimal starting point for international agencies. Only a few billion dollars per year would be needed for a certain improvement in human health.

## *New Sources or New Combinations of Food*

There may be food sources which human beings have not yet recognized. Many "filling substances" would not be used as food except in dire circumstances, and some not even then. Nevertheless, scientists continue to seek possibilities for increasing the supply of foods for human consumption.

It would be possible, though at present it is too expensive, to cultivate algae in water or even on petroleum or the sewage from our cities. The algae, after processing, could serve as food or could aid in the cultivation of yeast.

Grown on the wastes of human beings, the wastes from cane sugar production, or on the wastes from pulp factories, yeast could become an efficient and inexpensive source of protein. But, since yeast is not self-generating, it is as limited in supply as the waste matter upon which it grows.

Many of the new high-yield varieties of grains have lower protein content than prewar varieties. Research is now concentrating on developing and testing grain varieties with higher protein content as well as possible additives to enrich the present varieties.

*Incaparina*, a combination of corn, high-protein cottonseed meal, vitamin A, and tortulla yeast (a source of vitamin B), was announced to the world in 1957 and was heavily promoted in a pilot project in Colombia. After more than ten years of determined effort and investment, however, the Quaker Oats Company is still losing money on the product. People apparently do not like its unaccustomed taste and texture.

A tasteless and odorless fish protein concentrate has recently been developed for use as a food additive, especially for the hungry peoples of the world. It has the advantage of not interfering with the tastes and textures desired by the various peoples of the world. It can be unobtrusively added to the basic food, whether cornmeal, wheat, rice, or potatoes. In 1968 the world production of fish meal neared ten percent of the total tonnage caught. Like the coarser fish meal, the protein concentrate can be produced from inedible fish or parts of fish. Like fish in general, however, the supply is limited. The processing factories also require investment funds, but the returns in value to the human diet are far greater than when the fish meal is fed to chickens and hogs. The later consumption of those chickens or hogs by human beings would provide only a fraction of the protein which could be derived from consuming the fish protein concentrate directly.

If human beings were to accept these unconventional sources of food, they might also derive animal protein from species that are presently unacceptable for consumption. Some persons in the United States have come, like some Europeans, to regard snails as a delicacy. Some cultures utilize snake meat, caterpillars, and so forth. Should the Indian come to define beef cattle, rodents, and monkeys as food sources, he would simultaneously add several sources of animal protein to his diet and save a portion of the grains eaten by those animals. A cultural pattern thousands of years old is not likely to be readily changed, however. Waves of starvation have occurred at many times in human history when sources of food defined as unacceptable were in plentiful supply. The Ehrlichs (1970, p. 110) point out that the hungriest people are precisely those who recognize the fewest items as food.

## *FOOD AND POPULATION—THE WRONG PROBLEM*

Although, as Malthus suggested, "ultimately" the human species cannot expand its numbers beyond the food supply, the precise quantity and quality of food considered necessary to keep human beings alive varies greatly according to the level of existence considered acceptable. The skeletal human beings found in some German concentration camps had continued breathing on daily rations 800–1000 calories per person per day. Yet an average daily ration of 2300 calories is judged inadequate to provide normal levels of energy and working men require well over 3000 calories per day. Calories alone are not enough. Vitamins, minerals, and daily supplies of protein are all necessary for human health and development.

There is a great difference, then, in food requirements necessary for a "bare" existence and those required for a healthy, energetic life. Given a choice, most people would obviously choose the latter for themselves and for mankind. When the choice becomes a conscious one, as we come to understand how rising populations have been nullifying the advances in food production, it makes sense to match our control over deaths with birth control. The human capacity to plan ahead allows us to reduce births in order to improve the quality of life. We are not left to the self-steering aspects of nature in either death control or birth control.

If mankind had been content to let the death rate find its "natural level," there would not already have been such rapid population growth. Human beings have made the decision to manipulate nature and soon we will have to decide whether to maximize the numbers of bodies to be kept alive at some low level or whether to maximize the creative, aesthetic, and intellectual capacities of all—in contrast to those of only a small proportion of the world's people. It is not possible to maximize both the quantity and the quality of human beings.

Ours is a world divided. And, by whatever measure is used, the gap between the haves and the have-nots is widening.

After an examination of the effects of population growth on natural resources, we will review the extent of the economic gap between the developed and less developed nations. Whether in the economic or material realm, in food production, housing, medical care, or education, whatever gains are made in the "developing" countries are approximately nullified by population growth. The gains become insignificant in light of the more rapid gains of the slower-growing, advanced nations.

## *SUMMARY*

A survey of the past, present, and future food situation of the world can hardly result in an optimistic view of the race between population and food. Although world food production has actually been proceeding at a slightly more rapid pace than has population growth, the increases in the underdeveloped countries have been little more than equal to population increases.

The increased production in recent years was brought about by great effort on the part of all the nations of the world and with the cooperative efforts of the United Nations agencies and private foundations. The increases *could* have allowed all the people of the world to have improved and adequate diets. Thereafter, man's improved health, vitality, productivity, and energy presumably would have contributed to general improvements in living standards. But population increase has nullified almost all of the gains made.

The developed nations must share an increasingly greater portion of their production with the underdeveloped countries. But even complete sharing will not solve the problems as long as population continues to increase.

The so-called "green revolution" is partial and spotty. New seed strains are not usable under all geographic, climatic, and soil conditions. Millions of people need to cooperate in order to achieve a maximization of food production with present facilities.

The possibilities for future expansion of agricultural output typically require vast investments in trained manpower, tools, fertilizers, water, new high-yield seeds and breeds, and the control of pests. The more primitive the agricultural methods of a particular society, the more these additions are needed and the less likely that the people will be willing to accept the necessary changes.

New and strange food products are also likely to meet resistance, not only among peasant populations but even among highly educated persons.

No single solution is probable for the food-population problem. Every approach to improving the production and distribution of food needs to be facilitated, with the long-term preservation of the soil and waters of the earth in mind. Whether per capita food supplies improve or worsen, the people of the world will improve their total situation more rapidly if population is soon brought under control.

## *REFERENCES*

BORGSTROM, GEORGE. 1965. *The hungry planet.* New York: Macmillan.

BORLAUG, NORMAN E. 1971. The green revolution, peace and humanity. Nobel Peace Prize acceptance speech, December 10, 1970. Reprinted: Washington, D.C.; Population Reference Bureau, Selection no. 35 (January).

BOULDING, KENNETH E. 1964. The utterly dismal theorem. In *Population, evolution, and birth control,* ed. Garrett Hardin, p. 81. San Francisco; W. H. Freeman.

BROWN, HARRISON. 1954. *The challenge of man's future.* New York: Viking Press.

BROWN, HARRISON, JAMES BONNER, AND JOHN WEIR. 1957. *The next hundred years.* New York: Viking Press.

BROWN, LESTER R. 1970. Human food production as a process in the biosphere. *Scientific American* 223, no. 3 (September): 161–70.

CHANDRASEKHAR, S. 1967. *Asia's population problems.* London: George Allen & Unwin.

EHRLICH, PAUL R., & ANNE H. EHRLICH. 1970. *Population, resources, environment: Issues in human ecology.* San Francisco: W. H. Freeman.

FISHER, JOSEPH L., & NEAL POTTER. 1963. Resources in the United States and the world. In *The population dilemma,* ed. Philip M. Hauser for the American Assembly, pp. 94–124. Englewood Cliffs, N. J.: Prentice-Hall.

FISHER, TADD. 1968. The many-faceted food problem. *Population Bulletin* 24 (December): 83–99. Washington, D.C.: Population Reference Bureau.

HENDRICKS, STERLING B. 1969. Food from the land. In *Resources and man: A study and recommendations by the Committee on Resources and Man of the Division of Earth Sciences, National Research Council with the cooperation of the Division of Biology and Agriculture,* pp. 65–86. San Francisco: W. H. Freeman.

HOLT, S. J. 1969. The food resources of the ocean. *Scientific American,* 223, no. 3 (September): 178–94.

LENSKI, GERHARD E. 1966. *Power and privilege.* New York: McGraw-Hill.

MAYER, JEAN. 1969. Food and population: The wrong problem? In *Population studies: Selected essays and research,* ed. Kenneth Kammeyer, pp. 459–72. Chicago: Rand McNally.

PADDOCK, WILLIAM, AND PAUL PADDOCK. 1967. *Famine—1975!* Boston: Little, Brown.

PINCHOT, GIFFORD B. 1970. Marine farming. *Scientific American* 223, no. 6 (December): 15–21.

UNITED NATIONS, Food and Agriculture Organization. 1969. *The state of food and agriculture 1969.* Rome: FAO.

———. 1970. *Monthly Bulletin of Agricultural Economics and Statistics,* 19 (January).

———. 1970. *Monthly Bulletin of Agricultural Economics and Statistics,* 19 (February).

United States Bureau of the Census. 1970. *Statistical abstract of the United States, 1970.* Washington, D.C.: United States Department of Commerce.

United States Congress, Senate, Committee on Government Operations. 1968. *Population Crisis,* Vol 2. Washington, D.C.: Government Printing Office.

United States Department of Agriculture. 1965. Changes in agriculture in twenty-six developing nations. 1948–1963. *Foreign Agricultural Economic Report* no. 27 (November). Washington, D.C.: Government Printing Office.

Zamenhof, Stephen, Edith van Marthens, and Frank L. Margolis. 1968. DNA (cell number) and protein in neonatal brain: Alteration by maternal dietary protein restriction. *Science* 160 (April 19): 322–23.

chapter 6

# THE EFFECTS OF POPULATION ON NATURAL RESOURCES AND POLLUTION OF RESOURCES

*As human beings, we do not need to apologize for the fact that we have succeeded in modifying and controlling our natural environment to our collective advantages. However, as the saturation level is approached, and space and resources are all in use, then the exploitive, wasteful approach becomes increasingly unadaptive and must be shifted to the opposite pole, to considerations of birth control, for example, or to legalized abortion, recycling and reuse of resources, regulation of land use, complete waste disposal treatment, law and order, civil rights, and the peaceful coexistence of man and nature in general.*

Eugene P. Odum, Ecologist (1970)

We will now turn to a discussion of the more general relationship between population and natural resources. The two are actually dependent upon one another: the population depends upon many kinds of resources and the supply of resources depends in turn upon the social group's definition of what is useful and valuable and its technological manipulation of potentially useful materials.

We will explore the types of natural resources and their expected supply levels in the immediate and distant future. Since each resource is limited, conservation will be seen as a long-run necessity, important not only for improving the quality of human life but even for insuring the survival of human life.

The present chapter will begin by looking at population in relation to the physical environment. Any given environment obviously is able to support more persons at a lower than at a higher standard of living. However, it is important to realize the ways in which different cultures may manipulate the relationship between population and resources. Five types of population-resource relationships will be examined.

The latter part of the chapter will review the most important kinds of natural resources and the supplies of each. Some of the effects of pollution on water, air, soil, and plant resources will also be examined. We will look at some recent findings on chemical hazards within the food chain that have frightening implications for the quality of human life.

Although pollution may differ in kind between underdeveloped countries and developed countries, many of the effects of pollution spread throughout the biosphere, the thin layer at the surface of the earth capable of supporting living matter. Some of the pollutants of water, air, and soil resources will be highlighted, but new sources of harm and new combinations of elements are still being discovered.

## *THE RELATIONSHIP BETWEEN POPULATION AND RESOURCES*

The earliest hunting and gathering groups must surely have recognized the relationship between the resources of their local area and the numbers and welfare of their group. The same holds true for contemporary tribal societies. Many modern people, in contrast, have lost their respect for nature in the manipulation of it.

A "resource" may be defined as any substance or physical property of a place that can be used in some way to satisfy a human need. Resources include the physical and biological potentialities of the minerals, soils, biota, water, and atmosphere of the locality—as they can be realized by its occupants—and whatever transportational, military, or recreational value may accrue through the interests and activities of local or distant people (Zelinsky, 1966, p. 103).

Resources must, in a broad analysis, be identified in terms not only of quantity, but also of quality and stability and of their relation to other conditioning features of the natural environment. The following discussion of the relationship between population and resources benefits from the work of Edward Ackerman (1959).

## *Numbers of People and the Physical Environment*

The most densely populated areas of the world are located at the important links in transportation and communication systems. Great cities are often situated at points of commodity exchange and transport connections. Access to raw materials at these points has allowed the development of manufacturing.

The most densely settled agricultural areas are in those regions which have had, in the past, the most productive agricultural lands: the Far East, the Indian peninsula, Southeast Asia, and Mediterranean Europe. Within these regions there is a further concentration of people in the great river valleys, where irrigation has promoted agricultural productivity.

The remainder of the world's population is sparsely settled on lands of three types: (1) high latitude and high altitude environments with infertile soils and short, undependable growing seasons; (2) arid and semiarid environments with evaporation potentials greater than precipitation; and (3) tropical savannas and rain forests that combine infertile soils, insects, and bacterial disease with unusable vegetation and fungus decay. In addition, in certain sparsely settled parts of the world there are dots of denser settlement that depend almost entirely on local resources, such as the oil fields in Arabia (Ackerman, 1959, p. 623).

The numbers of persons who can be supported in any given physical environment depend upon the demands of the people and the supplies available for their use.

## *Standards of Living in Relation to Resources for the Population*

More people can surely be kept alive at a lower standard of living than at a higher standard of living. There is no question but that there is increased demand for rising standards of living. In fact, the "rising expectations" of the peoples of the less developed nations of the world—and of more developed nations as well—are taken for granted. No one proposes research to determine whether or not people want more of whatever they define as the "good things of life." The assumption is that everybody wants a better life—more food, better health, housing, education, and so forth. Even though 75–90 percent of the peoples of the world have always been poor and probably hungry, they can now visualize that something better is possible. The mass media raise the desires of the population of the world, and politicians promise their people much that they have little hope of fulfilling. We will continue to elaborate on the many ways in which rapid population growth frustrates attempts to improve resource use on a per capita basis.

While the verbal demand for goods among the people of the less developed countries is increasing, the *effective* demand—the ability to buy —is not necessarily increasing at all. Meanwhile, in the modern industrial nations, demand (including effective demand) continues to rise. For instance, in electric consumption alone these nations range broadly from 150 to 8,000 kilowatt hours per year per residence. As more of the industrial nations produce and distribute the household electrical equipment taken for granted in the United States, the demand for electricity will soar.

The level of a culture—in terms of its technological complexity— influences both its *demand* for resources and the *supply* of resources for its use.

### *Cultural Manipulation*

Because various cultures define and use raw materials physically available in different ways, the culture of each social group affects its supply of resources.

> It is, perhaps, necessary only to remember that the American Indians possessed, but benefited little from, the fertile soil which formed an unprecedented source of wealth for the Colonists . . . that the Colonists gained little more than the grinding of their grain from the water power which made magnates of the early industrialists . . . that the early industrialists set little store by the deposits of petroleum and ore which served as a basis for the fortunes of the post-Civil War periods . . . that the industrial captains of the late nineteenth-century had no conception of the values that lay latent in water power for generating electricity, which would be developed by the enterprisers of the twentieth century . . . and that these early twentieth century enterprisers were as little able to capitalize the values of uranium as the Indians had been five centuries earlier. The social value of natural resources depends entirely upon the aptitude of society for using them (Potter, 1954, p. 85).

The technology of each culture, or the methods by which resources may be used, has generally been expanding both geographically and in kind. The technology of the United States, for instance, permits the utilization of resources from wide areas, while less advanced groups must depend upon limited areas of supply.

Furthermore, technology may give value to otherwise useless materials. Chinese peasant families have historically used dried grass for cooking fuel, although valuable beds of coal lay underground. Technology has done so much with materials formerly defined as useless that we have almost unlimited expectations of future technological marvels.

The territorial extent of each culture-area allows or restricts economics of scale and diversity of resources. A culture with a high degree of division of labor and an extended territory is likely to possess, employ, and exploit a great diversity of natural resources.

*TABLE 6-1 Five Population/Resource Types*

| Type | Numbers of People in Relation to Resources | Standard of Living: Desires | Standard of Living: Effective Demand (trading or purchase power) | Technological Level: Now | Technological Level: Trend |
|---|---|---|---|---|---|
| United States | low | high | high | high | increasing |
| European | high | high | high | high | increasing |
| Egyptian | high | high | low | low | increasing |
| Brazilian | low | high | low | low | increasing |
| Arctic-desert | low | low | low | low | low |

*Source:* Modified from the Ackerman (1959) and Zelinsky (1966) discussion.

Trading relations may make up for the small size of a political unit. Extensive trading has extended the standards of living of the Japanese, British, and Swiss far beyond the capacity of local resources. The growth of the European Economic Community demonstrates the mutual advantage of free trade areas.

Each culture inherits from the past its social institutions: certain ways of organizing group life, and certain attitudes related to their patterns of living. Economic habits, for instance, can favor or discourage savings and capital formation, the appearance of competent enterpreneurs, the provision of flexible and adequate training in skills, the coordination of resource development and planning, and so on. In some cultures lively family businesses are limited in growth because of objections to nonfamily participants. In some cultures small businesses cannot expand because the owners habitually turn all profits into gold (to be hidden) rather than investing it in the expansion of productive activities.

## *Types of Population-Resource Relations*

Figure 6-1 is a map of the five generalized population/resource regions of the world. The typology presented is not meant to be a detailed description of the broad areas indicated. There are many variations within each type and each geographical area. Nevertheless, it will be useful to review the broad characteristics of each type in light of the factors discussed above. Table 6-1 lists the five areas in relation to (1) the numbers of people in relation to the physical resources (the population/resource ratio), (2) the standards of living of the population, or their *demand*

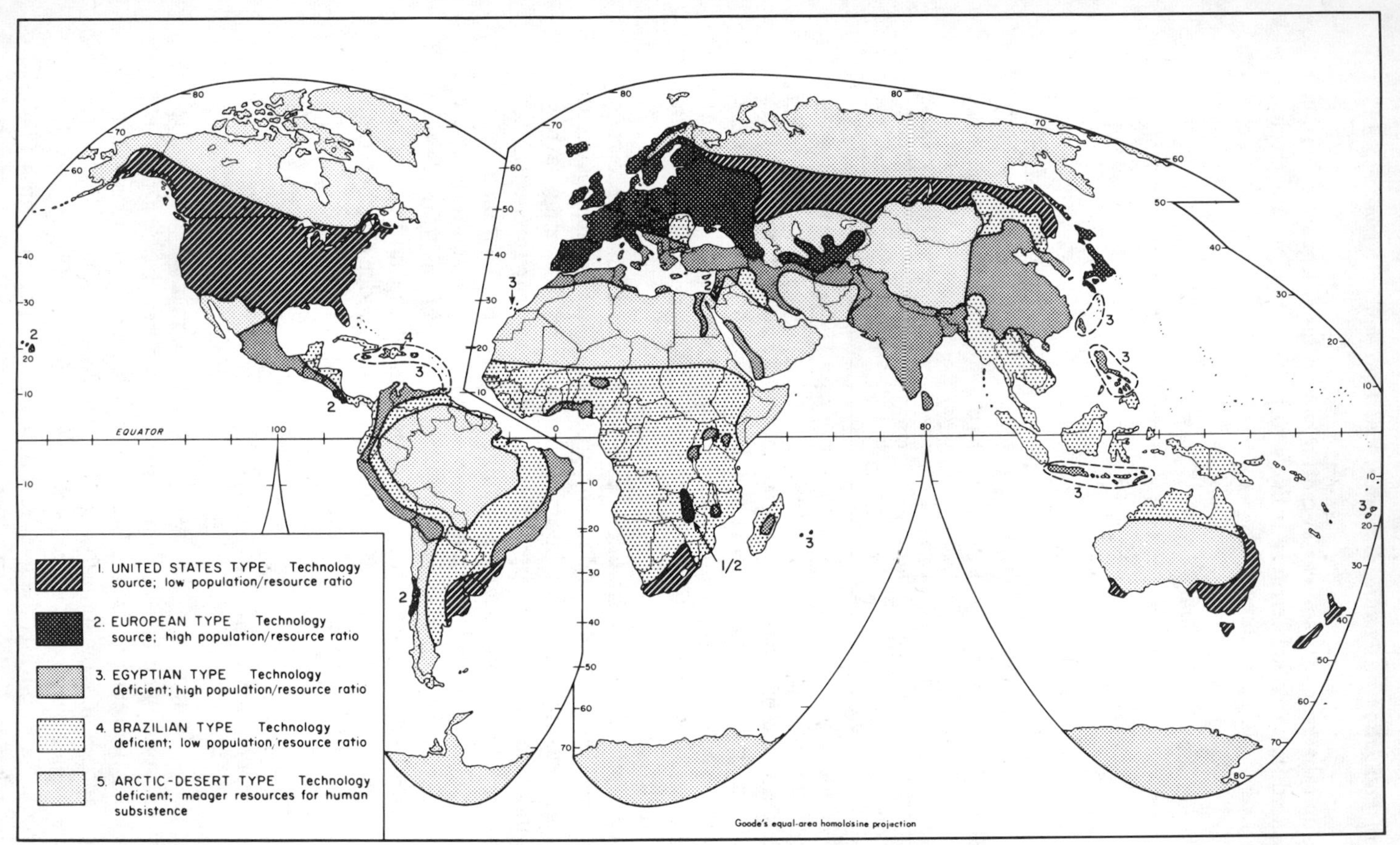


*Source:* Wilbur Zelinsky, A *Prologue to Population Geography*. Englewood Cliffs, N. J.: Prentice-Hall, Inc., © 1966, pp. 108–9.

FIG. 6–1 *Generalized Population/Resource Regions*

upon resources, and (3) the technological level, which determines the cultural manipulation of resources or *supply*.

The "rising expectations" of peoples around the world imply a high demand everywhere. However, the desires of people must be considered separately from the *effective demand*, the trading or purchasing power of a group which allows them to translate desires into real goods and services.

There are two aspects of the technological level as well. Because of the rapid diffusion of new techniques in the contemporary world, all areas (except the relatively uninhabited arctic or desert regions) and cultures are increasingly able to manipulate their resources. They begin, however, from very different technological bases. They may thus be distinguished on the basis of present levels of technology *and* upon the direction of technology. Zelinsky (1966) suggests that of the variables used in this scheme:

> the most critical would appear to be amount and quality of available technology. Where technology is highly developed and technicians are abundant, as in the United States and European types, then resources, and hence, prosperity, are at adequate, though not necessarily optimum, levels. This is true even when the national territory is cramped and the storehouse of physical resources is nearly empty. But neither small populations nor copious supplies of land and potential resources can, in themselves, make for adequate per capita levels of production and consumption. At best, they will keep the "overpopulation" of a nation under control for a certain term of years while the standard of living remains slightly above the distress level (p. 107).

On the other hand, it is necessary to recognize the possibility that the population itself may be growing so rapidly that it becomes an impediment to the society's attempts at technological development. The growth capital or resources of a social group may be required merely to sustain the additional numbers of people at the same low level, rather than contributing to an improvement in productivity, and, thereby, an increase in the level of life of the population.

Contemporary variations embrace the following types.

THE UNITED STATES TYPE. This includes Canada, New Zealand, and Australia in addition to the United States. These are the most enviable regions of the world: they have large territories well supplied with known resources; populations of small or moderate size; an advanced, rapidly expanding technology; skilled personnel; and the social means for maximizing national and individual affluence. The peoples of these areas have increasing desires, but they have the productivity and therefore the trading or purchasing power to augment their desired standards of living.

THE EUROPEAN TYPE. This group includes most of the countries of Northern Europe, all of Western Europe, and Poland and Hungary in Eastern Europe. Japan, the most rapidly advancing industrial nation of the world, is the only "non-Western" country of this type. These are densely populated areas, but population growth is slow and the people are high in social skills and ingenuity. These nations are more restricted in space and resources, however, than the first type. The prosperity of this group depends upon an elaborate system of international exchange of skilled services and advanced industrial goods for locally deficient fossil fuels, minerals, and so forth.

None of the European-type lands can escape the limitations of large populations and small territories. Zelinsky (1966) suggests that they represent the sort of *crowded, intricately geared way of life* that, at the moment, appears to be the only tolerable one to which the entire population of this planet can aspire. The standards of living and space of the first type are already out of reach for the world as a whole.

THE BRAZILIAN TYPE. Most fortunate among the technologically deficient lands in terms of resources is the Brazilian type. Their present position is a temporary one, however, since populations are growing so rapidly that they will shortly be transformed into one of the crowded types of land. Ghana, Angola, Panama, and portions of Peru, Nigeria, and Kenya are presently members of this type. Although population densities are well below the saturation point and physical resources could support more highly developed human populations than are presently found in this type of area, political and social barriers block advancement. Even with wise management, future technological advance would be questionable.

THE EGYPTIAN TYPE. This type is the most discouraging in its imbalance of excessive numbers of consumers and shortages of immediately available resources. Including India, China, Pakistan, Mexico, El Salvador, Tunisia, and sections of Nigeria, Indonesia, and Korea, these areas are not only the most populous, making up almost one-half of the population of the world, but they are also growing most rapidly in numbers. Zelinsky says that in some cases the physical endowment is so limited that even the most radically thorough-going approach to a community's development would seem to offer little chance of general betterment. Although such areas have existed at other times in human history, "only in modern times have technologically deficient folk reached such great numbers and excessive densities" (p. 114). Escape via migration to less populous regions is no longer possible because of the large numbers of human beings involved.

THE ARCTIC-DESERT TYPE. Included in this type are fairly large areas that because of aridity, cold, inaccessible terrain, remoteness, or other physical problems are either unsettled or only very sparsely inhabited. All of Antarctica and Greenland, most of Northern Canada and Eurasia, the Sahara, Amazonia, and Central Australia are included in this type. Their value lies not in their available land but in their raw materials—mineral ores and fuels, furs, marine life, and hydroelectric power. Settlement is likely to remain negligible, with only occasional and temporary scientific expeditions, hunting, mining, and sporting forays.

For all but the first two types the decline of death rates and consequent population growth has been unrelated to an overall technological advance within the countries. Cheap means of death control were introduced by the more advanced nations and by international agencies. Now populations of all but the Arctic and desert areas are either so large or growing so rapidly that birth rates must also be brought under control or there will eventually be a return to primitive death rates. The longer the equilibrium between births and deaths is delayed, the more difficult it will be to meet decent standards of human existence for all.

## *TYPES OF NATURAL RESOURCES AND SUPPLY*

The world's resources of land and water were mentioned in our discussion of the food crisis, but a brief review of the general availability of these resources, as well as of forest, energy, and mineral resources, will follow. Finally, the ways in which people have been polluting some of our most important natural assets will be considered.

### *Water*

It is hard to imagine, with water covering ⅔ of the surface of the earth at an average depth of 2½ miles, that there is any need to concern ourselves with water as a natural resource. However, ocean water is obviously not suitable for drinking. Moreover, even minute amounts of salt in agricultural irrigation can be fatal not only to current crops, but also to future growth. Fresh water, then, is the resource in heavy demand and the supply is extremely limited.

For personal use each individual in the advanced countries consumes an average of fifty gallons of water per day: one gallon is drinking water; six gallons for laundry; five gallons for personal hygiene; and about eight or nine gallons for flushing toilets. In addition, many persons take a 25-gallon bath or shower. In many United States cities the personal use of water has reached 115 to 150 gallons per day (Borgstrom, 1965, p. 413).

These quantities do not include the water used in industrial manufacturing or the water required for food production. "The cost of all the water used by U.S. householders, industry, and agriculture is around $5 billion a year; about 1 percent of the gross national product. The less-developed countries, where raw materials are a major component of the economy, cannot afford water prices that would be acceptable in the United States" (Revelle, 1963, p. 55).

Table 6-2 lists water requirements for food production. While wheat

*TABLE 6-2 Water Requirements in Food Production*

| | *Pounds of Water per Pound of Organic Matter* |
|---|---|
| Wheat | 300–500 |
| Potatoes | 600–800 |
| Rice | 1,500–2,000 |
| Vegetables | 3,000–5,000 |
| Milk | 10,000 |
| Meat | 20,000–50,000 |

*Source:* Reprinted with permission of The Macmillan Company from *The Hungry Planet* by George Borgstrom, p. 414. Copyright © by George Borgstrom, 1965.

requires from 300–500 pounds of water per pound of organic matter, rice and vegetables require thousands of pounds of water per pound of produce. For each pound of milk produced an average of 10,000 pounds of water are used.

Water has been pumped from underground sources more rapidly than it can be replaced naturally, so it is simply a matter of time until ground sources are exhausted. River water tapped for irrigation has been depositing minute amounts of salt in the Imperial Valley in Southern California. Over the years, the salt content has built up until the land is increasingly unusable for crop production. Rainwater remains a major long-term source of fresh water for agriculture. Borgstrom's illustration of the hydrologic cycle (Figure 6-2) aids our appreciation of the recycling process which water naturally goes through and the advantages of rainwater as a source of fresh water.

Industrial uses do not always require pure water sources and may involve recycling water supplies. Nevertheless, industry in general has had little concern for the way in which it used fresh water supplies or the way contaminants might be discharged into fresh water rivers and lakes. The amounts of water required by industry are enormous. The production of one ton of steel requires 160 to 260 tons of water; newsprint production requires 900 to 1,000 tons of water per ton; coal and rubber require upwards

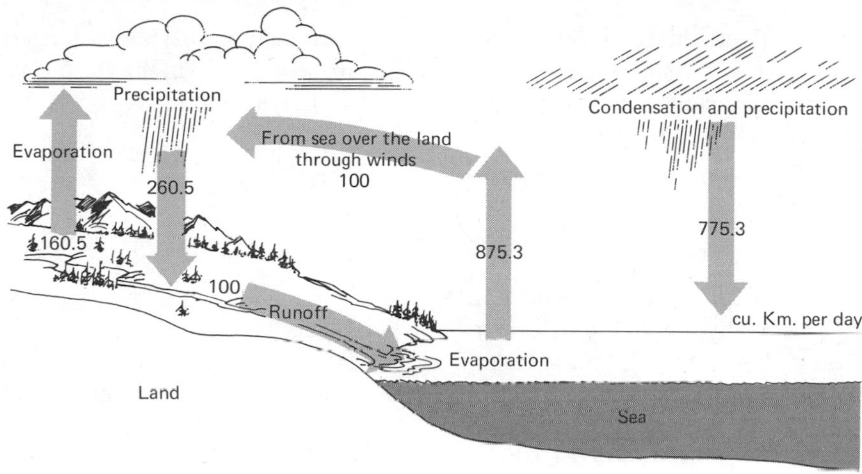


*Source:* Redrawn after George Borgstrom, from *Too Many*, copyright © by George Borgstrom, 1969. Used by permission of Macmillan Company.

FIG. 6–2 *The Hydrologic Cycle of the Earth (in cubic kilometers per day)*

of 2,250 tons of water per ton (Borgstrom, 1965, p. 423). Most of the less developed countries are already using nearly all of their present water resources, which will complicate attempts at industrialization.

In the affluent United States more than a thousand communities have had to put at least seasonal restrictions on the use of water.

> Americans use so much water—about 1,700 gallons a day per capita—that capital costs for water development are comparable to other kinds of investment. Although the water diverted from streams and pumped from the ground is equivalent to only about 7 percent of the rain and snow falling on the United States, this is still an enormous quantity: 200 times more than the weight of any other material used except air. The annual capital expenditure for water structures in the United States—dams, community and industrial water works, sewage-treatment plants, pipelines and drains, irrigation canals, river-control structure, and hydroelectric works—is about $10 billion (Revelle, 1963, p. 56).

The Feather River Project, estimated to cost $2 billion and to take thirty years to complete, will transport most remaining surface waters of northern California to the Los Angeles area. Opponents are concerned that it will simply increase the congestion of the southern area, while siphoning off the pure water of the north, but the southern population outnumber and, therefore, outvote those in northern California.

In all cases, the limited nature of our water resources must be recognized and treated with concern for the future. Not population alone, but the uses to which people put our water resources determine the relative scarcity of present and future quantities. Since each of us has a longer life expectancy than earlier generations, it is to everyone's best interest as well as to the interest of future generations that available resources be guarded.

## *Land*

Although about one-fourth of the world's 32 billion acres are classified as "potentially arable," only one-half of that is actually under cultivation. Most of the potentially arable land not already in use requires more investment in knowledgeable labor and capital inputs than the crop return would be worth.

Another fourth of the world acreage could be used for grazing, but would be unsuitable for cultivation. The remaining half of the world's land area, which includes deserts, mountains, arctic wastelands, and so forth, is very limited for human use. Forests cover some of these areas as well as parts of the more useful first half of the world's land.

As population pressure increases, land becomes more valuable. The most densely populated areas of the world utilize almost all of their "potentially arable" land for the cultivation of crops. The Asian and European continents have very little additional acreage that could be utilized in the production of food.

The productivity per cultivated acre varies greatly from one area to another. Japan, the Netherlands, Egypt, and the United Kingdom, countries which maximize the productive use of their arable lands, contain the largest numbers of persons per acre of tilled land (see Table 6-3). These nations support from four to nine times as many persons per acre tilled as the world average of eight-tenths of one person per cultivated acre of land.

The industrially well-developed countries can better afford high inputs of irrigation, fertilizers, and machinery. Because of advanced educational systems they also have a high degree of advanced technical knowledge, and they apply it in the field. For example, the amount of fertilizer used on arable land in Europe is twelve times that used in Asia and Africa. In 1960 the number of tractors in Europe and North America was four times that in the rest of the world (Christian, 1965, p. 158). Favorable prices for agricultural produce are possible in industrial countries because of the high average income of the populations. The trend in these nations is to use land even more efficiently and to raise the yield per acre still higher.

Nevertheless, these lands must be carefully managed in order that they are not overused and depleted of life-giving properties. Fairfield Osborn (1948) warns that under existing methods of rapid crop produc-

*TABLE 6-3 Number of People in Relation to Tilled Acreage (1958–1959)*

| | *Number of People per Acre Tilled Land* | *Tilled Acreage in Acres per Person* |
|---|---|---|
| Japan | 7.4 | 0.14 |
| Netherlands | 4.4 | 0.23 |
| Egypt | 3.9 | 0.26 |
| U.K. | 2.9 | 0.34 |
| China | 2.5 | 0.40 |
| Peru | 2.4 | 0.42 |
| Indonesia | 2.0 | 0.50 |
| Norway | 1.7 | 0.59 |
| Brazil | 1.4 | 0.71 |
| Italy | 1.2 | 0.83 |
| India | 1.1 | 0.91 |
| WORLD | 0.80 | 1.25 |
| Mexico | 0.70 | 1.43 |
| Nigeria | 0.60 | 1.67 |
| U.S. and USSR | 0.38 | 2.63 |
| Argentina | 0.28 | 3.17 |
| Australia and Canada | 0.17 | 5.86 |

*Source:* Reprinted with permission of The Macmillan Company from *The Hungry Planet* by George Borgstrom, p. 5. Copyright © by George Borgstrom, 1965.

tion, the mineral elements that nourish plant growth are removed from the soil faster than they can be replaced by natural processes. The deterioration of the life-giving elements of the earth may be checked but cannot be cured by the use of chemical fertilizers. It has been estimated that in the last few decades the loss of productive soil has been greater than the accumulated loss over all previous time.

Borgstrom (1969) recently claimed that more man-made desert acres are *created* per year than are reclaimed by irrigation!

There are two reasons why artificial processes, unless recognized as simple complements to nature, will fail to provide a solution to the present land problems of the world.

The first is that the *erosion of topsoil* (which has been proceeding rapidly as a result of man's mismanagement) *can never be reversed by man.* Osborn (1948) reminds us that fertile soil is *alive,* that it harbors many different kinds of living organisms that provide the health and productivity of the soil. Animal life in the soil ranges in size and kind from burrowing rodents, insects, and earthworms down through the scale to animals and life forms of microscopic size, such as protozoa and bacteria. These living things cultivate or aerate the soil and transform organic remains and combine them with the minerals in the soil. Once the "life" of the soil has been destroyed, or the topsoil eroded, "science" cannot re-create the life that is lost.

The second reason is that even if, in theory, knowledge of soil recreation were available, it would be impossible to teach the millions of farm workers (many of whom are illiterate and tradition-bound) the intricate procedures necessary for the reclamation job.

Land, then, is a very precious and scarce resource. The greater the pressure of population, the more valuable our limited land supply becomes. Urban sprawl in the United States alone removes one million acres of good land from production each year. Misuse of land is even more destructive.

> Today, the world is faced with large areas of land where the natural process of wind and water erosion has been accelerated and surface soil has been lost; where continued cultivation and the removal of nutrients in crop and animal products, particularly under monoculture, has led to a substantial reduction in soil fertility and deterioration of soil structure; where excessive or unwise irrigation, without adequate drainage, or irrigation of unsuitable types of land, has led to rising water tables, waterlogging, and salting, to the point where crop production is no longer possible; where forests have been overexploited and valuable species eliminated, and where the removal of forests has changed the hydrological regime of an area, affecting stream flow and underground water; where overgrazing or bad grassland management has caused the loss of better pasture species with their replacement by bare ground or by inedible or less nutritious competitors (Christian, 1965, p. 161).

### *Forests*

Trees are important to mankind because the roots hold and protect the soil of the land from erosion, because the forests themselves protect wildlife, and because wood products play an important role in maintaining living standards.

The problem of erosion is not a pretty one. In the Congo, where forests were cleared to facilitate hunting and cultivation, 30,000 square kilometers of soil were destroyed in six years. In Madagascar, the degradation took sixty years. Once covered with forests, the island is now "occupied by an ocean of tough grasses, ravaged by fire and unsuitable even for the feeding of herds. In short, we are in the throes of apparently irreversible progressive *reduction* of the surface of cultivable lands" (Bouillenne, 1962, p. 709).

> In the poorer countries [man's] expanding need for fuel [and land] has forced him to cut forests far in excess of their ability to renew themselves. The areas largely stripped of forest include mainland China and the subcontinent of India and Pakistan, where much of the population must now use cow dung [manure] for fuel (Brown, 1970, p. 164).

Man can learn from past history if he is interested. The great oak forests of the Hittite Empire have disappeared, as have the groves of cypress and palms that once made lush the plains of Iraq. The Rienows (1967) ask why there is no trace of the forests of Phoenicia, whose great timbers allowed the culture's rise as a naval power. When the cedars of Lebanon were cut for the Temple of Solomon, why didn't that thriving tree community reseed and recover from the shock? And why has the Sahara Desert been moving southward—for the last 500 years—at the rate of at least a mile a year across a front some 18,000 miles wide (the estimate of K. H. Oedekovan, forestry researcher for the United Nations Food and Agriculture Organization)? "When man scalps the land, he outrages the ecology; he destroys the humus, evaporates the water, erodes the soil, alters the climate, and so shocks the environment that never again can the conditions that brought these choice climax forests into being prevail" (Rienow and Rienow, 1967, p. 40).

The results of clearing tropical forests for agriculture are equally clear. When the cover of insulating foliage is removed, the recycling of soil nutrients is interrupted. Although it seems incredible that the lush jungles, rain forests, and savannas of the tropics hide unproductive soils, McNeil (1964) observes that "put to plow, these lands yield an amazingly small return and soon become completely infertile. . . . A lateritic soil (commonly found between latitudes of 30 degrees North and 30 degrees South) is rich in iron and aluminum, low in silica and chemically acidic" (pp. 97, 98). Where slash-and-burn agriculture is practiced on a small scale, clearings may be farmed for a year or two and then the jungle growth returns while the farmer moves on to clear another section. Increasing population pressure has promoted attempts to farm more acres over a longer time. However, once *large* fields are cleared, they may harden into stony laterite, a brick-like form of rock. "As a result of laterization vast areas of the earth's soil have been converted into deposits of bauxite (aluminum ore) and into hematite and limonite ores of iron" (p. 98). Such lands are premanently lost to agriculture.

Soils, then, do have a life of their own. Man tampers with them at some risk, sometimes improving and sometimes spoiling the resource. Forests protect not only soil, but also the wildlife of a region. In India, where forests have been cleared for farm land, the wild predators of some of their overpopulous species have virtually disappeared. One forest preserve has been so reduced in size that scientists are able to count as the Indian lion, a unique species, becomes extinct. The latest estimates are that only 160 remain.

Forests are equally important for the welfare of man. In addition to their aesthetic value, wood products are used in building and construction, for fuel, and as a source of new products and export incomes. There are large national differences in the use of wood. The per capita amount of pulp products used for newsprint in the Pacific area in 1956–1968 was 25 times that used in Asia (Christian, 1965, p. 166). Timber requirements in the United States alone are expected to *triple* between 1960 and 2000 if population grows only at the medium projections of the United Nations (Fisher & Potter, 1963, p. 102). The more educational development and industrialization occur in the less developed countries, the greater their demands for wood and paper products will become. The expansion in the use of our forest resources, therefore, is likely to be even more rapid than the growth of population. Although forests are potentially renewable, complete clearing is likely to mean total destruction unless care of the soil and replanting occurs. The developing as well as the developed nations need to improve their forest management practices. Although almost 20 percent of the world's forests are subject to some form of management, only a small fraction of those are used in accordance with advanced techniques of selective cutting and reforestation.

The rate of wood removals from the forests of the world between 1946 and 1960 increased about 50 percent. Projecting to the year 2000, Joseph Fisher and Neal Potter (1963, p. 118) estimate a possible quadrupling of lumber output and a sevenfold increase in pulpwood. They are dubious that the world's forests will be able to stand the drain. However, half of the world's output of sawlogs and 40 percent of its total wood came from North America and Western Europe in 1960, and those areas hold only 20 percent of the world's total forested acreage. If the output of the rest of the world could be brought to the European–American level, output could be doubled.

With increasing population, however, the world demand for forest products may well become more and more difficult to meet. International trade in lumber, pulp, and paper does facilitate the provision of products for those countries which have little in the way of local forest resources. Although demand may be met in the short run, neither more efficient cutting and processing, nor international trade will solve the long run problems of renewal of forest resources to meet the demands of increasing numbers of persons.

### *Minerals*

The future demand for minerals, like that for the other resources on our list, will be doubly complicated by increases in populations and by economic development. Estimates of the lifetimes of some of the most important mineral resources known and capable of being mined with present-day techniques are represented in Figure 6-3. These estimates are most reliable for the fossil fuels. We assume that our knowledge about

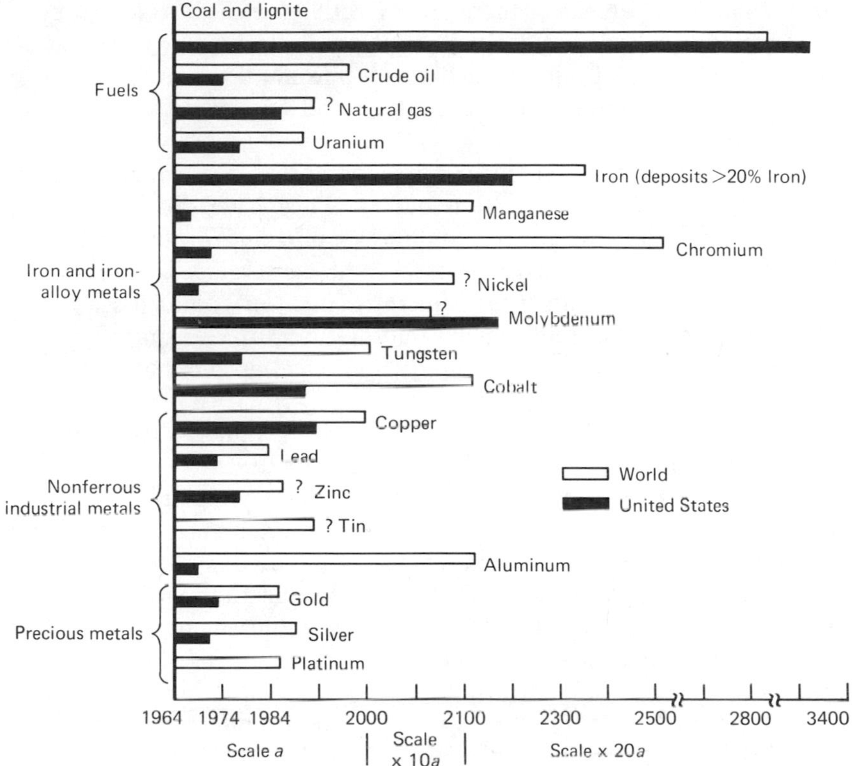


*Source:* Paul R. Ehrlich and Anne H. Ehrlich, *Population, Resources, Environment: Issues in Human Ecology*. San Francisco: W. H. Freeman and Company, copyright © 1970, p. 60. Drawing after Cloud, 1968.

FIG. 6–3 *Lifetimes of Estimated Recoverable Reserves of Mineral Resources. (Reserves are those that are of high enough grade to be mined with today's techniques. Increasing population and consumption rates, unknown deposits, and future use of presently submarginal ores are not considered.)*

reserves of the other minerals is incomplete: they are generally concealed and occur in erratically varying concentrations.

Whether a particular type and grade of mineral, concentrated at a particular location in the earth's crust, is or can become an ore (a deposit that can be worked at a profit) depends upon a number of economic factors, including mining, transportation, and extractive technology. Even with the high value placed upon gold, the limits of supply and extractive technology led Piddington (1956) to conclude that increases in the gold supply cannot keep up with population increases. On that account alone, the gold standard is not practical for the world.

The total volume of workable mineral deposits makes up only a small fraction of 1 percent of the earth's crust and each deposit represents some geological accident in the remote past. Deposits must be mined where they occur—often far from the centers of consumption. Each deposit is also limited: if it is worked long enough, it will be exhausted (Lovering, 1969, p. 110).

The industrialized nations control more than an equitable share of the world's supply of mineral resources. They have the incentive to search out, and the investment capital to mine and/or buy, whatever metals are needed by their economies. The underdeveloped countries are often only too eager to turn their mineral dposits, or "quick assets," into export commodities. Yet they may be trading their future industrial potential for immediate cash or credit. Mineral resources are nonrenewable and many are already in short supply.

Meanwhile, the demand for goods requiring mineral raw materials will probably increase exponentially for at least the next fifty years, as both populations and their demands rise. Even without population increases, the underdeveloped but aspiring countries would experience a tremendous increase in the demand for the nonrenewable resources of the world. The more quickly they push toward industrialization and the more their populations increase, the greater the crisis in resource requirements will become.

Lovering (1969) concludes that:

> It may well be true that science and technology will continue to provide satisfactory answers to our mineral resource problems far into the future. This can take place, however, only insofar as long-range foresight, lead time, exploration, and research keep pace with diminishing grade, changes in minerology and the need to exploit entirely different types of deposits—it will not happen automatically. Above all, new discovery is required that, together with technological innovation, will develop reserves of mineral resources at an exponential rate until *population control* and relatively constant or *decreasing* per capita *demand* can be achieved—both *inevitable requirements on our finite earth* (pp. 128–29; italics mine).

## *Energy*

Energy may be thought of either as the capacity to produce power or as the actual production of power. There is actually a continuous flux of energy into and out of the earth's surface environment. As Hubbert (1969) notes, "the largest source of this energy flux is solar radiation, a small fraction of which is captured by the leaves of plants and stored as chemical energy. This chemicallly stored solar energy becomes the essential biological energy source for the entire animal kingdom" (p. 157).

"Diffuse energy," which cannot be harnessed by man, will not be reviewed here. There are four types of energy which man has been able to use: animal energy, the burning of fuels, water power, and atomic power.

Man's own energy is dependent upon his food supply—its quantity and quality. Malnourishment and malnutrition are greatest in precisely those areas of the world that depend most upon the energy of human beings alone. Of course, man has learned to supplement his own muscle power by harnessing the energy of subhuman species. However, these power sources are inadequate for the process of industrializing the less developed nations of the world. Even farming must become industrialized if the world's billions are to be fed. Animal power alone, then, is not enough to raise mankind above the bare subsistence level.

The burning of fuels has historically been the major source of energy for the world. As people learned to utilize carbonaceous fuel—first lumber, then coal, petroleum, and natural gas—they multiplied their power many times over. The expansion in the use of these energy sources has allowed the earth to support increasing numbers of human beings, but that expansion is nearing an end.

We have already noted the problems of forest reserves. Because of the 20- to 100-year lag in growing new stands of timber, the decreasing forested acres (as agriculture requires more land), and the insignificant amount of careful reforestation, wood cannot remain a major contributor to the fuel supply of the world.

Yet the time lag for fossil fuels runs to millions of years.

> During geologic history a minute fraction of the organic matter of former plants and animals became buried in sedimentary sand, muds, and limes, under conditions of incomplete oxidation. This has become the source of our present supply of fossil fuels—coal, petroleum, and natural gas. . . . Since the earth's deposits of fossil fuels are finite in amount and nonrenewable during time periods of less than millions of years, it follows that energy from this source can be obtained for only a limited period of time (Hubbert, 1969, pp. 157–58).

Although the world's supply of coal is expected to last for at least another century, it is likely to be used more and more as other fuels are reduced in availability (see Figure 6-3). The world supply of crude oil is considered sufficient to last beyond the year 2000. Although the United States will not command an adequate supply, buying power on the world market will supplement internal supplies. Estimates of natural gas reserves, while not as certain as for some of the other resources of the world, indicate that world supplies will be exhausted sometime between the years 1990 and 2000.

Energy resources, like so many of the earth's goods, are used unevenly by the nations of the world. The gap in energy consumption between the developed and underdeveloped countries is very wide. Table 6-4 lists the

*TABLE 6-4 Projections of Energy Consumed in 2000 Compared to 1960 Actual by World Areas (Billions of metric tons of coal equivalent)*

| | | Year 2000 if: | | | |
|---|---|---|---|---|---|
| | 1960 Actual | Trend in Consumption From 1950 to 1960 Continues (1) | World Consumption is at U.S. 1960 Level (2) | World Consumption is at W. Europe 1960 Level (3) | N. Am., Eur., USSR, & Oceania at U.S. 1960; Rest at Europe 1960 Level (4) |
| World | 4.2 | 20.8 | 50.3 | 16.1 | 23.2 |
| North America | 1.55 | 2.56 | 2.50 | .80 | 2.50 |
| Latin America | .14 | 2.89 | 4.74 | 1.52 | 1.52 |
| Western Europe | .79 | 2.77 | 3.20 | 1.03 | 3.20 |
| Eastern Europe & USSR | .90 | 4.5 | 4.40 | 1.41 | 4.40 |
| Communist Asia | .40 | 4.5? | 12.8 | 4.1 | 4.1 |
| Non-Communist Asia | .24 | 2.7 | 18.4 | 5.9 | 5.9 |
| Africa | .08 | .77 | 4.14 | 1.33 | 1.33 |
| Oceania | .05 | .10 | .23 | .07 | .23 |

*Source:* Joseph L. Fisher and Neal Potter, "Resources in the United States and the World," p. 112, in Philip M. Hauser, ed., *The Population Dilemma*, 1963, by The American Assembly, Columbia University. By permission of Prentice-Hall, Inc.

actual energy consumption by the major areas of the world for 1960 and projects energy consumption to the year 2000 under various assumptions.

In 1960 North America, with about 6.5 percent of the population of the world, used 37 percent of the total world consumption of energy. Communist Asia, with well over 20 percent of the world's population, consumed less than 10 percent of the world's energy.

Using the medium population projections of the United Nations to the year 2000, world energy supplies would require a fourfold increase in order to meet the 1960 West European level. But the most advanced nations are already at a higher per capita consumption than the 1960 West European level. For the world to meet U.S. standards of energy consumption by the year 2000 would require a twelvefold increase. Yet only a tripling of energy supplies is projected by Brown *et al.* (1957), who assume that an exponential increase in the use of atomic energy will begin in about 1970 (see Figure 6-4).

Water power supplies only about 2 percent of the world's energy supply. The remaining potential for development lies mainly in Africa and Latin America, which (except for Oceania) are lowest in consumption of energy. As these continents begin to tap their potential water power, the direct and indirect costs of hydroelectric power are being recognized. Harnessing the tides might increase the potential water power of the world by 1 percent, but even if *all* such sources could be utilized, only a tiny fraction of the power requirements of the world would be met.

The future energy needs of the world, therefore, will not be provided by water power. Nor is there very much time left before the supplies of petroleum and natural gas are depleted. The change-over from these fuels must begin at once. The energy needs of the world in the immediate future can be met by reliance on coal resources, which should last for another century. However, even these are exhaustible. Research and development of other sources of energy must be increased.

The direct production of power from solar energy would be an ideal solution, but large-scale production appears technologically unpromising. Recently, a system for obtaining power from algae grown in a closed system has been described. Estimates indicate that electricity *might* be produced from such a source at a cost of 2.5 to 5 cents per kilowatt-hour and liquid fuels at a cost of about $150.00 per ton (Brown *et al.*, 1957, p. 105).

> Geothermal and tidal energy is now being exploited in a few suitable sites around the world, but the ultimate amount of power from these sources does not promise to be larger than a small fraction of the world's present power requirements. This leaves us with nuclear energy as the only remaining energy source of sufficient magnitude and practicability of exploitation to meet the world's future energy needs at either present or increased rates of consumption. Of the possible sources of nuclear energy, that from (1) fusion has not yet been achieved and may never be. Power from (2) the fission of uranium-235 is an accomplished fact, and reactors in the 500 to 1,000 megawatt-capacity range, fueled principally by this isotope, are rapidly being constructed. However, the supply of uranium-235 is such that serious shortages in the United States are already anticipated within the next two decades.
>
> In the light of present technology, we are left then with the development of (3) full-breeding nuclear reactors capable of consuming all of natural uranium or of thorium as our only adequate source of long-range industrial power. In view of the impending shortage of uranium-235, which is essential as an initial fuel for breeder reactors, it is urgent that the present generation of light-water reactors using uranium-235 be replaced by full breeders at as early a date as possible (Hubbert, 1969, pp. 158–59).

The anticipated world energy consumption in the next hundred years,

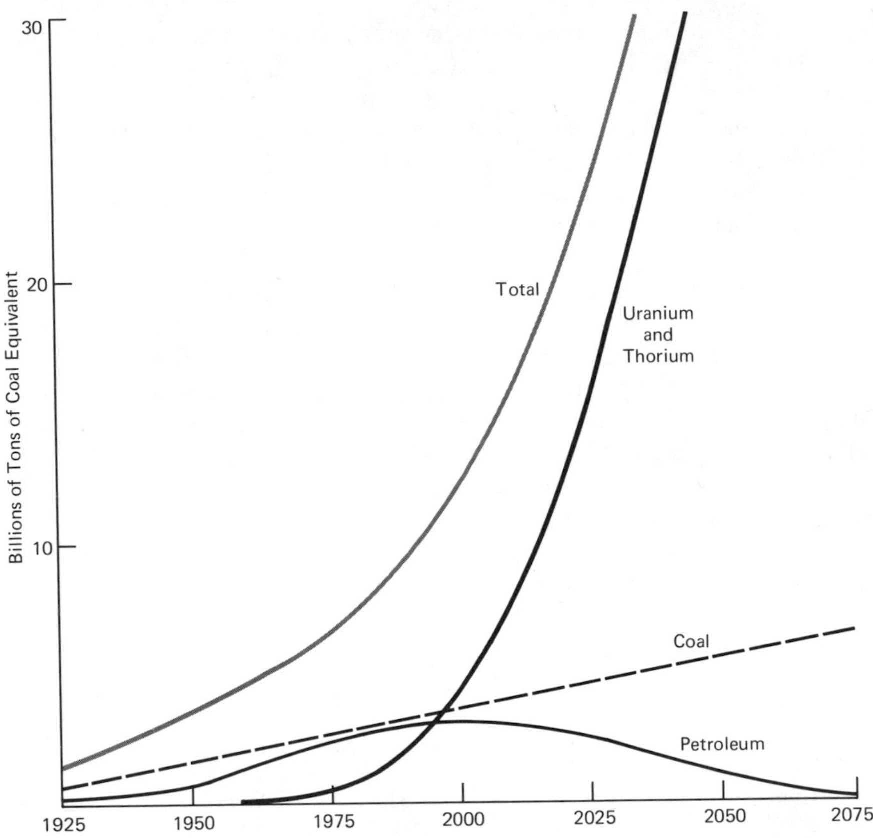


*Source:* Harrison Brown, James Bonner, John Weir, *The Next Hundred Years*. New York: The Viking Press, Inc., copyright © 1957, p. 110. By permission of The Viking Press, Inc.

FIG. 6–4 *World Energy Consumption in the Next Century—A Possible Pattern*

as graphed by Brown *et al.* (1957), is reproduced in Figure 6-4. The exhaustion of petroleum and increased use of coal are plotted, together with the phenomenal rise expected in nuclear power sources. If the full-breeding reactors can be put into operation soon, there need be little worry about the supplies of uranium and thorium.

Our concern then will be transferred to the frightening increase in pollution from these sources. As Garrett De Bell says, "all power pollutes." In the next section we will summarize some of the effects of increasing numbers of persons using, ever more rapidly, the world's renewable and nonrenewable resources.

## *POLLUTION*

A great many books have been written on the causes and consequences of pollution. I want to touch only briefly on how pollution problems are compounded by population pressures. We will review some of the causes of pollution, examine some of the differences in pollution between underdeveloped and developed countries, and, finally, survey the way in which different parts of the biosphere are affected by pollutants.

Pollution is the accumulation, in the air, the waters, and the soils of the biosphere, of substances harmful to living things. Since, by definition, substances in the air, water, or soil are not pollutants until they are of sufficient quantity to be harmful to living things, man is still discovering specific pollutants. Furthermore, since the chemical composition of the parts of our biosphere is very complex, it is not always clear which substances, in what concentrations, over what period of time, become harmful and to what extent.

### *Causes*

The population explosion and the technological explosion together cause the increasing pollution of our environment. It has become commonplace to note that the increasing affluence of persons in advanced countries has contributed more to pollution than a simple rise in population numbers. Recognizing the truth of the statement, however, does not close the issue. People are not overwhelmingly eager to give up the niceties recently acquired. And, as we are trying to eliminate or reduce pollution from some sources, it increases from other sources (note the increase in camper-wagons, power boats and motorcycles as well as newsprint and educational materials). It is precisely because we hope to raise the level of life for *all* that population numbers are a major concern in relation to pollution. It is no coincidence that pollution has been recognized as a very real problem in the last few years. The population explosion and implosion are very recent phenomena. Not only people themselves, but all sorts of activities and products related to the maintenance of people contribute to the spoiling of our natural resources and of the environment in general. Twice as many people at a constant standard of living would produce twice as much garbage, whether the waste were discharged into the air, the waters, or dumped on land. If the number of "things" people possess or use up increases, so does the potential destructive power of the useless remains. Old automobiles don't just fade away, and the metallic content is seldom recycled. They have been piling up in ugly heaps.

Pollution occurs, then, partially as a result of the population increase and the rise in standards of living. It is also a consequence of the time lag in our recognition of the problems created by people pollution and our lack of concern or inability to remedy the problems.

### *A Comparison of the Developing and Developed Countries*

In the less developed countries pollution is more directly a result of the population explosion. Although there were instances of water and soil pollution in the past, the problem on a broad scale is a very recent phenomenon. No one who has seen the rivers flowing through some of the more populous underdeveloped countries of the world can doubt that people are polluting these rivers directly. Anyone who watches people bathe and brush their teeth in water from the river that carries the sewage past Bangkok knows that increased population means increased pollution.

Chemical pollutants have several interrelated effects upon the people of the less developed nations. Many of these products have been introduced in recent years to destroy disease-carrying agents or crop pests. Pesticides have helped save crops from destruction by insects, and chemical fertilizers have helped increase crop yields. The chemical products have helped lower the death rate, resulting in the population explosion. In addition, many people who would otherwise have died at an early age are able to add their waste products to the ever-expanding disposal problem. The same chemicals have polluted the air, the water, and in some cases the soils of the countries involved.

In the developed countries, where population has been growing less rapidly than in the underdeveloped nations, there has been an explosion in the number of "things" produced for use by people. They have contributed far greater quantities of pollutants to the biosphere than have the less developed countries, generally.

There is some logic to the argument that to insure continued increases in their standards of living, the affluent nations should be working toward a *negative population growth rate.* The North American standard of living is impossible for the overpopulated, impoverished areas of the world. The 6.5 percent of the world population presently living in the United States and Canada are using up approximately one-half of the world's yield of resources. Philip Hauser has computed that *at our standard of living the total products of the world would support about a half a billion people:* only one-seventh the number presently alive.

It serves no one's interest to add to the number of world consumers.

The affluent create one problem by consuming more than their share of the world's resources and another problem by throwing away so much waste. Solid wastes now average over four pounds per American per day. Urban areas especially are having real problems trying to dispose of these wastes. Yet most city governments, Chambers of Commerce, and citizens at large still plan for and encourage expansion. Without great and immediate effort the continued growth of cities will lead to increased pollution of all kinds.

The interrelations between human consumption and pollution in the industrial nations of the world are illustrated in Figure 6-5. Man has used the natural resources of the earth to supply the energy to produce the

**Man and his machine**

*Source:* LePelley in *The Christian Science Monitor,* June 10, 1969. Reprinted by permission from *The Christian Science Monitor,* © 1969, The Christian Science Publishing Society. All rights reserved.

FIG. 6–5

products he thinks he needs and wants. In time (often a very short time, thanks to planned obsolescence) the products themselves become garbage and new things must take their place. Meanwhile, productive equipment has spewn its waste materials into the air and waters of the community. One wonders whether the machine was made for man or man for the machine.[1]

A part of the problem in the developed countries is that the substances which pollute the environment are usually the residue from some product or service. It would be easy to halt pollution if those products or substances had only negative consequences. However, driving a car is usually more convenient than walking, riding a bicycle, or taking a train or bus. It is less trouble to throw bottles and newspapers into the garbage can than to save them for recycling. Pesticides, fertilizers, and even defoliants have positive uses, not merely negative consequences.

The effects of pollution, moreover, are no longer confined merely to the region of pollution. Developed countries are increasingly banning the use of DDT, but they will receive the residues from its use in less developed countries. DDT, which now threatens lives indirectly, has been saving millions of lives directly. The leaders of certain United Nations agencies (the World Health Organization and the Food and Agricultural Organization) are unwilling to ban DDT and other persistent pesticides on the basis of probable future harm to human beings, because of its immediate life-saving capacity in malaria control. They argue that holding off on the use of DDT as a caution against the possible and even probable long-term effects is a luxury that the less developed nations cannot afford. Time will certainly tell.

## *POLLUTION IN VARIOUS PARTS OF THE BIOSPHERE*

Many different agents are involved in the pollution of water, air, soil, and living species. The same hazardous chemical agents often permeate several or all of the areas of the biosphere. DDT is the best-known example: it is carried by air and in the waters and soils of the earth and affects insects (the target), grazing animals that eat the same grasses and grains as the insects, fish that eat the green plants of the ocean, birds, animals, and human beings who eat the fish, the grazing animals, or the grains that have been sprayed.

[1] I had always assumed that the machines were made for man. Recently, however, statements indicate that the Japanese and Germans are becoming interested in increasing their rate of population growth in order to increase the labor force needed for their continued industrialization.

## *Water Pollution*

Soil erosion may be aggravated by a lack of care of the land or by the mass clearing of forests. Precious topsoil may fill streams that were once clear with mud that is carried downstream to dammed areas, natural lakes, and the ocean.

These water sources may become overloaded with mud and silt and the land, meanwhile, has lost some of its initial richness. Knowledgeable farmers typically use fertilizers to restore the agricultural yield. The fertilizer itself results in another type of pollution. As the fertilized land is watered by rain or irrigation, nitrate nitrogen from the fertilizer is carried by the water to streams and lakes, killing the living species of those waters. The amount of nitrate nitrogen entering Lake Erie from the farm lands in the Erie watershed is equal to the amount of pollution entering from Detroit and all the other major cities that have been dumping sewage into the lake. Lake Erie has been widely publicized as a dead lake, its natural species having been killed by pollution. It is also dangerous for swimming and human enjoyment.

The increased use of Lake Tahoe in California by the expanding population of that state and by visiting tourists has endangered the life of that lake. The increase in seasonal and year-round population at Tahoe has caused pollution, silting, and algae to mar the natural beauty of the lake. Although construction that would add more raw sewage to the lake has been halted, there is no way to retract the previous contamination. A new $3 million experimental sewage treatment plant at the south end of the lake pumps treated water 14 miles to the Indian Creek reservoir. It arrives colorless, odorless, tasteless, and stripped of harmful wastes. The plant is an expensive experiment and serves only a portion of the lakeside population. However, if the purification procedure proves itself over time, the costs for future treatment facilities could be cut by pumping pure water back into the lake.

Most people have assumed that the *oceans* are too big to pollute, but marine biologists say that the oceans too are becoming polluted at an increasing rate. Lead is one of the substances which man is dumping into the sea in unprecedented quantities. The lead used in antiknock gasolines is discharged into the atmosphere, is rained out, and eventually finds its way to the ocean. Lead is found in the upper layers of the entire ocean, in greatest concentration near the coastlines. Since lead is toxic to most living things (including human beings) even in minute amounts, it is most threatening in the portions of the oceans near the shoreline, which normally carry the greatest variety and quantity of living species.

Dr. Edward E. Goldberg of the Scripps Institution of Oceanography has said that an estimated one million tons of oil a year are leaked or spilled into the Atlantic Ocean from tankers and other ships ("Oceans polluted . . . ," 1969). Seamen have reported finding oil droplets all along the Atlantic route from the Middle East to Central America.

Vast amounts of dry cleaning fluid and freon, the gas used in aerosol cans, may be finding their way into the oceans. Dr. Goldberg said there is no idea what the effects might be on the life of the sea.

Ocean pollution affects everyone. What one nation or group does affects many others. President Nixon proposed recently that the United Nations be allocated the management of resources and the income from the oceans of the world (beyond the 12-mile limit claimed by most nations). Presumably the plan would not only provide the U.N. with an independent source of income, but would invest the organization with responsibility for the protection of a world resource.

### *Air Pollution*

Mankind is now taxing the capacity of our atmosphere to absorb and carry away the enormous amount of emissions from areas of high population density. Almost every major city of the world has serious air pollution problems. Even more important, the entire atmosphere of our planet is now afflicted to some degree. Pollution at times reduces the amount of sunlight reaching New York City by nearly 25 percent, and that reaching Chicago by approximately 40 percent (Ehrlich & Ehrlich, 1970, p. 118).

There is a growing recognition of the problem (most people cannot escape seeing, smelling, and tasting the smog) and the Air Quality Act of 1967 states that the U.S. goal is not only to protect the nation's air shed from further harm, but to *enhance* the quality of air. However, new pollutants are being added faster than the old ones can be controlled.

Some appreciation of the problem of trying to halt air pollution may be gleaned from a review of the sources of air pollution (see Table 6-5). Over 140 million tons of air pollutants were estimated to have been re-

*TABLE 6-5 Sources of Air Pollution (in millions of tons annually)*

| | *Carbon Monoxide* | *Sulfur Oxides* | *Nitrogen Oxides* | *Hydro-carbons* | *Particulate Matter* | *Totals* |
|---|---|---|---|---|---|---|
| Motor vehicles | 66 | 1 | 6 | 12 | 1 | 86 |
| Industry | 2 | 9 | 2 | 4 | 6 | 23 |
| Power plants | 1 | 12 | 3 | 1 | 3 | 20 |
| Space heating | 2 | 3 | 1 | 1 | 1 | 8 |
| Refuse disposal | 1 | 1 | 1 | 1 | 1 | 5 |
| Totals | 72 | 26 | 13 | 19 | 12 | 142 |

*Source:* Population Reference Bureau, "The Thin Slice of Life," *Population Bulletin,* 24 (December 1968), 117.

leased by Americans in 1968. Motor vehicles contribute about 60 percent of the total and an even greater proportion of carbon monoxide and hydrocarbons.

All of the pollutants are deadly in greater amounts, but even in small doses they are believed to contribute to deaths from lung cancer, pneumonia, chronic bronchitis, and emphysema. Dr. John T. Middleton, Director of the National Air Pollution Control Administration, says:

> On any busy thoroughfare you'll certainly breathe in lead . . . nitrogen oxide . . . carbon monoxide and organic matter such as the polynuclear hydrocarbons, . . . sulfur oxides, a variety of particulates and oxides of iron, aluminum and other metals. . . . Both the gases and particulates can be harmful by themselves. But what greatly disturbs us is the fact that a mixture of them is often even more harmful. It's not just an additive effect—it's an enhancing one (*Population Bulletin*, 1968, p. 118).

Wherever and whenever *thermal inversion* (a warm layer or "lid" over a cooler layer of air) occurs, the pollutants cannot rise and dissipate, so they build up close to the ground. Thermal inversions are very frequent around Los Angeles and account for much of the difference between the kinds of pollution on the East and West Coasts.

The Los Angeles Air Pollution Control District, one of the most able in operation anywhere, has established and enforced strict standards of control. Yet, although it has been possible to keep the density of smog from increasing, the volume of heavily polluted air has continued to increase in area and height. While the per capita amount of pollution has declined, the continued growth of population in the area leads to an ever-increasing total pollution. The geographical spread of the area and the lack of an adequate public transportation system, together with increasing numbers of people, mean that increasing numbers of automobiles are on the roadways. The United States as a whole has one motor vehicle registration for every two persons of all ages (United States Bureau of the Census, 1970). Los Angeles has more than its share.

The smog generated in the Los Angeles basin is destroying 100,000 acres of Ponderosa and Jeffrey pine trees 60 miles from the city. The smog oxidants destroy the leaf tissue that carry on the vital process of photosynthesis by which the trees are nourished. Smog levels near Santa Cruz in northern California are now sufficient to damage the Monterey Pines. It is suspected that trees in many other areas are also being damaged.

### *Soil Pollution*

Among the factors that cause deterioration of productive soils is erosion. The soils harbor a very complex system of interconnected species, and erosion destroys the entire network at once. Man cannot re-create the living organisms of the soils once they are gone. Yet, deforestation continues to expose additional topsoil to erosion by wind and water. Borgstrom (1969) estimates that "in many parts of the globe the available [farm] land should be shrunk (reduced) in order to save the topsoil. More than half of India's tilled land is afflicted by soil erosion, one-third so seriously as to jeopardize the future of the topsoil" (p. 69).

In his attempt to renew some of the exhausted nutrients of the soil, man has developed all sorts of soil additives. Most of these have already proved to be helpful in increasing crop yields when they are added over great acreage, but not all are helpful to the soil itself. Fertilizers are likely to be used if they increase yields per acre. Yet it is not known how often the fertilizer, or the accompanying chemicals, are likely to be harmful to the soils, especially over a long period of time.

While both the total acreage and the proportion of agricultural land under irrigation are increasing yearly, the salts deposited with irrigated water threaten the ultimate destruction of soil productivity.

> Rainwater is essentially salt-free, but water for irrigation having come in contact with the minerals and fossil salts of soils and geologic materials may contain several tons of dissolved salts per acre foot. Plants grown by irrigation absorb and transpire the water but leave nearly all of the salt behind in the soil, where it accumulates and eventually prevents plant growth unless removed by leaching and drainage (Bower, 1966, pp. 4, 5).

An annual leaching by heavy rainfall can be counted on in only 4 of the 21 countries having more than one million hectares of irrigated land. In the other countries, salinity of the soil is a potential hazard.

Several civilizations that flourished in the distant past left evidence of irrigation systems that failed because they did not provide for salinity control.

On the basis of his acquaintance with salinity literature, contact with foreign salinity specialists, and travel in Latin America, the U.S.S.R. and the Near and Far East, Dr. C. A. Bower, Director of the U.S. Salinity Laboratory in Riverside, California, estimates (1966) that "salinity reduces crop yields on one-fourth to one-third of the world's irrigated land" (p. 6). He notes further that:

> Designers of irrigation developments during the last 50 to 75 years have usually been aware of salinity hazards but in many cases they failed to provide control measures, particularly artificial drainage. This has led to the development of much salt-affected soil in presently irrigated areas and has necessitated extensive remedial measures. Fortunately, there is scarcely an irrigation development planned today that does not take into account the need for salinity control (p. 5).

The $250 million agricultural empire in Southern California's Imperial Valley is an excellent natural laboratory for the study of salt-poisoning of the soil. Farmers are postponing the destruction of the soils via a vast network of underground drainage tubes to carry off saline water before it destroys the roots of the crops. The tubes have already been installed under 400,000 acres at a cost of from $100 to $490 per acre. In all, more than 16,000 miles of tile have been laid, enough to go through the center of the earth to the other side and back again. Farmers who laid tubes 200 feet apart five or ten years ago are already going back to lay tubes 100 feet, 50 feet, or even 25 feet apart ("Salt may be. . . ," 1970).

Others could learn from this natural laboratory in order to prevent a repetition of the same mistakes all over the globe. However, neither the press of population nor immediate profit incentives will allow the world the luxury of holding extensive acreage out of maximum production. Long-term results may well increase the problems of feeding the peoples of the earth. If deserts continue to be created faster than new acreage is put under the plow, there will be no long-term human solutions.

### *Defoliants*

Chemical weed-killers have been used for many years. Treatment of small spots and larger areas with light amounts of defoliants is an acceptable means of eradicating unwanted plant growths. When used under controlled conditions and in very light concentration, there do not seem to be any long-term negative effects.

However, for the first time, high concentrations of herbicides are being used over wide areas as a part of U.S. military policy in Viet Nam. Most of the defoliation has occurred along roads and rivers, around military establishments, and along the Cambodian and Laotian borders. The mangroves along the Nha Bo River, the main shipping channel to Saigon, have been heavily defoliated.

Observations on the ground indicate that one application leads to a modest kill of canopy trees, but not seedlings. A year after spraying, the timber could still be harvested for commercial use. The smaller trees then could continue to grow in the area.

Since the program began in 1962 the acreage defoliated has increased so rapidly that by the end of 1968 the Department of Defense estimated that 3.5 million acres had been defoliated. As much as 20–25 percent of the forests of Viet Nam have been sprayed *more than once* (Orians and Pfeiffer, 1970, p. 544), so that all seedlings are also destroyed.

The targets and concentrations of poisons have been pinpointed precisely, which will allow the future study of the consequences of different rates of application. Agriculturalists, biologists, and zoologists should be immediately involved in studying the effects not only on the trees themselves, but also on other plant life, and on the birds, fish, and wildlife of the areas.

The problem of defoliation lies in the fact that *no one knows the long-term effects.* Military goals must be balanced by other long-term considerations. If, as Orians and Pfeiffer (1970) suggest, the attitude of the South Vietnamese toward Americans has soured because of defoliation, the war could be lost even though, and perhaps because, some battles have been made easier to fight.

Defoliation is a drastic measure in a world whose population is increasing so rapidly that it needs every bit of useful acreage. Even during the war in Viet Nam, the populations of both the north and the south have almost doubled. Although short-term military advantage is possible, the long-term effects of defoliation are not known, but are likely to be detrimental.

## *Chemical Pollutants and the Food Chain*

"Persistent" pesticides are those that do not break down and disappear in time. A light spray each year builds up over time and may be carried by wind and water. It is concentrated by many organisms and passed up the food chain to higher animals. The last species in the food chain is man.

The best known of the "persistent" pesticides is DDT. It was introduced commercially only 26 years ago (in 1946) to control malarial mosquitoes and various insects that are harmful to crops.

DDT is actually less toxic than many newer poisons. Endrin is estimated to be 50 times more harmful than DDT, with dieldrin, aldrin, chlordane, and toxaphene ranging between the two.

The United States Department of Agriculture has been criticized by the Rienows (1967, p. 210) for claiming that it cannot set up recommendations on most poisons because it knows too little about them. The Department had in fact for years registered dieldrin and aldrin as safe. Then in 1966 they canceled its registered use. How can the widespread use of *any* poisons be allowed if too little is known about them?

DDT was once hailed as a marvelous find, but only the immediate advantages were known. Now some of the relatively long-term disadvantages are appearing, even though not enough time has lapsed to *maximize* their intensity in human beings.

The increasing dangers of DDT may be seen by considering its concentration in the food chain within a single estuary. Only 70 parts per billion in drifting microscopic plants of the water eventually resulted in 800 parts per million in the fat of porpoises, a 10,000 fold concentration. A few parts per million can kill, and food fish, shrimp, and crabs die in several weeks. No one knows how often or in how many places these food sources may be disappearing without our being able to identify the cause of loss.

Birds of prey also concentrate the persistent poisons, since they feed upon species which have themselves concentrated small amounts. Eagles, ospreys, and some great hawks have been laying infertile eggs or eggs whose membranes are too thin to protect their delicate interiors. It is now established that DDT has been traveling through the insect-fish-bird feed cycle, accumulating in greater density at each link in the chain and impairing the birds' ability to reproduce. Several species are now threatened with complete extinction.

The same build-up occurs on land. Hay and grasses that have been sprayed are eaten by grazing animals, chickens, and so forth. Human beings then consume the milk and meat, as well as the original grains. The concentration multiplies in each link in the food chain—and becomes most highly concentrated in the last link—man. The DDT intake of infants around the world is now about twice the daily maximum deemed safe by the World Health Organization. Concentrations of more than 12 parts per million have been found in human fat and as high as 5 parts per million in human milk (though the usual range is some 0.05 to 0.26 parts per million). The DDT concentrations in mothers' milk in the United States now exceeds the tolerance levels established for foodstuffs by the Food and Drug Administration (Brown, 1970, p. 169).

Because the heavy and widespread use of the persistent pesticides is a very recent phenomenon, the long-term effects are still unknown. Biologists have every reason to believe that these biologically active molecules are dangerous. One study, the results of which were obtained by autopsies, showed a correlation between DDT levels in human fat and cause of death. Concentrations of DDT and its breakdown products, DDE and DDD, were significantly high in the fat of patients who had died of softening of the brain, cerebral hemorrhage, hypertension, portal cirrhosis of the liver, and various cancers than in groups of patients who had died of infectious diseases. Neurophysiologist Alan Steinbach of the University of California at Berkeley claims that DDT is an irreversible nerve poison. Experiments with animals indicate that exposure to chlorinated hydrocarbons, of which DDT is one, caused changes in the central nervous system (quoted in Ehrlich and Ehrlich, 1970, p. 132).

As more is learned about chemical pollution of the environment, perhaps man will become more cautious. Perhaps too, mankind will recognize that it is the basic population pressure that encourages the use of products that provide immediate results, but may have numerous long-term hazards.

## *SUMMARY*

An overview of the relationship between population and resources revealed that there are and have been distinctive patterns of human settlement in relation to the characteristics of the physical environment. Concentrations of people have tended to occur near productive land, near trade routes, and, especially, near exchange points.

The relationship between population and resources has both demand and supply aspects. The standards of living and cultural values affect the demand side; the level of technology affects the uses to which resources may be put—the productivity of a group—or the supply side of the relationship.

Five distinctive types of population/resource relationships were discussed. Although variation among and even within societies is very great, the five types are useful approximations of actual national differences.

The capacity of the world's available resources to satisfy the needs of the population has been investigated. Supplies of water, land, forests, minerals, and even energy are limited. If people care about the human situation in the long run, it should be clear that careful management of the world's resources *and* some limitations on population are both necessary.

Pollution was viewed as the result of increasing numbers of people using up and discarding ever greater quantities of chemicals and waste materials. Pollution, like population itself, is increasing at an exponential rate. Not only population controls, but also greater wisdom and more effective control of the ways in which people harm the environment are needed. In the final analysis, men must be protected from the harm they cause themselves.

## *REFERENCES*


Ackerman, Edward A. 1959. Population and natural resources. *The study of population,* ed. P. M. Hauser and O. D. Duncan, pp. 621–48. Chicago: The University of Chicago Press.

Borgstrom, Georg. 1965. *The hungry planet.* New York: Macmillan.

———. 1969. *Too many: A study of earth's biological limitations.* New York: Macmillan.

Bouillene, Raymond. 1962. Man, the destroying biotype. *Science,* 135, 3505 (March 2): 706–12.

BOWER, C. A. 1966. Irrigation, salinity and the world food problem. Paper presented at the joint meeting of the Crop Science Society of America and Soil Science Society of America, Stillwater, Oklahoma, August 22.

BROWN, HARRISON, JAMES BONNER, AND JOHN WEIR. 1957. *The next hundred years.* New York: Viking Press.

BROWN, LESTER R. 1970. Human food production as a process in the biosphere. *Scientific American* 223, no. 3 (September): 161–70.

CHRISTIAN, C. S. 1965. The use and abuse of land and water. *The population crisis,* ed. Larry K. Y. Ng and Stuart Mudd, pp. 157–77. Bloomington, Ind.: Indiana University Press.

*The Christian Science Monitor.* Boston: The Christian Science Publishing Society.

CLOUD, PRESTON E., JR. 1968. Realities of mineral distribution. *Texas Quarterly* 11, no. 2 (Summer): 102–24.

EHRLICH, PAUL R., AND ANNE H. EHRLICH. 1970. *Population, resources, environment: Issues in human ecology.* San Francisco: W. H. Freeman & Co.

FISHER, JOSEPH L., AND NEAL POTTER. 1963. Resources in the United States and the world. In *The population dilemma,* ed. Philip M. Hauser, pp. 94–124. Englewood Cliffs, N.J.: Prentice-Hall.

HUBBERT, M. KING. 1969. Energy resources. In *Resources and man: A study and recommendations by the Committee of Resources and Man of the Division of Earth Sciences, National Academy of Sciences, National Research Council with the cooperation of the Division of Biology and Agriculture,* pp. 157–239. San Francisco: W. H. Freeman & Co.

LOVERING, THOMAS S. 1969. Mineral resources from the land. In *Resources and Man: A study and recommendations by the Committee on Resources and Man of the Division of Earth Sciences, National Academy of Sciences, National Research Council with the cooperation of the Division of Biology and Agriculture,* pp. 109–33. San Francisco: W. H. Freeman & Co.

MCNEIL, MARY. 1964. Lateritic Soils. *Scientific American* (November): pp. 96–102.

Oceans polluted by lead wastes. 1969. *Oakland Tribune* (November 2).

ORIANS, GORDON H., AND E. W. PFEIFFER. 1970. Ecological effects of the war in Vietnam. *Science* 168 (May 1): 544–45.

OSBORN, FAIRFIELD. 1948. *Our plundered planet.* Boston: Little, Brown.

PIDDINGTON, R. A. 1956. *The limits of mankind: A philosophy of population.* Bristol, England: John Wright & Sons.

POPULATION REFERENCE BUREAU. 1968. The thin slice of life. *Population Bulletin* 24 (December).

POTTER, DAVID M. 1954. *People of plenty.* Chicago: University of Chicago Press.

REVELLE, ROGER. 1963. Water. In *Technology and economic development,* ed. Scientific American, pp. 53–69. New York: Alfred A. Knopf.

RIENOW, ROBERT, AND LEONA TRAIN RIENOW. 1967. *Moment in the sun.* New York: Ballantine Books.

Salt may be kiss of death to lush Imperial Valley. 1970. *Oakland Tribune* (January 4).

UNITED STATES BUREAU OF THE CENSUS. 1970. *Statistical abstract of the United States, 1970*. Washington, D.C.: United States Department of Commerce.

ZELINSKY, WILBUR. 1966. *A prologue to population geography*. Englewood Cliffs, N.J.: Prentice-Hall.

chapter 7

# ECONOMIC ASPECTS OF THE POPULATION EXPLOSION

*It may yet be discovered that the economics of labour quality and population control have a much greater potential than ordinary capital investment for purposes of economic development.*

Stephen Enke, Economist (1963)

*Under all conditions of economic performance considerable advantage, in terms of per capita output and consumption, is apparent when fertility is controlled.*

Theodore K. Ruprecht, Economist (1967)

The United Nations, in its *Report on the World Social Situation* (1969), sums up the three major ways in which rapid population growth in the developing and underdeveloped countries adversely affect its economic and social development:

> First, it can increase the pressure of population on land that is already densely settled and so retard increases in the productivity of agricultural labour. . . .
>
> Second, accelerating population growth can aggravate the problem of capital shortage, which is one of the most important obstacles to economic development of nearly all underdeveloped countries. The faster the population grows, the larger the share of each year's income which must be invested in increasing the stock of productive equipment merely to maintain the existing level of equipment per worker. . . .
>
> Third, the high birth rates of the underdeveloped countries create a heavy load of dependent children for the working population. . . . The percentages of children under 15 years of age in the less developed countries of Asia, Africa, and Latin America are generally in the order of

> 40 percent or more of the total population, while the range of this ratio in the European countries is from about 20 to 30 percent (p. 127).

We have investigated the first of these major economic consequences in chapters 4 and 5. Dependency is considered in chapters 2 and 8. The second major consequence—capital shortage—is a major focus of the present chapter.

The interrelatedness of the many consequences of the population explosion may be seen most clearly when examining the economic factors associated with rapid population growth. The solution to most of the problems resulting from the rise in human numbers, as well as the alleviation of rapid population growth itself will require substantial monetary investments.

No government in the world has enough money to meet all of the demands upon it. Even the affluent nations are unable to cover all of their "urgent needs." In part, of course, this is due to the changing definitions of need, and in part it is due to the nature of investment.

Money itself is an abstraction, a symbolic medium of exchange. And, according to Sauvy (1961), "Investment means work without the immediate fruits of one's labor" (p. 113). However, most of us do not like to postpone rewards. Even where the desire to save and invest for the future is present, the closer a people are to bare subsistence, the less capable they are of postponing consumption.

In this chapter we will examine some of the problems faced by national leaders in trying to obtain sufficient capital investment merely to meet the subsistence needs of the increased numbers of persons and to raise the levels of living for the peoples of the world. No matter how optimistic one might try to be, it is clear that the rapid increase of the species is a barrier to improving the lives of all.

The economic gap between the developed and the less developed countries will be highlighted. After a review of economic development difficulties, the un- and underemployment of persons and their consequent underproduction will be investigated. Finally, we will look at the costs and economic benefits of checking population growth.

Economic development is not an *end* in itself, but rather a *means* to better human life.

> The object of economic development is the welfare and dignity of the individual human being. We must concern ourselves, not with aggregate statistics, but with the progress made in assuring each person a full and satisfactory life—adequate levels of personal consumption, including food and housing, health and education, and also satisfaction of those political, cultural, and spiritual needs that are fundamental to all men.
>
> If the condition of the individual, and not gross statistics, is to be the measure of our progress, then it is absolutely essential that we be con-

cerned with population trends. So long as we are concerned with the quality of life we have no choice but to be concerned with the quantity of life (Gardner, 1965, p. 286).

## *THE GAP BETWEEN THE DEVELOPED AND UNDERDEVELOPED COUNTRIES*

The inequality of national incomes resembles the highly stratified hierarchy of individual incomes within some nations. In 1958 the United States, with only 6 percent of the world's population, produced (and consumed) about 35 percent of the world's economic goods and services. The more developed nations as a group, with only 32 percent of the world's population, together produced about 82 percent of the world's goods and services. By 1968 their share of world production had increased even further, to 87 percent of the total.

| | *Share of World Population* | *Share of World Production* |
|---|---|---|
| Developed countries | | |
| 1958 | 32% | 82% |
| 1968 | 30 | 87 |
| Underdeveloped countries | | |
| 1958 | 68 | 18 |
| 1968 | 70 | 13 |

The less developed nations, with a more rapid increase in population and thus an increasing percentage of the people of the world, produced a lower proportion of the world's goods and services in 1968 than in 1958.

The per capita value of goods produced was over 30 times higher in the United States than in India or China.[1] The most recent estimates of per capita gross national product are indicated for some selected nations in Table 7-1.

In spite of the very low per capita product of many nations, some developmental progress has been made in certain less developed countries. Indeed, how else could they be called "developing nations"? Yet their relative proportion of world production has declined. Although the world has been focusing on improving the least advanced nations, the "developed" countries are actually "developing" at a more rapid rate. Those nations are still expanding and innovating at a quickening pace. *The gap between the two groups of nations is growing wider despite the tremendous effort in recent years to help develop the underdeveloped countries.* The

[1] For a review of some of the problems involved in these international comparisons and an attempt to improve comparability, see Gilbert and Kravis (1954).

*TABLE 7-1 Estimates of Per Capita Gross National Product (converted to U.S. dollar value), Selected Countries, 1967*

| *Country* | *Per Capita Product* |
|---|---|
| *Developed countries* | |
| United States | 3,670 |
| France | 1,950 |
| West Germany | 1,750 |
| United Kingdom | 1,700 |
| Italy | 1,120 |
| Japan | 1,000 |
| USSR | 970 |
| Poland | 780 |
| Spain | 680 |
| *Developing countries* | |
| Mexico | 490 |
| Cuba | 330 |
| Colombia | 300 |
| Brazil | 250 |
| Algeria | 250 |
| U.A.R. (Egypt) | 160 |
| Thailand | 130 |
| South Vietnam | 120 |
| North Vietnam | 100 |
| Indonesia | 100 |
| China | 90 |
| Pakistan | 90 |
| India | 90 |
| Nigeria | 80 |
| Ethiopia | 60 |

*Source:* International Bank for Reconstruction and Development, reported on 1970 World Population Data Sheet, Table 2-1.

whole world has been getting more prosperous, but the relative inequality among nations has increased.

Why are the differences widening? One reason is the lower pace of development in the less developed countries; another is the more rapid population growth in the underdeveloped nations. The underdeveloped countries would have improved their per capita production if they had been able to reduce their birth rates and rates of natural increase.

## *Population Growth and Costs of Production*

Population growth can affect economic unit costs of production in one of two ways. In some situations it can cause a reduction, in others a rise in unit costs.

Where population is very sparse, *economies of scale* may be obtained by an increase in population. In parts of Canada, Australia, and the

U.S.S.R. there might be an increase in efficiency or in the division of labor if the population were not so sparsely settled. Russian attempts to encourage people to move to Siberia are, at least in part, an attempt to take better advantage of the economies of scale.

There are now very few places in the world where increasing population might lower production and distribution costs. In the past, however, the unit cost of producing many items decreased as a result of gradually increasing population. The world is presently in a unique historical period in which rapid population growth is likely to lead not to economies of scale, but to the opposite.

The *law of diminishing marginal returns* suggests that, at some point, additional labor inputs begin having a detrimental effect on unit costs of a product. Where population density is adequate for a division of labor or too great to obtain any economies of scale or where population is growing too rapidly for the level of social organization, the law of diminishing marginal returns may apply. Of course, any increase in population results in lower natural resources per capita so that there is automatically a diminishing per capita productive potential (at any given level of technology).

At what point does population maximize the economies of scale without moving on to the point at which diminishing marginal returns set in? What is the "optimum population"? Many people talk in terms of an optimum level of population for the economy of a nation; others refer to aesthetic optimum or food-adequate optimums. There is as yet no precise way of determining the optimum level of population for a given nation. Many social factors, cultural values, and national goals must be considered in any debate about the *ideal* population size of a nation. The economic factor is only one aspect of the question.

Diminishing marginal returns can be seen in the less developed countries, where additions to the numbers of farm laborers do not increase the agricultural yield but simply mean that the production must be divided among more consumers. The point has been made more emphatically by Petersen (1969): "On a true Sahara more people bring no benefits" (p. 166).

In the advanced countries, diminishing returns can be detected in the costs of maintaining increasing numbers of persons: if increasing numbers mean higher per capita school costs, increased crime rates, increased costs to remedy pollution and control crime, then diminishing returns have set in. Further additions to the population increase the per capita costs of maintenance and, therefore, lower the net productivity per person.

Since increasing population does not always yield increased production and income, it does not necessarily mean an increase in purchasing power. An expanding market, therefore, does *not* require an increasing population, but rather an increase in production and in purchasing power.

### *Relationship Between Natural Increase and Gross National Product*

It is not possible to establish a causal relationship between rapid population growth and slow growth in total gross national product. There are too many interconnected factors in social causation to point to a single variable, such as population growth, as *the* cause of something else.

Numerous economists are, however, convinced that a 2 or 3 percent rate of natural increase is a principal *barrier* to development. There is evidence that rapid population growth lowers the *potential* economic development of the less developed nations. In the first place, a rapid increase in numbers means that most of the money or effort that could have been invested in improving the long-term economic, educational, and living conditions of the present population must instead be used to keep the additional persons functioning at the subsistence level. It also means a more rapid depletion of a nation's natural resources and continued inadequacy in education. Lauchlin Currie (1967) finds that a rapid growth in population in underdeveloped areas today prevents the people in these areas from utilizing technology to achieve an assured dominance or control over their social, economic, cultural, or political environment.

Economic analysis usually focuses on the per capita unit of economic productivity as it relates to population growth. That is probably the best indicator of the relative ability of a nation to provide its people with human necessities. It is also an excellent measure of long-term trends, independent of population increments. Continuous low per capita production, furthermore, is an indicator of the *failure of economic development*. Recognizing these advantages of the per capita measure, Simon Kuznets nevertheless recommended (1955) that *total* gross national product should be the measure analyzed over time, so that population will continue to be included in the factors influencing the aggregate outcome in production. He suggests that if the unreduced totals show long-term increases, while per capita or per worker levels of production are relatively constant, there has *not* been economic growth but simply "extensive expansion" (p. 12). More persons producing and living at the same level do not indicate economic growth, but rather stagnation.

While for some purposes economists may prefer to examine the population factor separately, we are most interested in per capita production as an indicator of growth or stagnation and of the level of living.

NEED VS. EFFECTIVE DEMAND. Some people believe that rapid growth in population creates new or increased demands and is therefore good for business and thus development. That view confuses "needs" with "effective demand." The fallacy of the argument may be seen by comparing the low effective demand of over 500 million people in India with the very high effective demand of 50 million British. Increasing the numbers of poor, uneducated persons creates little additional effective demand.

On the other hand, a stationary population does not mean a stationary buying power. On the contrary, as a general rule, the more slowly a population increases, the more rapid is the growth of both its gross income and its per capita income and, hence, of its buying power in absolute terms (Currie, 1967, p. 30). Ansley J. Coale and Edgar M. Hoover flatly state (1958) that *there is no way in which rapid population growth could be expected to assist economic development by increasing demand.* The needs and hopes of the populations of less developed countries are already high. What is needed is an increase in "effective demand" or buying power. Rapid population increase, in fact, may reduce buying power. Economist Joseph J. Spengler, addressing American businessmen (1966), suggests that:

> Much of the importance that some writers attach to population growth as a stimulator of profits at the firm level is without foundation. . . . A mere increase in population, or in its rate of growth, will not by itself make a firm's sales prospects better or worse. There will be more buyers, it is true, but there will also be more suppliers. . . . In the future, economic growth will depend mainly upon invention, innovation, technical progress, and capital formation, upon institutionalized growth-favoring arrangements. . . . It is high time, therefore, that businessmen cease looking upon the stork as a bird of good omen" (pp. 3, 5).

THE DEVELOPED VS. UNDERDEVELOPED NATIONS. The developed countries as a group have since 1950 been growing less rapidly than the less developed countries in population and more rapidly in both total gross domestic product (GDP) and per capita GDP. This is true for *any* set of dates between 1950 to 1966 listed in the United Nations *Statistical Yearbook for 1967*. For the more recent years, 1960 through 1966, the developed countries together registered a 35.6 percent increase in total GDP and 25.3 percent per capita increase. At the same time the less developed nations reported a phenomenal (for them) 29.5 percent increase in total GDP, but population increase reduced that to only 11.6 percent increase in per capita GDP. The increase for the people in the less developed countries would have been almost three times as much *if* population had stabilized for the seven-year period. Since there is a 15- to 20-year lag from birth to productive involvement in the economy, the population additions have added nothing to production but have lowered average production and income.

Computing the future advantages of a 50 percent reduction in birth rates in India over the years from 1956 to 1986, Coale and Hoover (1958) concluded that "per-consumer income would attain a level about 40 percent higher by 1986 with reduced fertility than with continued high fertility" (p. 284). Furthermore, with fewer births, malnutrition could be checked. The rise in labor force energy and productivity could be expected to continue the improvement into the future. They estimate that for at least 25 or 30 years a lower birth rate would bring a larger *total* national product as well as a smaller population, than would a high birth rate.[2]

In general, the lower the rate of natural increase the greater the per capita increase in gross domestic product. The exceptions are noteworthy. Both Mexico and Venezuela have recently had high rates of growth in both population and production. Unusual, favorable factors were involved. Nevertheless, their per capita gain (1958–1966) was only about one-third of their total gain. Over the same period of time, Japan, the only non-Western country to complete the transition to low birth and death rates, was able to translate a tripling of GDP into a near tripling in the per capita product as well.[3]

There seems little hope of narrowing the economic gap between the developed and the less developed countries. In spite of postwar aid, advances in the underdeveloped nations have been significantly reduced and even nullified by population increases. The gap has, therefore, been growing wider and will probably continue to do so. There is no doubt that the advanced nations need to contribute far more than they have to the less advantaged countries, but their resources are not limitless. They are unlikely to spend *more* abroad than at home and anything less will not resolve the world's development problems.

Imagine that with a commitment to liberalism and equalitarianism, we might divide the gross national product of the United States among all the people of the world. The hypothetical income would be a windfall to the truly poor of the world, but a one-time largess would not cure their poverty or alleviate their lack of educational, housing, and medical needs, much less provide them with the tools to become productive over the long run. It is not possible to make such a division, even if Americans willed it. Yet, present United States aid would probably need to increase

[2] Carrying this line of analysis to the extreme, Julian Simon (1970) points out that "the optimal birth rate for at least the next 20 years is *zero* births per thousand" (p. 371). But that possibility would have obvious long-run disadvantages. "The general conclusion, then, is that per capita income *alone* cannot be a satisfactory criterion for a rational national natality policy. At best it can be but one factor to be taken into consideration in such a policy decision" (p. 378).

[3] For the debate on the possible advantages and disadvantages of population growth with regard to per capita income in *developed* countries, see Universities-National Bureau Committee for Economic Research (1960).

tenfold to effectively *begin* to stimulate the economies of the less developed countries.

The problem of development narrows down to one of maximizing the mental and physical capacities of each person so that societal goals—aesthetic, material, health, and independence—may be attained. Education, of all the social processes, requires the greatest investment of time and talent without the immediate realization of the fruits of one's labor. An educated population, then, may be the greatest wealth of a nation, with wealth in machine goods a result, as well as a cause, of national wealth. The problems of improving the educational level of a population while the numbers of people are rapidly increasing will be investigated in Chapter 8.

People have marvelled for years at the rapid recovery of Germany and Japan from the destruction of World War II. With relatively small amounts of foreign aid, economic development went far beyond prewar levels. It is recognized that the populations were both skilled and well educated, but the full implications of that fact may not be realized. Foreign aid could hardly do as well for the less developed countries; more than economic aid is required there. How can millions of persons be moved from illiteracy to technological proficiency and from a superstitious to a rational approach to decision making? The economic gap between rich and poor nations may well be largely a result of the gaps in knowledge and rational behavior (relating means to goals). Reasoned action would include controlling reproduction at levels that allow improvement in the quality of human life over the long run.

Since education takes a very long time and since the young make up the greatest proportion of persons in the less developed countries, the educational gap may continue to increase. Education in the need for population control, accompanied by direct incentives for restricting reproduction, might be a profitable place to begin.

## *ECONOMIC DEVELOPMENT DIFFICULTIES*

People of all nations want economic expansion. Do any national governments suggest curtailing production? The problems of organizing for continued development are probably universal, but they are much more intense in the least developed nations.

### *Land, Natural, and Human Resource Requirements*

Economic development requires land, not only for building sites, but also for the construction of streets, highways, railways, and airports to facilitate the transportation of new goods produced. Piddington (1956) estimates that the miles of roadway required simply to bring the less developed countries up to the "inadequate level" of British transportation would require acreage equal to the agricultural livelihood of 47 million persons. Piddington suggests that England is the first nation to run out of land: there are no spare acres for roads, housing, airfields, recreation, reservoirs, schools, playing fields, or even cemeteries. The more that nations increase their standards of living, the more limited will be the availability of land.

The limits on natural resources were considered in the last chapter. So much of the world's resources have already been used up that Brown *et al.* (1957) suggest that if the exhaustion of critical components were to continue and the industrial network of the world were somehow destroyed, it is doubtful that the natural resources for a second industrial revolution would be available. Mankind would be trapped in a primitive, agrarian struggle for survival. We must learn to work with what is presently available and to prevent the continued destruction of resources.

Even where adequate land and natural resources are available, it would appear that economic development can proceed no faster than human resources can be trained to keep an economy in operation. A literate population is necessary even to apply existing technology; a still higher average level of education is necessary before a nation can adapt current technology to special local conditions; and a higher level yet before a nation can be instrumental in pioneering the development of new technology (Heer, 1968, p. 91).

It has been common to ascribe all of the difficulties of the less developed countries to a lack of capital and to the ways in which population growth has made it more difficult to obtain investment capital through savings or taxation. I have been trying to suggest that many factors other than a lack of funds contribute to development problems. Simon Kuznets (1966) is among those who play down the primacy of the role of capital in development:

> Evidence suggests that capital formation is far less important than a variety of other factors that can affect the rate and efficiency of capital utilization. Different rates of population . . . may be significant, not in terms of the rather obvious demands upon capital product, but of what they signify for the capacity of people to shape their lives and institutions so as to exploit properly the large potential of modern economic growth (p. 389).

In addition to these general values, a high motivation to work, the diffusion of knowledge, and the establishment of contractual law, one of the major direct determinants of economic growth is the amount of income-producing equipment in use per worker. The rate at which output per worker increases over time is conditioned by the rate at which his tools and equipment improve. Thus the rate at which a nation saves and uses its savings to increase the amount of equipment in use per worker is important. The United Nations Economics Commission for Asia and the Far East (1959) stressed that the capital required depends not only on the number of jobs to be provided, but also on the nature and productiveness of the jobs. Estimates for the average amount of capital required to supply the tools, building, and equipment to employ workers usefully in underdeveloped countries range from $1,100 to $2,500. Capital is required, however, to provide useful employment not only for new entrants into the labor force, but also for those previously unemployed or underemployed. Moreover, there is a limit to possible reductions in the amount of capital needed per worker. Certain basic facilities that require large amounts of capital per worker, such as railways and electricity, are essential for general economic development. Moreover, certain labor-intensive methods of production may rule out the chance of maximizing output and income.

Output per capita is also conditioned by the amount of investment made in the person: in his physical well-being, his technical education, his occupational training, and his social discipline (Spengler, in Kuznets, *et al.* 1955).

Every nation would like to maximize its investment per worker in order to increase production. How is this possible in a world of limited resources? What are the means of facilitating investment internationally? What are the more specific sources of investment within individual nations? And how may population growth affect them?

## *International Monetary Problems*

There is so much misunderstanding about the basis of national and international monetary exchange that a cursory review of the gold exchange standard, monetary value, and paper gold may help us understand the very great difficulty of obtaining investment capital.

GOLD STANDARD. Around the turn of the present century many of the advanced industrial countries based their paper currency on gold. The paper money initially represented a promise to pay in gold, the "only genuine international currency." The willingness to redeem paper with gold guaranteed that nations would not increase the quantity of paper money in circulation beyond their own capacity to trade production commodities for gold.

The monetary crises connected with both the First World War and the great depression ended the old gold standard. Since gold reserves have never been more than a small percentage of the outstanding paper currency of any nation, a dangerous run on gold would threaten with each inflationary spiral. The elimination of a willingness to redeem paper money for the citizens *within* nations removed a part of the danger.

Until 1971 gold was still used to balance international accounts. However, in the decade of the 1960's the United States had continued to spend abroad much more than it received, until in 1968 the dollars held by foreign governments and central banks were about 50 percent greater than the U.S. Gold reserves. The government thereafter simply declined to give up gold for outstanding dollars, effectively ending the gold-exchange standard internationally.

A basic problem is that the gold supply of the world has no relation to the need for money. The value of gold held in reserves could be multiplied about tenfold through the ability of central and commercial banks to lend many times the amount required in reserve. Nevertheless, the supply of gold has not been adequate to the traditional concept of an international currency.

Years ago R. A. Piddington (1956) computed that if the mining of gold could be brought up to 1400 million dollars' worth per annum (a rate actually achieved from 1964 through 1970) and maintained,

> . . . it would still take 450 years for the International Bank to accumulate enough gold in its vaults to supply the investment needs of all the backward areas. By that time, however, unless there is a universal drop in birth rates, the population of the world will be at least a hundred times larger than it is today and the gold mines, even should they prove inexhaustible, would be more than fifty thousand years' output short of their target (pp. 91, 92).

MONETARY VALUE. The printed paper that we call money has no intrinsic value. In each nation the money used *symbolizes* something of value. Any government that has tried to print more money, without relating it to something of worth, has found that the paper becomes about as valueless as the paper money we use in the game of *Monopoly*. As Piddington suggests (1956), "money that is conjured out of thin air dissolves back into thin air at the slightest breath of skepticism" (p. 90). Confidence in any monetary system is related to what the money symbolizes. Productivity levels influence how much the paper money will purchase—its symbolic value.

Therefore, a stable nation which can guarantee that its paper currency can be used to purchase *valued* items in the marketplace does not need to depend upon gold backing. Britain and France recently devalued the pound and franc not because of any change in gold supply, but rather because of a decline of productivity relative to other countries. The German mark was, of course, worth more in relation to the British pound and French franc after their devaluation. Indeed, German productivity was so high that the mark continued to be more valuable in exchange with the dollar and with the currency of other nations. It is natural that because each country differs in its monetary policy relating to the supply of its currency and differs from time to time in its level of productivity, there will need to be periods of readjustment in currency exchange. Allowing the German mark and the dollar to "float" permits these currencies to normalize their values in relation to others. The dependability of national productivity gives people confidence in the paper money of any nation. If that same confidence and dependability in national productivity could be extended to the international sphere, the world could widen its trading capacities independent of gold.

PAPER GOLD. In January of 1970 the International Monetary Fund began a historic attempt to broaden international credit. The IMF established Special Drawing Rights (SDRs), as kind of money to be used only by the monetary authorities of each participating nation. One hundred and nine of the one hundred and fourteen (non-Communist) members of the IMF are participating in a new international experiment, as described by David Francis (1960):

> The basic purpose of the SDR's is to supplement the existing reserve assets—gold, reserve currencies such as the United States dollar and sterling, and automatic borrowing rights in the IMF. . . . Such reserves . . . are used to pay international bills when a country's balance of payments is in deficit. They give a nation some time to adjust its domestic economy to restore balance in its international payments.
>
> Since the amount of gold held by IMF members has ceased to grow and most major nations are reluctant to hold more dollars in their reserves, a substitute had to be found or the price of gold raised. Thus the SDR's are often called paper gold. . . . The amount of SDR's each nation gets on the first distribution will be equivalent to between 16 and 17 percent of its regular IMF quota (p. 14).

The use of Special Drawing Rights will mean an expansion of credit ranging from many millions of dollars for the advanced nations down to about half a million for the smallest countries.

The fact that nations chose a credit type of reserve asset indicates a growing trust between non-Communist member nations. Countries that are about to go to war do not usually grant credit to each other. The advantages to be gained from this expansion of credit will continue only if the plan is used in such a way as to sustain the confidence needed for its success.

A major disadvantage is that, like any credit, once the SDRs are spent, they are gone and need to be repaid. Although the plan facilitates international trade, it is not a permanent solution. In the long run, economic expansion requires an increase in production, especially in per capita production.

### *Raising Gross National Product*

People can survive by picking berries or catching fish or hunting game animals (if any are available). However, if they are to produce more of the goods and services that they need and want, some tools and training are necessary. That means that an investment—a postponed gratification—is required of some one or some group.

Economists and development experts seem to be in general agreement that if the less developed nations reinvested 9 to 10 percent of their *total* gross national product each year, their GNP would increase an average of 3 percent each following year (a one-third return on investment). It sounds great: one-tenth of GNP reinvested once should return itself in only three years and then—gravy. Why aren't all countries taking advantage of these conditions to promote a rapid increase in GNP? Japan did in fact reinvest about 25 percent of her national income in the period from 1952 to 1957 and her national income rose about 7 percent per year (United Nations, Economic Commission for Asia and the Far East, 1959). The rise in Japan's national income has been even greater in the 1960s.

Most other nations have also tried to take advantage of the opportunity to invest toward an increase in GNP. The less developed nations as a group did increase GNP by 30 percent between 1960 and 1966. Why isn't there worldwide rejoicing at the success of the "first development decade"?

Two factors inhibit our joy. One is the conviction that the less developed nations cannot sustain the reinvestment necessary to continue growing. The other is the reduction of even that 30 percent gain by the rapid increase in populations.

Jean Bourgeois-Pichat (1966) claims that uninflated economic growth is probably incapable of exceeding 5 or 6 percent per year over a period of time. It is more likely to average three or four percent. In addition, it becomes increasingly difficult for the less developed countries to skim off 10 percent of their own GNP for reinvestment purposes.

Even when investment funds are obtained from outside sources, a 3 percent increase in GNP in any given year is cancelled by a 3 percent increase in population. Another 10 percent needs to be obtained for reinvestment *each* year just to keep even with population growth. The overall increase of 30 percent for the less developed countries between 1960 and 1966 was actually reduced to 11 percent per capita increase, because over those few years the population of the group of nations had grown by 18 percent.

Thus, although the stabilization of the population cannot guarantee to initiate economic development, rapid increases in population make a per person improvement extremely difficult to attain. Rapid population growth makes it more difficult to obtain investment capital via saving or taxation, and it also eats away any aggregate gains that occur.

## *HOW MAY CAPITAL INVESTMENT BE INCREASED?*

Since we have seen that money is an abstraction, that investment means work without the immediate fruits of that work, and that some investment is necessary for economic development, what are the possibilities of obtaining money for development, especially for the less developed countries?

### *Outside Sources of Investment Funds*

There are three potential sources of capital outside of the nation itself: gifts, loans, and foreign investments. Each has specific drawbacks as a source of investment capital.

GIFTS. Unconditional gifts from nations or from individuals are rare. They would be an ideal source of developmental funds if they were large enough. Probably the only nation which has had significant contributions from individuals and other nations is the small state of Israel. An equal division of the GNP of the U.S. would not amount to much for each individual on earth, but it would prevent those sources from supplying any capital in the future. Germaine Tillion, professor at the Sorbonne, in analyzing the complexity of the economic problems and solutions of Algeria, recognized that France had been second only to the United States in expenditures for foreign aid, with much of their outlay going to help Algeria. Miss Tillion offered what she called a conservative estimate of what was needed to help Algeria. Yet in converting her per person estimates into national needs, including industrial investment for only *half* of the males aged between 20 to 59 (and nothing for female workers), it turned out that Algeria would have required over one-fourth of the gross national product of France. In 1958, the year before Miss Tillion's book was published, there were about five-and-a-half times as many Frenchmen as Algerians. In the years since then the population of Algeria, one of the fastest growing in the world, has increased from nine to fourteen million. The problems have enlarged with the population and solutions have become more difficult, if not impossible. It is important to make suggestions, but one has a responsibility to compute the costs of those recommendations and the likelihood of meeting the requirements proposed. Clearly the 48 million people of France are unlikely to contribute one-fourth of their GNP to the far smaller numbers of Algerians, no matter how "responsible" they may be. For this reason, gifts have been and continue to be an unlikely source of significant developmental capital.

TABLE 7-2 *The Flow of Long-Term Financial Resources to Developing Countries and Multilateral Agencies by Major Categories, 1961 (disbursements in millions of U.S. dollars)*

| *Donor Countries* | *Grants and Grant-Like Contributions* | *Official Net Lending* | *Total Official Flow* | *Total Private Flow* | *Total Flow* |
|---|---|---|---|---|---|
| Belgium | 107.4 | —1.0 | 106.4 | n.a. | n.a. |
| Canada | 64.4 | —3.4 | 61.0 | n.a. | n.a. |
| France | 880.1 | 72.6 | 952.7 | 311.8 | 1,264.5 |
| Germany | 169.2 | 404.4 | 573.6 | 210.9 | 784.5 |
| Italy | 47.2 | 21.0 | 68.2 | 165.5 | 233.7 |
| Japan | 80.4 | 151.2 | 231.6 | 144.5 | 376.1 |
| Netherlands | 69.8 | —1.3 | 69.0 | 126.5 | 195.5 |
| Portugal | 11.2 | 18.6 | 31.5 | n.a. | 31.5 |
| United Kingdom | 248.0 | 199.0 | 445.0 | 429.0 | 874.0 |
| United States | 2,853.0 | 561.0 | 3,414.0 | 1,218.0 | 4,632.0 |
| Total Development Assistance Committee countries | 4,530.7 | 1,422.1 | 5,953.0 | 2,750.8 | 8,703.8 |
| Communist countries | | | About 300.0 | | 300.0 |

*Source:* Annabelle Desmond, "Population Growth and Economic Development," *Population Bulletin,* 19, 1 (February 1963), 12.

LOANS. These are equally problematic. Table 7-2 indicates that in 1961 the total amount lent by the major countries of the world was only one-third as great as the amount of outright grants. One of the main problems with loans, aside from their scarcity, is that they must be repaid, usually with interest. Many of the less developed countries are now borrowing to repay the interest on loans they made ten or more years ago. Furthermore, as with gifts, the lending or contributing countries often want to attach conditions to the use of the funds. Governing officials in the borrowing nations are often insulted by such conditions, despite some prior cases of misuse of such currency.

FOREIGN INVESTMENT. This typically involves the double disadvantage of risk for the investor and aggravation or resentment by the borrowing country. These disadvantages are mediated for the investor by the possibility of obtaining a desired product and profit, and for the population of the borrowing nation by the increases in employment, skills, and income. If any of us were to put our savings into an enterprise in another country, we would probably want to oversee its use. Because of the constant threat of nationalization or failure of the enterprise, investors usually want to get quick returns on their investment. The profits, furthermore, do not do the investor much good unless he can take them out of the country. If he leaves them, he must further postpone the gratification he might obtain from alternative use of the funds and he must reinvest the profits in the same or other risk ventures. If the investing person, firm, or nation leaves the money in the less developed nation, there will be maneuvering for high profits or for some other means of gaining from the investment. On the other hand, if the profits are withdrawn from the country, the investment has been of little value to the developing nation, beyond furnishing training and employment to some of its citizens.

Profits from foreign investments would not need to be excessive if the fear of nationalization could be reduced. A proposal that came before the United Nations in 1955 to guarantee international contracts might have resolved the problem and increased the willingness of savers to invest in the less developed nations at a lower rate of return. The proposal was rejected, however, by a vote of the United Nations General Assembly. It was thought to be a threat to the "sovereignty" of nations (Sauvy, 1961). The rejection itself may have made for even greater hesistancy and a decline in potential foreign investments.

The total flow of private financial resources from the more developed to the less developed countries in 1961 was 2.7 billion dollars or about 30 percent of all long-term commitments.

The total flow from these three types of financial resources may appear to be quite sizable. But U.S. economic aid, more than one-half of the total aid in 1961, amounted to less than $2 per person per year in the receiving countries over the entire period from 1952 to 1961. In South Korea, the single exception, the average during that particular time period was over $10 per person (Desmond, 1963). Over the long run these sources could not begin to meet the development needs of those countries that are not self-propelled. As Alfred Sauvy (1961) suggested, "industrialization doesn't occur in a vacuum. . . . *Industrialization is a social environment*" (p. 133). He sees capital as being second in importance to a supply of qualified workers. Both must come mainly from within.

### *Internal Sources of Investment*

Ultimately capital investment must come, for the most part at least, from within each country. Outside capital, whether in the form of gifts, loans, or foreign investment, is surrounded with problems. There are not enough rich nations to supply the many poor ones, even if they were to make major sacrifices.

Internal development capital may be raised by encouraging savings and investment or by confiscating or taxing by the governing body. Either way the countries that need capital most will have the greatest difficulty in obtaining it.

The encouragement of savings presumes investment. People are encouraged to put their money in a bank or to buy stock by the offer of reward: either interest or growth in the value of the stock certificate. Banks and corporations use the money invested in them to expand jobs and increase the tools of production, and thus make a return on the investment. Even in Russia, people are now offered interest on their bank accounts. The greater the risk of any given investment, the greater the likelihood of attaining *either* significant returns *or* complete losses. The more developed countries have greater economic surplus available for investment. Faaland (1966) explains it thus:

> Taking savings capacity more or less as a residual above basic consumption requirements, a larger population will have proportionately lower per capita income, leaving capacity to generate savings correspondingly smaller. . . . This is a trivial finding on which no disagreement is reasonably possible (p. 297).

Both confiscation or taxation by the government for the purpose of investing in government-owned capital equipment have sometimes been considered elements of socialism. A government that maintains total control may, rather than levy a tax, simply withhold whatever portion of wages they determine to reinvest. There are limits to the amounts they are able to hold back: workers produce more if they are highly motivated, both by wages received and by the capacity to purchase what they want with their wages. Governments of any form can get away with only as much as the people will allow. Clearly, the more destitute the population, the less the government can obtain by confiscation or taxation, much less by saving.

One might suppose that the governments of the least developed nations would be the most highly motivated to control population growth in order to release the capital needed for highways, railroads, communication systems, electric power generators, factories, and so forth. Yet, as we will see in chapter 11, government officials are just beginning to recognize the way in which rapid population growth may restrict national investment and productivity.

## *UN- AND UNDEREMPLOYMENT*

Both unemployment and underemployment occur in many countries as both a direct and an indirect result of population growth. Most discussions consider only *unemployment*: the number of persons, or the proportion of the labor force, actively seeking jobs. Underemployment is much more difficult to measure and yet is more pervasive in the underdeveloped nations. *Underemployment* may be defined as a situation in which reducing the number of persons in a given activity would not reduce total output. Underemployment, then, contributes to the low productivity of the poorest nations of the world and of any activity within any nation. It is directly related to the concept of the diminishing marginal utility of adding extra workers. Wherever more employees or self-employed persons are involved in a task that fewer persons could competently handle, underemployment exists. In India, grown men are "underemployed" in selling matches on the street corners. In parts of the Near and Far East, clerks and owners of small shops are idle most of the day because there are not enough customers to support the numerous shops carrying exactly the same products.

The percentages of visibly underemployed, in terms of involuntary participation in employment of less than normal hours or duration, range from 1 percent in Israel, to 12.5 percent in the Philippines, to 22 percent of the employed persons in Pakistan. In India, some 15 to 18 million persons are underemployed. The flow of workers from rural to urban areas increases the un- and underemployment in and around cities. Meanwhile, population growth is so rapid that, despite the increase in the nonagricultural proportion of the labor force, millions are still being added to the rural underemployed. If the proportion in the labor force dependent on agriculture declined from 70 percent in 1961 to 60 percent in 1976, 23 million would still be added to the underemployed agricultural work force of India (Sadie, 1966, p. 225).

Full employment is a nearly universal goal. Economic development involves more than increasing the income per capita in the less developed nations. Other goals, such as improved health and education, are ends in themselves as well as means to higher incomes by way of more specialized and efficient labor. Productive employment for male adults and for a proportion of adult women is also valuable in its own right, because of the degrading effect of unemployment or of unproductive employment (Coale, 1963, p. 65).

### *Youth Un- and Underemployment*

Un- and underemployment of young people differs in kind in the developed and underdeveloped countries.

IN THE DEVELOPED COUNTRIES. Unemployment among youth is related to a lack of skills or to uneven population growth in developed countries. Richard Easterlin (1966) has demonstrated that in the United States the recent increase in young workers has meant, in spite of their relatively high beginning wage, a lower median income relative to 35- 44-year-olds. In other words, while wages have increased overall, they have not increased as rapidly for the large supply of young as for the older worker. Furthermore, when they enter the labor force, the very youngest age group often lacks the education and training which is in demand in the more developed countries. The previous educational advantage of the young over the old shows little prospect of continuing. On the whole, Easterlin suggests, "a substantial reversal of the situation in the preceding period as to the relative quantity and quality of younger versus older persons is now in progress" (p. 67). Moreover, at each age, the lower the education, the higher the proportion unemployed.

In the United States the post-Warld War II "baby boom" has created problems not only for the educational system, but also for the labor force. By 1960 a million persons were being added to the labor force each year. The projections of the United States Bureau of the Census, based upon births which had already occurred, indicate that by 1970 1.5 million new jobs would have to be provided *each year* in order not to increase the numbers unemployed (see Table 7-3).

TABLE 7-3 *United States Labor Force in Millions of Persons and Yearly Increase*

| *Year* | *Labor Force (millions)* | *Increase per Year (millions)* |
|---|---|---|
| 1960 | 73 | 1.0 |
| 1965 | 79 | 1.2 |
| 1970 | 87 | 1.5 |
| 1975 | 94 | 1.4 |
| 1980 | 100 | 1.3 |

*Source:* Donald J. Bogue, "Population Growth in the United States," p. 80, in *The Population Dilemma*, Philip M. Hauser, ed. © 1963 by The American Assembly, Columbia University. By permission of Prentice-Hall, Inc.

FIG. 7–1 *In many countries young children participate in the agricultural labor force, but the opportunity to learn advanced skills is limited. Wide World Photo*

The yearly additions to the labor force projected in Table 7-3 would challenge any system to absorb them. There will be a 50 percent increase in the U.S. labor force from 1960 to 1980. Add to the numerical increase the fact that the additions, as well as the replacements for those who retire are all in the youngest age group, without work experience and often without the skills needed in an advanced industrial society. The unemployed in the United States are basically the very young and unskilled members of the labor force including disproportionately high numbers of blacks and high school dropouts, among whom unemployment runs as high as 30 percent. In the past, Negroes were more likely to be unemployed or underemployed than were whites of the same educational level. In the late 1960s, however, both employment and wages were rising faster for educated blacks than for their white or their less educated black counterparts (United States Bureau of the Census, 1970).

By 1970 the baby boom babies who had graduated from college were finding that they were not always prepared with the skills most needed in the job market. In a democracy the people decide daily whether they are willing to pay for more teachers, doctors, nurses, military personnel, machine operators, sports stars, scientists, or philosophers. They are yet undecided whether education should be broad and general or specialized and technical.

Unemployment in general is likely to be aggravated for as long as fifteen to twenty years after the very rapid population growth of the post-war years in the developed countries.

IN THE LESS DEVELOPED COUNTRIES. Some of the same problems occur in less developed countries. In addition to the rapid increase in the number of persons entering the labor force, the underdeveloped nations face far greater difficulty than the more developed nations in providing the new young workers with the necessary skills and tools. Furthermore, in the underdeveloped countries the numbers entering the labor force will be entering at an even earlier age and with much less education, on the average, than is true in the advanced nations. In Latin America, for instance, 60 percent of the nearly three million young entering the labor force each year do not even have a basic primary education. (Population Reference Bureau, 1968). As a group, the underdeveloped countries are having great difficulty increasing the investment in the labor force they already have, and yet yearly the proportional increase will be far greater than that faced by the United States.

Unemployment in the large cities of the "developing" countries is staggering. Apart from the waste that it implies (and that a poor country can ill afford) and apart from the deprivation it entails, unemployment is a serious threat to the political stability that development policy requires (Olin, 1965). The absence of opportunities for productive employment in the cities of the underdeveloped countries is the result of insufficient productive equipment and resources for labor to work with and also of the lack of education and training of the labor force itself.

In the past the process of industrialization brought about employment along increasingly diverse, nonagricultural lines. All of the more highly industrialized countries have already reached or passed through a phase in which the number of persons employed in agriculture remains constant, so that all of the increases in the labor force have to be absorbed by the nonagricultural sectors of the economy (Coale, 1963).

Because of their high rate of population growth, the underdeveloped countries cannot provide nonagricultural employment opportunities for all of the additions to their labor forces; and because of the small landholding that high density implies, additions to the agricultural labor force merely add to underemployment in this sector. Ansley Coale has computed that if all of the increased labor force of a population growing at 3 percent per year were to be employed *outside* of farming, it would require annual increases in nonagricultural employment of between 4.8 and 7.3 percent for at least 20 years. That would require a doubling of the nonagricultural labor force every 10 to 14 years. No one believes that that can be accomplished. Therefore, an increase in un- and underemployment in the less developed countries is to be expected.

If fertility could be cut in half in a relatively short period of time, it would still take approximately 30 years before the labor force would be relieved of the rising pressure. By 40 or 50 years hence the reduction of population increases would play a crucial role in attaining the goal of adequate employment opportunities, not to mention the closely related but not identical goal of insuring a more rapid increase in income per consumer (see Coale, 1963, p. 68, for precise computations).

At the 1965 World Population Conference in Belgrade, A. Zimmerman proposed the formation of national development armies, modeled on the military draft system, into which "youths of superior stock," who might be molded into potential leaders, would be conscripted at about the age of 18.

> While strict armylike discipline would be observed, they would be instructed in reading, writing, and arithmetic, and, in specialized camps, taught to handle tools, machinery, building materials, financial accounts, and monetary matters, while those returning to the land would learn about modern agricultural methods. While in the camps the youths would be able to make a useful contribution through the construction of roads, simple dwelling units, irrigation and drainage systems, the opening up of new territories for settlement, etc. (in Sadie, 1966, p. 228).

The proposed plan could occupy young people in useful developmental projects while teaching them skills beyond traditional patterns. To implement such a plan on a significant scale, however, would require funds which are in very short supply.

### *Female Employment*

Labor force computations have not always taken into account the possibility of increasing the female contribution to the productive labor force. Yet we know that in the advanced nations the female contribution to gross national product is relatively high and has been increasing. Women make up over one-third of the labor force in the United States (United States Bureau of the Census, 1970, p. 214). The more educated women become, the greater the role they may play in the entire economy. Yet high birth rates retard the possibility of female participation in the industrial sector of the economy. The absence of females from the nonagricultural labor force seems both to result from and to contribute to high fertility.

Whether in advanced or less developed countries, when childbearing begins at an early age, the education of women is interrupted. In the developed countries a small but still problematic proportion of women begin having children in their early and middle teens. In the underdeveloped countries that is often the accepted cultural pattern.

Uneducated women have even fewer job opportunities than uneducated men. Some nations list these women as part-time unpaid family workers. They may work in the fields or in some cottage "industry," but their contribution to the total economy is small.

In the Middle Eastern countries and in some other less developed areas of the world, religious, political, familial, and economic sectors all reinforce the traditional pattern of "seclusion and exclusion" for women. Without acceptable alternatives, women can aspire only to marriage and motherhood (Youssef, 1970). The release of women from domination by males could both release a productive potential and lessen the reproductive performance of the species.

M. Gendell finds evidence of an inverse correlation between the number of minor children at home and a woman's rate of labor force participation, but the age of the youngest child is of even greater consequence than their number. Freedman and his colleagues have found that in the U.S., working wives are more likely to use the most effective contraceptive methods and consequently to have fewer children. If this were to hold true generally, particularly in the developing countries, the entry of females into the organized labor market—as distinct from domestic services—would promise a solution to high birthrates (in Sadie, 1966, p. 221). The working woman contributes to the higher income of her family and to the support of the society (via taxes), has fewer children on the average, and performs needed services for the social group (women are primarily involved in teaching, nursing, and other service occupations).

## *Automation and Education*

Both automation and education interact to affect the levels of employment and productivity in less developed as well as developed countries. Automation may create or eliminate tedious jobs. Marx complained that assembly-line industry alienated man from his work and, in the end, from himself as well. However, it is difficult to imagine that spinning wool or weaving cloth could be much less boring in 12–14 hours at home than in a factory. Granting that early factory conditions were horrible, work in the fields or in home industries was not much better (see Laslett, 1965; Smelser, 1959). Overall, the mechanization of tedious work has freed people to do more varied types of work in fewer hours than previously and true assembly-line work now occupies a very small proportion of the labor force. For instance, in the automobile industry, assembly-line operation par excellence, less than 5 percent of all jobs are on the line itself (Broom and Selznick, 1968, p. 483). One reason for the decline in the proportion of assembly-line workers is that in the advanced countries a larger proportion of the total labor force is more involved in services than in manufacturing and construction. Even in construction jobs, however, ditches might just as well be dug by machine with a single operator so that many other men may be free to continue their education, to be social workers or doctors, to build homes, and so forth.

At the same time, the introduction of automation naturally requires readjustments. It is difficult, but not impossible, to plan the reorganization of the work force and work skills. Automation itself and the resulting increase in the proportion of service jobs both require a more educated, skilled labor force. Complex equipment and industrial methods call for the talents of highly skilled mechanics, engineers, and workers who are able to understand them. The connected services of transportation, buying and selling, communication, accounting, and coordination require training or advanced education.

Those who object that automation reduces jobs and therefore is bad for employment cannot see its positive aspects. The number of persons in the labor force in the United States, one of the most highly automated countries in the world, has increased from about 11 million in 1860 to over 80 million in 1970. Jobs have obviously increased along with automation. At the same time the hours of work have decreased, and production and income have risen fantastically.

The problem for the less developed countries is to tap the advantages of automation and at the same time to find jobs for the rapidly increasing numbers of persons.

In the past, the relatively slow population growth in the now industrialized nations was absorbed by employment opportunities in the factories. There was what has been called a "pull" to urban–industrial occupations. Since excess population cannot be absorbed on the rural farms, they are, as we mentioned earlier, being "pushed" into urban areas with small hope of finding useful employment there.

## *COSTS AND ECONOMIC BENEFITS OF CHECKING POPULATION GROWTH*

Over 16 years ago Frank Lorimer (1954) pointed out that:

> The record is clear on two negative points of theoretical importance: first, a trend toward increased control of fertility is not necessarily de-

> pendent on large-scale industrialization; secondly, the rapid introduction of mechanical industries into a previously non-industrial society does not *automatically* bring a trend toward increased control of fertility (p. 217).

If we agree that fertility control or the prevention of births must be initiated without waiting for economic development, what would be involved in economic costs and benefits?

There have been so many attempts at wide-scale birth control programs that the costs are already well known. The larger the population, of course, the more costly is any program aimed at reducing births. Some government leaders have balked at the total costs of such a program and have budgeted only insignificant amounts for spotty programs. The question is not merely one of total costs, however, but of what benefits may arise and how those benefits compare with the returns from other investments.

Coale and Hoover (1958) claim that because of the difficulty of finding useful employment for a rapidly growing labor force and because the necessity of devoting time to child care limits women's labor, total output would grow faster with reduced fertility than with continued high fertility. We have already seen that fewer births in recent years could have contributed to increased per capita incomes in the less developed countries. What then are the costs of reducing the growth rate?

### *Costs*

The cost of a birth control program depends on the number of participants, the methods of contraception they use, and the presumed fertility of participants, were they not practicing birth control. Stephen Enke and Richard G. Zind (1969) estimate the average cost of a program to be $2 a year for each participant, using such methods as the pill and the coil. And if, as is the case in many less developed countries, one woman in every five in the childbearing years had been giving birth each year, the cost of preventing one birth would be about $10. (If the costs were to be calculated for whole populations, a modest program would average about 30 cents per person per year.)

### *Benefits*

Assuming that 50 percent of all women in the childbearing ages were to accept birth control (gradually at first but reaching 50 percent participation[4] by the end of 30 years), Enke and Zind estimate that the undiscounted *returns* on investment would be 13 times the cost in the first five years, 26 times cost at the end of ten years, 50 times cost at the end of twenty years, and 80 times cost at the end of thirty years. (The estimated returns were computed by dividing the extra income for the existing population, at past actual increase in GNP for the less developed nations, by the cost of increasing birth control.) No other investment program could be expected to bring such high returns. The authors suggest that over thirty years the yield on investment in birth control is about 15 times what could be expected from investment in capital goods. Although the assumptions underlying such calculations may be questioned, the probability of benefits deriving from birth control programs is clearly very high.

Internal saving for investment purposes would have to be about two or three times as great as is assumed to be typical if similar per capita income increases were to be realized without birth control.

The value of *permanently* preventing a birth in an under developed country is equal to twice the per capita income of that country. In view of the low costs and lack of reasonable alternatives, investment in birth control by the less developed countries would seem to be highly advantageous. Although total costs may seem high to policy makers, 30 cents per capita compares favorably with total expenditures for economic development in less developed countries, which ranges around $10 per person per year. A full birth control program, including one-half of *all* fertile women in every age group, would take only about 3 percent of all current expenditures for economic development. The best investment in economic development does seem to be an investment in birth control. With the program described, 97 percent of most development budgets would still be available for increasing health, education, and real capital investment.

Coale and Hoover (1958) cite the probably unquantifiable influences on economic development which could accrue from reduced fertility: fewer pressures on the food supply might allow an improvement in nutrition, which would lead to greater energy and thus greater production per laborer; as advances begin to occur and a lower proportion of total funds are needed merely to stay alive, there might be an increase in incentives and a decrease in widespread apathy among the populations in the less developed nations.

There are many *means* of birth control. For the most part, however, the nations of the world have not yet decided that population control is a high-priority goal. As Frank Notestein (1966) has said:

[4] Since some women in the childbearing age group will be trying to conceive, and others will be bearing a child, and still others will be unmarried, widowed, or divorced, a 50 percent participation rate may be all that is realistic even after 30 years.

> Since all people covet health, the reduction of the death rate involves only the question of obtaining efficient means. The control of fertility, however, requires changes of *both* ends and means. It seems probable that death rates will always decline *before* birth rates. The problem is to minimize the lag in order to simplify the difficulties of economic development. . . . There is ample evidence that special efforts to foster the practices of family planning are successful in speeding the reduction of fertility (p. 98; italics added).

Widespread efforts to lower fertility could help greatly in reducing the lag between the decline in death rates and the decline in birth rates. Notestein assumes that fertility will decline in the future, or death rates will surely rise.

> In the long run, [population] growth, far from inevitable, is impossible. . . . in the short run, immediate curtailment of the rate of population growth will greatly facilitate the kind of technological development that can provide long-run support for populations both large and prosperous. The major difficulties are not ultimate but immediate, not hypothetical but real and urgent. They are those of at once reducing the rate of growth in order to foster economic development. If growth can soon be reduced, the risks of temporary and tragic failure in modernization will be greatly lessened. Once the major transformation has been made, mankind will have an excellent chance for the first time in history to attain health, education and reasonable prosperity for all (pp. 99–100).

Because 3–5 percent of national income could be saved by reducing population growth about 1 percent per year and because human behavior responds to reward, Spengler (1966), among others, suggests state intervention to promote direct rewards to potential childbearers for *not* producing children.

The various proposals for family planning or population control will be reviewed in the last chapter. At this point we have simply established its economic feasibility and described the benefits to be gained from fertility reduction.

## *SUMMARY*

The enormous economic gulf between the "developed" and "developing" countries has been growing ever greater. In fact, the advanced countries are advancing more rapidly than those countries typically categorized as "developing nations."

In many places in the past and in a few places now, economies of scale could allow advantages to be gained by increasing population density.

However, in most countries of the world the law of diminishing marginal returns has set in: the disadvantages, or costs, of increasing population outweigh the advantages, or returns. On neither the production (labor supply) nor the consumption (effective demand) side is much to be gained by adding to national populations.

Since there are more than enough human laborers in relation to land and natural resources, improvements in production require capital investment in tools and human skills. Current monetary supplies are already invested, however, so that new investment requires postponed gratification by real human beings. Monetary systems only facilitate exchange. Paper money printed without relation to the productivity of a nation (that is, without being related to the value of what it will buy) becomes quickly devalued or worthless. International and national monetary supplies, therefore, are inadequate sources of the capital needed.

Gifts, loans, and investments from outside any given nation all have disadvantages, and none can be obtained in sufficient amounts. Therefore, internal investment is basic to the growth of a national economy. The poorer the nation, the more difficult it is to obtain investment capital internally—by savings, confiscation, or taxation. Population growth greatly exaggerates the problem by eating up potential investment funds merely to keep people alive.

Being short on investment funds and long on labor supply, the less developed nations have high un- and underemployment. Even in the developed countries the postwar baby boom has meant that huge numbers of additional jobs must be created each year if unemployment is not to rise.

Female employment complicates the situation. On the one hand, frequent childbearing keeps women from making more productive contributions to family and national income. On the other hand, without skills or tools there is little that women can contribute, and so their alternatives to childbearing are limited.

Tools, especially automated machinery, help each worker to be more productive. However, fewer workers are then required. Those who are displaced must be retrained and reorganized, often at great expense.

All of these conditions imply that nations might be better off if populations were shrinking instead of expanding. Estimates of the costs and economic benefits of checking population growth indicate that a return of 80 times the cost of prevention of births is possible in a 30-year period. No other investment would be expected to reap such high returns.

Clearly, we must consider more than economic benefits alone. The quality of life is not measured in dollars. Better health, education, housing, nutrition, and pure water and air, however, all require investments which cannot be made when mere survival is the primary need.

A small proportion of investment funds (as little as 3 percent of national government investments) applied to birth control would reap huge economic benefits and thereby facilitate a general increase in the quality of life.

## *REFERENCES*

BOURGEOIS-PICHAT, JEAN. 1966. *Population growth and development.* New York: Carnegie Endowment for International Peace.

BROOM, LEONARD, AND PHILIP SELZNICK. 1968. *Sociology (a text with adapted readings).* New York: Harper & Row.

BROWN, HARRISON, JAMES BONNER, AND JOHN WEIR. 1957. *The next hundred years.* New York: Viking Press, 1957.

COALE, ANSLEY J. 1963. Population and economic development. *The population dilemma,* ed. Philip M. Hauser, pp. 46–69. Englewood Cliffs, N.J.: Prentice-Hall.

COALE, ANSLEY J., AND EDGAR M. HOOVER. 1958. *Population growth and economic development in low-income countries.* Princeton, N.J.: Princeton University Press.

CURRIE, LAUCHLIN. 1967. The tangled crisis. *Population Bulletin,* 23:2 (April), 25–43.

DESMOND, ANNABELLE. 1963. Population growth and economic development. *Population Bulletin,* 19, no. 1 (February), 12.

EASTERLIN, RICHARD A. 1966. On the relation of economic factors to recent and projected fertility changes. *Demography,* 3, no. 1, 131–53.

———. 1968. *Population, Labor Force and Long Swings in Economic Growth.* New York: Columbia University Press.

ENKE, STEPHEN, AND RICHARD G. ZIND. 1969. Effect of fewer births on average income. *Journal of Biosocial Science* 1, 41–55.

FAALAND, J. 1966. Demographic aspects of savings, investments, technological development and industrialization. Statement by the Moderator, Meeting A.9. *Proceedings of the 1965 World Population Conference,* Vol. 1. New York: United Nations.

FRANCIS, DAVID R. 1969. International monetary fund plan. *The Christian Science Monitor* (December 26).

GARDNER, RICHARD N. 1965. The politics of population: a blueprint for international cooperation. In *The population crisis,* ed. Larry K. Y. Ng and Stuart Mudd, p. 286. Bloomington, Indiana: Indiana University Press.

GILBERT, MILTON, AND IRVING B. KRAVIS. 1954. *An International Comparison of National Products and the Purchasing Power of Currencies.* Paris: The Organization for European Economic Cooperation.

HEER, DAVID M. 1968. *Society and population.* Englewood Cliffs, N.J.: Prentice-Hall.

KUZNETS, SIMON. 1966. Demographic aspects of economic growth. Statement by the moderator, Meeting A. 10. *Proceedings of the 1965 World Population Conference,* Vol. 1. New York: United Nations.

KUZNETS, SIMON, *et al.* 1955. *Economic growth: Brazil, India, Japan.* Durham, N. C.: Duke University Press.

LASLETT, PETER. 1965. *The world we have lost.* London: Methuen & Co.

LORIMER, FRANK. 1954. General theory. Part one. In UNESCO, *Culture and human fertility,* pp. 13–247. Zurich: UNESCO.

NOTESTEIN, FRANK W. 1966. Some economic aspects of population change in the developing countries. In *Population Dilemma in Latin America,* ed. Mayone Stycos and Joyce Arias, pp. 86–100. Washington, D.C.: Potomac Books.

OLIN, ULLA. 1965. Population growth and problems of employment in Asia and the Far East. *Proceedings of the 1965 World Population Conference,* Vol. 4, p. 314. New York: United Nations.

PETERSEN, WILLIAM. 1969. *Population.* New York: Macmillan.

PIDDINGTON, R. A. 1956. *The limits of mankind: A philosophy of population.* Bristol, England: John Wright & Sons.

POPULATION REFERENCE BUREAU. 1968. Demographic awakening in Latin America. *Population Bulletin,* 24, 1 (February), 1–21.

SADIE, JAN L. 1966. Demographic aspects of labor supply and employment. Statement by the Moderator. Meeting A. 5. *Proceedings of the 1965 World Population Conference,* Vol. 1. New York: United Nations.

SAUVY, ALFRED. 1961. *Fertility and survival.* New York: Criterion Books. Translated from French ed: 1958.

SIMON, JULIAN L. 1970. The per-capita income criterion and natality policies in poor countries. *Demography,* 7, no. 3 (August), 369–78.

SMELSER, NEIL J. 1959. Social change in the industrial revolution: an application of theory to the British cotton industry. Chicago: University of Chicago Press.

SPENGLER, JOSEPH J. 1966. Implication of population changes for business. *Population Reference Bureau,* selection 19 (December).

TILLION, GERMAINE. 1959. *Algeria.* New York: Alfred A. Knopf.

UNITED NATIONS Department of Economic and Social Affairs. 1959. *1957 Report on the World Social Situation.* New York: United Nations.

UNITED NATIONS Economic Commission for Asia and the Far East. 1959. Population trends and related problems of economic development in the ECAFE region. *Economic Bulletin for Asia and the Far East,* 10, no. 1 (June), 1–78.

UNITED NATIONS Economic and Social Council. 1968. *Statistical yearbook, 1967.* New York: United Nations.

UNITED STATES Bureau of the Census. 1970. *Statistical abstract of the United States, 1970.* Washington, D.C.: United States Department of Commerce.

UNIVERSITIES-NATIONAL Bureau Committee for Economic Research. 1960. *Demographic and economic change in developed countries.* Princeton, N.J.: Princeton University Press.

YOUSSEF, NADIA. 1970. *Social structure and female labor force participation in developing countries: A comparison of Latin American and Middle-East countries.* Doctoral dissertation, University of California, Berkeley.

chapter 8

# THE SOCIAL CONSEQUENCES OF POPULATION GROWTH

*The Government* [*of India*] *realized that a rapidly growing population in an underdeveloped agrarian country like India is more a hindrance than a help in raising the nation's standard of living, for with a high birth rate every increase in national effort was being used up to maintain the existing low standard of living.*

S. Chandresekhar, Indian demographer (1967)

*If population growth is not stabilized, all our efforts in health and welfare will go for naught.*

Dr. Roger Egeberg, Assistant Secretary of Health, Education and Welfare (1969)

The social aspect of human group life involves the ways in which people interact in work, play, and daily living. Human groups and societies differ in what they contribute to the survival and enrichment of the lives of their members.

"Social" considerations, in the sense of human behavior or attitudes that are directed toward or influenced by other people, are in some way central to all of the chapters of this book. The fact that some of the major factors under discussion (especially in the economic, social, cultural, and political questions) overlap follows from the basic unity of the social sciences. A separation of areas occurs as we learn more details of any subject. Yet a periodic attempt to bring the areas back together is necessary in order to maintain a sense of perspective and to summarize for the beginning student the specialized knowledge of each particular field.

In this chapter we will examine the aspects of population growth that have to do with the interaction and welfare of the members of a society. In this sense, of course, economic development, cultural attitudes, and political organization also have something to do with the welfare of the group. We will include here, however, mainly those aspects that might be broadly construed as related to the psychological and physical health and the general social welfare of the members of a society. The per capita standard of living is one indicator of society-wide levels of social welfare, but nowhere is wealth distributed equally throughout a society's population. We will examine the proportional distribution of wealth *within* societies to gain an understanding of the relative affluence and poverty within specified countries.

Specific aspects of social welfare—including the ability of the social group to provide health and medical care for the young and elderly, to provide housing, and to furnish means of travel—will be compared across nations. The general differences between the developed and less developed nations will be highlighted. Because of its profound effect on the knowledge and belief systems of social groups, education will be considered in the following chapter.

## *SOCIAL INTERACTION AND ORGANIZATION IN RELATION TO POPULATION SIZE*

We have already seen that population growth affects not only the likelihood of human contact, but also the quality of interaction. A number of changes in social interaction and social organization occur as the size of any group increases (see Mott, 1965, for a list of related propositions).

As population size increases, a smaller proportion of all contacts consists of primary relationships. The larger the social group, the more formalized the relationships and the norms of interaction. The larger the city, the less likely we are to care *who* drives the bus, serves the lunch, rings up a sale, runs the elevator, and so forth, as long as the service is within the expected form. Yet it is the primary relationship, in which people are valued for themselves and not just for the services they perform, that makes for satisfaction in living.

There are a number of indications that the more potential contacts a person has, the more superficial they become. The United States census reports indicate a far greater proportion of individuals living by themselves in large cities, rather than in small cities. While residential pattern is only one indication, people actually are likely to have fewer primary relationships in large cities than in rural areas or small communities. As Konrad Lorenz (1966), writing *On Aggression*, states:

> It is definitely detrimental to the bond of friendship if a person has too many friends. It is proverbial that one can have only a few really close friends. To have a large number of "acquaintances," many of whom may be faithful allies with legitimate claim to be regarded as real friends, overtaxes a man's capacity for personal love and dilutes the intensity of his emotional attachment. The close crowding of many individuals in a small space brings about a fatigue of all social reactions. Every inhabitant of a modern city is familiar with the surfeit of social relationships and responsibilities and knows the disturbing feeling of not being as pleased as he ought to be at the visit of a friend, even if he is genuinely fond of him and has not seen him for a long time. A tendency to bad temper is experienced when the telephone rings after dinner. That crowding increases the propensity to aggressive behavior has long been known and demonstrated experimentally by sociological research. . . . The increase in number of individuals belonging to the same community is in itself sufficient to upset the balance between the personal bonds and the aggressive drive (p. 244).

Not only does crowding increase aggressive behavior, directly, but visible cultural differences, which are more likely to increase as population grows, also offer ready targets for aggression.

To prevent or minimize the potential conflicts, social organization develops increasingly complex rules of conduct, levels of hierarchy, separation of hierarchies (that is, political, religious, educational, business), avoidance rituals, and so forth.

With reduced interaction (and more formalization) between hierachical levels, with occupational specialization, and with increasing opportunities for deviant or different life styles, people may find it more difficult to identify with all of their fellow citizens.

Social tensions and emotionalism may *actually* be at continual high levels (as suggested by D. O. Hebb, 1968, and Konrad Lorenz, 1966) with only the organization of self-controls and societal curbs to limit our capacity for violence. We see the underlying tensions *expressed* only when some event, often insignificant in itself, triggers an unorganizd aggregate to mob violence.

The size of a population thus influences the organization of human group life in many ways. It is also important to consider the rate of increase. The higher the rate of population increase, the less time available for all of the many adjustments required with increasing size. The slower the rate of increase, the more capable the community or organization or whole society may be to deal with the resultant problems.

## *STANDARDS OF LIVING*

While population increase clearly affects social organization, the level of social organization also influences the capacity of a social group to provide for the existence of more persons. The organization of health and medical services, for example, has a most profound impact on the numbers of persons who survive various diseases and to what age they live. The improvement of world wide public health and medicine has, in fact, allowed so many persons to survive that the world is now faced with a population explosion.

In one of the few serious attempts to convert the factors that determine population size into a theoretically solvable equation, Ed Ackerman (1959, p. 622) produced the following equation:

$$P = \frac{RQ\ (TAS_t) + E_s + T_r \mp F - W}{S}$$

The symbols have the following meanings:

$P$ —number of people
$S$ —standard of living
$R$ —amount of resources
$Q$ —factor for natural quality of resources
$T$ —physical technology factor
$A$ —administrative techniques factor
$S_t$ —resource stability factor
$E_s$—scale economies element (size of territory, and so forth)
$T_r$—resources added in trade
$W$—frugality element (wastage or intensity of use)
$F$ —institutional advantage and "friction" loss element consequent upon institutional characteristics of society

Although it is not possible to attach precise mathematical values to each of the elements, the equation is a valuable way to examine the interrelationships of the factors. Elements $A$, $E_s$, $F$, and $W$ involve organizational aspects of the society. Ackerman is interested in solving the equation for $P$, the number of people who can be supported by a social unit at a given standard of living.

It would be equally useful to solve the equation for $S$, the standard of living. In this case, all of the other factors—resources and their quality, technology and organization, resource stability, scale and trade advantages, and institutional factors less wastage—become divisible by the numbers of people:

$$S = \frac{RQ\,(TAS_t) + E_s + T_r \pm F - W}{P}$$

The formula now indicates that whatever the advantages or disadvantages of a specific social group, division among larger numbers of persons makes for a lower standard of living for all. (The only exception would be a society where a decline in population would also mean a drastic lowering of the economies of scale, $E_s$.)

Although there are many readily available indicators of standards of living, there is no single measure with which to compare all the various nations of the world. It does appear, however, that whatever indicators are used, the developed countries' standards of living appear to be higher than those of less developed countries. While per capita space may be greater in Africa than in the more densely settled European nations, recreational development per person on the space available is undoubtedly farther along in Europe. Facilities for travel and recreational pursuits will be examined among other more obvious indicators of standards of living. Health and medical care, social welfare, and housing and recreational opportunities will be examined in turn.

### *Health and Medical Standards*

Although the death rates for most of the nations of the world have declined very dramatically in recent years, there is still a great deal of room for improvement.

The infant mortality rate is probably the best indicator of overall health and medical standards. Wherever infant mortality is high, it is likely that the nutritional standards of the adult population are inadequate; that public health, sanitation, and disease control are poorly developed; and that the proportion of medical personnel to total population is very low.

The number of deaths within the first year of life for each 1,000 births is estimated to vary from about 13 in Norway and Sweden to 259 in Zambia. In the past it was expected that about one child in every four or five would die before it reached one year of age. It is rare for infant mortality to be that high now (see Table 8-1). In addition, the higher the rate of death within the first year of life, the higher it is likely to be within the first ten years of life as well. Thus the average age of death in India in the nineteenth century was about 20 years of age, not because most of the population died at that age, but because most deaths occurred before age 10, and a smaller proportion occurred in the later age groups.

If the European average of about 20 infant deaths per 1,000 births is taken as a health goal, the less developed nations have a long way to go to attain that low level. As infant mortality continues to decline, population growth will be further inflated. Yet there is a general conviction that infant deaths must be brought under control before the control of births will become more acceptable. The nutritional standards of the less developed nations would need to be raised in order for prospective mothers to provide improved fetal environment. Even in the advanced countries, prenatal care by medical doctors and health workers has a direct effect on lowered infant mortality, as well as on fetal mortality.

The number of physicians in relation to the total population may be taken as another measure of the adequacy of medical care. Although the training and proficiency of medical doctors varies among the nations of the world, the numbers still give some idea of the ability of the society to attend to the needs of the population. Table 8-1 lists the number of inhabitants per physician in a number of countries. (Data are not available for all countries of the world.) The range is again very wide, with over 68 thousand persons for each medical doctor in Ethiopia and only 410 persons per physician in Israel. The most advantaged countries are most adequately supplied, but the United States is not in its usual favored position. There is some evidence that because the "baby boom" was most pronounced in the United States, our population growth has been more rapid than the increase in medical doctors.

Other nations have complained that the so-called "brain drain" has been most pronounced in the medical field. While the United States has allowed the immigration of physicians from England, the British have been accepting those from India and Pakistan, which countries, with seven times as many persons per physician, can hardly afford to lose their few trained doctors. In 1967 physicians, surgeons, and dentists made up about 1 percent of the total immigration to the United State. The number, 3,557 (Population Reference Bureau, 1969), means less than does the *proportion.* Among the immigrants there are 99 persons per doctor. Not even Israel has so favorable a population per doctor ratio. Even if we assume that one-fourth of these are dentists, which might be a typical proportion, the United States gains from the movement of these highly medical personnel. Other countries have invested a great deal in their education and training, and many need them even more than the United States does.

Although we have witnessed an unprecedented decline in death rates, physicians are not miracle workers, they are human beings who are still learning about many of the afflictions of the human system. They are limited in numbers and especially scarce in the less developed countries. In those areas, public health administrators with mass campaigns, vaccines, and residual insecticides have served large areas well. Yet Dr. M. G. Candau, Director-General of the World Health Organization, points out

*TABLE 8-1 The Number of Inhabitants per Physician and Infant Death Rates (deaths per 1,000 births)*

| *Country* | *Date* | *Inhabitants per Physician* | *Infant Death Rates (latest year)* |
|---|---|---|---|
| Less Developed Countries | | | |
| Ethiopia | 1965 | 68,520 | (unknown) |
| Nigeria | 1965 | 44,230 | (unknown) |
| Viet Nam, Rep. | 1965 | 37,430 | (unknown) |
| Congo, Dem. Rep. | 1965 | 31,250 | (unknown) |
| Indonesia | 1967 | 28,000 | 125 |
| Angola | 1965 | 13,140 | (unknown) |
| Congo | 1965 | 11,640 | 104 |
| Zambia | 1968 | 11,500 | 259 |
| Algeria | 1965 | 8,950 | (unknown) |
| India | 1965 | 5,780 | 139 |
| Pakistan | 1967 | 5,620 | 142 |
| Syria | 1965 | 5,110 | (unknown) |
| Guatemala | 1969 | 4,030 | 89 |
| Brazil | 1966 | 2,160 | 170 |
| U.A.R. (Egypt) | 1968 | 2,080 | 117 |
| Mexico | 1968 | 1,850 | 64 |
| Paraguay | 1965 | 1,850 | 52 |
| South Africa | 1967 | 1,500 | (unknown) |
| Chile | 1968 | 1,380 | 100 |
| Venezuela | 1968 | 1,120 | 46 |
| Argentina | 1968 | 520 | 58 |
| More Developed Countries | | | |
| Ireland | 1966 | 960 | 24.4 |
| Japan | 1967 | 920 | 15 |
| France | 1965 | 900 | 20.4 |
| Sweden | 1967 | 850 | 12.9 |
| Great Britain | 1965 | 830 | 18.8 |
| Spain | 1968 | 760 | 32.0 |
| United States | 1965 | 670 | 21.2 |
| Belguim | 1967 | 660 | 22.9 |
| Austria | 1965 | 550 | 25.5 |
| Hungary | 1968 | 520 | 35.8 |
| Israel | 1965 | 410 | 26 |

*Sources:* 1965 figures from United Nations Economic and Social Council, *Demographic Yearbook, 1966* (1967), Table 201; 1966–1969 figures from United Nations, *World Health Organization, 1969 Report* (1970).

that nearly 380 million human beings in the malarious areas of the world are still without the protection of eradication schemes. There are probably even now around ten million sufferers from leprosy, and more than 4.5 million from yaws. There are possibly 400 million who suffer from trachoma, 200 million from bilharziasis (a debilitating intestinal disease), and 20 million from onchocerciasis (a parasitic disease that sometimes causes blindness). It is estimated that in certain countries bilharziasis affects 30–40 percent of the population at one time or another in their lives. Even more astonishing to those who take their own advantages for granted are estimates that about 70 percent of the *world's* population lacks an adequate and safe water supply and 85 percent has to depend on the most primitive methods for the disposal of excreta and refuse (United Nations, 1963). All of these problems would be within the realm of health and medical control if only there were adequate numbers of medical workers and auxiliary services.

The variation in availability of other medical personnel and facilities is not much different than that of doctors. Since the number of inhabitants per physician shows such wide discrepancy from one nation to another, one would hope that a part of the gap might be made up by additional nurses or auxiliary medical personnel.

The data for Latin America are discouraging on this count, however. It would appear that nations that are deficient in physicians are likely to lack adequate numbers of nurses, auxiliary personnel, and dentists as well. Figure 8-1 shows that North America, with a high ratio of physicians to

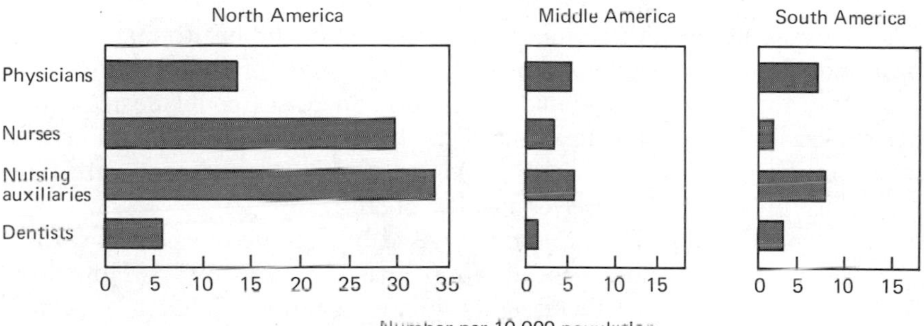


*Source:* Abraham Horwitz and Mary H. Burke, "Health, Population, and Development," in *Population Dilemma in Latin America*, Mayone Stycos and Jorge Arias, eds., The American Assembly, Columbia University. Washington, D. C.: Potomac Books, 1966, p. 181.

FIG. 8–1 *Number of Physicians, Nurses, Nursing Auxiliaries, and Dentists per 10,000 Population in the Three Regions of the Americas, 1962*

population, has an even higher ratio of nurses and nursing auxiliaries than either Middle or South America. The ratio of dentists to population is two to seven times more advantageous in North than in Middle or South America.

The universities of Latin America are graduating just enough dentists each year to maintain the present ratios. Improvements in the proportion of dentists per 10,000 population are unlikely as long as population growth continues as at present.

Although the number of medical schools in Latin America has doubled in the last 20 years, population growth is likely to keep pace with the numbers of medical graduates. Current ratios will be maintained, but improvements in the physicians per population ratio are unlikely through 1980 (Horwitz and Burke, 1966).

It was reported at the population and development conference in Caracas, Venezuela, in 1967, that little if any progress had been made in health care since 1960 in Latin America. Although 1,700 new hospitals were built between 1960 and 1964, the 1960 ratio of 3.2 hospital beds per 1,000 population was barely maintained. Population growth had nullified any per capita advantage that might have accrued from the new construction. Dr. Jorge Eliecer Ruiz of Bogota, commented that:

> No proponent of public health can deny that, although there has been a vertical drop in mortality, at the same time the infant mortality rate has remained constant, abortion is still the most frequent cause of maternal death, and the general condition of the population is little more than subhuman (quoted in Cerda, 1968, p. 9).

Because of the long training time required in the health and medical professions and only slightly shorter time required for hospital construction and sanitary facilities, rapid population increases could decrease the current level of services in health and medicine. One proposal is to certify less competent medical personnel. Many people may approve of that possibility until they themselves need a doctor.

One of the most basic questions raised by any examination of health and welfare concerns how a social group cares for its members. How does the group or society distribute rights and obligations? What is expected in the way of contributions? And how are the dependent persons defined and cared for? We cannot answer all of these questions, but we will investigate broad national differences in youth and aged dependency and in absolute and relative inequality.

### *Welfare and Dependency*

Population specialists have developed dependency ratios to facilitate international comparisons. *Youth dependency* is defined by the United Nations as the ratio of those aged 0 through 14 per hundred persons aged 15 through 59. The *aged dependency* ratio is found by dividing the number of persons aged 60 or more by those aged 15 through 59 and multiplying by 100. The *total dependency* ratio is simply the sum of youth and aged dependency. (Alternative cut-off points used by some authors are 20 and 65.) The youth dependency ratio compares persons in a 15-year age range

(0–14) to those in a 45-year age range (15–59). A ratio of 100 would indicate equal numbers of people in the two categories.

The dependency ratios of some of the countries of the world whose data allowed the computations are presented in Table 8-2. The very high

TABLE 8-2 *The Dependency Ratios of Selected Countries Presented in Descending Order of Magnitude of Their Total Dependency Ratios: Latest Data Available*

| *Country* | *Year* | *Dependency Ratio* Youth | Aged | Total |
|---|---|---|---|---|
| (1) Iraq | 1957 | 94 | 15 | 109 |
| (2) Mexico | 1966 | 95 | 11 | 106 |
| (3) Philippines | 1966 | 95 | 8 | 103 |
| (4) Pakistan | 1961 | 90 | 12 | 102 |
| (5) Kenya | 1962 | 89 | 9 | 98 |
| (6) UAR | 1960 | 84 | 12 | 96 |
| (7) Brazil | 1960 | 81 | 6 | 87 |
| (8) India | 1961 | 77 | 11 | 88 |
| (9) South Africa | 1960 | 74 | 11 | 85 |
| (10) Israel | 1965 | 62 | 17 | 79 |
| (11) United States | 1966 | 54 | 24 | 78 |
| (12) France | 1965 | 43 | 31 | 74 |
| (13) Poland | 1965 | 54 | 19 | 73 |
| (14) USSR | 1961 | 55 | 17 | 72 |
| (15) Australia | 1965 | 51 | 21 | 72 |
| (16) United Kingdom | 1966 | 39 | 30 | 69 |
| (17) Czechoslovakia | 1964 | 43 | 25 | 68 |
| (18) West Germany | 1964 | 38 | 29 | 67 |
| (19) Argentina | 1965 | 50 | 16 | 66 |
| (20) Italy | 1964 | 39 | 23 | 62 |
| (21) Hungary | 1965 | 38 | 24 | 62 |
| (22) Japan | 1966 | 38 | 15 | 53 |

*Source:* Computations from data in United Nations Economic and Social Council, *Demographic Yearbook, 1966* (1967).

ratios of young in the less developed countries have already been discussed. All of the countries listed with very high youth dependency ratios are poor countries. Not only do they have extremely high ratios of youth dependency—70–95 young persons for every 100 in the productive years—but also half of those in the productive years—the women—are less likely to be in the labor force than are women in the more advanced nations. In many of the least developed countries then, only about one person in four is economically productive: one worker must support four persons. Iraq, for instance, has almost as many youth as it does persons in the productive years. Yet only about half of the persons aged 15–59 are economically active in that country. The less industrialized the country, the more difficult it would be for one person's work to provide for the bare survival of three or four people. The dependency ratios imply some of the problems nations face in caring for the most clearly dependent segments of their population. It is interesting that Japan, the country with the *lowest* total dependency ratio, has been increasing total and per capita national production more rapidly than any other nation.

The aged dependency ratios of the less developed countries are low, mainly because of the very high birth rates and the consequent concentration of the population in the lower age groups. Aged dependency ratios vary between 6 and 10 for the less developed nations. In these countries the elderly typically are cared for by their own offspring. In rural settings, they may be able to contribute some small labor. If even the younger members of the work force suffer from malnutrition and lack of energy, however, the contributions of the elderly cannot be very great.

The more developed countries have both lower youth dependency ratios and higher aged dependency ratios. Although youth dependency is often only half as great in the developed as in the underdeveloped nations, their expenditures for education and training of the young is very much greater.

Aged dependency ratios are about three times higher in the developed than in the less developed nations. The aged are not so often as completely dependent as are children and they may continue to contribute to the society during some of their aged years. However, Kingsley Davis (1960) indicates that approximately 35 percent of American men aged 65 or more are either in institutions or are ill or disabled. He suggests that one of the most vital questions facing industrialized civilization is whether the prolonging of life to ever more advanced ages will be an extension of senility or an extension of vigor (p. 15). Medical care is undoubtedly far more costly for the elderly than for any other age group. As the capacity to prolong life is maximized, the costs of the medical care required to achieve that goal rise rapidly. No one suggests that heart transplants are practical for the population in general, but where does one draw the line on extending the excellence (and the cost) of medical marvels to all? Longer life is one goal, but good health and vitality are also desired by all. Particularly because the care of the elderly in industrial societies has been transferred from the offspring to the society, and because the proportions of elderly are likely to increase, some innovations in care are badly needed. Furthermore, those who are healthy will want useful and enjoyable things to do.

The range of total dependency ratios is much smaller than that for either youth or aged dependency ratios. Nonetheless, even though the higher aged dependency ratios of the industrialized countries partly balance the high youth dependency of the underdeveloped countries, the total dependency ratio remains considerably higher in the nations least able to afford the burdens. How do various societies handle these burdens? The age ratios mean different things in different parts of the world. In the United States the dependency of the young is actually extended far beyond the fourteenth year of life. A large proportion of the U.S. youth are dependent upon partial or full support by their parents or the society through college and even long years of graduate school.[1] In fact, demographers extend the age of youth dependency through 19 when considering the United States alone. Such elongation of dependency may mean that a more valuable contribution will be made to the social group in future years, but it does add to the immediate burden on the society. In some of the less developed countries, by way of contrast, participation in the labor force may extend down to the five- to nine-year-old group. When visiting Egypt, I watched boys no older than my eleven-year-old son carrying large baskets of rocks on their backs. Interestingly enough, huge road graders were being used on the same construction project. The juxtaposition of the old and new methods can undoubtedly be seen in many countries working toward a transition to industrialization. The young probably are needed in the labor force, but they also desperately need schooling to enable them to help the society develop.

While the aged dependency ratios may remain near their current levels, the numbers of aged will probably increase in all countries. Rich and poor nations need to concern themselves with the welfare of this group. What may be adequate social security at one point in time becomes insignificant in another. Most of the less developed nations have very little in the way of public welfare programs. One proposal is to initiate pensions for the aged who have two or fewer children to care for them, thereby removing the "old-age security" reason for producing many children.

### *Poverty*

It is difficult to discuss poverty in and of itself, since its effects are found in other factors under discussion—low incomes, inadequate medical care, inadequate housing, and low education and literacy.

In the less developed countries absolute poverty predominates throughout the entire population, with the exclusion of the very well educated or the very wealthy. It is most apparent in low nutritional levels, in high infant mortality rates, in crowded housing, and in low levels of education and high illiteracy.

[1] The costs of education increase as the level of education rises. Yearly costs of graduate training at the university level approximate $3,000. Tuitions normally cover only a small part of the costs, and other sources of funds (tax revenues, alumni contributions, etc.) must provide for the additional needs.

There is no doubt that poverty in the less developed countries would have been somewhat relieved in recent years if population growth had not been so rapid. Yet poverty has been the human condition throughout history. Substantive poverty may be taken for granted when most of a population is poor. Individuals need to realize that something better is possible if they are to organize their lives so that something better does follow. On the other hand, whole nations do not change from traditional agricultural societies into modern industrial societies overnight. The very great advances of recent years have not been transferred into equivalent per capita advance because the rapid population growth has absorbed so much of the gain. Annual average percentage gains in total and per capita GNP for 1960 to 1966 for a few representative countries are listed in Table 8-3.

The increases for individual countries and for the less developed countries as a group would have been substantial without the simultaneous increase in population. The most rapidly developing countries economically—South Korea, Taiwan, Iran, Syria, and Thailand—would have approximately doubled their real gross domestic product in only ten years at these rates. However, the national advance cannot be translated into an equal per capita advance as long as rapid population growth continues.

Relative poverty occurs everywhere. Even in those countries which have equality as an ideal, there are vast differences in the proportion of national income received by the educated people, the politicians, or the monetary leaders. In Bulgaria, where the average per capita income in U.S. dollars is equivalent to $690 per year, I talked with a government official who was interested in exchanging income information. His salary was the equivalent of $18,000 per year. The style of life of educated people probably differs less from country to country than does the style of life of the poor, less educated people around the world.

The gap between the proportion of national income received by the lowest 20 percent and that received by the highest 5 percent of income units within each country is greatest in the less developed nations (see Table 8-4).

Income units are far more likely to be single individuals in the lower group than at the upper income levels, so per capita differences would not be quite as great as the variation for family or tax units. Nevertheless, the distribution of income within nations differs greatly. The top 5 percent of income units in the less developed countries typically received one-third to one-half of all income.

These tremendous economic inequalities are indicative of more general social inequalities within the less developed countries. The enormity of the differences can only add to the apathy and despair of the tradition-bound, uneducated masses. A reduction of these inequalities and

TABLE 8-3 *Percentage Increase in Total versus Per Capita Annual Real Gross Domestic Product, 1960–1966 (representative nations)*

| Countries | *Average Annual Percentage Increase* Total | Per Capita |
|---|---|---|
| *Less Developed* | | |
| Africa | | |
| Nigeria (1960–1962) | 4.5 | 2.5 |
| Sudan | 4.5 | 1.6 |
| U.A.R. (1960–1961) | 3.5 | 0.6 |
| Latin America | | |
| Bolivia | 5.4 | 3.9 |
| Brazil | 4.3 | 1.2 |
| Colombia | 4.4 | 1.2 |
| Honduras | 4.6 | 1.2 |
| Mexico | 6.0 | 2.5 |
| Panama | 8.5 | 5.1 |
| Venezuela | 4.5 | 1.0 |
| Asia | | |
| South Korea | 7.5 | 4.6 |
| India | 2.1 | −0.2 |
| Indonesia | 2.9 | 0.5 |
| Iran | 6.4 | 3.4 |
| Syria | 7.0 | 3.8 |
| Thailand | 7.0 | 3.9 |
| *More Developed* | | |
| European | | |
| France | 5.2 | 3.8 |
| Italy | 4.9 | 4.1 |
| Sweden | 5.0 | 4.3 |
| United Kingdom | 2.8 | 2.0 |
| Other | | |
| Japan | 9.8 | 8.7 |
| Canada | 5.7 | 3.7 |
| United States | 5.0 | 3.5 |

*Source:* United Nations, *Statistical Yearbook* 1967. Nortman, Dorothy, Population and Family Planning Programs: a Factbook. New York: The Population Council, July 1970, Tables 4, 5.

an opening of the rigid class and caste systems must occur if the masses are to be motivated to work for the improvement of their own lives. We have already noted that the "laziness" of people in the underdeveloped countries may be due in part to malnutrition. Yet malnutrition can be cured only by increased motivation and effort, together with population limitation.

The more developed the country, the lower the proportions (20–25 percent) of total income received by the upper 5 percent of income units. The difference between what the top 5 percent and lowest 20 percent of income units received was twice as great for Mexico as it was for Great

TABLE 8-4 *Shares of Ordinal Groups of Income Units (families or tax returns) and Concentration Ratios, Selected Countries, Late 1940s and Early 1950s*

| *Country and Year* | *Shares of Ordinal Groups* 0–20% | *Shares of Ordinal Groups* Top 5% | *Top 5% Minus Lowest 20%* | *Concentration Ratio* [1] |
|---|---|---|---|---|
| Southern Rhodesia, 1946 | n.a. | 65.3 | — | 0.62 (1946) |
| Kenya, 1949 | n.a. | 50.9+ (2.9%) | — | 0.41 (1949) |
| Northern Rhodesia, 1946 | n.a. | 45.3+ (1.4%) | — | 0.54 (1946) |
| Columbia, 1953 | n.a. | 41.6 | — | 0.18 (1951) |
| Mexico, 1950 | 6.1 | 40.0 | 33.9 | — |
| Mexico, 1957 | 4.4 | 37.0 | 32.6 | — |
| El Salvador, 1946 | n.a. | 35.5 | — | 0.29 (1950) |
| Guatamela, 1947–48 | n.a. | 34.5 | — | — |
| India, 1950 | 7.8 | 33.4 | 25.6 | 0.21 (1951) |
| India, 1955–56 | n.a. | 23.6 | — | — |
| Ceylon, 1952–53 | 5.1 | 31.0 | 25.9 | 0.14 |
| Netherlands, 1950 | 4.2 | 24.6 | 20.4 | 0.15 (1947) |
| Italy, 1948 | 6.1 | 24.1 | 18.0 | 0.15 (1951) |
| West Germany, 1950 | 4.0 | 23.6 | 19.6 | 0.11 (1959) |
| Puerto Rico, 1953 | 5.6 | 23.4 | 17.8 | 0.31 (1950) |
| Great Britain, 1951–52 | 5.4 | 20.9 | 15.5 | 0.06 (1951) U.K. |
| United States, 1950 | 4.8 | 20.4 | 15.6 | 0.12 (1950) |
| Denmark, 1952 | 3.4 | 20.1 | 16.7 | 0.13 (1955) |
| Sweden, 1948 | 3.2 | 20.1 | 16.9 | — |
| USSR [2] | n.a. | n.a. | — | 0.22 (av. 1950–58) |

[1] The concentration ratio is the ratio of the area between the Lorenz curve (the cumulative income percent to income units) and the curve of complete equality. The ratio ranges from 0 for complete equality to 1.0 for maximum inequality.

[2] Kuznets notes that the measure of inequality increases during the period.

*Source:* Simon Kuznets, Quantitative Aspects of the Economic Growth of Nations: VIII. Distribution of Income by Size. *Economic Development and Cultural Change*, 11, no. 2, Part II (January 1963). Data on shares of ordinal groups are from Table 1; data on concentration ratios are from Appendix, Tables 1 and 5; data on the USSR are from p. 22.

Britain, the United States, Denmark, or Sweden. Kuznets (1963) found the same phenomenon for individual states within the United States: the higher the per capita income in a state, the lower the inequality in distribution.

The top 5 or 10 percent of the income units receive a lower proportion of national income and pay higher taxes in the most developed countries—Denmark, Sweden, the United States, and Great Britain—than do their counterparts in the least developed countries. Unfortunately, not all countries publish data which allow these computations. Kuznets has computed a "concentration ratio" as another indicator of income inequality within nations (see Table 8-4, right-hand column). The concentration ratios indicate again that inequality is greater within the less developed countries. The advanced democracies not only have lower inequality than the less developed countries, but measure more equal income distribution than the Soviet Union, with its ideological commitment to equality. Kuznets has also computed and reported relatively high concentration ratios for the East European Communist Countries (see his Table 6).

In spite of the more equal distribution of income in the advanced industrialized countries, it is quite possible that relative poverty is felt more desperately in the midst of general affluence. Michael Harrington (1963) suggests that the poor are less visible to the majority, and the affluence of the majority is highly visible to the poor in contemporary, mobile, televized societies. Certainly it does no good to compare the impoverished in the United States with the poor of India or Africa.

The largest group of people classified as below the "poverty line" [2] in the United States are the elderly. The second largest group are "fatherless" families. Thus the problem of poverty within the United States may well be related to some aspects of our system that have both advantages and disadvantages. Nathan Glazer (1965) points out that the individualism and freedom from familial controls that are in many ways advantageous also mean that our society has not yet answered the question of whether adults are to be held responsible for their elderly parents. And are adult men to be held responsible for their children? The greater cultural

[2] The definition of the "poverty line" has changed over time and from one researcher to another. Whatever the definition, the groups comprising the lowest income category remain approximately the same. In the 1960 census, 20 percent of the families reported 1959 incomes of less than $3,000. (Unrelated individuals were even more likely to have had low incomes, with half reporting less than $1,000 income in 1959). Part of the problem of classification is that the poor may be elderly, living alone, and unemployed. Classifying families more than once, Miller (1964) reports 31 percent aged, 28 percent with no worker in the family, 24 percent mother and children, 21 percent non-white families with 1959 incomes below $3,000. The proportions have changed very little since 1951 (pp. 76–81).

FIG. 8–2 *Without adequate housing, thousands sleep on the sidewalks of Calcutta. Wide World Photo*

and ethnic uniformity of Sweden, Germany, and England may make it easier to answer such questions. Moreover, local (vs. federal) control, while advantageous in some respects, has allowed states and even counties to determine whether or not they will pass on federal welfare, food, and medical coverage to the poor. It allows some states to give less than $50 and others as much as $500 per month to destitute families. The new Family Assistance Program will enforce a federal minimum based on family size.

It is possible to provide a poverty floor, to be held up by welfare payments, which could by definition eliminate poverty. But the definition of poverty has changed over time, and a minimal support provided by a government does not eliminate relative income differences, even though it would make life less difficult for completely dependent persons.

## *Housing*

Housing needs everywhere have been aggravated by rapid population growth. Housing requirements may be viewed in terms of (1) present deficits, (2) replacement of dilapidated units and shacks made from scrap materials, (3) future needs resulting from population growth, and (4) future needs as a result of urban growth.

Present housing deficits are most apparent in the less developed nations, some of which, Nigeria, Mexico, Pakistan, and the Central African Republic, report averages of three or more persons per room. Even if half the population may be slightly less crowded, the other half lives in even more crowded conditions than the average.

Table 8-5 indicates that the average number of persons per room in India is 2.6 while the more advanced countries have less than one person per room. The data tell us nothing about average room size, but more than likely rooms are smallest where the average number of persons per room is largest. Also, other amenities, such as sanitary facilities, and running water, are usually lacking in the developing countries.

Mexico has made a tremendous effort to provide improved housing for its population. Indeed, between 1950 and 1960 one million units were added. In 1950 dwellings averaged 1.9 rooms per unit. The additional units did not change the average size, but population growth during the ten years was so great that even with a million new units there was an increase in the average number of persons per room and per dwelling!

Replacement of dilapidated units is necessary even in the most advanced nations. The definition of dilapidated will, of course, vary from one country to another. Some people in the United States may be eager to tear down and "renew" urban housing that in some countries might be jealously preserved as landmarks. Nevertheless, some units are so bad that virtually all would agree on the need to be rid of them. "Makeshift" structures of such materials as mud, old boards, straw, scrap metal, and so forth, are "home" for millions of persons around the world. The Calcutta Metropolitan Planning Board (1966) reported that (in 1961) 33.8 percent of the housing units had nonpermanent walls. For the city as a whole there was an average of 4.76 persons per household unit, or 2.99 persons per room. A United Nations report on world housing estimated that over 900 million persons in Africa, Asia, and Latin America are without proper

*TABLE 8-5 Average Number of Persons per Room in Housing, for Specified Countries and Dates*

| Country | Date | Average Density (persons per room) |
|---|---|---|
| Underdeveloped Countries | | |
| Central Africa Republic | 1955–60 | 3.4 |
| Pakistan | 1960 | 3.1 |
| Nigeria | 1961 | 3.0 |
| Mexico | 1960 | 2.9 |
| India | 1960 | 2.6 |
| Ecuador | 1962 | 2.5 |
| Syria | 1961–62 | 2.3 |
| Jamaica | 1960 | 1.9 |
| China (Taiwàn) | 1966 | 1.9 |
| Israel | 1963 | 1.8 |
| U.A.R. (Egypt) | 1960 | 1.6 |
| Argentina | 1960 | 1.4 |
| Brazil | 1960 | 1.3 |
| Puerto Rico | 1960 | 1.1 |
| Developed Countries | | |
| Yugoslavia | 1961 | 1.6 |
| USSR | 1956 | 1.5 |
| Hungary | 1963 | 1.5 |
| Bulgaria | 1965 | 1.2 |
| Germany, East | 1961 | 1.2 |
| Japan | 1962 | 1.2 |
| France | 1962 | 1.0 |
| Austria | 1961 | 0.9 |
| Germany, West | 1960 | 0.9 |
| Sweden | 1965 | 0.8 |
| Australia | 1961 | 0.7 |
| New Zealand | 1961 | 0.7 |
| United States | 1960 | 0.7 |
| Canada | 1961 | 0.7 |
| United Kingdom (England & Wales) | 1966 | 0.6 |

*Source:* United Nations Economic and Social Council, *Statistical Yearbook 1967* (1968), Table 202.

housing (in Cook and Gulhati, 1965, p. 114). Many old, unstable, or "dilapidated" units lack such basic facilities as piped water, sanitary service, and so forth.

### *Future Needs Resulting from Population Growth*

If the world population is to double by the year 2000, housing units equal to all of those presently available would presumably have to be built just to keep up with present inadequate standards. If one allows, as the U.N. estimates do, that the average life of a dwelling unit is from 20 to 30 years, replacement plus new units for the additional population would require that more than twice as many units as are presently available be built within the next 30–35 years. Again there is no allowance for improvement of worldwide housing conditions; those units would be necessary simply to maintain present standards. The rate of construction in the last decade does not offer much hope that the needs of increased numbers of people can be met.

United Nations estimates of annual housing needs in Africa, Asia, and Latin America for the years 1960 and 1975 are reproduced in Table 8-6.

TABLE 8-6 *Estimated Annual Housing Needs in Africa, Asia, and Latin America, 1960 and 1975 (in millions of dwelling units)*

| | *1960* | *1975* | | *1960* | *1975* |
|---|---|---|---|---|---|
| Due to population increase | | | To replace the old stock * | | |
| Africa | 0.84 | 1.50 | Africa | 1.03 | 1.03 |
| Asia | 5.30 | 9.40 | Asia | 7.10 | 7.10 |
| Latin America | 1.10 | 1.70 | Latin America | .90 | .90 |
| To eliminate the present deficit or shortage in 30 years | | | Total new housing needed | | |
| Africa | .73 | .73 | Africa | 2.60 | 3.26 |
| Asia | 4.80 | 4.80 | Asia | 17.20 | 21.30 |
| Latin America | .60 | .60 | Latin America | 2.60 | 3.20 |
| | | | Total | 22.40 | 27.76 |

* Average life of dwelling unit is assumed to be 30 years in urban and 20 years in rural areas. In 1975 figures do not take into account increments of stock between 1960 and 1975.

*Source:* Robert C. Cook and Kaval Gulhati, Housing and Population Growth in Africa, Asia, and Latin America, in *The Population Crisis,* ed. Larry K. Y. Ng and Stuart Mudd, Bloomington, Ind.: Indiana University Press, p. 23.

By 1975, almost 28 million units *per year* would be needed. Population increase alone would contribute over 45 percent of that need.

### *Future Needs Resulting from Urban Growth*

Metropolitan areas of every size have been increasing in population at an even faster rate than have nations. In the less developed countries urban populations are growing at rates twice as high as those for overall population. In 1960, 275 million Africans, Asians, and Latin Americans

FIG. 8–3 *With the press of urban populations even relatively expensive housing may lack individuality. These are $35,000 homes in Daly City, one of the many suburbs south of San Francisco. Photo by Robert A. Isaacs*

were living in cities of over 100,000 people. By 1975, only 15 years later, the number is expected to be twice as great.

While housing in rural areas may present some problems, land is cheaper than in cities, shelters are often constructed of local materials, and the movement to urban areas reduces the relative pressures of housing in agricultural areas.

Rural migrants tend to move to the largest urban centers, frequently with short stays in moderately sized cities on the way. Most of these new urban residents lack money to rent, much less buy, a place to live. In their 1967 Report on the World Social Situation, the United Nations Department of Economic and Social Affairs (1969) states that:

> An increasing proportion of urban development is uncontrolled: squatting, illicit subdivision, unapproved buildings—very often on steep slopes, in ravines and in flood plains. . . .
>
> Rapid growth, high population density, and uncontrolled development, reflecting a lack of resources on the one hand and an ineffective urbanization strategy on the other, pose enormous hurdles of future development. The costs may well be several times that of development on new land and involve the loss of many years of investment by the people, as well as a serious social dislocation through demolition and relocation (p. 46).

To illustrate the way in which urban growth aggravates already severe housing shortages, Cook and Gulhati (1965) report:

> The population of Bombay grew by almost 70 percent during 1950–60. About one-half of the population lives in substandard housing and a large number live on footpaths. Bombay's slums contain over half a million persons living in 9,000 dilapidated units. Another million live in 200,000 single-room tenements scattered over the city. In some cases, 7 to 10 persons consisting of 2 or 3 families share 1 room. . . .
>
> By 1960 Rio de Janerio's population had added nearly 1 million people to the 1950 total of 3 million. In 1950, Rio's slums, known as "favelas," contained about 14.3 percent of the population. A 1948 survey showed that two-thirds of the "houses" were worth less than $108. Three-fourths had no toilets and about 90 percent had no piped water.
>
> The population of the federal district surrounding Mexico City grew by 160 percent between 1940 and 1950. The city proper grew by 53 percent during the same period.
>
> A citywide housing survey in 1952 showed that 34 percent of the population lived in "turgurios"—one-room apartments opening on a courtyard or passageway. Another 11 percent were living in rented "jacales"—shacks made from scrap materials. The jacales had about 34 persons per toilet but most of the toilets were out of order and the jacale dwellers used the waste land around their shacks (pp. 121–22).

Can there be any doubt that continued population growth under these circumstances simply increases the misery of all?

In Buenaventura, Colombia, Octavio Cabello (1966) estimated that 80 percent of the population live in slums. In Chile, the people who occupy tenements, shacks, and housing of this nature increased from 10 percent of the population in 1952 to 14 percent in 1960. In Peruvian cities the proportion is even higher, reaching a maximum of 70 percent in Chimbote and 40 percent in Arequipa.

Abraham Horwitz and Mary H. Burke (1966) have produced a nation by nation count of housing deficits in Latin America and of housing units required annually to meet population growth and replacement needs. They compared these deficits and future needs to current annual construction in each of the nations. Overall construction is running about 30 percent of requirements, which means that about 70 percent of yearly needs are unmet and that the deficits are growing greater each year. Although there is wide variation from one nation to another, in no case does annual construction reach more than two-thirds of annual requirements.

For the world as a whole housing output has steadily lagged behind needs during the most recent, the so-called "Development Decade" (1960–1970). The United Nations (1969) reports that:

> The estimated requirement of ten new dwelling units per 1,000 inhabitants per year has been met only in a few industrialized countries. In many of the developing countries it has not been higher than two or three units per 1,000 inhabitants.
>
> Problems of financing for housing and community facilities continue to be a major source of concern in both the industrialized and the developing countries. Even though there has been an over-all increase in the flow of external capital for housing and urban development over the past five-year period, it is recognized that the overwhelming bulk of resources required in the developing countries must come from internal sources (p. 49).

The few outstanding examples of successful projects, such as those at Piura in northern Peru, Lima, and Panama City, demonstrate that low-cost but sanitary housing can be provided; but nowhere is construction in the less developed countries adequate to meet increasing needs. Much of the physical planning and construction which does occur is uncoordinated with regional and national planning. "Perhaps the greatest single bottleneck to progress in urban development in the developing countries is the lack of trained planners, especially those at the highest level. The number of planning schools is inadequate, and their enrollments very small" (United Nations Department of Economic and Social Affairs, 1969, p. 49). The construction industries of the less developed countries also lack persons educated for middle level jobs; draftsmen, technicians, foremen and building craftsmen.

### *Travel, Recreation, Transportation, and Communication Facilities*

Travel is no longer limited to the affluent minority of the world's population. In all of the advanced countries even semiskilled workingmen and their families have the time and the money to travel. Nine or ten months of the year, the highways of the United States are crowded with cars and trailers. In fact, camping and house-trailer units of all kinds comprised one of the fastest growing segments of the U.S. construction and sales industries in the sixties.

Piddington (1956) suggests that "travel is a universal passion that grips like a drug, and demands satisfaction even by borrowing or stealing" (p. 71). Indeed, he indicates that some eight million persons travelled on the Indian State Railways in 1953 without paying their fare. For the most part, poor farmers travel only to see relatives or on important business, but all other classes conceive of holiday travel for pleasure. It is not easy to imagine *billions* of people on the move for two weeks each year, but most of us have experienced the seasonal crowding and increased prices of accommodations in the most desirable vacation spots.

The shortage of hotel rooms and the higher "in-season" costs are annoying, but even if people were to carry their pads on their backs, the crowding would hardly be relieved. Many people travel in order to see the interesting cities of the world, most of which are already overcrowded without tourists. There is only one Tower of London, but when tourists fill the inner walls, it is difficult for any of them to appreciate the experience. There is only one Sistine Chapel and it is very large as chapels go. But even if the visitor lines up well before opening time he can barely move about when he finally arrives inside. Later in the day, the noisy crowds distract one's attention from the magnificence of Michelangelo's masterpiece.

> In Paris, where tourist traffic increased 20 percent from 1953 to 1954, a day's record of 14,069 admissions was set up at the Eiffel Tower on April 19. Clearly the limits of capacity are being reached. What is the solution? Imagination boggles at the thought of two Eiffel Towers in Paris, but that monstrous feat could just be achieved. Two Royal Mints for London, two Windsor Castles for Windsor, two Vaticans for Rome, and two Stratfords for Stratford-on-Avon are not, however, within the power of even the Atomic Age to supply (Piddington, 1956, p. 73).

In spite of the crowds and the difficulty of serving their needs, most communities and nations appeal to the tourist trade. There are important economic benefits to the areas visited and many communities and nations are now competing to attract the tourist and his money. Former President Johnson expressed concern that the eagerness with which Americans spent dollars abroad had contributed to U.S. monetary exchange problems in the 1960's. One of the principal reasons behind the "Discover America" program has been to keep more American travel dollars at home (Lee, 1968, p. 53). England has established strict limitations on the money its citizens are allowed to spend abroad.

The growth of international travel in terms of numbers of persons and millions of dollars spent may be seen in Table 8-7. Estimates for 1966 show five times as many international travelers as in 1950. The dollars spent multiplied by six over the same period of time. The greatest gains in tourist receipts were in the Near and Middle East and Asia and Australia, regions which had been lowest in 1950 receipts. Europe has maintained its leads in numbers of tourists crossing national borders and in total tourist receipts.

Travel has far more than economic significance, however. One hopes that travel will increase understanding among human beings with various styles of life. The ability of all human beings to share in the great art, archi-

TABLE 8-7 *The Growth of International Travel, for Major Regions of the World, at Specific Dates*

| *Region* | *Tourist Arrivals (thousands of persons)* | | | | *Tourist Receipts (millions of $)* | | | | *Times* |
|---|---|---|---|---|---|---|---|---|---|
| | *1950* | *1963* | *1965* | *1966 ** | *1950* | *1963* | *1965* | *1966 ** | *Increased* |
| Europe | 16,839 | 66,163 | 85,933 | 95,500 | 890 | 5,437 | 7,249 | 8,120 | 9 |
| North America | 6,180 | 16,449 | 19,394 | 20,750 | 668 | 1,483 | 1,903 | 2,130 | 3 |
| Near and Middle East | 197 | 2,090 | 2,835 | 3,290 | 26 | 164 | 197 | 340 | 13 |
| Latin America and the Caribbean | 1,305 | 3,247 | 3,579 | 4,150 | 392 | 1,253 | 1,265 | 1,502 | 4 |
| Africa | 523 | 1,299 | 2,083 | 2,250 | 88 | 225 | 296 | 325 | 4 |
| Asia and Australia | 237 | 1,616 | 1,829 | 2,050 | 36 | — | 524 | 580 | 16 |
| Total | 25,281 | 90,864 | 115,893 | 127,990 | 2,100 | 9,051 | 11,634 | 12,997 | 6 |

* IUOTO (International Union of Official Travel Organizations) estimates.

*Source:* Ronald F. Lee, *Public Use of the National Park System 1872–2000*. Washington, D.C.: National Park Service, U.S. Department of Interior, 1968, p. 53.

tectural, and natural beauties of the world is one part of the increasing quality of human life. Furthermore, the more crowded cities become, the more important that people have opportunities to get out of that congestion to a place of calm. The exodus from urban centers on weekends and vacation times is taken for granted in most advanced countries. It implies greater mobility and the desire to escape the urban pressures for rest and recreation.

FIG. 8–4 *A Weekend at the Beach. Photo by Bill Eppridge, LIFE Magazine, © Time, Inc., 1971.*

Most nations have some locations that are prized as "naturally" beautiful. Often the rush of tourists to see these areas has resulted in hastily constructed gaudy buildings to house, feed, and sell to the tourist trade. National and state parks often restrict the uses to which areas will be put. Nevertheless, the simple multiplication of tourists can cause the gradual ruin of the very qualities each visitor hopes to enjoy. (See any conservationist publication on the garbage left on hiking trails.)

Not all countries are as fortunate as the United States in the amount of space available and the protection given to natural, historical, and recreation areas. Recent visitors to some of these areas are, however, as awed by the crowds as by the sights themselves. Traffic jams have become such a problem on the floor of Yosemite Valley that cars have been banned from portions of that area. Some idea of the multiplication of use of the national parks within the U.S. is indicated in Table 8-8. Throughout the

*TABLE 8-8 The Increase in the Numbers of Visitors to the National Parks of the United States, at Specific Dates*

| | *Actual 1950* | *Actual 1960* | *Estimated 1967* | *Projection 1976* |
|---|---|---|---|---|
| Natural Areas | | | | |
| Yosemite | 821,000 | 1,150,400 | 2,091,000 | 3,010,000 |
| Yellowstone | 1,110,500 | 1,443,300 | 2,283,000 | 3,281,000 |
| Great Smokies | 1,843,600 | 4,528,600 | 7,263,000 | 9,934,000 |
| Historical Areas | | | | |
| Independence (1951) | 769,200 | 1,595,000 | 2,960,000 | 4,888,000 |
| Lincoln Memorial | 2,065,600 | 2,488,200 | 4,884,000 | 8,103,000 |
| Gettysburg | 656,000 | 1,336,000 | 4,562,000 | 10,392,000 |
| Recreation Areas | | | | |
| Blue Ridge | 1,996,400 | 5,503,200 | 8,638,000 | 12,527,000 |
| Lake Mead | 1,798,300 | 2,254,200 | 3,843,000 | 4,953,000 |
| Cape Hatteras (1955) | 264,500 | 467,300 | 1,179,000 | 1,594,000 |

*Source:* Lee (1968), p. 63.

park system, traffic is expected to be ten times greater in 1976 than it was in 1950. Increasing affluence plus the increase in population could lead to astronomical figures in the future.

Travel implies a means of transportation. There are only three possibilities—one may move by land, by sea, or by air. All become increasingly complicated as the number of people who travel increases.

In 1970 the United States already had one mile of paved road for every square mile of land. There is one automobile for every two and one half persons. It is difficult to imagine that the peoples of other nations will want to meet U.S. standards, and some countries simply do not have the space to supply a comparable system of roadways. Yet the increasing numbers of cars in European countries and Japan will require increases in the valuable land which must be given over to concrete and asphalt. Systems of public transport, while more practical in many ways, hold little appeal where automobiles are available.

Sea transport is too slow to attract most international travelers. The seas have the capacity to greatly expand their share of transport and will continue to increase with the expansion of foreign trade. However, the traveler is more likely to continue to choose the use of the airplane.

Air travel is much faster and less expensive than travel by sea. Reduced tourist fares have allowed more persons to move greater distances. The increasing demand for air travel, however, also requires large areas of land for airports. Since the demand is for flights that start and terminate near the great urban centers of the world, land for airports is expensive and often difficult to obtain. Airfields may ultimately prove to be a more insatiable earth-grabber than railways or highways. France has been planning ahead for 756 airports (Piddington, 1956, p. 85). Since airports are also very expensive to construct, one would suppose that the nations of the world will be hard-pressed to meet the increasing demands.

If the standards of living do not decline, the problems of travel and transport are bound to increase. If standards of living can increase, only a real decline in the numbers of people on earth would facilitate travel. The preservation of the most beautiful natural areas of the world will become more difficult if unlimited numbers of human beings are to be encouraged to enjoy the scenic, cultural, and historic sights of the world.

One might hope for some new means of transport for the billions of persons on earth. Table 8-9 indicates the vast discrepancies in numbers of persons per automobile in the nations of the world. If the U.S. standards of automobile ownership were overnight spread worldwide, the present world roadways would become parking lots.

Communication facilities indicate little or nothing about the quality of actual communication. However, the opportunity to communicate with others allows an extension of individual vision beyond the immediate village or community surroundings.

For most people the ability to travel by car, rail, air, or sea, the capacity to communicate with others by phone, and the opportunity to receive communication by way of television contribute to an improvement in the quality of human life.

The variations in availability of transportation and communication facilities can be seen in Table 8-9. Even among the developed countries there are significant differences in the availability of cars, telephones, and television sets. These conveniences are not absent, but they are in relatively short supply in most of the less developed nations (an indication of the shortage of consumer goods in general). Clearly, Brazil, Mexico, Venezuela, and Taiwan are less deprived than many of the other less developed countries. In fact, in Bulgaria, Yugoslavia, and Russia, these three items appear to be hardly more readily available.

Television could play an expanded role in educating the many largely unschooled persons around the world. However, mass-media facilities are in short supply in many parts of the earth. While "in some advanced countries, there are for every 100 people as many as 58 copies of daily newspapers, 94 radio receivers, 13 cinema seats, and 32 television receivers," in most nations the distribution of these facilities is thinly scattered (United Nations, 1963, p. 152).

TABLE 8-9 *The Numbers of Persons per Automobile, Phone, and Television Set, Specified Countries, 1967*

| | *Persons per* | | |
|---|---|---|---|
| | *Automobile* | *Telephone* | *Television* |
| Less Developed Countries | | | |
| Algeria | 8,950 | 89 | 86 |
| Brazil | 58 | 60 | 15 |
| Cambodia | 302 | 1,111 | 262 |
| China (Mainland) | 20,803 | 3,196 | 7,800 |
| Egypt (UAR) | 288 | 93 | 63 |
| India | 1,150 | 527 | 74,842 |
| Indonesia | 614 | 672 | 1,578 |
| Jamaica | 33 | 34 | 34 |
| Mexico | 53 | 45 | 21 |
| Nigeria | 853 | 837 | 1,175 |
| Pakistan | 981 | 799 | 3,250 |
| Taiwan (Nationalist China) | 536 | 58 | 45 |
| Venezuela | 21 | 30 | 14 |
| Developed Countries | | | |
| Bulgaria | 937 | 24 | 44 |
| Canada | 4 | 2 | 3 |
| Czechoslovakia | 37 | 9 | 5 |
| Denmark | 6 | 3 | 4 |
| France | 5 | 7 | 6 |
| Germany, East | 24 | 10 | 4 |
| Germany, West | 6 | 6 | 3 |
| Great Britain | 5 | 5 | 4 |
| Hungary | 6 | 3 | 7 |
| Israel | 28 | 8 | 55 |
| Japan | 26 | 6 | 5 |
| Sweden | 4 | 2 | 3 |
| United States | 2.5 | 2 | 2.4 |
| USSR | 216 | 26 | 12 |
| Yugoslavia | 57 | 40 | 16 |

*Source:* United Nations Economics and Social Council, *Statistical Yearbook, 1968*, New York: United Nations.

UNESCO has suggested, as an immediate target, that a country should aim to provide for every 100 of its inhabitants at least 10 copies of daily newspapers, 5 radio receivers, 2 cinema seats, and 2 television receivers. Yet . . . 100 states and territories in Africa, Asia, and Latin America fall below this very low "minimum" level for *all* 4 of the mass media. These countries have a combined population of 1,910 million, or 66 percent of the world total (p. 152; emphasis mine).

## *SUMMARY*

The social consequences of large and increasing population size all point in the direction of increasing complexity and formality. The more superficial human contacts one has the less satisfying these become and the more likely that people will *feel* alienated even when surrounded by other human beings. Sometimes these feelings are expressed in anti-social behaviors—acted out aggressively or implied in some form of withdrawal.

Even though the current population explosion is the result of a very sharp drop in death rates, one must not assume that the battle for human health is won. On the contrary, efforts continue to further reduce mortality and improve health. One reason population growth is expected to continue is that even if birth rates decline, death rates may decline even more sharply.

Whether we examine infant mortality or the proportion of physicians, nurses, dentists, or hospital facilities to population, the less developed countries are far behind the industrialized ones. Great efforts have been made to catch up, but population growth has usually been more rapid than the increases in hospital beds and medical personnel in the disadvantaged countries. Like Alice and the Queen of Hearts, these nations must run ever faster just to keep up with their beginning position.

Housing needs so outdistance the recent production of units and the possibilities for meeting them in the future that the attempts would be futile without greatly increased efforts to limit population growth.

The minimal needs for human sustenance, health, and shelter have not been adequately met. Even if these could be covered, a growing population with increasing desires for travel, recreation, transportation, and communication would create new complications. The standards of living cannot be raised for all if the total numbers of human beings continue to multiply.

In the less developed countries there appears to be an actual decline in some aspects of the quality of life—in housing, in the proportion of the dependent population, and in social organization itself. In other aspects—the supply of hospital beds and medical personnel, per capita incomes, and so forth—conditions remain at the same average low level despite attempts to improve them. Finally, in such aspects of life as travel, transportation, and communication, even though facilities have increased, population growth has lowered the per capita gains that might have occurred.

In the advanced countries improvements in some aspects of standards of living—such as the spread of automobile ownership and air travel—have lowered the quality of other aspects of life—by causing overused highways, increasing pollution, and crowds at recreational and historic areas. Even the advanced countries are limited in their ability to increase health and welfare care for expanding populations with rising expectations. Only limiting the growth of population would turn improvements in housing, medicine, transportation, and so forth into *net gains* for individuals.

## *REFERENCES*


ACKERMAN, EDWARD A. 1959. Population and natural resources. *The study of population*, eds. P. M. Hauser and D. D. Duncan, pp. 621–48. Chicago: University of Chicago Press.

CABELLO, OCTAVIO. 1966. Housing, population growth, and economic development. In *Population dilemma in Latin America*, eds. Mayone Stycos and Jorge Arias, pp. 101–22. Washington, D.C.: Potomac Books.

CALCUTTA METROPOLITAN PLANNING ORGANIZATION. 1966. *Basic development plan for the Calcutta metropolitan district 1966–1986*. Calcutta: Development and Planning Dept. of the Government of West Bengal.

CERDA, LUIS ESCOBAR. 1968. After Caracas: Problems and perspectives. *Population Bulletin* 24, no. 1 (February).

CHANDRASEKHAR, SRIPATI. 1967. Asia's population problems and solutions. In *Asia's population problems*, pp. 7–47. London: George Allen & Unwin.

COOK, ROBERT C. AND KAVAL GULHATI. 1965. Housing and population growth in Africa, Asia, and Latin America. *The population crisis*, ed. Larry K. Y. Ng and Stuart Mudd, pp. 114–24. Bloomington, Ind.: Indiana University Press.

DAVIS, KINGSLEY. 1960. *Population and welfare in industrial societies.* Fourth annual Dorothy Nyswander Lecture (April 6). Health Education Monographs no. 9. The Society of Public Health Educators.

GLAZER, NATHAN. 1965. A sociologist's view of poverty. In *Poverty in America*, ed. Margaret S. Gordon, pp. 12–26. San Francisco: Chandler Publishing Co.

HARRINGTON, MICHAEL. 1963. *The other America.* New York: Macmillan.

HEBB, D. O. AND W. R. THOMPSON. 1968. The social significance of animal studies. *The handbook of social psychology*, eds. G. Lindzey and E. Aronson, Vol. 2, 729–74. Reading, Mass.: Addison-Wesley.

HORWITZ, ABRAHAM AND MARY H. BURKE. 1966. Health, population and development. In *Population dilemma in Latin America*, eds. Mayone Stycos and Jorge Arias, pp. 145–95. Washington, D.C.: Potomac Books.

KUZNETS, SIMON. 1963. Quantitative aspects of the economic growth of nations: VIII. Distribution of income by size. *Economic Development and Cultural Change*, 11, no. 2, Part II (January), 1–80.

LEE, RONALD F. 1968. *Public use of the national park system 1872–2000.* Washington, D.C.: National Park Service, U.S. Department of Interior.

LORENZ, KONRAD. 1966. *On aggression*. New York: Bantam Books. (Original copyright Vienna, 1963.)

MILLER, HERMAN P. 1964. Rich man poor man. New York: Thomas Y. Crowell Company.

MOTT, PAUL E. 1965. *The organization of society*. Englewood Cliffs, N.J.: Prentice-Hall.

MYRDAL, GUNNAR. 1970. *The challenge of world poverty*. New York: Panthion Books.

NORTMAN, DOROTHY. 1970. Population and family planning programs: A factbook. *Reports on population/family planning*. New York (July).

PIDDINGTON, R. A. 1956. *The limits of mankind: A philosophy of population*. Bristol, England: John Wright & Sons.

POPULATION REFERENCE BUREAU. 1969. The brain drain: Fact or fiction? *Population Bulletin* 25: 3 (June), 57–87.

UNITED NATIONS. 1963. Science and technology for development. *Report on the United Nations conference on the application of science and technology for the benefit of the less developed areas*. vol. VI. *Education and training*. New York: United Nations.

UNITED NATIONS. 1970. *World Health Organization, 1969 report*. New York: United Nations.

UNITED NATIONS Department of Economic and Social Affairs. 1969. *1967 Report on the world social situation*. New York: United Nations.

UNITED NATIONS Economic and Social Council. 1967. *Demographic yearbook, 1966*. New York: United Nations.

———. 1968. *Statistical yearbook, 1967*. New York: United Nations.

———. 1969. *Statistical yearbook, 1968*. New York: United Nations.

chapter 9

# CULTURAL CONSEQUENCES OF POPULATION GROWTH

*No matter what technological advances are made in contraception and no matter what coercive controls are employed, population limitation will not succeed unless human attitudes are changed. The basic problem lies in educating people to the fact that mankind will breed itself into extinction. The quality of life will continue downward until that ultimate end. Thus a cultural change must be wrought. People must come to desire and be proud of small families. They must see their own responsibility to their children and to the human race. Only when people expect to have two children or less will the fight to halt over-population have some chance of succeeding.*

Zero Population Growth (1970)

Attitudes about population result from certain aspects of shared culture—knowledge, values, expectations, and so forth—which are in turn influenced by population variables. This reciprocal process can result in either change or stability in the social system. Throughout most of history change in attitudes and behavior relative to family size was imperceptible or very slow.

The pace of *social change* picked up in the West during the industrial revolution. Now that mortality has been reduced rapidly, populations in most of the nations of the world have increased so quickly that we are faced with a totally new human experience. How will these unprecedented changes in the social structure influence changes in cultural systems? Will people alter their high fertility goals? Studies indicate that the higher the level of formal education, the lower fertility is likely to be. According to Carleton (1966), the advanced education of women in the less developed countries is the strongest predictor of low fertility, but, at the same time, the rapid population growth in these countries limits their capacity to educate their young. Because of the importance of education in lowering fertility, as well as in providing the skills and aspirations that will lead to an improved life, the differences in educational levels from one country to another will be considered in some detail.

On the historical relationship between education and economic development Easterlin (1965) notes:

> In the nineteenth century the countries to which modern technology spread most rapidly—the United States, Germany, Switzerland, the Low Countries, Scandinavia, and perhaps France—almost uniformly had relatively high school enrollment ratios as early as 1830. . . .
>
> . . . In *all* countries which have achieved substantial and sustained economic growth, formal education was either already at a high level or was raised to a high level in fairly short order (p. 423).

Although it was once possible for educational systems merely to pass on the narrow traditional beliefs and behavioral patterns of the past, increased exposure to international communications make this less probable today than ever before in human history.

Basic literacy—the minimal ability to read and write—varies greatly from one country to another. It is likely to be extremely difficult to educate the young of a nation where adult illiteracy is widespread. In this chapter we will be especially concerned with how population expansion complicates the job of educating youth. School enrollment and the supply of teachers also vary greatly among countries.

After comparing variations in educational indicators, international differences in other cultural variables will be highlighted. How do the knowledge and beliefs, the values and the expectations people hold (specifically with regard to family size) vary from one country to another? Government leaders have often assumed, for example, that the people of the less developed countries want many children. Studies indicate that this is not uniformly the case, but only in recent years has anyone asked the people themselves. While many studies indicate that uneducated persons are interested in limiting the number of children they produce, their knowledge of the means of birth control is severely limited and often inaccurate.

In addition to examining some of these factors and the way they interact, the possibility of widespread alienation, the feeling of social isolation as a result of increased population, will be considered.

## *EDUCATION*

M. S. Thacker, president of the United Nations Conference on Science and Technology for Development (United Nations, 1963), urged that the highest priority be given to the development of human resources: "The tremendous growth which we have witnessed in the science and technology is the result of one thing—a better use by man of his mental capacities. . . . Developing human resources, training of minds, resources still largely untapped, constitute man's real hope for the future" (p. 25).

It is impossible to make an accurate cross-national comparison of the quality of education. "The educational statistics are probably even less satisfactory than statistics in almost every other field pertinent to underdevelopment and development" (Myrdal, 1970, p. 164). Although there are a number of indicators of levels of education, none is wholly satisfactory for analysis. Yet, an examination of several different measures of education will give an overall idea of the contrast among nations.

### *Literacy*

Recent estimates of literacy in a number of developing and developed countries may be reviewed in Table 9-1. The history of widespread education within the developed group of nations is evident in the nearly unanimous high levels of literacy, 96 percent and above.

The range of literacy rates among the less developed countries, however, is very great: from Ethiopia's 5 percent literate and India's 28 percent literate, to Chile's 85 percent and Taiwan's 97 percent. South American nations, in general, seem to report a higher proportion literate than the African or Asian regions.

Since there is no international uniformity in the definition of literacy, these reports must be taken as indicators rather than absolute measures of the extent of a population's ability to read and write. In many of the countries listed, a census taker probably records the claim to literacy without any knowledge of performance. Since admission of illiteracy has negative connotations, one would anticipate a bias in the upward direction.

In 1963, UNESCO's Director-General reported (United Nations, 1963) that as far as adults are concerned (persons more than 15 years of

TABLE 9-1 *Indicators of Educational Levels*

| | *Percent of Adult Population Literate, 1970 Estimate* | *School Enrollment Ratio, 1965* [1] | *People per Teacher, 1970* |
|---|---|---|---|
| *Developing Countries* | | | |
| Africa | | | |
| Algeria | 19% | 34 | 334 |
| Ethiopia | 5 | 6 | 2,000 |
| Ghana | 25 | 57 | 151 |
| Kenya | 30 | 39 | 287 |
| Nigeria | 30–35 | 23 | 531 |
| South Africa | 45 | 57 | 219 |
| UAR | 35 | 43 | 210 |
| Latin America | | | |
| Brazil | 61 | 41 | 174 |
| Chile | 85 | 61 | 207 |
| Colombia | 63 | 38 | 187 |
| Mexico | 65 | 49 | 220 |
| Asia | | | |
| Cambodia | 31 | 42 | 327 |
| China (Mainland) | 60 | 46 | ? |
| Korea (South) | 82 | 58 | 244 |
| India | 28 | 38 | 267 |
| Indonesia | 60 | 38 | 313 |
| Pakistan | 19 | 22 | 370 |
| Taiwan | 97 | 61 | 138 |
| Thailand | 70 | 38 | 213 |
| *Developed Countries* | | | |
| France | 96 | 73 | 98 |
| W. Germany | 99 | 78 | 157 |
| Italy | 98 | 61 | 103 |
| Japan | 99 | 74 | 103 |
| Sweden | 98 | 74 | 91 |
| USSR | 98 | 71 | 84 |
| United Kingdom | 99 | 88 | 116 |
| United States | 98 | 87 | 85 |
| Canada | 99 | 81 | 85 |
| Hungary | 99 | 66 | 72 |

[1] Number of students enrolled in primary and secondary schools per hundred 5–19 year olds.

*Source:* United Nations Economic and Social Council, *Statistical Yearbook 1968*, 1969, Table 2.5.

age), "we are obliged to make approximations, and in 1957 found that there were approximately 700 million people who are assumed to be illiterate. This represents more than *two-fifths* of the adult population of the world. . . ." (p. 12). Under present conditions of educational development and population growth, 20 to 25 million new illiterates will be added to the world population during each of the next six to seven years.

Even though the proportions of literate adults have been growing, population has grown so rapidly that the numbers of illiterate persons have also increased. As has been true in so many other areas, the rapid increase in population has made it very difficult to raise the standards in literacy and in education in general.

Reporting the proportion of the adult population said to be "literate" reflects, for the most part, the past history of education in any particular nation. There may be considerable variation in literacy from one age group to another within a nation. Persons who are currently nearing 80 years of age, for example, would have had their early educational experience around the turn of the century. The educational efforts of the past twenty years are reflected only in data on young adult literacy.

Furthermore, because knowledge of the actual abilities of persons to read and write is limited, one should not rely on literacy reports alone as an indication of educational levels in various countries of the world.

Because of the length of time involved in childhood education and the low literacy rates in many of the underdeveloped countries, one would expect adult literacy classes to receive heavy emphasis. Yet Myrdal (1970) finds to his dismay that the South Asian countries have downgraded adult education, particularly literacy classes:

> UNESCO itself has indicated that only if each year a considerable number of the illiterate adults are given an opportunity to take a literacy course are there good prospects for the eradication of illiteracy within a reasonably short time. *Adult education not only should be more important in underdeveloped than in developed countries, where almost all are literate, but poses quite different problems.*
>
> For another thing, *adult education, with emphasis on literacy, should help to make the school education of children more effective.* All the information we have suggests that children of illiterate parents tend to fall behind in scholastic achievement and that they more easily lapse into illiteracy (p. 179).

Without a very great commitment by the intellectuals of each country or a massive "each one teach one" program, adult illiteracy will remain widespread for many years to come.

### *School Enrollment*

Using an indicator of educational development based on the enrollment in secondary schools and universities in 75 countries, Harbison (1963) found the coefficient of correlation between educational level and the gross national product per capita to be 0.888. He concluded that "the best single indicator of a country's wealth in human resources is the proportion of its young people enrolled in secondary schools" (p. 102). Yet, 400 million of the world's children have no school to go to. For the great mass of the earth's population the boundless riches of man's scientific genius have barely touched their primitive economies" (United Nations, 1963, p. 9). The imbalance among countries is difficult to remedy because the least educated are reproducing most rapidly.

The number of children enrolled in primary or secondary schools in relation to the population aged 5 through 19 offers a fair idea of the current educational efforts of a nation. The advanced countries, as a group, report a large proportion of youth enrolled in the school system in 1965 (see Table 9-1).

The variation in the school enrollment ratios in the less developed countries ranges from 6 to 61 enrollments for each 100 young people. Unfortunately, most of the largest nations have low enrollment ratios: 23 per 100 in Nigeria, 22 in Pakistan, 38 in India and Indonesia, and 46 in Mainland China.

Again, there is no uniformity in the meaning of "enrollment." In some places it may indicate merely registration, with or without attendance. Even where attendance is indicated, there is often no evidence of the number of hours per day or days per year. The figures can be taken only as a rough indication of the dispersion of education among the young of various nations. The Population Reference Bureau (1966) calculated from United Nations data that 70 percent of school-aged children in the less developed countries were *not* in school. The situation has been more favorable in Latin America than in Asia or Africa. Yet, "for Brazilians who enter school, the average number of years of education completed is 2.62; for Venezeulans 2.63; and for Panamanians, 3.6. In Brazil only 8.42 percent of the school children ever reach grades 4 through 6" (p. 2).

Since their still-expanding populations are already very heavily weighted by young persons, the less developed countries face tremendous problems in attempting to increase the proportion of young persons in school. During the time it takes to build and organize schools and train more teachers, an attempt to double enrollment *ratios* involves a much more than twofold increase in the *numbers* of students. For instance, the computations of Masihur Rahman Kahn (1967) reveal that to raise the enrollment ratio for Pakistan in the age group 5–14 from 25.2 percent in 1962 to 67.5 percent in 1985, the enrollments would have to increase from 7.2 million to 49.5 million with constant age-specific fertility and declining mortality or to 32.7 million if a rapid decline in fertility should occur. Thus, to attain a 2.7 fold increase in enrollment ratios in Pakistan, the number of school enrollees needs to be increased 4.5–6.8 times. That would still leave 32.5 percent of the school-aged population outside the system. Kahn thus concludes that:

> The educational objectives of the Pakistan long-term-perspective plan are thus not only highly optimistic, they are rather unrealistic, and especially so under the sustained high fertility assumption of the population. Under the constraint of limited funds and resources available for educational investments, it is only a fast declining fertility that can help alleviate the magnitude of illiteracy in Pakistan (p. 198).

Neither the numbers registered nor the years of education completed can indicate the quality of education received. As in the case with the other variables we have examined, the quality of education is highly unequal around the world. The educational system of Mainland China has expanded rapidly under the Communists. Yet two-thirds of classes are said to be without texts and teachers have had little training. One province claimed to have set up 44 universities in two days (National Science Foundation, 1960). One is likely to be skeptical of the quality of education under such arrangements.

## *Teachers*

Although the numbers of persons in the total population per teacher is not a direct indicator of the numbers of pupils, on the average per teacher, it is one more measure of the total educational commitment of a nation.

The developed countries report slightly more or less than 100 persons per teacher. Since about one-fourth of the total population in these countries is of school age, there are probably 25 pupils, on the average, per teacher.

The less developed nations not only have many more persons per teacher, but the school-aged population makes up a much higher proportion of the total population. If the 40–45 percent of the total populations who are of school age were all in school, the teachers of the less developed nations would average from 60 to 200 pupils each, depending upon the specific national ratio of teachers to population.[1]

There is no way to measure the education, training, talent, or commitment of the teachers who are available. Not only are their abilities likely to vary among countries (as they do within countries), but again the most disadvantaged nations will probably be weaker, on the average,

[1] This estimate does not even consider the case of Ethiopia, where teachers are so scarce as to make such a calculation absurd.

*Source:* Courtesy Professor Gerald D. Berreman and the University of California Press, from *Hindus of the Himalayas,* © 1963, Berkeley.

FIG. 9–1 *In the North Indian village of Sirkanda, untouched by even dirt roads, this school is a small beginning in the movement toward modernizing values and behavior. Note that two students are spinning wool thread while reciting their lessons.*

than the more advanced countries. In most of the less developed countries of the world teaching, except at university level, is a low status, low paying job. The less developed the nation, the more their well-educated persons are in demand for many important jobs, and the less likely they are to have many well-qualified persons in the teaching profession.

## *Variations in National Spending*

The material aids to learning—books, equipment, and the like, as well as teachers' salaries—vary proportionately from nation to nation in much the same way as the other indications of educational adequacy. The enormity of the differences can be seen by comparing national spending on education in India and the United States.

In 1966 India spent an average of 31 rupees per primary school pupil, the equivalent of $6.00 per year. In the United States an average of $567.00 per pupil was spent for the year, or nearly 100 times more. At the college level India spent about $172 per student and the United States about $1,724 per student, or 10 times as much.

India can do little to alleviate her situation. With approximately three-and-a-half times as many school-aged children in India as in the United States, the Indian people simply do not have the means to educate all of their young for the twentieth century. In fact, in 1966 the United States, with fewer children, spent more ($32.8 billion) on the recurring expenses of primary education (excluding such costs as building construction) than the total national income of India (United Nations, Economic and Social Council, 1969, Tables 2-19, 2-20).

The absolute lack of formal education for some, together with the low quality of education for others in the less developed countries, discourages attempts to raise the levels of living generally. The problem is increasingly complicated by the continued rapid increase of population. Each year there are many more children ready to feed into the educational systems than places for them. Even if the rate of population growth were to slow down next year, the educational system would not feel the lessened demand until six years later. Some mechanical jobs do not, of course, require an elaborate educational background, but the move from a superstitious to a rational view of life is advanced by formal education.

After a comprehensive study of 75 countries, Charles A. Myers and Frederick Harbison concluded that:

> The progress of a nation depends first and foremost on the progress of its people. Unless it develops their spirit and human potentialities it cannot develop much else—materially, economically, politically, or culturally. The basic problem of most of the underdeveloped countries is not a poverty of natural resources but the underdevelopment of their human resources. Hence their first task must be to build up their human capital—in more human terms, to improve the education, skills, the hopefulness, and thus the mental and physical health, of their men, women, and children (p. 95).

## *COMPONENTS OF THE CULTURAL SYSTEM*

In chapter 3 we considered some general aspects of cultural systems. It is important to remember that cultural systems do not stand alone. Rather, the knowledge and beliefs, the values and norms, or expectations of various groups are related both to one another (and heavily influenced by education) but, also, related to actual patterns of human relationships or social structures.

The man on the street, as much as the social scientist, expects some congruence between what the individual or the social group claims to value (and expect) and their actual behavior. When these are very divergent or inconsistent over time, the individual or the society is labeled "disorganized." The existence of social change, however, leads one to expect periods of disorganization, followed by or joined to periods of reorganization. Only when reorganization does not seem to be in process may the individual or society be labeled "psychotic" or "sick."

One of the most pervasive social changes of the mid-twentieth century is the very rapid increase in populations. It is natural for there to be a "cultural lag" between the increase itself and a recognition of the increase. Because people everywhere are glad to have death rates reduced, they have seldom allowed their joy to be marred by a realization of the problems that can follow from lowering the number of deaths. Since people are still striving to reduce mortality, a decrease in population growth rates can be achieved *only* by lowering birth rates.

The need for a reorganization of values and expectations and people's behavior with regard to childbearing is quickly becoming evident to those who have studied population. This book is an attempt to expand the circle of those who are informed about the causes and consequences of rapid population growth.

One of our tasks is to understand that all people do not think as we do. Our assumptions about the knowledge and beliefs of social groups may be verified or disproved empirically by research on the questions of interest. We can assume that past societies valued high fertility, since they would not otherwise have survived the high death rates. The assumption that these high fertility values have carried over to the present is now being tested by surveys of knowledge, attitudes, and practice (KAP) of persons in various countries or sections of countries. KAP studies should not be accepted uncritically, since they are conducted by persons with a variety of goals. Yet they are a better indication of the knowledge and beliefs, the values and expectations about fertility than were previously available, and they will serve as a yardstick for future studies within the same countries. The following review of KAP studies relies heavily on a summary by Bernard Berelson (1966), which was presented to the International Conference on Family Planning Programs in Geneva in August of 1965.

### *Knowledge and Beliefs*

Because KAP (knowledge, attitudes, and practice) studies have been designed by many different persons for different settings, they do not all ask precisely the same questions. The number of questions asked varies from about 100 to over 300. Those studies that focus especially on the knowledge and beliefs of respondents may be grouped into four subject areas: (1) expressions that indicate whether or not the interviewee recognizes that childhood mortality has decreased; (2) knowledge about the physiology of reproduction; (3) recognition that control of reproduction is possible; and (4) knowledge about specific means of fertility control. Another important consideration is the effect of the KAP surveys in improving the knowledge available to political leaders about the views of their people.

1. Of those populations which have been asked, large proportions know that child mortality is lower in their areas than during their parents' generation. In Turkey 40 percent verbalized such a recognition and in Thailand 76 percent did so. One might expect that the knowledge that more children are living to maturity would be most evident in joint-family households. The survival of two or three extra children in a nuclear family might not be so immediately evident as the nondisappearance of six to nine children in a joint household.

2. Knowledge about the physiology of reproduction is very low. Somewhat less than 10 percent of the Turkish and Thai women who were interviewed knew on which days of the menstrual cycle conception is possible.

3. A great proportion of survey respondents know that control of fertility is possible. By itself, however, that knowledge is not very useful if it is accompanied by superstition or ineffectual contraceptive practices. In many countries those who could supply accurate birth-control information (doctors and nurses, for example) are in extremely short supply. Furthermore, women in many areas of the world would not consider going to a male doctor for advice on fertility control. Unless midwives have had special training, their knowledge of effective birth-control methods may not be much better than that of the women.

4. Although a fairly large proportion of those interviewed seem to know that contraceptive methods are available, the proportions who do not know what any of them are range from over 40 percent in Turkey to 65 percent in rural Thailand to 85 percent in Tunisia. Over two-thirds of the respondents verbalized an interest in learning about fertility control; 57 percent in Thailand and 75 percent in Turkey said they wanted the government to develop a birth-control program.

Many government leaders assume that their populations would be hostile to the introduction of family planning programs. The KAP studies have been a source of enlightenment for everyone concerned. Governmental and political officers, the medical fraternity, the press, the business community, and other professional and lay groups have all gained new insight into the potential for family planning programs. It is important to correct the impression of leaders who believe that the masses of their own people, especially those low in status and life positions, are not interested in fertility control. The wide attention given to the 1963 KAP study in Turkey, for instance, contributed to that country's recent change in national population policy. Contrary to the typical impression of national elites, there may be more potential for political gain than risk in this area.

## *Values*

Surveys have come to separate questions about values, ideals, or desires from those about expectations. Both verbalized desires and expectations may differ from actual behavior. In most of the less developed countries studied, the "ideal" family size of those interviewed is considerably smaller than the average completed family size of women over forty years of age.

TABLE 9-2 *Completed and "Ideal" Family Size (approximate)*

| Country | *Completed Family Size* [1] | *"Ideal" Family Size* | *"Ideal" as Percent of Completed Family Size* |
|---|---|---|---|
| Ghana (urban) [a] | 7.0 | 5.3 | 76 |
| Tunisia (national) [a] | 5.9 | 4.3 | 73 |
| Korea (national) [a] | 5.4 | 4.2 | 78 |
| Taiwan (urban) [a] | 5.5 | 3.9 | 71 |
| Thailand (rural) [a] | 5.2 | 3.8 | 73 |
| Turkey (national) [a] | 5.8 | 3.5 | 60 |
| Colombia (urban) [a] | 4.8 | 3.6 | 75 |
| Venezuela (urban) [a] | 4.3 | 3.5 | 81 |
| Mexico (urban) [a] | 5.0 | 4.2 | 84 |
| Panama (urban) [a] | 3.8 | 3.5 | 92 |
| Brazil (urban) [a] | 3.3 | 2.7 | 82 |
| Costa Rica (urban) [a] | 4.3 | 3.6 | 83 |
| Japan (national) [b] | 2.0 | 2.8 | 140 [c] |
| Hungary (national) [b] | 2.5 | 2.4 | 96 [c] |
| France (national) [b] | 2.8 | 2.7 | 96 [c] |
| United States (national) | 3.4 | 3.3 | 97 [c] |
| Philippines (urban/rural) [b] | 5.9 | 5.0 | 85 [c] |

[1] Completed family size is usually the number of living children for women of the highest age group, for example, over 40.

*Sources:* (a) Data taken from the Mauldin article and more recent surveys (e.g., Tunisia, Thailand, Latin America) as reported in B. Berelson, ed., *Family Planning and Population Programs,* Chicago and London: University of Chicago Press, 1966, p. 658, Table 2; (b) Berelson (1966), p. 658, footnote 4; (c) my calculations.

Table 9-2 lists the 17 nations for which such a comparison was possible. Of the 17 nations listed, only in Hungary, France, and the United States are the completed family sizes almost the same as the "ideal." Only the Japanese report a smaller completed than "ideal" family size. For the most part, the poorer the country the greater the divergence between the ideal and real. Furthermore, the differences are greater in rural areas than in cities, where most of these surveys were taken. Berelson (1966) estimated that if couples were able to do what they said they wanted to do, and if all other conditions remained the same, the birth rate of the typical developing country would decline about ten points, which would mean a decline of about 10 per thousand population, and would mean a decline of 1 percent in the growth rate (i.e., from 3 percent to 2 percent increase).

In Korea, the Philippines, Panama, Turkey, Costa Rica, Colombia, Mexico, Brazil, and Thailand 50 percent or more of the respondents said they wanted no more children. The main reason expressed was the economic welfare of the family, including the provision of educational and occupational opportunities for the childern. There appears to be an initial and natural motivation toward family planning in the countries that have been studied. The desire to have no more children, moreover, is directly tied to the number of children the respondents already have. Among persons with more than three or four children the proportion who wanted no more children increases rapidly (see Table 9-3). Verbalized desires seem to imply that family planning programs would be most effective in reduc-

*TABLE 9-3 Percentage Not Wanting More Children by Number of Children*

| | Number of Children | | | | | |
|---|---|---|---|---|---|---|
| *Country* | *0* | *1* | *2* | *3* | *4* | *5 or More* |
| Ceylon | 2 | 8 | 29 | 57 | 69 | 88 |
| India | 2 | 7 | 25 | 43 | 74 | 88 |
| Pakistan | 4 | 5 | 25 | 42 | 67 | 74 |
| Taiwan | 0 | 1 | 24 | 54 | 76 | 88 |
| Thailand | 12 | 30 | 48 | 71 | 85 | 96 |
| Turkey | 19 | 34 | 58 | 68 | 67 | 76 |
| Philippines | 3 | 24 | 42 | 56 | 68 | 85 |
| Korea | 1 | 8 | 28 | 65 | 81 | 94 |
| Tunisia | 1 | 9 | 26 | 44 | 68 | 87 |
| Brazil | 21 | 53 | 85 | 95 | 93 | 93 |
| Colombia | 15 | 45 | 55 | 67 | 79 | 93 |
| Costa Rica | 20 | 45 | 60 | 67 | 78 | 86 |
| Mexico | 16 | 30 | 48 | 64 | 76 | 86 |
| Panama | 11 | 35 | 51 | 70 | 86 | 94 |
| United States | 8 | 20 | 57 | 62 | 81 | 74 |

*Source:* Berelson (1966), p. 662.

ing birth rates in Brazil, Colombia, and Costa Rica and least effective in Pakistan and India.

## *Norms: Expectations of Behavior*

In almost all countries the poorer and less educated the population, the more likely people are to say that they expect to have more children than they want to have. The differences between expectation and desire is especially obvious among the Negro population of the United States. Even here, where contraceptive information is supposedly widespread, it would appear that those who are deprived of health knowledge and care also lack knowledge and advice about family planning.

For whole nations, the lower the per capita GNP, the lower the percentage enrolled in schools and the higher the proportion illiterate, the greater the percentage *wanting,* as well as *expecting,* four or more children.

These specific aspects of the knowledge, values, and expectations of people in various countries must be considered in any plan to implement fertility control.

## *Means to Achieve Goals*

Even though research continues, a number of simple and effective tools of contraception are already available. While only the rhythm method is officially sanctioned by the Catholic Church, most individuals find more than one means of control acceptable. Although the intrauterine device, or IUD, has been widely used in less developed countries in recent years, it may be expelled without the user's knowledge and is therefore not as efficient as the pill, when this is used correctly. Male or female sterilization is, of course, the most certain means of birth control. It has been widely used in India, which reports over five million vasectomies. Because it is permanent and immediately effective, sterilization actually costs less over the long run than do methods which must be used repeatedly.

The most important consideration when comparing birth-control methods is their acceptability to the prospective users. Therefore, most family planning clinics now offer several different means of birth control.

The probable number of pregnancies per 100 women per year for each of the major methods of contraception is given in Table 9-4. For all methods except sterilization (male or female), the pill, and the IUD, the probabilities of conception in any given year are quite high. At the rate

TABLE 9-4 *Various Means of Contraception, Measured Effectiveness and Possible Side Effects*

| *Method* | *Effectiveness (Number of likely pregnancies among 100 women in 1 year)* | *Possible Side Effects* |
|---|---|---|
| Sterilization | 0.003 (100%) | None |
| The pill | 0.3 (up to 100%) | Weight gain, nausea, usually ending after several months |
| Intrauterine devices | Spiral 1.8<br>Loop 2.4 (up to 98%)<br>Bow 5.7<br>Ring 7.5 | Irregular bleeding, discomfort in beginning |
| Diaphragm with jelly | 12 (85 to 90%) | Jelly may cause minor irritation |
| Condom | 14 (80 to 90%) | None |
| Withdrawal | 18 | Psychological effects |
| Chemical barriers (foam most effective) | 20 | Minor irritation |
| Rhythm | 24 | None |
| Douche | 31 | None |

of 20 pregnancies per 100 females, one fifth of the cases conceive each year.

A distinction should be made between contraception and birth control. The former include all methods of avoiding or preventing conception, while the latter includes all methods of avoiding births. Thus abortion would be a method of birth control, but not a method of contraception. The history of changing attitudes and governmental policies on abortion is extensive (see Lader, 1966).

The use of birth control methods clearly affects population growth and the growth rate, in turn, helps determine how many children people want within their own families. As more persons perceive that a greater proportion of children are living to maturity, there is a greater desire for knowledge about the means of birth control. As more persons recognize the population problem and its worldwide implications, they are more likely to expect responsible parents to limit their families to no more than two children each, replacing the parents and no more.

### *Tangible and Intangible Values*

Besides fertility values themselves, other aspects of the world's cultures are likely to be affected by the press of increasing numbers of people.

TANGIBLE VALUES. It has often been said that "human life is cheap" wherever there are heavy concentrations of impoverished people. Of course, it is always someone else's life that is cheap or expendable, never one's own or those of one's family.

The human desire for space is evidenced by the commuter's willingness to spend time traveling to and from the city to work so that he may live in a suburb with larger lots and more greenery. Wherever people can afford the time and expense, they tend to choose the suburban home environment. Early returns from the 1970 census showed that many of the largest U.S. cities had grown less rapidly than their surrounding areas or had even declined in population.

The rising interest in saving forests, shorelines, and wilderness areas indicates an increasing awareness of their nonmonetary value to human life.

INTANGIBLE VALUES. It is rather difficult to measure the intangible values of various social groups or societies. How highly do people value education? Can we measure the desire to learn to read? Dollars spent on formal education may simply indicate the availability of money for such expenditures. Individuals in Africa who walk many miles each day to take lessons in the open air from an unpaid or poorly paid teacher may have a far greater desire to learn than those in the more advanced countries who can take education for granted.

Different cultures have widely different concepts of the purpose of existence. At one extreme, people believe that the individual's principal duty is to fulfill caste duties in order to be reincarnated into a better position in the social system and at the other extreme they want to see visible daily improvements in life.

Such intangibles as the pursuit of excellence, a sense of security, an appreciation of beauty, and the joy of living may be declining with the continued growth of population. Although most of these values cannot be measured, there is adequate evidence that the natural resources of the world are being rapidly spoiled. This fact alone limits some of the possibilities for increasing the quality of life.

Roger Revelle (1969) noted a series of factors which combined to bring about contemporary prosperity in certain locations. Most of the factors on his list are cultural components. The first is a belief that the world is rational. It is possible to search for the means to achieve specific goals, only if one perceives an orderly rather than random sequence to life's events. Second, democratic capitalism and the rule of law combined to give people the incentive to postpone gratification and to work within established rules which might be changed only in an orderly manner. In contrast to totalitarianism, this allowed human beings to organize rationally for the future. The third factor, the "Protestant Ethic," combines the beliefs that honesty is best, that the purpose of life is to work, and that public morality supersedes even family responsibility. When people hire family members instead of persons of superior qualification, whatever enterprise is underway will suffer. Many cultures have rules against "nepotism" because family favoritism is so prevalent. Fourth, an interest in power technology and in the scientific method increases the prosperity of whole societies and of the individuals within them. Revelle reminds us that contemporary prosperity is a departure from the normal human condition in the past. Fifth, the rise of a large middle class is a new phenomenon. Nevertheless, Revelle suggests that the present gulf between the rich and poor of the world cannot continue. If the conditions of existence for the poor are not improved, the decline of the rich Western countries is very likely. The people of the poor nations of the world want to benefit from the knowledge and experience of the rich nations. Indeed they may, but they do not yet share the cultural beliefs that are most compatible with the application of the scientific method and rational organization.

In three volumes of detail on the interrelated aspects of Asian social systems, Gunnar Myrdal (1968) poignantly describes the vicious circle that keeps these societies backward. On cultural factors, he says:

> The prevailing attitudes and patterns of individual performance in life and at work are from the development point of view deficient in various respects: low levels of work discipline, punctuality, and orderliness; superstitious beliefs and irrational outlook; lack of alertness, adaptability, ambition, and general readiness for change and experiment; contempt for manual work; submissiveness to authority and exploitation; low aptitude for cooperation; low standards of personal hygiene; and so on.
>
> To these attitudes should be added unreadiness for deliberate and sustained birth control (p. 1862).

It may be possible, though difficult, to teach scientific methods on the scale that is needed. But objectivity, pragmatism, and optimism are prerequisites. How can these be communicated to people bound by superstition?

People need to *believe* that they can affect the outcome of their own lives or they will not be motivated to work for results: whether for increased production, for plans for the future, or for seeing the relationship between population increase and poverty and thus for limiting offspring. The beliefs people hold, the formal structure of social relations, and the social sanctions on behavior are powerful motivators of human contact.

The necessary attitude or cultural changes would give rise to numerous conflicts of values. Where large families are valued now, people must be shown that one or two children can be provided with better food, education, job opportunities, and so forth. The emphasis must shift from the number of children to the quality of life they and their parents may enjoy. Even the language used in discussing population problems indicates a need to shift from valuing the quantity of children to valuing the quality of children. That our ethical system regards each person as worthwhile is one reason people have worked so diligently to reduce deaths. Yet we are more and more burdened with too much of a good thing and the result is often a decrease in personal significance.

## VARIATION IN PERSONAL SIGNIFICANCE

Although worldwide population pressures are recent, regional crowding is an old problem. Overpopulation in specific social groups was often met in the past by exposing infants, abandoning the aged, or conquest of the lands of others (Shinn, 1970). Human values no longer regard these as acceptable measures, yet there is no worldwide commitment to any other means of resolving population pressures.

### *Decrease in Individual Importance*

As the numbers of persons in any nation or community increase, the individual will have less economic, political, and social influence. The more consumers there are, the less concerned manufacturers need to be with providing satisfactory products. Advertising and selling may take precedence over quality control. Government may set up a multiplicity of rules to regulate the production and marketing of goods, but the individual inevitably *feels* less important as a consumer. If he is not satisfied with his new television, car, or suit, rarely can he find any one to complain to. In stores with many potential customers, the importance of any individual customer is lessened. When customers are drawn from a large and mobile community, stores may have little concern for the satisfaction of customers they may never see again. In contrast, the salespeople in a small local community have a limited clientele who must be served well if the stores are to remain in business. Large populations can make their influence felt by forming consumer groups, but their importance as individuals is decreased.

As the numbers of people increase, the influence of a single vote in any election decreases. With the growth in population it becomes difficult for political candidates to discuss complex issues with any significant proportion of the voters. Thus the growth of mass communications makes it increasingly tempting for politicians to appear to the mass of voters with repetitious slogans that actually say very little. The importance of the press in questioning candidates and officeholders may be increased, but individual citizens can participate only vicariously in the political forum. Letters to legislative representatives may be counted, but they will count for less as the population increases.

As individual influence declines, the importance of organized special interest groups increases. An individual who wants to influence legislation will be more effective if he forms or joins a group. However, the interests of the majority may be obscured as the small interest group promotes its goal. For instance, the pro-gun lobby in Washington was already organized and effective by the time citizens became concerned about unregulated sale and use of firearms. Although a majority of individuals may have wanted the registration and limitation of gun sales, the special interest groups were more effective in applying pressure on legislators.

With increasing population individuals also have fewer opportunities for achievement or leadership. One has a better chance of being a member of the national ballet, a star athlete, or even president in a nation of 8 million than in a nation of 200 million. Even within a school system, one has a better chance of being a school leader, or a star football player in a small than in a very large school.

Thus human interaction in social groups, and, especially, in whole societies, increases in complexity as the number of individuals increases. Consensus may prevail in small groups, but it is far less likely to occur in very large groups. In fact, the larger the group the greater the temptation to impose consensus. Leaders may assume power and propose to speak *for* "the people" without ever bothering to speak *with* the people.

Whether at the level of whole societies or small groups, high population density restricts freedom and individualism. Wolfram Eberhard (1970) relates the assumption of the Chinese culture that "society cannot function unless the individual relinquishes some of his freedoms" to the fact of their historically overcrowded condition. "Every society tries to avoid conflicts," he says, and this is easier where population density is low. In crowded societies like that of the Chinese "conflicts have to be avoided because one has to live together with others since there is no escape" (pp. 28–29).

*Increased Bureaucracy and Decreased Freedom*

No matter how complex or simple the government, the more persons in a nation, the more elaborate the bureaucracy required to deal with them. The more automobiles on the highway, the more complex the rules of the road.

As population grows, almost every aspect of life is coming to be licensed. As population becomes more dense, the behavior of an individual affects many other persons and therefore comes more and more under regulation by the group. When human beings were sparsely scattered over the American continent no one needed a license to fish or hunt or to own a dog or build a house, no permit was required to obtain water and dispose of sewage. Now each person is surrounded by rules relating to the welfare of all.

Individual freedom declines, then, as numbers increase. Although life permits neither total freedom nor total coercion, mankind cannot evade the dilemma of population growth versus individual freedom. Roger Shinn, professor of applied Christianity at Union Theological Seminary in New York, suggests (1970) that human dignity demands the limitation of population. He notes that in any crisis society qualifies personal rights, but argues that part of ethical wisdom is to *avoid crises* that permit only destructive choices. Immediate attention must be given to limiting population before it is too late to avoid destructive choices. There is little time in which to maximize free decisions and minimize coercion in the area of population. Social groups will undoubtedly attempt to steer a course between uninhibited freedom and overt coercion. Between these extremes lie many methods of persuasion and pressure. Prestige systems, economic pressures, taxation, housing policies, and skillfully contrived propaganda are a few of the devices which societies are likely to use as they see the necessity of limiting reproduction. Shinn argues that it is not wrong for society to use such pressures. Since society itself is under immense pressure, there is no reason why the families within it should be allowed to evade the pressures.

Yet there is danger in the propensity of a society to manipulate its members for their own good. Donald Michael has pointed to one of the basic conflicts of our time: man increasingly sees himself as a manipulable and manipulated object in social and physical systems; and he increasingly rebels with humanistic passion against the premise that he is a manipulable object.

Sociologists and psychologists have demonstrated many ways in which people may be influenced. The greater one's awareness of the sources and means of pressure, the greater is one's freedom to avoid being manipulated. Nevertheless, 200 million Americans require more than twice the bureaucracy of 100 million Americans to achieve their own desired goals. It is difficult to imagine the bureaucratic systems that will be required to coordinate and serve 300 or 400 million Americans.

We still have much to learn about the ways of relating personal freedom to social responsibility in this technological age. The more populous the group, the more individual freedoms are restricted by responsibilities to others (unseen others as well as "significant others"). People must learn how to promote and maintain their individual identity and dignity while acting responsibly within mass society.

## *ALIENATION*

Freedom may be very restricted without creating alienation as, for example, in a small tribe where a high degree of conformity is demanded. However, the restrictions on freedom that come from a large impersonal bureaucracy seem to lead to the resentment and alienation of individuals. Alienation may be viewed as an individual phenomenon, but when it is widespread, it becomes a cultural phenomenon. Whether we define alienation as self-estrangement, meaninglessness, political powerlessness, normlessness, or social isolation, the phenomenon seems to increase in the highest density urban areas. Almost all visitors to New York City comment on the fact that people avoid looking at or recognizing other human beings. We read about groups of people in our large cities watching while individuals are beaten or killed in city streets or parks. In one city, rape is so common that the city council has seriously considered setting up a 24 hour-a-day, 7 days-a-week rape clinic! The absence of any effort to help or even to call someone else to help a victim is the clearest evidence of alienation or separation—and of the lack of empathy for fellow human beings. Boredom with one's work, still another type of alienation, is nothing in comparison to the loss of shared human feelings. Yet the paradox is that social separation seems to be greatest precisely when potential human contacts are greatest.

Although we cannot specify optimum population densities, we should be able to recognize the signals of social pathology. Dramatic increases in four different types of crimes committed between persons—murder, rape, robbery, and assault—paralleled dramatically increases in city size and density in the United States in 1940, 1950, and 1960 (Kyllonen, 1967). No wonder people who can afford to will spend time and money commuting to and from the cities they do not want to live in. But what about those who are left? The problems of the alcoholic, the aged, the fatherless family, and the unemployed are exaggerated in the high density urban center. Yet people continue to move into the city in the search for something better than they left.

Unfortunately, slum renewal has been just that. Unless there can be a building of a sense of community, new physical structures will have little impact on the way of life of the urban poor. As an indication of the alienation and fear felt by residents of one of our famous urban-renewal projects, we may examine the comments reported by Lee Rainwater (1967). The Pruitt-Igoe public housing project in St. Louis is a complex of 33 eleven story buildings hailed by the Architectural Forum, but now

FIG. 9–2 *In the words of a resident, "They tore down one slum and built another." Pruitt-Igoe public housing project, North St. Louis. Associated Press Photo*

recognized as a failure. Although a majority of tenants feel their apartments are better than what they had previously, "only a minority demonstrate any real attachment to the project community, and most would very much like to move out to a neighborhood that would be nicer and safer" (p. 118). Rainwater summarized some of the statements of residents:

"Bottles and other dangerous things get thrown out of windows and hurt people."

"People who don't live in the project come in and make a lot of trouble with fights and stealing and drinking and the like."

"People use elevators and halls to go to the bathroom."

"The laundry rooms aren't safe: clothes get stolen, and people get attacked."

"Children run wild and cause all kinds of damage."

"A woman isn't safe in the halls, stairways, or elevators." And to sum it all up:

"They were trying to better poor people (but) they tore down one slum and built another."

Sociologists do know a little bit about *how* to organize communities. *Doing it* is another matter. The successful projects are all small in scale. It takes leadership and people who will work together and not at cross-purposes. Pleasant physical surroundings can help, but new buildings do not produce new communities. If we continue to bring together uprooted, alienated, frustrated individuals by the thousands we are likely to increase the "tangle of pathology." The large families of the poor make life more difficult for themselves and for those who would help them.

Just as these factors affect the internal dynamics of nations, they also influence international relations. Frank Lorimer (1969) has noted that:

> Trends which threaten the national aspirations of more than half the world's population present a problem to all nations. Frustration breeds envy, suspicion and violence. The security of the lucky nations with large natural resources, accumulated wealth and advanced techniques may be critically affected by the progress or reverses experienced in less fortunate nations during the next few decades. The development of American policies relating to population trends must, therefore, be framed in a world context (p. 169).

Although specific political aspects of population growth and questions of population policy will be considered in subsequent chapters, we have touched briefly on certain cultural aspects that are relevant to political and policy questions. Knowledge, values, expectations, and feelings do not determine individual or group behavior, but they do predispose individuals and groups to act in specific ways. It is because values and expectations may be redirected by new knowledge that an understanding of the influence of population growth on other aspects of life is fundamental to voluntary change in growth rates.

## *SUMMARY*

Several indicators of educational achievement highlight the great variations between the developed and the less developed groups of nations. In the more advanced countries very high proportions of the people are literate, high proportions of youth are enrolled in school, and there is a fairly high proportion of teachers to the total population. Although the less developed nations vary widely among themselves on all of these measures, most are at a real disadvantage in the educational sphere. Rapid population growth complicates their attempts to extend education. Teachers cannot be trained quickly and probably are not trained well where education is only one of many desperate needs. The underdeveloped countries can in no way provide the kind of investment in education that the developed countries can afford. The gap between rich and poor nations will continue to grow because of the educational imbalance between the two groups. As the less developed countries exert themselves to provide basic literacy to their expanding populations, educational standards within the developed nations will probably continue to rise. In the United States, for instance, the proportions of youth in college continue to increase. In 1969, 21 percent of females and 35 percent of males aged 18 to 24 were enrolled in college (U.S. Bureau of the Census, 1970, p. 107).

Different nations often have quite distinctive cultural systems. Social research has recently provided us with data about what people in various societies say they know or believe about child mortality, the physiology of reproduction, the possibility of fertility control and contraceptive methods. These surveys provide political leaders with information that often counteracts common assumptions. Furthermore, there is now a basis upon which to compare the actual average number of children in completed families with the "ideal" expressed by individual respondents. Presumably the difference indicates that there is an interest in family planning. The effectiveness of birth-control methods varies widely and the success of attempts at family planning will vary in a similar way. Nations or social groups can facilitate or retard the availability of, and the motivation to use, various means of avoiding conception.

Population growth affects both the tangible and intangible values that people within any nation hold. The values people hold influence, in turn, their attempts to rationally manipulate their destiny, including their attempts at family planning. Rational control may seem hopeless, however, since population increase implies a decrease in individual importance, a rise in bureaucracy, and a decrease in freedom and human dignity. In the advanced countries, educated persons expect increased individuality and personal recognition, but are more and more regimented as part of the growing masses. Increasing numbers require increasingly formalized rules and regulations. There is less room to *avoid* stepping on other people's toes or polluting the air and water shared by the group.

## *REFERENCES*

BERELSON, BERNARD. 1966. KAP studies on fertility. In *Family planning and population programs*, eds. Bernard Berelson, *et al.*, pp. 655–68. Chicago & London: University of Chicago Press.

CARLETON, ROBERT O. 1966. The effect of educational improvement on fertility trends in Latin America. *Proceedings of the 1965 World Population Conference*. New York: United Nations.

EASTERLIN, RICHARD A. 1965. A note on the evidence of history. In *Education and economic development*, eds. C. Arnold Anderson and Mary Jean Bowman, pp. 422–29. Chicago: Aldine Publishing Co.

EBERHARD, WOLFRAM. 1970. On three principles in Chinese social structure. Reprinted from *Chinese Culture*, Vol. 11, no. 1 (March).

HARBISON, FREDERICK. 1963. Education for development. In *Technology and economic development*, ed. Scientific American, pp. 95–103. New York: Alfred A. Knopf.

KAHN, MASIHUR RAHMAN. 1967. A demographic approach to educational planning in Pakistan. In International Union for the Scientific Study of Population, *Contributed papers*, Sydney Conference, Australia, August 21 to 25, pp. 192–98.

KYLLONEN, R. L. 1967. Crime rate vs. population density in United States cities: A model. *General Systems*, 12, 137–45.

LADER, LAWRENCE. 1966. *Abortion*. Boston: Beacon Press.

LORIMER, FRANK. 1969. Issues of population policy. In *The population dilemma*, ed. Philip M. Hauser, pp. 168–206. Englewood Cliffs, N.J.: Prentice-Hall.

MICHAEL, DONALD. 1965. *The next generation*. New York: Random House–Vantage Books.

MYRDAL, GUNNAR. 1968. *Asian Drama*. 3 vols. New York: The Twentieth Century Fund.

———. 1970. *The challenge of world poverty*. New York: Random House–Pantheon Books.

NATIONAL SCIENCE FOUNDATION. 1960. *Professional manpower and education in Communist China*. Washington, D.C.: Government Printing Office.

POPULATION REFERENCE BUREAU. 1966. The expanding "universe of the untutored," *Population Profile*. Washington, D.C. (September).

RAINWATER, LEE. 1967. The lessons of Pruitt-Igoe. In *The public interest*, 8 (Summer) pp. 116–26.

REVELLE, ROGER. 1969. *Lectures on the population problem and what can be done about it*. Hitchcock Professor at the University of California, Berkeley (May).

SHINN, ROGER L. 1970. Population and the dignity of man. In *The Christian Century* (April 15), pp. 442–48.

UNITED NATIONS. 1963. Science and technology for development. *Report on the United Nations conference on the application of science and technology for the benefit of the less developed areas.* Vol. 6. New York: United Nations.

UNITED NATIONS Economic and Social Council. 1969. *Statistical yearbook, 1968.* New York: United Nations.

U.S. BUREAU OF THE CENSUS. 1970. *Statistical abstract of the United States, 1970.* (91st edition.) Washington, D.C.: U.S. Department of Commerce.

chapter 10

# POLITICAL ASPECTS OF POPULATION GROWTH

> *. . . The best solution for ensuring world peace is the widespread promotion of contraception and abortion. . . . Moralizing factions that oppose it must face the fact that they are engaged in dangerous war mongering.*
>
> Desmond Morris (1967)

Increasingly national leaders are recognizing that in planning on a national scale they cannot overlook the crucial population variable, or leave it to "nature," while trying to manipulate other aspects of nature.

In this chapter we will explore the effects of population increase on the political power of individuals, groups, and nations. How does the influence of individuals and groups change as population grows? To what extent does population size or growth contribute to or detract from a nation's power?

Political power may be defined as the ability to influence groups or nations to engage in policies which they would not otherwise undertake. This power may be exercised by providing rewards for compliance with one's goal, threatening the use of force for failure to comply, or actually using force when compliance has not otherwise been induced (Heer, 1968, p. 95). Population size and growth affect the distribution of power both within and among nations and have implications for international conflict and cooperation.

## *INTRANATIONAL*

Population size and rate of growth affect individual and subcultural power in numerous ways. Furthermore, they affect the way the relationship between population control and other societal concerns is perceived.

### *Individual "Powerlessness"*

Whether a nation has 200,000 or 200,000,000 citizens, there can be only one effective head of state. Surely the potential power of the individual citizen in the larger country is less than that of the citizen in the smaller one. The probabilities of any given individual achieving national recognition in politics, sports, music, science, or any other field is lower in the larger country. Even if leadership opportunities were allocated solely on the basis of talent, skill, and creativity, they would be less likely to fall to any given individual in a very large society. The leader, however, once having attained his position, has more potential power in the larger country.

The larger the population, the less impact an individual has in voting, the lower his chance of communicating with the political leaders of a nation. Leaders and would-be leaders can always claim that they represent the "silent majority" while brushing aside individual complaints or suggestions. The "powerlessness," or inability of the individual to influence local or national government, has undoubtedly led to the formation and promotion of special interest groups and to the organization of mass rallies and demonstrations. Large cities facilitate crowd formation and collective actions on the basis of felt injustices. At the same time city officials, even if they wished it, would find it more difficult to be responsive to the needs of all citizens as size increases.

The United States National Advisory Commission on Civil Disorders (1968) found (contrary to the assumptions of some) that in the riot cities surveyed, Negroes were indeed disadvantaged—"that local government is often unresponsive to this fact; that federal programs have not yet reached a significantly large proportion of those in need; and that the result is a reservoir of unredressed grievance and frustration in the ghetto" (p. 136). Within each community the Commission investigated the objective conditions and also the attitudes expressed by the participants.

> In the Newark survey, respondents were asked how much they thought they could trust the local government. Only 4.8 percent of the self-reported rioters, compared with 13.7 percent of the noninvolved, said that they felt they could trust it most of the time; 44.2 percent of the self-reported rioters and 33.9 percent of the noninvolved reported that they could almost never trust the government.
>
> In the Detroit survey, self-reported rioters were much more likely to attribute the riot to anger about politicians and police than were the noninvolved. Of the self-reported rioters, 43.2 percent—but only 19.6 percent of the noninvolved—said anger at politicians had a great deal to do with causing the riot (p. 135).

We have already noted that the riot cities had grown in the proportions of black between 1950 and 1965 far more rapidly than nonriot cities. When felt injustice cannot find satisfaction in the political arena, street violence may be an effective way to communicate the frustrations of any group—to transform individual powerlessness to group power.

The larger the nation, the easier it becomes for anyone to appeal to the masses through slogans rather than rational discussion of alternative goals and possible means to their achievement. Even in a democracy the quantity of votes rather than the quality of (knowledgeable) decisions determines who will rule and for what purposes.

Those who are angered by personal feelings of powerlessness and frustrated by slogans and mass advertising may increasingly resort to similar emotional tactics. It is easier to idealize than to practice the rational approach to the problems we would like to have solved.

Many college students have learned in recent years that in large universities students have a difficult time influencing administrators. No matter how many turn out at a rally, they are almost always a minority. At the same time, those who want to influence policy at any level often feel that it is impossible to effect change.

Past experience indicates that mass demonstrations and shows of force are more likely to lead to a response in kind than to rational discussion of the problems of human beings trying to live together on an ever larger scale. If numbers continue to increase and concentrate, human group life will become more difficult. It will take increasing effort on the part of individuals and governments just to maintain current living conditions.

Lest the reader think that civil disturbances occur only in advanced countries, it should be pointed out that in many of the most populous nations demonstrations are so frequent as to lack news appeal. Politically motivated street fights and murders are a daily problem in Calcutta. Ulla Olin (1966) points out that "sporadic rioting is a common occurrence" within the nations of Asia and the Far East. The populations of these nations are "under constant stress. . . . The demands of adjustment and change are profound and incessant" (pp. 314–15). The outlook for the future is no better. The city populations of the less developed countries have had an influx of relatively young males. Freed from traditional bonds, they typically have few or no friends. Jobs are scarce and unstable; housing is inadequate and expensive; frustration runs high. If food problems decrease, even greater migration to the cities and increased unrest may be expected.

Individual feelings of frustration and powerlessness are in part the unintended consequences of the choices individuals have made. As individuals we have chosen to reduce deaths, to create more children than necessary to replace the parents, to move to already congested urban areas, to tempt the young with material goods, and to seek "freedom" from, rather than responsibility to, other human beings. As these individual choices are multiplied, the unintended consequences become social problems. Erich Fromm (1941) has suggested that under such circumstances individuals often look to a strong leader to solve their problems. It is too early to tell whether human beings will choose to escape from freedom or to organize themselves to understand and reduce the problems of human group life.

In his writing on anomie and alienation, Raymond Aron (1968) points out that even if food production is able to keep pace with future population growth, even if the rate of economic growth exceeds that of population growth:

> *Quantity* even in the developed countries runs the risk of impairing *quality*—that is, of reducing those qualities which cultured men throughout the centuries have held to be the highest. Great questions arise. Are states composed of hundreds of millions of men compatible with the known forms of political democracy? Would the actual participation of the citizen in public life, which is already so filled with malaise, be tolerable? Can men avoid an increasing and almost abstract rationalization of bureaucracy and the extension of impersonal relations to new domains—to universities, for instance? Some distinction again is inevitable between the *small number* of highly gifted individuals who warrant and may obtain special treatment and the *large number* who will receive only the training necessary to perform their jobs effectively. Is it feasible to think of educating every one so that each man can realize his full potential, if not in work, at least in leisure? Or is it not more likely to foresee a society in which these millions and millions of human beings will be able to enjoy certain comforts, but will be condemned to the creative existence of termites? (p. 114).

### *Group Power*

In complex contemporary societies the individual is most likely to seek to accomplish goals by joining with other individuals. Social organizations assume many forms and may employ a variety of means to achieve specified ends.

Many groups now assume that power comes from large numbers. Membership may be increased either by gaining converts or by reproducing from within. Such long-term collectivities as racial, religious, and ethnic groups may be quite eager to increase fertility and may promote large families under the supposition that the increased numbers will improve the relative position of the group within the larger society. Certain Black Power advocates within the United States have espoused such ideas. Yet, numerical superiority has never prevented the mistreatment of blacks in the south.

Whether a high rate of natural increase within a subcultural group is promoted or unplanned, it *may* diminish the group's power. In the United States, where blacks have been allowed to live only in restricted locales, high fertility and immigration into urban areas have complicated ghetto life. In Watts in 1965 approximately 30,000 persons were crowded into 1.9 square miles. The median ages of the nonwhite population were 13.5 for males and 17.1 for females, indicating that dependent youths far outnumbered adults. Yet whether from heredity or environment or both all studies show that children from small families score higher on the average than children from large families on a variety of tests of skill and intelligence, they have greater educational and occupational achievement (Carter, 1962). This is true even when social class background is held constant. Small family size, in turn, is most closely related to education, with well-educated blacks having very slightly lower fertility on the average than do whites of equal education. The children from these small families will be better able to take advantage of opportunities resulting from reductions in discrimination and increased civil rights than children from much larger ghetto families.

Many families are included in the poverty bracket, not because family income would automatically place them there, but because there are so many children to support on the given income (Gordon, 1965). In addition to tending to have small families, educated blacks have increased their incomes faster than any other group in American society (174 percent from 1960 to 1967).

Increases in occupational level and income may occur because small families are better able to take advantage of educational opportunities. American Jews, for example, make up only about 3 percent of the total population. Jewish immigrants started working in the lowest urban occupations, typically without knowledge of the English language. They stressed family and group ties and a high regard for education as a means of occupational advancement. With small, close-knit families, each child could receive attention and encouragement from "significant others."

Motivation to achieve remains high among this small group. Jewish fertility has been lower than that of any other religious group in the United States. Individual Jews have made tremendous strides in advancing their socioeconomic status, and surveys have shown that Jews have a higher average income and a generally higher occupational and educational status than either Catholics or Protestants (Bogue, 1959, pp. 701–6). Their political and economic influence is far greater than their proportion of the population.

Of course we cannot say that population size *never* determines political power, only that it is not *the* only determinant of power. Relative numbers mattered very much in the 1947 partitioning of India and Pakistan, decided on the basis of Hindu-Moslem majorities. Yet the disputed area of Kashmir, with a Moslem majority but a Hindu ruling class has been administrated by India.

Power is the ability to accomplish one's goals even over the objections of others. Throughout most of the history of the world, the poor made up the largest proportion of each country's population. Yet the poor clearly have not exercised great power. Even within those nations claiming to be "people's democracies," the division of power among various persons and groups is very unequal. It is not the size of the group, therefore, that determines its influence or power but rather its ability to motivate members to mobilize their resources and efforts to achieve valued goals.

## *The Competition of Groups for Power*

Even in most complex societies where there are many "power elites," influence is not equally distributed. The larger the society, the more likely that many small groups will form and compete for influence. This is true even when ethnic and religious differences are unimportant. The more individuals tend to identify with the group goals rather than with the overall society goals, the easier it becomes for them to press the advantage of the small unit even if the whole suffers. John Platt (1969) cites as an example the problem in New York City when the 1968 Ocean Hill-Brownsville teacher strike was combined with a police strike, a garbage strike, and a longshoreman's strike, all within a few days of each other.

Our dependence on one another makes us all vulnerable to such tie-ups. If each group continues to fight for the advantage of its own members without regard for the welfare of the larger society and the world, the life-chances of the human race are narrowed.

> Anyone who feels more hopeful about getting past the nightmares of the 1970s has only to look beyond them to the monsters of pollution and

**'I thought I was supposed to be in charge here'**

*Source:* LePelley in *The Christian Science Monitor,* December 11, 1970. Reprinted by permission from *The Christian Science Monitor,* © 1970, The Christian Science Publishing Society. All rights reserved.

FIG. 10–1

> population rising up in the 1980s and 1990s. Whether we have 10 years, or more like 20 or 30, unless we systematically find new large-scale solutions, we are in the gravest danger of destroying our society, our world, and ourselves in any of a number of different ways well before the end of this century. . . . [On the other hand] human predictions are always conditional. *The future always depends on what we do and can be made worse or better by stupid or intelligent action* (Platt, 1969, p. 1116; emphasis added).

## *Cultural Lag*

The "population explosion" is so recent a phenomenon that there has naturally been a lag in a general recognition of how population growth aggravates internal political problems. Citizens within the nations of the world may demand a reorganization of national priorities, but political leaders in even the most affluent countries of the world are not able to accomplish everything at once. Limiting population growth will not solve all of the world's problems. Yet the continued increase of human numbers retards current attempts to extend public health, to clean the waters and air, to provide housing, education, transportation, and recreational facilities. As populations increase, central governments will grow larger in order to provide more services to more persons in ever more tenuous relation to one another. Whether or not government policy facilitates the prevention of births, we expect the cultural lag to be bridged; people will eventually use new technology to reduce births. Considering the consequences of rapid growth in population, the sooner and the faster the drop in fertility, the better.[1]

## *INTERNATIONAL*

Population pressures within nations may also lead to political conflicts and war among nations. Much as we would like to believe that war cannot continue to be used to resolve disputes in a world that possesses the means of total destruction, evidence indicates that the main motivating force in international relations today is nationalism. On the one hand, "nationalism is the sine qua non of industrialization" (Davis, 1955, p. 294). It motivates the postponement of gratification and thus spurs development. On the other hand, it also offers an excuse for international political and military conflict.

Although for each nation to pursue its own best interests clearly does lead to the good of all, narrow nationalism does tend to dominate in international relations. The number of member nations of the United Nations has expanded rapidly in recent years and most of the new members are new nations or newly independent nations. Political leaders in these nations are working to promote feelings of national unity and to protect their national sovereignty.

Whether the national leadership regards its people as military potential, as producers, or as consumers affects the nature of the competition among nations for international superiority. Many people still would tend

[1] Small declines in crude birth rates, especially evident among many island nations, may hint at the beginning of a trend. There is even some evidence that where the decline has already been significant as in Puerto Rico and Taiwan the rate of decline is more rapid than among European nations 50–100 years ago (see Kirk, 1971). A great effort has been expended to aid the fertility decline in both Puerto Rico and Taiwan. If these serious efforts could be extended world-wide, the cultural and time lags between reduced mortality and fertility might be cut.

to see population growth as an advantage where military or productive competition is paramount. In the past the growth of human numbers was also seen as advantageous in that it raised the demand for market goods. Some persons are just now beginning to see the negative effects of population growth on international competition in military potential, in production, and in consumption standards.

### *People as Military Potential*

Throughout most of human history wars have been fought with relatively large numbers of soldiers. Young men have often been regarded as cannon fodder. Technological improvements in the tools of war have often made the difference between victory and defeat, but the contestants typically faced each other en masse, and large numbers of men were required to utilize the available weapons. Today battles are decided not by numbers, but by their training and skill in the use of modern weapons. Surely the Japanese surrender in 1945 came as a result not of the numbers of Americans in battle but of the use of a new and powerful means of destruction. Nuclear powers have resisted using these new weapons for twenty-five years, but if their national existence were threatened, it is unlikely that the nuclear retaliation would be withheld. It is inconceivable, for instance, that Russia would watch an invasion by millions of Chinese without using their nuclear stockpile. Thus even though the Chinese outnumber the Russians three to one, their numerical superiority is cancelled by the present technical superiority of the Russians.

An even more dramatic example is provided by the Arab-Israeli war of 1967. The Arabs outnumbered the Israelis by about 40 to 1; Egyptians alone outnumbered Israelis (including Israel's Arabs) by 12 to 1. Yet the training, skills, and technical weapons of the Israelis quickly proved superior to the numerical preponderance of Arab military. An increase in Arab training and in the sophisticated weapons supplied by Russia are now emphasized by the Arab group in recognition of the fact that numbers alone no longer win wars.

Although political leaders in the past viewed a large and growing population as an advantage in case of military adventure, some leaders are now reversing that historical pattern. Numerical superiority is no longer the deciding factor in military encounters; indeed, a large and rapidly growing population may be a drag on a nation that is attempting to advance its military technology. Even when military tools are provided by other nations, some type of exchange is usually required, if only allegiance or dependence. Newly sovereign nations have little to gain from exchanging one kind of dependent relationship for another.

### *People as Producers*

A large and rapidly growing population is a political disadvantage wherever the population as a whole is poor, which is the case in almost all countries with a high growth rate. Malnourished populations have little energy for either military or productive purposes. International trade is extremely limited because these nations have little to exchange for the many items they want and need. The political power and even respect commanded by nations whose populations are growing at a rapid pace may be quite limited.

Many national leaders have regarded people primarily as producers. Marx suggested that only by way of human labor can value be added to raw materials. It follows, according to Marxism, that human beings must be an asset to the productive capacity of a nation. Until very recently Communist nations have dogmatically adhered to this stance.

However, Communist as well as non-Communist nations have begun to recognize that people are more than producers or national assets, that people are also consumers or a liability even in a nation of workers. Productivity is affected by investments in workers themselves and in the capital goods they use. Even agricultural productivity is heavily influenced by monetary investment in machinery, fertilizer, seeds, water, and even in the training of farmers. Funds for such an investment are more difficult to obtain when population is large in relation to resources or is growing rapidly, whether the nation is primarily capitalistic or communistic in organization.

### *People as Consumers*

Only in totalitarian political or slave systems can human beings be regarded merely as machines of production. Whenever political leaders care, or are forced to care, about the living standards of their population, people come to be seen as consumers as well as producers. The provision of consumer goods can create internal problems for political leaders and can also influence political relationships among nations.

When the demand for consumer goods is high (and especially when a nation's production is inadequate to provide for the subsistence of a population), political leaders may be forced to beg, borrow, or steal the required goods. The poor of the world are no longer satisfied with their lot; they have "rising expectations" and demands for material advantages. Probably no developing country is capable of contracting for sufficient capital or of receiving outright gifts in amounts that will satisfy its people. When politicians are unable to satisfy the people's demands, or meet their own political promises (and sometimes even when they satisfy them partially), political turmoil may result.

The probability of political instability makes it difficult for government officials to contract for outside aid. Many countries average one or more political coups a year, making it difficult to arrange international agreements.

It has often been assumed that totalitarian leadership is more efficient in organizing a population for production. However, some China watchers interpret the "cultural revolution" as evidence to the contrary. Whether and to what extent consumption can be postponed in any political system is questionable. Political leaders all over the globe are watching the race for developments between India and China. While India is making an attempt to develop its production and raise the quality of its population through democratic means, China has a greater variety of means of persuasion at its disposal. Instead of *recommending* that farmers use new methods, it can communalize large areas and force new techniques.

Both countries have problems of population growth. Both will have to satisfy the increasing demands of those growing numbers. Both have had to import vast quantities of food to support their populations. Both are now committed to reducing the rate of population growth. Both have had difficulty implementing national *plans* to control population and development in general.

National planning, whether of the five-year variety or the long-range type, has become an international fad. Government plans are usually announced with great fanfare, but the results are frequently accompanied by apologies. According to Edward S. Mason (1963):

> The record shows that the espousal of planning, from country to country, is more eloquent than its execution. The plan as it emerges from the planning agency may fail to win acceptance as a program of action by political authority, or, if the plan is ratified by duly constituted authority, political pressures and interministerial rivalries may cause expenditures to depart from its prescriptions; or the resources and development requirements as envisioned by the plan may turn out to be so remote from actual capabilities that the plan loses significance as a set of policy directives (p. 192).

Any national plan requires the cooperation of both leaders and citizens. Plans must be realistic, or discouragement with the results may increase the people's dissatisfaction.

While India's problems and internal disagreements are in plain view of all the world, China's internal conflicts can only be estimated. We have little real knowledge of how many lives have been sacrificed, what kinds of internal disagreements led to the "cultural revolution," or whether regimentation of human beings will lead to better material conditions than can be achieved by the more democratic methods attempted in India. In order to improve the material conditions of life, both nations need the cooperation of their enormous populations. Whether they can be motivated by rational appeal or only by force is still not certain, but it is instructive that both nations are trying to limit population growth as a part of their attempts to improve both production and consumption.

More nations are likely to look to Japan as a model of economic advance with democratic means and a stabilization of population. The Japanese moved from a traditional policy of isolation from other nations to an attempt to win and settle other nations by war. One of the obvious motives of the Japanese was to disperse a rapidly increasing population. Several million Japanese had colonized other lands by the end of World War II. Since that time the Japanese have used rational means to limit their population growth and to expand their production and consumption. [The Japanese economy is now the third largest in the world, and its growth rate approached 15 percent per year by 1970.] Its economic growth rate is without precedent or parallel: 9 percent per year (in real terms) in the 1950s, more than 10 percent in the 1960s, and 13–14 percent in the past few years (Abegglen, 1970, p. 31). At this rate the per capita living standards of the Japanese could be the highest in the world before the turn of the century. What the Japanese could not obtain by war they may gain through their productivity.

### *International Power*

David Heer (1968) suggested that four variables, in combination, are necessary to explain a nation's power in relation to other nations. The variables were mentioned earlier, but it is important to stress their interdependence: (1) population size; (2) per capita production; (3) government motivation to achieve international goals; and (4) the efficiency of the government in mobilizing resources.

POPULATION SIZE. Although no very small nation can be considered powerful in the sense of coercing other nations to actions against their will, it may be influential in terms of the persuasive power of its international leadership, its education, or its productive skills. Thus Sweden, with a population of only eight million, has contributed individual and national leadership in international affairs.

It is becoming increasingly clear that large populations are not necessarily advantageous to national military or productive goals. The training and skills of a population and their productive tools are more important than their numbers alone.

PER CAPITA PRODUCTION AND INCOME. Of the top twenty nations in population size, only five, the United States, West Germany, United Kingdom, Italy, and France, are among the top twenty nations in per capita gross national product (see Table 10-1). Furthermore, of those nations in the top twenty in per capita GNP, only two (Kuwait and Puerto Rico) have populations that are increasing more rapidly than the world average of 2 percent per year. Each of these is a special case, Kuwait because of enormous oil resources and Puerto Rico because of very heavy investment from outside. Large populations and high per capita incomes, then, do *not* usually go together. The possibility of economic development is diminished wherever large populations with low per capita incomes are found. Most of the nation's production is needed simply to maintain the population at a minimum level of living. Little may be skimmed for reinvestment in capital goods, education, or international trade.

TOTAL NATIONAL INCOME. Although Kingsley Davis (1964) has suggested that the best indirect measure of national power may be total rather than per capita income, he also points out some of the disadvantages of that measure in comparison with the per capita income indicator. When total income is examined, China and India are among the top-ranking nations of the world, solely because of the size of their populations. On a per capita basis, they fall near the bottom of a rank ordering of nations. Their population size may be considered a handicap when they try to improve the efficiency of resource use, social organization, knowledge, level of skills, and so forth. Sweden surely has greater international influence and far higher living standards than either Mexico or Brazil, both of which have the same total national income. A subsistence level of life leaves nothing to invest in the "arts of war," improved tools of production, housing, and so forth. In an emergency, nations with a high per capita income are better able to mobilize their natural and human resources than are countries with very low per capita incomes. For these reasons, per capita income may be the best indicator of a nation's potential to influence other nations.

MOTIVATION. There are no easy measures of government motivation to achieve international goals or of efficiency in mobilizing resources. Unfortunately, most of the indicators that might supply clues to motivation and efficiency are related to war goals. Measures of prestige and influence within the United Nations or of advantages obtained in international trade agreements would require the attention of very specialized analysts. Widespread consensus on a complete rank ordering of nations according to international power is unlikely in the near future.

TABLE 10-1 *A Rank Ordering of the Top 20 Countries in Population, in Per Capita GNP, and in Total National Income, 1970*

| *Rank Order* | *Country* | *Population (in millions)* | *Rank Order* | *Country* | *Per Capita GNP (converted to U.S. $)* | *Rank Order* | *Country* | *Total National Income, 1968 in billions of U.S. $* |
|---|---|---|---|---|---|---|---|---|
| 1. | China | 760 | 1. | U.S. | 3,670 | 1. | U.S. | 880.7 |
| 2. | India | 554 | 2. | Kuwait | 3,563 | 2. | Russia | 235.3 |
| 3. | Russia | 242 | 3. | Sweden | 2,500 | 3. | Japan | 141.9 |
| 4. | U.S. | 205 | 4. | Canada | 2,380 | 4. | W. Germany | 132.7 |
| 5. | Pakistan | 137 | 5. | Switzerland | 2,310 | 5. | France | 126.6 |
| 6. | Indonesia | 121 | 6. | Australia | 1,970 | 6. | U.K. | 102.9 |
| 7. | Japan | 103 | 7. | Denmark | 1,950 | 7. | Italy | 74.8 |
| 8. | Brazil | 93 | 8. | France | 1,950 | 8. | China | 68.4 |
| 9. | West Germany | 59 | 9. | New Zealand | 1,890 | 9. | Canada | 62.3 |
| 10. | United Kingdon | 56 | 10. | Norway | 1,860 | 10. | India | 41.1 |
| 11. | Nigeria | 55 | 11. | W. Germany | 1,750 | 11. | Australia | 29.8 |
| 12. | Italy | 54 | 12. | Belgium | 1,740 | 12. | Brazil | 28.2 |
| 13. | France | 51 | 13. | U.K. | 1,700 | 13. | Mexico | 26.7 |
| 14. | Mexico | 51 | 14. | Finland | 1,660 | 14. | Sweden | 26.3 |
| 15. | Philippines | 38 | 15. | Netherlands | 1,520 | 15. | Poland | 25.7 |
| 16. | Thailand | 36 | 16. | E. Germany | 1,300 | 16. | Spain | 25.2 |
| 17. | Turkey | 36 | 17. | Austria | 1,210 | 17. | Netherlands | 25.2 |
| 18. | Egypt | 34 | 18. | Puerto Rico | 1,210 | 18. | E. Germany | 21.1 |
| 19. | Spain | 33 | 19. | Israel | 1,200 | 19. | Belgium | 20.7 |
| 20. | Poland | 33 | 20. | Italy | 1,120 | 20. | Pakistan | 15.3 |

*Sources:* Population Reference Bureau, *World Population Data Sheet* 1970 and United Nations, Economic and Social Council, *Statistical Yearbook, 1968*, 1969, Table 183.

Whether they are totalitarian or democratic, the capacities of governments for organization depend to some extent upon the efforts and coordination of the population. Government motivation to achieve international goals must receive the support of the population if the mobilization of national resources is to be efficient. That is one reason why ideological propaganda is used in so many countries. A charismatic leader may stir a population to solidify national commitments. In contrast, a government that is permeated by graft and corruption or that lacks organizational skills will be unable to make maximum use of available resources.

EFFICIENCY. In order to maximize its economic and political efficiency and therefore its [national] power, a government needs:

1. A population that is adequately nourished and free of debilitating diseases, thus being able to take advantage of opportunities.
2. A high proportion of the population educated, literate, and able to manipulate, perfect, and even invent complex tools.
3. A high proportion of the labor force in nonagricultural pursuits.
4. A low density of persons on agricultural land. In many Asian countries, the number of persons per square kilometer of agricultural land makes agriculture less efficient and possibly less productive.
5. A high proportion of the population in urban areas would allow more efficient land use, communication, and transportation. However, many less developed nations already find their cities congested even though they still contain very low proportions of the total population. At the same time the nations face high and increasing rural densities, which shows that the problem is the rate of population increase.
6. A combination of low birth and death rates. High birth and death rates can be said to be inefficient from a number of perspectives: high birth rates sap the energy and health of mothers and reduce their contribution to the labor force; high birth and death rates together indicate widespread ill health; ill health in general increases dependency for the population as a whole, while high birth rates increase the proportion of the population in the early dependent years; high birth rates retard the possibility of providing improved education for all children and high death rates result in lower investment in the young because of the high probability that they will die before reaching the productive years; the combination of high birth and death rates requires greater spending on the necessities, leaving fewer funds available for capital goods to increase the employment and efficiency of the labor force.

In population size, in rate of population growth, in per capita production and income, and in the ability and efficiency required to work toward national and international goals, the less developed nations are at a very great disadvantage. It is difficult to foresee any improvement without enormous effort on the part of the less developed countries and a sacrificial commitment on the part of the already advanced nations. A reversal of the growing gap in the quality of human life will require international cooperation in every sphere, including that of population limitation.

FIG. 10–2 *What are the standards of human existence implied by these people and the regulatory signs? This is the normal "out to lunch" crowd in New York City's financial district. UPI Photo*

In this atomic age all thoughtful persons should work toward a reduction of raw political power in the international arena. Political units might then cease considering a large and increasing population as support for either military machines or productive machines. Rather than people being valued for strengthening the state, the state or political unit could then exist in order to raise the quality of human life. Clearly such an outcome would require a reorganization of political thinking within most countries. It would both require and facilitate an extension of cooperative efforts among nations. Nations that do not aim to exert power by force of their numbers but that give priority to raising the standards of human existence are likely to begin the most effective programs of population limitation.

### *International Relations*

In the immediate future the very low standards of living, together with the rising expectations of people in the less developed countries, are likely to exaggerate political instability both within and among nations.

There are several different and even contradictory international political aspects of population growth.

On the one hand, differential rates of population growth have aggravated the gap between the "have" and "have not" nations, leading to greater tensions, less understanding, and fewer common interests between the two groups. In addition, population growth in the less developed countries has retarded the past efforts of the more developed countries to help the less developed group. In many quarters despair has resulted when past foreign aid has disappeared without leaving any apparent results.

On the other hand, the cooperative effort of the United Nations has led to improvement in the means of obtaining and analyzing population data. The data seem to be increasing recognition of the fact that population growth is not a problem merely for those countries with the most rapid increase but a world problem that will require an increase in international cooperation.

Many of these tendencies are at work simultaneously, some leading in the direction of increased conflict, others in the direction of greater cooperation among the nations of the world.

CONFLICT. Johan Galtung (1964) suggests that aggression is most likely to be instigated by nations in positions of "rank-disequilibrium," especially where other attempts to achieve equilibration have failed and the culture has had some previous practice in overt aggression. Although further evidence is required, the thesis is not without logical and empirical support. That is, war is most likely to be used by nations who rank themselves high on some important dimension (such as population or territorial size) and low on other important dimensions (such as per capita income). Nations that are low on all relevant rankings or that lack the ability to compare themselves with others will have little aggressive potential. "Rising expectations" and better international communication, however, increase the visibility and frustration of rank-disequilibrium and thereby enlarge its aggressive potential. (We saw the very great differences in rank-ordering of the few countries listed on Table 10-1). To the extent that aggression is perceived as a means of improving rank-position—when other routes have been closed off—or found ineffective—it is to be expected. Since national leaders have been eager to tell their people about aggregate improvements in GNP, health, and so forth, but reticent to confess per capita stagnation, the demands and frustration of the world's poor may be expected to multiply. One of the best ways to divert a population from their internal quarrels and dissatisfactions is to find a scapegoat outside the nation itself. Recognizing this social universal makes the behavior of political demagogues seem a rational, indeed necessary, attempt to solidify the national group. The ravings of a leader against the discrimination of country *x*, the border skirmishes of country *y*, or seen and unseen evil forces may weld a people together in a way that rational appeal never could. And the less a people have practiced rational behavior, the more effective is wild oratory. It is to be expected, therefore, that scapegoating will be used effectively among the poor and uneducated populations of the world, precisely those who can least afford to expend their energies on emotionalism. Border skirmishes or unproductive rivalries may be promoted in order to take people's minds off their own unhappy circumstances.

Real differences in levels of living and overcrowding may also be used as an excuse for military expansion. Population size or growth rates are not the only cause of international conflicts, but are considered a reason for attempts at political and military expansion—in the past, at present, and in the future.

Earlier in this century Germany, Italy, and Japan committed aggression against other nations and tried to justify their actions by insisting that they required living space. Very early in the thirties Japan claimed that her seizure of Manchuria was necessary to assure a food supply for Japan's growing population. In 1941 the Japanese foreign minister announced that Oceania could support 600–800 million people and that it must be made a place to which Asiatic people could migrate (Organski and Organski, 1961). Italy also thought herself overpopulated and justified the conquest of Ethiopia by calling it a settlement for Italians. Few Italians actually settled in Ethiopia, but that was irrelevant to the position of the expansionist leaders. It was the Germans who made *Lebensraum* a household word throughout the world. The Nazis repeatedly demanded their "fair share" of world space, citing facts and figures to back their claims that Germany was overpopulated compared with other nations and therefore entitled to the return of its colonies and further territorial expansion in Europe. The doctrine of *Lebensraum* was neither consistent nor altogether factually accurate, but the motivating power of beliefs does not depend upon their consistency and accuracy.

The call for *Lebensraum* is now greater than ever before in world history. Recent incursions of the Chinese into India and skirmishes at the Russian border are surely related to population problems. The North Vietnamese attempt to unify the whole of Vietnam may be motivated as much by the lower rural density and higher agricultural productivity of the South as by the ideological commitments of the North. The short war between Honduras and El Salvador in 1969 was clearly attributable to the press of population. Several hundred thousand Salvadoreans, densely crowded even on their agricultural land, spilled across the border looking for land and jobs in Honduras. Unfortunately, the people of Honduras, which is also growing rapidly, but is not yet as densely crowded as its neighbor (see Table 4-5), had troubles enough of their own. Resentments increased and when Hondurans finally tried to physically expel the newcomers, the two nations entered into open war. Fortunately the Organization of American States was successful in negotiating an early ceasefire. The root cause, however, will continue to plague the two countries. Each one is expected to double its population in only twenty-one years at the present rate of increase.

FIG. 10–3 *Millions of refugees recently crossed the Indian border from East Pakistan. With populations already at bare subsistence, any additional crisis, whether natural or manmade, increases the possibility of disease (the cholera epidemic), famine (as refugees depend on emergency food rations), and war (as threats between India and Pakistan increase).* Wide World Photo

Future prospects are not rosy. The futility of war is not yet evident to the people of the world. Warren Thompson concludes that under the pressure of population, the larger nations of the Far East may very well resort to force to gain access to additional resources. Small countries will probably be unable to resort to force by themselves, but will require increasing aid to prevent internal chaos or take-over by other nations. The larger nations, especially if authoritarian leadership prevails, could probably squeeze enough from an already weak population to wage some kind of war if they desired to do so (1959).

Finally, as Paul Ehrlich (1968) has pointed out:

> Thermonuclear war could provide us with an instant death rate solution. Nearly a billion people in China are pushing out of their biologically ruined country towards Siberia, India, and the Mekong Rice bowl. The suffering millions of Latin America are moving towards revolution and Communist governments. An Arab population boom, especially among Palestinian refugees, adds to tensions. The competition to loot the sea of its fishes creates international incidents. As more and more people have less and less, as the rich get richer and the poor poorer, the probability of war increases. The poor of the world know what we have, and they want it. They have what is known as rising expectations. For this reason alone a mere maintenance of current levels of living will be inadequate to maintain peace (p. 12).

In spite of the dismal prospects, international cooperation must be facilitated as our only hope to avoid the extermination of the human race.

COOPERATION. According to the United Nations (1963):

> Such instruments of joint action as the International Bank for Reconstruction and Development, the International Monetary Fund, the International Development Association, the International Finance Corporation, the Special Fund and the Expanded Programme of Technical Assistance, as well as special programmes like the World Food Programme and the United Nations Children's Fund (UNICEF), have thoroughly proved their worth even where inadequate funds have greatly restricted their operations. Their special contribution to, and close co-ordination within, the [Development] Decade are apparent (p. 17).

If, within the "Second Development Decade," the 1970s, cross-national aid for population control, education, and economic development could be increased (perhaps by taking an increasing proportion of the yearly increase in GNP of the developed nations) and channelled through those international agencies that have already proven themselves, many of the previous problems of such aid and many of the objections to it in the past might be greatly reduced.

With regard to population the United Nations agencies have both encouraged and aided the cooperative collection and publication of statistical data on population: total numbers and age distributions, marital status, births, deaths, health, population movement, labor force participation, education, and so forth. National statisticians have benefitted from the advice, training, and research assistance of the professional demographers of the United Nations. The data gathered by individual nations have been evaluated, organized, and published by the various departments of the U.N. Over the last 20 years these data have indicated that the source of a great many problems is the unprecedented population growth of the world as a whole, but especially that within the less developed countries. It is impossible to deny that population is and has been growing more rapidly than ever before in the history of the world and that the rate of growth has itself been increasing. In and of themselves, the data make it very difficult if not impossible for the old ideological arguments and slogans to hold any influence. It has become increasingly clear that population growth can no longer be ignored. As members of the less developed countries have recently overwhelmingly outvoted the Communist and Catholic blocs on the issue of aid to countries that request help in family planning, the Communists at least have begun to reassess their ideological position on population.

Not very long ago the United Nations agencies and most individual nations, including the United States, were refusing family planning help to countries that requested it. In fact, foreign aid for birth control services has always been extremely rare, due in part to the fact that even the developed countries have generally banned the promotion and sale of contraceptives. The decline of birth rates in the developed countries thus occurred in spite of, not as a result of, governmental policies. Changes in this policy area are recent and often still limited in nature.

Furthermore, aid and advice on birth control, even when countries have requested it, may be misinterpreted by segments of the population of the receiving country. Political opponents of the party in power have frequently accused birth control advisors of participating in a racial, ethnic, or religious plot to weaken their power. These accusations often work against the accusers, however, as the peoples rush to obtain information that will help them limit their numbers of offspring.

The Swedish were the earliest and have probably been the most effective single nation to share information on birth control. They began a research and action program in Ceylon in 1958, and since then have participated upon request in programs in Pakistan, Tunisia, and the Gaza Strip. Sweden has also been instrumental in bringing the question of international aid for population limitation to the forum of the United Nations. That international body can more adequately handle requests for aid on the scale needed than could any individual nation. It is also less likely to be accused of "imperialism" or "genocide." As General Assembly votes continue to favor family planning more and more strongly, the old dogmatic positions will lose more adherents than they will gain.

Whether increased cooperative effort in the field of population can lead to increased political cooperation in other areas is uncertain. It may be that, as limiting population and improving the quality of human life come to be viewed as world problems rather than problems of individual nations, joint efforts in population limitation may lead to increased cooperation in many political and cultural activities.

Recognizing the problem of rising human numbers and the simultaneous destruction of the environment, Aldous Huxley (1969) suggests:

> Power politics in the context of nationalism raises problems that, except by war, are practically insoluble. The problems of ecology, on the other hand, admit of a rational solution and can be tackled without the arousal of those violent passions always associated with dogmatic ideology and nationalistic idolatry. There may be arguments about the best way of raising wheat in a cold climate or of reforesting a denuded mountain. But such arguments never lead to organized slaughter. . . .
>
> Power politics, nationalism, and dogmatic ideology are luxuries that the human race can no longer afford. Nor, as a species, can we afford the luxury of ignoring man's ecological situation. By shifting our attention from the now completely irrelevant and anachronistic politics of nationalism and military power to the problems of the human species and the still enchoate politics of human ecology we shall be killing two birds with one stone—reducing the threat of sudden destruction by scientific war and at the same time reducing the threat of more gradual biological disaster (p. 19).

The challenge of international cooperation or conflict are plain to all. The stakes are high: we literally have everything to gain or everything to lose. The population explosion and the threat of nuclear war may force our political cooperation. As U Thant solemnly concluded at the twenty-fifth anniversary celebration of the United Nations:

> If there were any alternative, the success or failure of the United Nations would be relatively unimportant. . . . But, as far as I can see, there simply is no alternative means in sight for attempting to deal with the swarm of increasingly urgent global problems which now beset us, especially now that survival itself may be the critical question. . . .
>
> Population, poverty, food shortage, urbanization, the squandering of natural resources, the pollution of the whole environment—these are problems we have hardly begun to face. . . .
>
> Even if all our great political problems were miraculously to vanish overnight, we would still be confronted with some of the greatest challenges the human race has ever faced.
>
> It is intolerable that the peoples of the world should have to live indefinitely on the brink of disaster. . . . We must move from power politics to collective responsibility, from narrow national or commercial interests to a sense of earth patriotism and global solidarity. . . . (Oakland Tribune, 1970, p. 3c).

## *SUMMARY*

A number of political aspects of population growth have been discussed. Within countries the political influence of each individual is likely to decline as population increases. Political appeals to the masses by way of slogans will be more easily carried out than rational discussion of issues and alternatives.

Nevertheless, many religious, racial, and ethnic groups have supposed that larger numbers would bring increased political influence. The reverse may be the case wherever large numbers of children lower the family's or group's ability to maximize its opportunities. The fact that power is related to influence and not merely to numbers means that the quality of education, skills, and motivation are more important than numbers in the political process.

Since the population explosion is such a recent phenomenon, there has been a time lag within every nation in recognition of the multiplicity of effects. The lag in recognizing the negative aspects of population growth is due in part to the historical tendency to view large and growing populations as a national and political asset. Since people fought and died in wars, they were assumed to be a military asset. Since people produce "things," they were assumed to be a productive asset. Now, however, those who seriously consider the data will be likely to conclude that large numbers do not necessarily win wars, that rapid population growth may indeed be a military, economic, and, therefore, political liability to a nation.

All over the world national leaders have been trying to repair their dikes instead of working to control the floodwaters at their source. The United Nations has been a positive force in advancing knowledge about techniques for collecting and analyzing population information. As more specific knowledge has become available and as the rate of population increase has risen, more and more nations have begun to recognize that population growth is a block to many of their national goals.

Population growth may stimulate either international conflict or cooperation. It is sobering to think that in the matter of world war we are no longer playing a zero-sum game, in which one participant or group wins and the other loses. It is quite likely that international conflict will result in loss for everyone. On the other hand, an increase in international cooperation—dealing with population reduction, economic development, and increasing the quality of life—could produce a winner-winner game, advantageous to all.

## *REFERENCES*

Abegglen, James C. 1970. The economic growth of Japan. *Scientific American* 222 (March), 31–37.

Aron, Raymond. 1968. *Progress and disillusion*. New York: Frederick A. Praeger.

Bogue, Donald J. 1959. *The population of the United States*. Glencoe, Ill.: Free Press.

CARTER, C. O. 1962. *Human heredity*. Baltimore: Penguin Books.

DAVIS, KINGSLEY. 1955. Social and demographic aspects of economic development in India. In S. Kuznets *et al. Economic Growth: Brazil, India, Japan*. Durham, N. C.: Duke University Press.

———. 1964. The demographic foundations of national power. In *Freedom and control in modern society*, eds. Morroe Berger, *et al.*, pp. 206–42. New York: Octagon Books.

EHRLICH, PAUL R. 1968. The population explosion: Facts and fiction. *Sierra Club Bulletin* (October), pp. 11–14.

FROMM, ERIC. 1941. *Escape from freedom*. New York: Holt, Reinhard & Winston.

GALTUNG, JOHAN. 1964. A structural theory of aggression. *Journal of Peace Research* 1, 95–119.

GORDON, R. A. 1965. An economist's view of poverty. In *Poverty in America*, ed. Margaret S. Gordon, pp. 3–11. San Francisco: Chandler Publishing Co.

HEER, DAVID M. 1968. *Society and population*. Englewood Cliffs, N.J.: Prentice-Hall.

HUXLEY, ALDOUS. 1969. The politics of population. *Center Magazine*, a publication of the Center for the Study of Democratic Institutions, vol. 2 (March), 13–19.

KIRK, DUDLEY. 1971. A new demographic transition? In *Rapid population growth*, pp. 123–47. Prepared by a Study Committee of the Office of the Foreign Secretary National Academy of Sciences with the support of the Agency for International Development. Baltimore: Johns Hopkins Press.

KUZNETS, SIMON, *et al.* 1955. *Economic growth: Brazil, India, Japan*. Durham, N.C.: Duke University Press.

MASON, EDWARD S. 1963. The planning of development. In Scientific American, *Technology and economic development*. New York: Alfred A. Knopf.

*Oakland Tribune*. 1970. Thant pleads for collective effort. Oakland, Calif. (October 25), 3c.

OLIN, ULLA. 1966. Population growth and problems of employment in Asia and the Far East. *Proceedings of the World Population Conference, Belgrade, 1965*. Vol. 4, 314–16. New York: United Nations.

ORGANSKI, KATHERINE, & A. F. K. ORGANSKI. 1961. *Population and world power*. New York: Alfred A. Knopf.

PLATT, JOHN. 1969. What we must do. *Science* 166 (November 28), 1115–21.

POPULATION REFERENCE BUREAU. 1970. *World population data sheet*. Washington, D.C.

THOMPSON, W. S. 1959. *Population and progress in the Far East*. Chicago: University of Chicago Press.

UNITED NATIONS. 1963. *Science and technology for development. Report on the conference on the application of science and technology for the benefit of the less developed areas*. Vol. 6. New York: United Nations.

UNITED NATIONS Economic and Social Council. 1969. *Statistical Yearbook, 1968*. New York: United Nations.

UNITED STATES Bureau of the Census. 1966. Characteristics of the south and east Los Angeles areas: November 1965. *Current Population Reports*

Series p. 23, no. 18 (June 28). Washington, D.C.: Department of Commerce.

United States National Advisory Commission on Civil Disorders. 1968. *Report of the National Advisory Commission on Civil Disorders.* New York: Bantam Books.

chapter II

# POSSIBILITIES: FAMILY PLANNING OR POPULATION CONTROL?

*Once, as President, I thought and said that birth control was not the business of our Federal Government. The facts changed my mind. . . . I have come to believe that the population explosion is the world's most critical problem.*

Dwight D. Eisenhower (1968)

The ideas people hold spring from cultural values and past experiences and, in turn, influence present and future behavior. Thus it is important to review some of the dominant themes about population that have circulated within and among various societies and in the United Nations in recent years.

After highlighting the major population theories and ideologies, we will investigate their influence on national and international policy. For the most part these policies have revolved around the concept of "family planning." Nations have either promoted, been permissive toward, or indifferent to, or forbidden family planning programs within their borders. There is considerable disagreement as to the past and present effect of family planning programs. A distinction between these approaches and population control leads to a search for new possibilities beyond family planning.

## *THEORIES AND IDEOLOGIES*

Social scientists, either explicitly or implicitly, try to make a distinction between theories and ideologies. *Theories* are those sets of propositions about relationships that are held up to critical questioning and testing. To test our ideas means to look for evidence that will either prove or disprove our preconceptions. Yet, to search for evidence that may destroy one's "images" is not typical human behavior. Few persons are as scrupulous as Darwin, who noted every bit of evidence that could conceivably contradict his own theory. Darwin realized that it is easy to remember evidence in favor of our ideas and just as easy to forget or fail to notice evidence that might disprove our notions. It takes scientific commitment, therefore, to continue questioning one's theories.

*Ideology,* in contrast, is an *un*questioned pattern of beliefs and concepts that attempt to explain complex social phenomena in a simplified manner. An ideology usually offers answers to the questions bothering people as well as defining directions for the choices faced by individuals and groups. Ideologies aim at total explanation. They offer a dogma, a closed set of beliefs to be accepted in toto. Marx and Engels (1939) saw ideologies as forms of false consciousness, as systems of distorted and misleading ideas based upon illusions, in contrast to scientific theory. Of course, they considered their own ideas "scientific."

Our problem in attempting to distinguish between theory and ideology is that the theories that are developed often become ends in themselves. That is, theories may come to be accepted as "truth" by their proponents. Beyond that point a theory is no longer tested by groups of adherents. Evidence from outside the group itself is denounced, "proven wrong," ignored, or absorbed. When any theory is closed to critical questioning and testing (as Marxism and various religious creeds have sometimes been), it becomes an ideology.

Just as some religious dogmas have fallen in the face of overwhelming and undeniable contradictory evidence, some contemporary ideologies about population are being weakened by the flood of factual data on population growth and its consequences. The real problem concerns the probable influence of theories and ideologies on individuals and government bodies. How have theories influenced the collection of data for testing propositions? And, even more important in this current consideration, how long and to what extent will Catholic and Marxist ideology continue to retard the possibility of lowering the rate of population growth?

## *Theories of Population*

A review of population theory usually begins with the Malthusian scheme, but there were allusions to some current themes much earlier.[1]

[1] See United Nations (1953) and D. E. C. Eversley (1959) for details on historical references to population theories.

Both Plato and Aristotle suggested that the "good life" could be attained only if the population were large enough to be economically self-sufficient and capable of defending itself, but not too large for constitutional government. (Plato considered 5,040 as the number of citizens most likely to be useful to all cities.)

THE MALTHUSIAN THEORY. This theory was first published in 1798 in the famous *Essay on the Principle of Population, as It Affects the Future Improvement of Society*. Thomas Robert Malthus, economist, mathematician, and curate, wrote in response to the speculations of Condorcet and Godwin regarding the "perfectibility of man." Malthus's purpose was "to investigate the causes that have hitherto impeded the progress of mankind towards happiness; and to examine the probability of the total or partial removal of these causes in the future" (1960, p. 151—reproduction of 7th Edition, 1872).

The impediment to progress that Malthus thought had been almost totally overlooked was "the constant tendency in all animate life to increase beyond the nourishment prepared for it" (p. 151). Malthus noted that in plants and irrational animals numbers were restricted simply by a lack of nourishment and space. Man, however, had the ability to rationally control his numbers. Reason might interrupt "the instinct to increase the species" (p. 152). Unchecked, however, population would go on doubling itself every 25 years, or increasing at a geometrical ratio. Because of the limits of land and agricultural complexity, Malthus concluded that the maximum increases in food production would be in arithmetic ratio. Thus while human beings could reproduce themselves as the numbers 1, 2, 4, 8, 16, 32, food could be increased only arithmetically—1, 2, 3, 4, 5, 6. Obviously a six-fold increase in food supply would not meet the needs of a 32-fold increase in population. Although population cannot increase more rapidly than the food necessary for survival, there is a wide range between minimal survival needs and food adequacy. The food/population dilemma is still with us, as Malthus suggested it could be.

Malthusian theory advances a tautology: on the one hand, "the ultimate check to population appears to be a want of food, arising necessarily from the different ratios according to which population and food increase"; on the other hand, "the ultimate check is never the immediate check, except in cases of actual famine." Two types of general checks on population are discussed: the preventive and the positive. "The preventive check, as far as it is voluntary, is peculiar to man, and arises from that distinctive superiority in his reasoning faculties which enables him to calculate distant consequences" (p. 158). Malthus never considered contraceptives as acceptable preventatives, but thought that educated man's reason could lead him to "moral restraint," or late marriage and postponement of sexual intercourse. Nonmarital sexual intercourse, with or without contraception, was viewed as vice.

Since Malthus recognized that education and, therefore presumably, reason were rare, he was convinced that the positive checks would arise unavoidably. Some of these arise from the laws of nature and may be called misery; those which human beings bring upon themselves, such as wars, excesses and many other tragedies which it would be in their power to avoid, are of a mixed nature. They are brought on by vice and their consequences are misery.

Malthus spent a lifetime elaborating the theme. Inadequate though collection techniques were in his time, Malthus gathered a great deal of demographic data to examine the population checks at work in specific countries of the world. He made numerous errors in his thinking and in the data he used (see Davis, 1955), but his work remains pertinent because of the questions he raised and the way in which his essay stimulated further dialogue and research. His supporters and opponents both realized the need for more adequate information about population trends, and their causes and consequences—the relationship between a multiplicity of biological and sociological factors. Eversley (1959) suggests that "after Malthus, every writer became a Malthusian, an anti-Malthusian or a neo-Malthusian" (p. 10). While the lines may not be so easily drawn, there is no doubt that all current interest and progress in the field owes something to the early work of Malthus.

OPTIMUM THEORIES. Included in this group are all theories of population that indicate that population is too large or too small, thereby implying that there is some most advantageous, or "optimum," level of persons for any given society or region at some point in time. Presumably the optimum might change with alterations in resources, tools, capital goods, or organizational efficiency.

The work of Malthus stressed the possibility of population being too large. Durkheim (1933) suggested that in past history, and in some places in the late nineteenth century, population was too sparsely settled. Only as population increased in "physical density" could societies develop in "moral density" or in what is now called patterns of communication and interaction. These were assumed by Durkheim to be necessary for the development of specialization and the division of labor in society.

The advantages of the economics of scale, achieved when sparsely settled populations increased their numbers, were reviewed in Chapter 7. The advantages in transportation, communication, and social organization (including such things as mass production) are relatively obvious. However, most economists and thoughtful persons recognize that the continual addition of persons may lead, and in many countries has already led, to a situation of diminishing returns. In very simple terms, the growth of population in relation to land and tools may at one point in time lead to a per capita advantage for the entire group; continued growth may add a proportionate increase in production and per capita income, but will finally lead to a decreasing return.

It is clear that in many countries of the world population growth has led to diminishing returns. Not only has the land/man ratio fallen drastically, but population growth has been so great that incomes are almost completely used up on current consumption rather than being diverted in part to the tools and supplies that would help raise per capita output.

Unfortunately, discussions of optimum population are typically phrased in economic language. In most of the less developed countries the problem of overpopulation may be most easily understood in terms of raw economic disadvantages. However, large and growing populations may be detrimental to the advanced countries even if per capita dollar production is increasing. Populations may already be too large and growing too rapidly for us to cope with the multiplying problems of crowding, maintaining adequate nutrition, conserving natural resources (of the world, not just of the advanced nations), preventing the pollution of our planet, raising educational levels and living standards in general, and improving international relations.

It should be evident, then, that optimum population cannot be conceived in purely economic terms. Many other values are at work simultaneously in any given society. The concept of "optimum" should be expanded to include human welfare in general. More and more, the abundance of "things" produced is being recognized as constituting only one aspect of human welfare. The material effluence of America has not guaranteed, and may in some respects reduce, the physical and mental health of the population. The effects of the pollution "explosion" are being brought to our attention every day. It will take a great deal of time and commitment for these effects to be reversed and the multiplication of polluters complicates the job.

In many of the aspects of life that concern us most and in the sum of what we call the quality of human existence, there is no way to directly measure an "optimum population." The idea of an optimum may be viewed as a way of speculating about population levels rather than as a theory including testable propositions.

THE LOGISTIC "LAW." This law of population growth is related to the actual growth curve found among many insect and subhuman animal species. The logistic curve and the theory from which it is derived, particularly as developed by Pearl and Reed, suggest that human population in a limited physical environment will increase from a lower level at an ever-accelerating rate until the limiting factors of food and space are brought into play. The proportional rate of increase will then decline until the numbers of the population level off. The theory is expressed in a general way in the "S"-shaped curve in Figure 11-1.

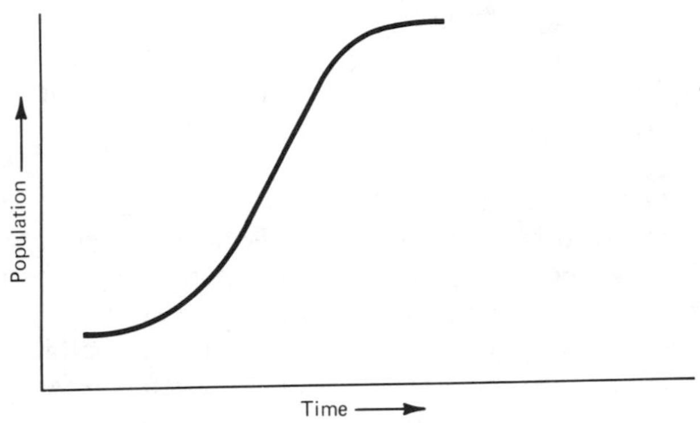


FIG. 11–1 *A Logistic Curve of Growth*

A number of different curves could be produced from the formula developed by Pearl and Reed. The formula has been used to describe the actual growth of populations and to predict the future growth of groups of people. Although it was developed by observing the actual multiplication of fruit flies, it has also been used with some success to produce logistic curves that fit the populations of Germany, England, and Canada. Furthermore, in 1920 Pearl and Reed were able to predict the 1950 population of the United States with an error of only about 1 percent (Petersen, 1969).

There are a number of problems with the scheme. It should be evident that for human populations it cannot be considered a "law." Since human beings intervene in and manipulate their environment, it is rare to find a limited physical environment that remains static over any long period of time. The logistic law is heavily biological in orientation, but human beings are able to exert some control not only over their physical environment, including the production of food, but also over their own biological reproduction. Man's ability to foresee the negative consequences of breeding up to the limit of food and space should enable the species to level off well *below* the absolute limits of food and space. Many advanced nations have already leveled population [for all practical purposes] well below the "ultimate" limit. The culture, especially in its level of knowledge and distribution of education, exerts a multiplicity of influences on human behavior, including reproductive behavior. Even where the logistic curve seems to fit the past population growth of a nation, it is not necessarily a good predictor of the future.

THE THEORY OF THE "DEMOGRAPHIC TRANSITION." This theory suggests stages of demographic evolution. After an initial stage of high birth and high death rates with little or no growth, a population begins to control the death rate. As the death rate declines slowly, the birth rate also begins to come under control. With some time lag, then, the birth rate is supposed to follow the death rate down to where both are at a low level and under firm control. The population, in theory, again produces little or no growth.

In Chapter 3 we noted that the theory of the demographic transition was both descriptive of what had occurred in many of the now developed countries during their period of industrialization, and it was used to predict what would occur in the less developed countries as they became industrialized. A great deal of our discussion has revolved around an examination of why the demographic transition has not occurred as was expected in the two-thirds of the world that is now underdeveloped. Although in the past slow population growth may have been advantageous to nations in the early stages of development, the rapid growth of populations now occurring in the underdeveloped nations retards the possibility of economic and industrial advance. Furthermore, even slow growth, continuing as it is in the advanced nations, may aggravate the problems that arise as unintended consequences of the advance of industry and affluence.

As a theory, the demographic transition implies flexibility. The time period and the birth and death rates may vary for specific nations of the world. It incorporates not one but many elements, since all of the positive and negative factors that affect fertility and mortality may be examined. Measurement of the factors involved may be recorded with a precision not possible in alternate theories. In itself, however, the theory is a model and not an explanation.

"Transition" implies that the growth is or will be overcome. Growth has not stopped completely in the advanced nations and has hardly begun to slow down in the less developed countries. The time lag between the decline in mortality and the drop in fertility has been very great, with little or no indication that fertility has begun to drop in most of the largest underdeveloped countries. The theory has the added disadvantage of having caused many world leaders to focus on economic development in the belief that with industrialization birth rates would automatically decline. It has taken some 25 years to realize the inadequacy of such a focus.

Concepcion and Murphy (1967) wrote:

> What is required is not a re-examination of the theory of demographic transition. What is needed is the creation of a theory that will tell us what

> fundamental relationships were involved in the historical transitions, what the key variables were, how the transition came about in the past, and how it might be repeated in the future (p. 6).

THE THEORY OF CHANGE AND RESPONSE. This is one of the most recent attempts to explain changing population trends. Davis (1963) suggests that population change and response "is not only *continuous,* but also *reflexive* and *behavioral*" (p. 345; emphasis added). It is reflexive in that after one component changes it is itself eventually altered because of the change it has induced in other components. It is behavioral in the sense that the process involves human decisions in the search for goals with the various means available to the individuals in a given environment. The study of population, then, includes a study of the biological, social, and cultural factors that may influence population levels and trends. According to Davis, "the subject has frightening complexity" (p. 345).

Japan is one example of a nation in which, "faced with a persistent high rate of natural increase resulting from past success in controlling mortality, families tended to use *every* demographic means possible to maximize their new opportunities and to avoid relative loss of status" (p. 362; emphasis added). An understanding of this process has been inhibited by the failure to visualize the many phases and variables involved.

A grasp of the complexity of population change may eliminate the hope for simplistic solutions. If we are not to wait for starvation as the "ultimate" check or to assume that the "demographic transition" is just around the corner, we must learn about all of the motivations that might encourage human beings to limit their numbers. It is not enough to provide many means of birth control or greater knowledge about how to use them. We need to learn more about *why* people actually do use them more or less effectively. Fear of hunger has been around for a long time, but it has not yet motivated birth control. The economic situation, even early industrialization, is only one factor in population study. Faith in the theory of transition will not guarantee economic improvement or declining birth rates. Individual human beings must recognize that their behavior will affect their futures. If hope for a better way of life can be linked to the importance of family limitation, people may alter their child-bearing behavior. But will the masses around the world realize (and realize soon) that they have an impact on their own future lives? It is not simply up to government leaders, or help from abroad, or fate, or technology, or unseen spirits, to bring about the progress that is possible, yet unrealized. Each person plays a part in human group life. The decisions or drift of millions of individuals add to or decrease the quality of life for all.

## *Ideologies and Population Policy*

Most of the world's great religions have offered sets of beliefs that are relatively closed. Not all of these dogmas have a direct influence on population policy.

NON-WESTERN RELIGIONS. Petersen (1969) has detailed the ambivalence of non-Western religions on the question of contraception. Hinduism seems contradictory in its frank sexuality on the one hand and its call to "dama," or self-restraint, on the other. "We should reduce our wants and be prepared to suffer in the interest of truth. Austerity, chastity, solitude and silence are the way to attain self-control" (*Radhakrishnan,* quoted in Petersen, p. 582). Among the most orthodox Hindus, marital coitus is a semireligious rite. There is some disagreement as to whether avoidance of procreation is permitted or denied in the sacred texts. Opposition to contraception is not an important part of Hindu dogma, however, and has not been an impediment to the birth-control movement in India. Yet, the belief in reincarnation could work against birth prevention, since spirits need bodies into which to be reincarnated.

"Buddhist texts say nothing directly upon the subject of contraception" (Ryan, quoted in Petersen, p. 583). A sampling of the opinions of monks and priests revealed differences according to their education. None of the best-educated found any objection to contraception in Buddhism. Forty-one percent of a middle group and 90 percent of the least-educated disagreed, feeling that to willfully prevent birth is tantamount to killing.

Confucianism was the ethical basis of the old family culture of China. Although Confucian scholars condemned abortion and infanticide, both seem to have continued among, respectively, the urban gentry and the peasantry.

Islam has appeared to be pronatalist in its emphasis on continuance of the family line. Sons, in particular, are essential to a marriage, and the cultural desire for a son or several sons tends to increase the average family size. The necessity of a male heir, however, does not require a ban on contraception. The Koran contains conflicting statements and is open to various interpretations with regard to contraceptive intent. Although Islam does not directly forbid birth control, Dudley Kirk (1966) concludes that of all of the world's great religions, the interrelated beliefs and practices of the Moslems (i.e., the early and universal marriage of women, the acceptance of polygamy, etc.) lead to high fertility.

The influence of Christian missionaries on the contraceptive beliefs and policies of non-Western nations has been in the direction of opposing the spread of knowledge about and availability of contraception as well as abortion and infanticide. Until very recently (about 1954) the Protestant, as well as Catholic, organizations opposed the spread of contraceptive practices.

WESTERN RELIGIONS ON BIRTH CONTROL. The origins of this thought are the same as those of the Protestant and Jewish religions. The tendency of Protestant denominations to encourage individuals to interpret the meanings of the scripture for themselves has meant that their organizational leadership has generally been more easily influenced by the membership than has the Catholic hierarchy. Changed social conditions, such as the population explosion, have influenced policy in the Protestant churches more easily than in the Catholic. Nevertheless, both branches of Christianity share the same Biblical heritage and early church teachings.

The Old Testament injunction to "be fruitful and multiply" (Genesis 1:28) is interpreted by some as a social, not a religious requirement. Throughout the Old Testament one finds marriage expected of everyone, with the assumption that marriage means sexual intercourse and that both pleasure and offspring result (Cole, 1955). The only clear example in the Old Testament of an act with contraceptive intent involved *coitus interruptus*, probably the most universal and most commonly practiced method of averting conception through the ages. The "sin of Onan" was interpreted by Augustine as the avoidance of parenthood, and "the Lord killed him for it" (Fagley, 1960, p. 171). As one of the four founding fathers of the early Church, Augustine has influenced all of Christianity, and his teachings are of tremendous importance in the contemporary doctrine of the Roman Catholic Church. St. Augustine declared that no attempt must ever be made either by wrong desire or evil appliance to prevent procreation. Any who sink to such depths are guilty of animal conduct. He could not under any circumstances allow sex for pleasure or the expression of love alone; there must always be at least the possibility of impregnation. He strictly forbade birth control, abortion, or the exposure of unwanted children. He even condemned what was later called the "rhythm" method of birth control (Cole, 1955).

Thomas Aquinas, in synthesizing Augustinian and Aristotelian thought, stressed procreation as the primary purpose of marriage. Monogamous unions were thought to be particularly characteristic of those species, especially the human, in which the young need the care of both parents.

Since underpopulation was a continuing problem in Europe because of very high death rates, the reformation of Luther and Calvin had no reason to suggest a change in the major purpose of marriage. The layman's responsibility for interpreting the scripture, however, opened the door to denominational splits in many areas, not the least of which has been contraceptive ideology.

Catholic doctrine, on the other hand, has not been open to interpretation by the laity. It is rather a set of beliefs to be interpreted by Priests for the laity. It is a total belief system, to be accepted as a whole, and to change one part may challenge the infallibility of the entire doctrine. The authority of the Pope has been complete in the past. It is increasingly under challenge in some places. The findings of the advisory committee on population and the regulation of procreation, established by Pope John XXIII and formalized by Paul VI, were suppressed and ignored by the Pope. However, members of that commission later "leaked" their conclusions to the press. Seventy of the 84 members thought that the final responsibility for decisions in the area of family planning should rest with the conscience of individuals in consultation with their spiritual and medical advisors (Lorimer, 1969).

Meanwhile, birth records and research questionnaires indicate that most educated Catholics in the advanced countries have been using, at least since the turn of the century, available means of contraception to limit family size. The declines in birth rates over the last 100 years in the Catholic countries of Europe differ very little from those in the non-Catholic nations (see Figure 11-2). Altogether the 11 Roman Catholic countries (Ireland, Austria, Belgium, France, Luxembourg, Czechoslovakia, Hungary, Poland, Italy, Portugal, and Spain) had an average annual birth rate virtually the same as that of the non-Catholic nations: 18.1 and 18.0, respectively (Population Reference Bureau, 1968).

The problem with Roman Catholic dogma is the political influence it carried in Latin America, where birth rates average 40 for the continent. Religious leaders have encouraged the legislators of each nation to forbid the distribution of the means of birth control.

Yet a United Nations study in six Latin American cities found that women who attended Mass most frequently produced slightly fewer children on the average than women who were only "nominally" Catholic. The strongest correlation was an inverse one between education and fertility (reported by Population Reference Bureau, 1968). Those with least education have the greatest difficulty learning about and finding the tools of contraception, because their availability is restricted.

However, Catholic influence is felt in its ability to restrict formal birth-control programs for the educated and the uneducated alike. With contraceptives unavailable, abortion is widely used to limit births. In Uruguay, some sources report that there are three abortions for every live birth. In Chile where statistics are more reliable studies show that one-fourth of all pregnancies end in induced abortions (Population Reference Bureau). Abortion is the most expensive form of birth control

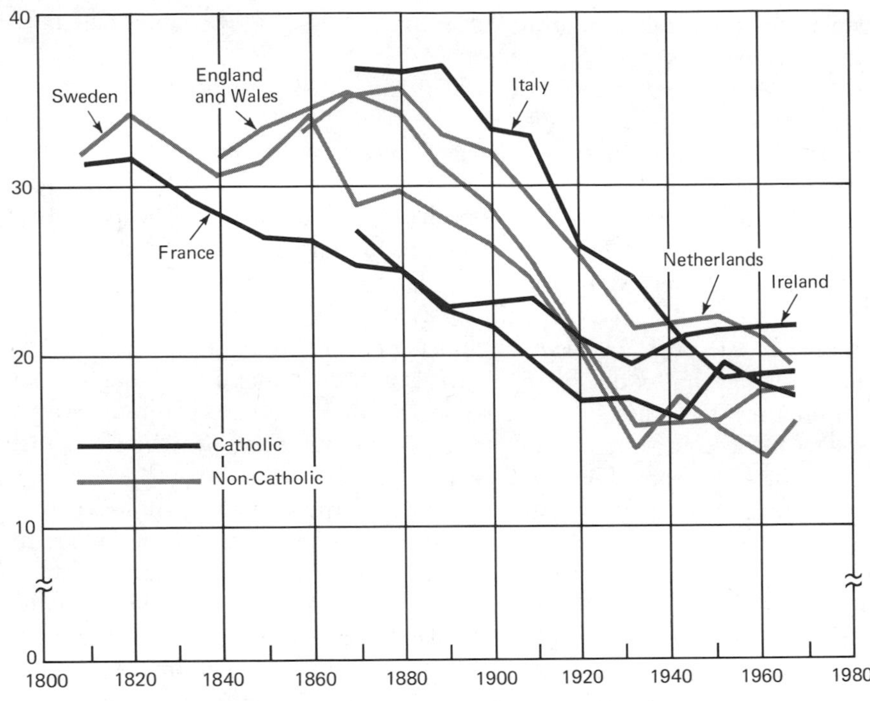


*Source:* Population Reference Bureau, Population Profile, July 1968, p. 1.

FIG. 11–2 *Birth Rate Trends: Selected Catholic and Non-Catholic Countries of Europe*

in terms of the time and energy of the mother and the physician, the use of hospital beds, and so forth. Because of Church objections, abortions are usually performed illegally, without the safeguards of medical knowledge, and often are followed by complications requiring hospitalization. The suppression of the knowledge and tools of contraception, then, may be simply increasing the costs of limiting births for people who are determined to do so. The Vatican recognizes the dangers of the population explosion, but offers only two unlikely means of birth control: complete or periodic abstinence.

Not only has the Catholic Church retarded the spread of knowledge and means of birth control within nations where it has direct political influence, but it has also opposed aid proposals that might be implemented through the United Nations. The Catholic countries, together with those of the Communist bloc, have stalled U.N. activity in the field of family planning.

MARX ON POPULATION. Marx mounted a personal as well as ideological attack on Malthus, not because Marx had an opposing set of ideas regarding population, but rather because Malthus' biological law was in conflict with the Marxian "law" of economics. Marx wrote:

> If Malthus' theory of population is correct, then I can *not* abolish this [iron law of wages] even if I abolish wage-labor a hundred times, because this law is not only paramount over the system of wage-labor but also over *every* social system. Stepping straight from this, the economists proved fifty years ago or more that Socialism cannot abolish poverty, which is based on nature, but only *communalize* it, distribute it equally over the whole surface of society! (Marx, 1933, p. 40).

Marx saw that if there was indeed a tendency for the human species to reproduce up to the capacity of the food supply, then common ownership of the means of production could not prevent poverty but only distribute it equally. Marx argued, therefore, that overpopulation could occur only under the capitalist system of ownership. That system required unemployment or "relative surplus labor," he claimed.

Not only do contemporary Germany and Japan provide examples to the contrary, but the biggest unemployment problem is to be found among the large and rapidly growing populations of the agrarian nations of the world, even those in which there is little or no private ownership of the means of production.

According to Marx, human labor alone added value to raw materials; it followed that additional labor must be advantageous in a socialist system moving toward communism. However, the possibility of diminishing returns from additional units of labor, with a given supply of tools and machinery, implies a lower per capita return. If labor alone added value, nations would have little incentive to industrialize, either by private or common ownership.

The twentieth-century problem, then, cannot be resolved by dogmatists of either the Malthusian or the Marxian school. Both are partly correct, but both are limited. Neither economic reorganization nor population limitation alone can raise the standards of human life. The focus has been primarily on economic structures. Increasingly, the necessity of combining population planning with economic planning is being recognized. However, just as a few Russian Marxists are beginning to recognize the problems incurred by populations that are doubling in 20–25 years, some contemporary leftists in the U.S. following the arguments of Lenin, oppose anything, including birth control, which might lessen the misery of the proletariat and postpone revolution. They even oppose discussion of population problems as diverting attention from the real problems of the world (see *Concerned Demography*, January, 1971). Responding to these critics Leon Bouvier (1971) suggests, "There is no concrete evidence that rapid population growth (and the accompanying large proportion of youth) will necessarily result in social revolution. Indeed, one could argue that social revolutions will come only *after* some progress has taken place—perhaps as a result of declining population growth" (p. 38).

THE RUSSIAN RESPONSE. According to the Population Reference Bureau, 1967b, this has followed the Marxian line, in so far as possible, and political advantage, in so far as necessary. The Marxist–Leninist doctrine on population has been used for its propaganda value both within and outside of the Soviet Union. The verbiage is instructive. At the 34th anniversary celebration of the Union of Soviet Socialist Republics in 1951, Lavrenti P. Beria said:

> Whereas, in the camp of the capitalists, the imperialist cannibals are employed in inventing various "scientific" means for wiping out the better part of humanity and reducing the birth rate, in our country Comrade Stalin has said, "People are the most precious capital and their well being and happiness are the government's great concern" (Population Reference Bureau, 1967b, p. 90).

In 1955, even after the waning of Stalinism, Khrushchev spoke in similar words: "Bourgeois ideology invented many cannibalistic theories, among them the theory of overpopulation" (p. 91).

In this century, the Russian population has been reduced by wars, revolution, political repression, and natural disasters. Soviet losses, due to exceptionally high death rates, birth reductions, and emigration, have been estimated to range up to 70 or 80 million. Population growth from 1913 to 1959, a period of almost 50 years, was only 30 percent. (In the same period United States growth was 80 percent and in Brazil the population tripled.)

The Soviet government changed its internal population policy radically a number of times during those years. In 1920 abortions were legalized, and both marriage and divorce were made easy formalities. The apparent purpose was to increase the freedom of women and facilitate their participation in the labor force. By 1936 there had been a complete reversal, including a tightening of marriage and divorce laws and a redefinition of abortion as a criminal offense. At that time the concern seemed to center on the declining birth rate at a time when Stalinist policy required additional labor for agricultural and industrial development. The relegalization of abortion in 1955 made the USSR appear to be pronatalist and antinatalist at the same time. Some rationale for each of these shifts was found in Marxian dogma.

Strict adherence to the Marxist theory of population was publicly questioned within the Soviet Union for the first time late in 1965, just a few months after the World Population Conference. Professor Boris T. Urlanis of the Institute of Economics of the Soviet Academy of Sciences, in a reply to a Soviet critique of an American article, suggested that problems of population:

> are not at all imaginary; they are quite real. . . . it is important that the population problem for most of these underdeveloped countries be solved right now. . . . Therefore, a definite population policy is as significant for them as are the problems of the development of the economy and culture (quoted in Brackett, 1968, p. 165).

A month later M. Kolganov, a colleague of Urlanis, drew attention to the physical limitation of space and air and distinguished between a merely quantitative and a qualitative way of life. The debate continued among the limited readership of the Russian journal *Literaturnaya Gazeta*. Late in 1966 it was noted that "in the abstract, increased manpower should favor social and economic development, but the concrete reality in the Afro-Asian countries is such that this favorable factor changes into its antithesis." Professor Arab-Olgy, Section Chief in the Laboratory for Population Problems, Department of Economics, Moscow University, points out that a society must choose: "Does it prefer to double the prosperity of an unchanging population every 20 years, say, or to double the population in approximately the same time while preserving the same standard of living?" (quoted in Brackett, 1968, p. 170).

Each of these articles was answered by those repeating the old line, but the mere fact that such a public debate could take place indicates some progress and openness to data. Finally, articles have been produced for the world audience indicating a new direction. In the September 1966 issue of *International Affairs*, published in English and French as in Russian and considered to be the showcase of Soviet thinking on foreign affairs, an article by Y. Guzavaty focuses on the population problems of developing countries. As an example he cites the United Arab Republic (Egypt), which long ago confiscated large landholdings, nationalized the Suez Canal and other foreign property, and assumed state ownership of 90 percent of the means of production. Yet the population problem continues. The average size of a peasant's farm plot in 1960 had shrunk to about three-fifths what is was in 1927, and even irrigation from the Aswan Dam will not alleviate the food shortage.

Recognition of the problems related to population growth by these Russian scientists has recently been matched by a changed behavior of the Soviet bloc within the United Nations. Policy changes within that international body will be examined after a brief look at the Chinese response to Marxist dogma in relation to their own population growth.

THE CHINESE RESPONSE. This response is more difficult to assess because so little is actually known about the situation within China. In 1953 the first census taken after the Communists gained power registered 583 million persons. The count was well over the estimates of most Western demographers by 100–150 million. The *official* Chinese reaction, however, was neither shock nor dismay, but jubilation. The situation was interpreted in terms of Marxist ideology: the people were producers for the state and thus China could count on increased production. Very soon, however, the government began to encourage the limitation of births. By 1956 birth control propaganda was legitimized. Sterilization and abortion were permitted and the legal minimum age of marriage was raised (to 18 for females, 20 for men). During the intellectual "flowering" many specialists spoke out in favor of birth control as a means of limiting the population. Wu Ching-Ch'ao, professor in the China People's University, asserted: "Our goal is to reduce the present birth rate of 3.7 percent to 1.7 percent." The purpose was to improve the health of mothers and babies and to "make our production fall in line with the basic economic law of socialism and the law of development. . . ." Dr. Ma Yin-ch'u, Chinese economist and President of Peking University, said in a speech before the First National People's Congress in Peking (1957) "As we have a big population our consumption expenditure is enormous and not much national income can be saved for capital accumulation, which must be distributed among many production departments" (quoted in North, 1964, pp. 92–93).

Party spokesmen countered that, "as all of us know, the national income is the material wealth newly produced by the toiling people in the process of production" (p. 97). By 1958 the government had done an about-face and proclaimed a manpower shortage; birth control was played down. The population of China—in line with Marxist-Leninist-Maoist theory—was expected to transform the environment rather than to adapt itself by limiting its numbers.

With the falterings of the Great Leap Forward, the leaders again reversed direction. They campaigned against early marriage and premature unions motivated by "bourgeois affection." Sterilization was made easier, contraception encouraged, and abortion again permitted. The organization of the Chinese peasants into 20–30,000 communes that often separated the sexes surely limited births, whether intentionally or not.

By the mid-1960s propaganda efforts promoted the late twenties as an "appropriate" age for marriage and advised a limit of two children per family. Most party members do in fact have small families and "undisciplined" procreation is frowned upon. In an interview with E. Snow in 1964, Chou En-lai spoke of attempting to reduce the population growth of 2.5 percent per year to below 2 percent. He indicated that Chinese scientists had been working on an oral contraceptive and he expressed an interest in the American product (Snow, 1964).

With a population presently of about 800 million, even a 1 percent yearly increase would add eight million persons each year. An estimated natural increase of 2 percent would add about 16 million persons yearly. As in Russia, the reality of the increase has forced an accommodation between the ideology and the facts of population growth. It may even be that the reality of Chinese growth near the Russian border has hastened Soviet recognition of the population problem.

## *THE UNITED NATIONS ON POPULATION*

Very soon after the United Nations Charter was signed in 1945, the growth and movement of population was recognized by some as disruptive of the peace and an impediment to improving the level of living. The idea that population growth could threaten the objectives of that Charter may have been a factor in the establishment in 1946 of a Population Commission, charged with studying "population changes, the factors associated with such changes, and the policies designed to influence these factors" (Population Reference Bureau, 1967a, p. 2).

From the beginning, however, the members had trouble trying to implement the mandate to study action programs. The communist nations took every opportunity to use the international forum to repeat the Marxist line that "overpopulation is impossible." The accusations used by the communists to attack those who suggested that living standards might be improved by limiting population growth, included "cannibalism," "genocidal tendencies," "hatred against humanity," and "the crazy thought of Malthus" (p. 90). Delegates from the Catholic countries meanwhile claimed that policies that might imply fertility control were not even proper subjects for discussion. For 20 years the communist-Catholic axis, voting as a bloc in this one area, prevented any advance by the commission in policy or action.

Fortunately, the secretariat of the Population Division has made consistent and significant contributions to the collection and analysis of population statistics for the nations of the world. The publication of the *Demographic Yearbook* calls attention to the annual and trend data on fertility, mortality, and migration, together with related data on such factors as marital status and age structure. The U.N. has also sponsored two world conferences on population, in 1954 and 1965, which brought specialists from many countries together to share ideas and information. Because of the process of gathering data and comparing them over time and among nations, it has become more difficult to deny the very real problems implied by the rapidity of growth.

The first break in the ideological logjam came in December 1966—the "Statement by the Heads of Twelve States." The statement has been a major turning point in international recognition of the implications of population growth. The signers were leaders of both advanced and less developed nations in different parts of the globe. They made it clear that there was little propaganda value to be gained in further opposition to family planning.

Following an introduction recognizing population growth of the past, possible growth to the year 2000, and the social implication of both, the document states:

> As heads of governments actively concerned with the population problem we share the following convictions:
>
> *We believe* that the population problem must be recognized as a principal element in long-range national planning if governments are to achieve their economic goals and fulfill the aspirations of their people.
>
> *We believe* that the great majority of parents desire to have the knowledge and the means to plan their families; that the opportunity to decide the number and spacing of children is a basic human right.
>
> *We believe* that lasting and meaningful peace will depend to a considerable measure upon how the challenge of population growth is met.
>
> *We believe* the objective of family planning is the enrichment of human life, not its restriction; that family planning, by assuring greater opportunity to each person, frees man to attain his individual dignity and reach his full potential.
>
> Recognizing that family planning is in the vital interest of both the nation and the family, we, the undersigned, earnestly hope that leaders around the world will share our views and join with us in this great challenge for the well-being and happiness of people everywhere.
>
> Signators:
> Colombia, Dr. Carlos Lleras Restrepo
> Finland, Dr. D. Urho Kekkonen
> Malaysia, Tunku Abdul Rahman
> Morocco, King Hassan II
> Nepal, King Mahendra
> Singapore, Lee Kwan Yew
> Korea, General Chung Hee Park
> Sweden, Tage Erlander
> Tunisia, Habib Bourguiba
> United Arab Republic, Gamal Abdel Nasser
> Yugoslavia, Marshal Jospi Broz Tito
> India, Mr. Indira Gandhi
>
> (United Nations, 1966).

Just eight days after U Thant's presentation of the above statement, the General Assembly of the United Nations adopted Population Resolution #2211, which "requested the Secretary-General to pursue, within the limits of available resources, the implementation of the work programme covering training, research, information, and advisory services in the field of population. . . ." (Population Reference Bureau, 1967a, p. 23). For the first time approval was given for U.N. agencies to provide training, information, and advice when requested in addition to simply conducting research into population matters. Although the Soviet Union had voted against such proposals in May and June of 1966, the December resolution was approved by a unanimous vote, including that of the USSR.

The financing of such projects proved an immediate limitation. Total expenditures in the population area rose slightly from $1.07 million in 1965 to $1.66 million in 1966, but the sum is still only 1.4 percent of the total U.N. budget. One-fourth of the funds went to establish or support research training centers. [Very little is available for world-wide training, information, and advice on family planning.]

The changed attitudes among United Nations members is tremendously important. The actual possibility of providing significant aid in population limitation, however, is still very slight. It is important to recognize that time is of the essence. In the twenty years during which action and even debate was stalled within the United Nations the world population grew by one billion persons. And the rate of yearly growth is greater in 1970 than it was in 1966, when in turn it was far greater than it was in 1956, or 1946, or even before in the history of the world.

A 1969 panel on world population recommended a population commissioner for the United Nations and an increase in funding to $100 million per year. Since funding is a more reliable sign of commitment than mere verbal approval, we should watch to see how far the recommended increase will be implemented in the years to come. In 1966 the world spent 1,543 times the recommended $100 million on "national defense" (Population Reference Bureau, 1968). In view of the implications of the population crisis for world peace, a small diversion would not be out of order.

## *FAMILY PLANNING AS POPULATION POLICY*

Population policy is often strictly defined as only the legislation intentionally designed to influence one or more aspects of a nation's population, but intent is not always obvious. If we are concerned with population we must be aware of all the national and international policies that affect the phenomenon, either purposefully or unintentionally.

Changes in population must come about through the three major variables: fertility, mortality, and migration. The latter is of relatively minor importance even in those few countries still allowing immigration. The United States, for instance, still absorbs 400,000 and more net immigrants each year. These individuals make up about 20 percent of the annual increase in population (United States Bureau of the Census, 1970).

National and international policies have worked in a single direction in recent years—to drive mortality down. Although international effort to prevent wars have had only limited success, nowhere have casualties in the localized wars of the last 25 years made much of a dent in overall population growth. The reduction of mortality has, in fact, been the major source of the "population explosion." Policies continue to work toward further reduction of deaths. No one seriously recommends reversing mortality trends in order to limit population growth.

An interest in lowering population growth must, therefore, focus on manipulating the fertility variable. However, national policies that work toward a reduction of fertility are contrary to all precedents. Even today most countries have pronatalist policies, either on purpose or unintentionally. Most countries have restrictions on some, if not all, birth-control measures. Thirty nations have family allowances, often unrelated to need. Single and childless persons typically pay higher taxes. These policies are often taken for granted and their potential for maintaining fertility often goes unrecognized.

Antinatalist policies are very recent in origin and frequently only half-hearted. Commitment, as measured in terms of monetary expenditures, is insignificant. Table 11-1 lists the government positions on family

*TABLE 11-1 Government Position on Family Planning Programs and Policies, for 67 Specified Countries in the Developing World: Current Data* [1]

| *Region and Country* | *1970 Population (in millions)* | *Governmental Position* | | | *Date of Policy or Support (if known)* |
|---|---|---|---|---|---|
| | | *Policy and Program* [2] | *Support but no Policy* [3] | *No Support or Policy* [4] | |
| Algeria | 13.8 | | | X | |
| Cameroon | 5.8 | | | X | |
| Congo Democratic Republic | 17.5 | | | X | |
| Dahomey | 2.8 | | X | | 1969 |
| Ethiopia | 25.4 | | | X | |
| Gambia (The) | 0.38 | | X | | 1969 |
| Ghana | 9.0 | X | | | 1969 |
| Kenya | 10.8 | X | | | 1966 |
| Madagascar | 6.8 | | | X | |
| Mauritius | 0.87 | X | | | 1965 |
| Morocco | 15.5 | X | | | 1965 |
| Nigeria | 66.4 [5] | | X | | 1969 |
| Rhodesia | 5.2 | | X | | 1968 |
| Senegal | 4.0 | | X | | 1970 |
| South Africa | 20.2 | | | X | |
| Sudan | 15.8 | | | X | |
| Tanzania | 13.2 | | | X | |
| Tunisia | 5.0 | X | | | 1964 |

| Region and Country | 1970 Population (in millions) | Governmental Position: Policy and Program[2] | Support but no Policy[3] | No Support or Policy[4] | Date of Policy or Support (if known) |
|---|---|---|---|---|---|
| Uganda | 8.5 | | | X | |
| United Arab Republic | 33.3 | X | | | 1965 |
| LATIN AMERICA[6] | | | | | |
| Barbados | 0.3 | X | | | 1967 |
| Bolivia | 4.8 | | X | | 1968 |
| Brazil | 93.4 | | | X | |
| Chile | 9.8 | | X | | 1965 |
| Colombia | 22.1 | | X | | 1967 |
| Costa Rica | 1.8 | | X | | 1968 |
| Cuba | 8.4 | | X | | |
| Dominican Republic | 4.3 | X | | | 1967 |
| Ecuador | 6.1 | | X | | 1968 |
| El Salvador | 3.4 | | X | | 1967 |
| Honduras | 2.6 | | X | | 1965 |
| Jamaica | 2.0 | X | | | 1966 |
| Mexico | 50.7 | | | X | |
| Nicaragua | 2.0 | | X | | 1963 |
| Panama | 1.5 | | X | | 1969 |
| Peru | 13.6 | | | X | |
| Puerto Rico[7] | 2.8 | X | | | 1970 |
| Trinidad and Tobago | 1.1 | X | | | 1967 |
| Venezuela | 10.8 | | X | | 1965 |
| EAST ASIA[8] | | | | | |
| China (Mainland) | 850–900 | X | | | 1962 |
| Hong Kong[7] | 4.1 | | X | | 1956 |
| Korea (North) | 13.4 | | | X | |
| Korea (South) | 31.9 | X | | | 1961 |
| Taiwan | 14.2 | X | | | 1969 |
| BALANCE OF ASIA[9] | | | | | |
| Afghanistan | 16.9 | | | X | |
| Burma | 27.7 | | | X | |
| Cambodia | 6.9 | | | X | |
| Ceylon | 12.5 | X | | | 1965 |
| India | 552 | X | | | 1952 |
| Indonesia | 118 | X | | | 1968 |
| Iran | 28.7 | X | | | 1967 |
| Iraq | 9.0 | | | X | |
| Jordan | 2.4 | | | X | |
| Laos | 3.0 | | | X | |
| Lebanon | 2.7 | | | X | |
| Malaysia[10] | 10.4 | X | | | 1966 |
| Nepal | 11.1 | X | | | 1966 |
| Pakistan | 134 | X | | | 1960 |
| Philippines | 38.4 | X | | | 1970 |
| Saudi Arabia | 7.4 | | | X | |

*TABLE 11-1 (cont.)*

| Region and Country | 1970 Population (in millions) | Governmental Position: Policy and Program [2] | Support but no Policy [3] | No Support or Policy [4] | Date of Policy or Support (if known) |
|---|---|---|---|---|---|
| Singapore | 2.1 | X | | | 1965 |
| Syria | 6.1 | | | X | |
| Thailand | 35.7 | X | | | 1970 |
| Turkey | 35.5 | X | | | 1965 |
| Vietnam (North) | 21.3 | | | X | |
| Vietnam (South) | 18.3 | | | X | |
| Yemen | 5–6 | | | X | |

[1] Governmental positions are based on the latest information available, and population data are estimates for 1970. For a full description of the criteria used to classify governmental positions and the problems encountered, see text. Not shown separately in this table are a number of countries with small populations that have given little or no support to family planning activities or policies. The total estimated 1970 population of these countries is 73, 15, and 5 millions, respectively, for Africa, Latin America, and East Asia.

[2] Official antinatalist policy and a family planning program.

[3] Support of family planning activities but no official policy.

[4] Little or no support of family planning activities and no official antinatalist policy.

[5] Based on United Nations estimate for 1969 which may be high.

[6] Comprises the Caribbean area, and Central and South America, except for Argentina and Uruguay both of which have low fertility.

[7] Nonsovereign territory.

[8] Comprises China (Mainland), Hong Kong, North Korea, South Korea, and Taiwan; excludes Japan, which has low fertility.

[9] Excludes Israel, which has low fertility.

[10] Excludes Sabah and Sarawak.

*Source:* Dorothy Nortman, "Population and Family Planning Programs: A Factbook," *Reports on Population Planning*. The Population Council, July 1970.

planning in 67 of the less developed countries of the world. Only 25 have both an official antinatalist policy and a family planning program. All but four national programs are very recent in origin (1965 or later). Because of the newness of these commitments to reducing the rate of population growth, it is very difficult to evaluate their potentialities for effecting change.

The very earliest antinatalist policy and family planning program were those of India. In 1952 the government committed itself to reducing the rate of population growth. The weakness of the commitment may be indicated by the fact that even by 1956 expenditures from all sources totaled only one cent (U.S. equivalent) for every twenty persons per year! By 1964 the per capita spending on family planning programs had increased to almost three cents per capita (Nortman, 1970). The fourth five-year plan (1969–1974) has a budget of 15 cents per capita from government funds. The Indian government now leads other nations in the share of government funds (1 percent) budgeted for family planning—see Table 11-2. Other nations, clearly less serious about their support, have

*TABLE 11-2 Estimated Proportion of Married Women Aged 15 to 44 Currently Using Some Means of Birth Control, Per Capita Budget, and Percentage of Total Government Budget Allocated to Family Planning, Specified Countries, Latest Available Year, Usually 1969 or 1970*

| *Country* | *Percent Current Users* | *Annual Per Capita Budget (U.S. cents)* | *Percent of Total Government Budget* |
|---|---|---|---|
| Ceylon | 8.2 | — | 0.01 |
| India | 12.0 | 7.7 | 1.0 |
| Indonesia | — | 4.1 | — |
| Iran | 11.2 | 3.6 | 0.02 |
| Kenya | 1.0 | 3.3 | 0.1 |
| Korea (South) | 32.0 | 10.4 | 0.12 |
| Malaysia | 7.0 | 8.6 | 0.10 |
| Morocco | 1.0 | 1.6 | 0.11 |
| Pakistan | — | 17.2 | 0.9 |
| Philippines | — | 2.7 | — |
| Taiwan | 36.0 | 6.0 | 0.14 |
| Thailand | >7.6 | 3.0 | 0.01 |
| Tunisia | 10.0 | 22.2 | — |
| Turkey | 3.0 | 4.6 | 0.05 |
| U.A.R. | — | 5.7 | — |

*Source:* Data from Dorothy Nortman, "Population and Family Planning Programs: A Factbook," *Reports on Population Planning*, The Population Council, July 1970, Tables 15, 16, 18.

budgeted as little as 0.01 percent of government funds to aid family planning programs. A verbalized policy may, therefore, be viewed as a beginning step, but it should not lead us to assume with Bogue (1967) that "instead of a 'population explosion' the world is on the threshold of a 'contraception adoption explosion' " (p. 19).

In Pakistan, where an antinatalist policy and government support for family planning were initiated in 1960 and where expenditures increased from about 1 to 17 cents per person per year in the years since then, the hope was to reduce the crude birth rate from 50 to 40 per 1,000 and to reduce population growth from 3 to 2.5 percent each year. The goal remains as elusive as when it was established. Estimates for 1970, in fact, indicate a birth rate of over 50 and growth at 3.3 percent per year.

Very little actual data on mainland China's population is available. There is widespread doubt about the rates released by the government

(Chandrasekhar, 1967). The only other countries with antinatalist policies and long-term support for family planning programs are South Korea and Taiwan. Expenditures by government and outside sources have been relatively large over the last decade in those two countries (Nortman, 1970). Of all the less developed countries, these two report the highest proportion of women (aged 15–44 who are or have been married) who have ever accepted family planning information and the highest proportion of estimated current users of contraceptives (see Table 11-2). The results in South Korea and Taiwan have given population "optimists" (like Donald Bogue and Ronald Freedman) cause to visualize an end to the population explosion. Some of the objections to such an optimistic stand will be reviewed below, but it should be noted here that both of these nations received from the United States massive dollar aid and high-level expertise, which simply could not be provided to larger nations on the same proportional scale.

This is not to suggest that U.S. aid has not, cannot, or will not make a very great difference in what can be accomplished through family planning. Sizeable aid has barely begun, so it is not yet possible to specify results. United States foreign aid for family planning and research has increased from only $2.1 million in 1965 to $50 million in 1969. The last three presidents of the United States have recognized the importance of population growth in the world. On July 21, 1969, Nixon delivered to Congress the first presidential address devoted solely to the topic of population growth. Recognizing the causes of population growth and its rapidity, he said:

> As a result, many already impoverished nations are struggling under a handicap of intense population increase which the industrialized nations never had to bear. Even though most of these countries have made rapid progress in total economic growth—faster in percentage terms than many of the more industrialized nations—their far greater rates of population growth have made development in per capita terms very slow. Their standards of living are not rising quickly, and the gap between life in the rich nations and life in the poor nations is not closing (Nixon, 1969, p. 2).

The president pledged cooperation with international bodies and attention to family planning and research by the U.S. Agency for International Development.

The President's message also noted that the doubling of the U.S. population between 1917 and 1967 strained our capacity to educate youth, to provide privacy and living space, to maintain the processes of open, democratic government (p. 3).

The recently established Commission on Population Growth and the American Future has been studying the probable course of population growth and its environmental, economic, political, and social implications. The Commission called for the early implementation of the Family Planning Services and Population Research Act of 1970, which had been passed by overwhelming majorities of both the House and the Senate. The Act would encourage family planning and assist couples in preventing unwanted conceptions. A comprehensive national effort has been approved as policy (United States Commission on Population Growth, 1971). However, even if immigration were to stop altogether and if couples were to start having no more than an average of 2.0 children, the population of the United States "would continue to grow until the year 2037 when it would be a third larger than it is now (United States Commission on Population Growth . . ., 1971, p. 8). Figure 11-3 contrasts the growth of the U.S. population in the next 100 years on a two vs. three child average per family.

The United Nations General Assembly and the leaders of many of the nations of the world have recognized the multiple problems created by population growth. They support, at least verbally, programs of family planning. Can we thus assume that it is just a matter of time until the "explosion" is halted?

## *Rapid Growth Despite Family Planning*

National and international population policies have been developed to counteract the negative effects of continued rapid growth rates. The means usually suggested to reduce growth is "family planning." The terms "population control" and "population planning" are often used synonymously in family planning discussions, but even where family planning has been widespread, population is not necessarily under control.

The increased acceptance of family planning by national leaders and by individual families may be accompanied by continued population growth. Discussion of family planning focuses on the "right of parents to decide" the numbers and spacing of the children they wish to produce. Studies indicate that on the average parents want well over 2.0 children (see Table 11-3).

The debate continues between those who see family planning as a solution and those who caution that by itself it is no cure for population growth. The opposing points of view may be reviewed by reference to the writings of Donald Bogue and Ronald Freedman, as representatives of the optimists, and Kingsley Davis and Garrett Hardin, as spokesmen for the case against complete reliance on "family planning."

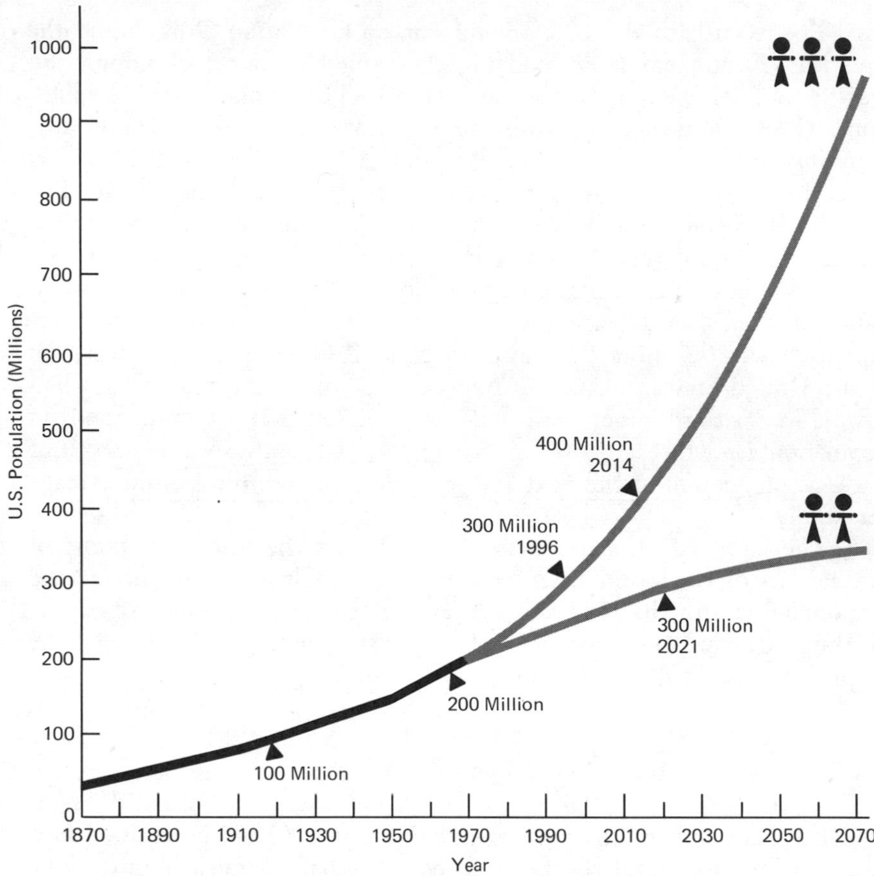


*Source:* United States Commission on Population Growth and the American Future, "Population Growth and America's Future—An Interim Report to the President and the Congress," March 1971, Washington, D. C.: Government Printing Office, p. 10.

FIG. 11–3 *Will the U.S. Add a Fourth 100 Million to Its Population? Effect of 3–Child Family vs. 2–Child Family.*

## *The Case for Family Planning*

At a time when most population specialists are seriously disturbed by the actual data on population growth, Donald Bogue (1967) has boldly predicted an end to the population explosion. He suggests:

> The exact time at which this "switch-over" took place cannot be known exactly, but we estimate it to have occurred about 1965. From 1965 onward, therefore, the rate of world population growth may be expected to

> decline with each passing year. The growth will slacken at such a pace that it will be zero or near zero at about the year 2000, so that population growth will not be regarded as a major social problem except in isolated and small "retarded" areas (p. 19).

Bogue presents a number of justifications for what he terms a "relatively optimistic prospect." It would be comforting to believe that "the end of the population explosion" is just around the corner, but both positive and negative aspects of recent developments must be ascertained.

Bogue claims:

> 1. Grass roots approval. All over the world, wherever surveys of the attitudes of the public with respect to fertility have been taken, it has uniformly been found that a majority of couples with three living children wish to have no more. . . . Objections to family planning among the masses on cultural, moral, or religious grounds are minor (p. 13).

However, three children on the average would be 50 percent above mere replacement of the mother and father; with considerable proportions wanting four or more (see Table 11-3), the averages are far higher. In Taiwan intensive studies have provided materials for the optimists, yet Freedman (1963) found that the average number of children wanted was four; only 9 percent wanted fewer than 3; and 20 percent wanted 5 or more (p. 232). Kingsley Davis (1967) reported that even in the "advanced" United States an average of 3.4 children was considered ideal by white women aged 21 or over in 1966. In Tunisia 4.3 were considered ideal, while studies found ideals of 4.3 in a Japanese village, 4.0 in a village near New Delhi, and 4.2 in a village in Mysore, India. In the city of Bengalore, the number of offspring desired by married women was 3.7, by married men 4.1. In seven Latin American capital cities, the average ideal was 3.4 children. Even if all children are planned and wanted, population growth will continue at a rapid pace, particularly in view of the high proportion of youth who will be entering the reproductive years in most countries.

> 2. Aroused political leadership . . . [is] accepting family planning as a moral and rational solution (p. 13).

The underlying assumptions here are that accepting family planning is the same thing as achieving zero growth and that individual families will want to procreate at the limited level that is good for the nation and the world. The family planning program in Taiwan has been encouraged at every leadership level. For all practical intents, the program has been a success. Yet, if Taiwan's age-specific birth and death rates were to remain at their 1968 level, the crude rates of natural increase would fluctuate

TABLE 11-3 *Desired Family Size in Selected Countries, Early 1960s* *

| | *Average Number of Children* | *Percentage Wanting 4 or More* |
|---|---|---|
| Austria | 2.0 | 4 |
| W. Germany | 2.2 | 4 |
| Great Britain | 2.8 | 23 |
| France | 2.8 | 17 |
| Switzerland | 2.9 | 22 |
| Italy | 3.1 | 18 |
| Norway | 3.1 | 25 |
| Netherlands | 3.3 | 39 |
| U.S.A. | 3.3 | 40 |
| Canada | 4.2 | 70 |
| Turkey | 3.2 | 36 |
| Japan | 2.8 | — |
| Ceylon (M) | 3.2 | 25 |
| Jamaica | 3.4–4.2 | 48 |
| Taiwan | 3.9 | 62 |
| Thailand | 3.8 | 54 |
| Pakistan | 3.9 | 64 |
| Chile | 4.1 | 58 |
| India: | | |
| Central India (M & F) | 3.8 | 57 |
| New Delhi | 4.2 | 63 |
| Indonesia (M & F) | 4.3 | 66 |
| Korea | 4.4 | 80 |
| Ghana | 5.1 | 88 |
| Philippines | 5.0 | 71 |

* With very few exceptions, these studies date from 1960–63; none go back farther than 1957. Respondents are women, except where otherwise noted.

*Source:* W. Parker Mauldin, "Fertility studies: Knowledge, Attitude, and Practice," *Studies in Family Planning,* No. 7, Population Council, June 1965, p. 4.

around 2.5 percent per year, and the population would double every 25–31 years. It would quadruple by the year 2028. "Even if its fertility decline were so accelerated that the two-child family became the average at once for all new families, there would be continued substantial growth for at least 60 years" (Avery & Freedman, 1970, p. 1). The reason is that Taiwan, like most of the developing countries, has a very young population with many in early childbearing years. "With age-specific vital rates constant at the 1968 level, the population of Taiwan would increase from 14.0 million in 1970 to 23.0 million in 1988 to 37.4 million in 2008 and to 60.8 million in 2028" (p. 2). Since the people of Taiwan show no desire to limit families to an average of two children each, aroused leadership and family planning will not necessarily lead to zero growth.

> 3. Accelerated professional and research activity. . . . Universities, both in the United States and abroad, have undertaken large-scale and sus-

> tained research activities in the fields of family planning. Their activities cover the entire range of topics—medical, sociological, and psychological (p. 14).

The studies conducted by Ronald Freedman and his colleagues in Taiwan have provided a model for numerous other national research and action programs. The qualifications of the staff have yet to be equalled. Yet the decline in birth rates from 50.0 in 1951 to 32.7 in 1965 cannot be attributed to a campaign which began only in 1963. Davis (1967) estimates that perfect contraceptive behavior with present desires would produce over four births per woman. If life expectancy is raised to 70 years, the rate of natural increase would be close to 3 percent per year. Freedman correctly points out that a goal of four children as an average is halfway between the six children of older women and the two children needed for replacement of the parents, yet there is no indication that desires and actual reproduction will fall below the four-child average.

> 4. The slackening of progress in death control. . . . Further progress in death control will be slower, because the remaining problems are those for which a solution is more difficult or is as yet unknown (p. 14).

Once life expectancy reaches 65 or 70 years of age, further prolongation of life is either impossible or extremely costly, in terms of medical skills required for reduction of such conditions as heart disease and cancer. Nevertheless, the discussion in chapter 3 of mortality in the less developed countries clearly indicated that in most of these countries life expectancy had not only increased rapidly, but could be expected to increase much further. In the larger nations in Latin America life expectancy ranges between 50 and 59 years of age. In Asia the range is wider—from 35 to the low 60s, with India at 46. In Africa only one large nation reports a life expectancy of over 60; most are in the low 40s and low 50s. The very high proportion of young people in these countries means that as deaths come under increasing control, their crude death rates can be driven lower than in the advanced countries, where there are higher proportions of elderly persons.

> 5. A variety of sociological and psychological phenomena, previously unknown or underappreciated, are promoting the rapid adoption of family planning by the mass of the people (p. 15).

Bogue (1969) says:

> The overall picture seems to be that on almost every continent birth rates are falling. Moreover, they appear to be falling faster than death rates. Thus what little evidence we have, and as crude as it is, suggests that the

> peak has been passed; the growth of world population may be decelerating (p. 881).

As evidence he presents a graph of actual and projected trends in crude birth rates in 16 countries, most of which have had more rapid actual declines than anticipated. The graph includes such countries as Brunei, Malaya, Albania, Singapore, Taiwan, West Samoa, Guadeloupe, and Hong Kong. Although "almost every continent" is represented, not one large underdeveloped country is shown. The United States is included, even though Bogue himself had pointed out at a much earlier date (1963) that U.S. births would increase as the number of women aged 20–29 increased from 11 million in 1960 to 20 million in 1980. In fact, Enke (1969) has demonstrated by analyzing the age structure of U.S. women that even at an average of only two children each it would take until the year 2050 for this country to achieve zero population growth. The same principle holds for most countries: there are larger proportions of young persons available to produce children, so that even with two offspring per couple they will produce new lives much faster than the elderly die. Tomas Frejka (1970) has computed that "in order to attain and maintain a zero population growth, during the next two decades U.S. women must have an average of only slightly more than one child. This would mean that the crude birth rate would have to drop to under 10 per thousand population. That this could happen seems very unlikely" (p. 2).

> 6. Improved technology in contraception promotes massive adoption by uneducated people at a rapid pace. Oral contraceptives and the intrauterine devices have both proved to be highly acceptable after only short periods of instruction and familiarity (p. 15).

This is true, and for many years population specialists have been encouraged by reports of long line-ups of women at mobile family planning clinics. Not only could women be talked into birth-control devices, but they were willing to walk miles for the opportunity. However, recent studies of the childbearing history of participants at family planning clinics have found that women generally seek family planning relatively late in their childbearing careers. According to Davis (1967): "among 5,196 women coming to rural Punjabi family planning centers [in India], 38 percent were over 35 years old, 67 percent over 30. These women had married early, nearly a third of them before age 15; some 14 percent had eight or more living children when they reached the clinic, 51 percent had six or more" (p. 736).

As clinics become more available, women will probably come to them at younger ages and before they have had quite so many children. Nevertheless, there is no indication that they will seek advice before they have more than reproduced themselves. In the study cited above, only 1.8 percent of clinic users had fewer than three children.

The work of Ronald Freedman and his colleagues in Taiwan, and of others all around the world, has been significant. It does offer some hope—but is it enough?

## *POPULATION CONTROL*

Although the concept of population control is often implied, and the term is sometimes used in family planning literature, for some the "control" aspect conjures up a specter of invasion of the bedroom by the state. Control, however, need not mean coercion. It is not merely a choice between persons producing children as they please *or* state control; there is a wide range of possibilities between the two extremes. Every nation uses a system of rewards and punishments to help motivate people not to harm one another—to drive motor vehicles in specified places under specified rules, to pay taxes for the common good, and so forth.

Why haven't individuals voluntarily seen the wisdom of controlling their reproduction for the good of all? Garrett Hardin (1968) writes that in the case of population it is not true that each individual intent on his own gain will promote the public interest. He draws an analogy between the family interest in offspring and the tragedy of freedom in a commons:

> Picture a pasture open to all. It is to be expected that each herdsman will try to keep as many cattle as possible on the commons. Such an arrangement may work reasonably satisfactorily for centuries because tribal wars, poaching, and disease keep the numbers of both man and beast well below the carrying capacity of the land. Finally . . . social stability becomes a reality. . . . As a rational being, each herdsman seeks to maximize his gain. . . . The addition of each animal is a positive gain to the individual herdsman, . . . [while] the negative effects of overgrazing are shared by all. . . . The rational herdsman concludes that the only sensible course for him to pursue is to add another animal to his herd. And another; and another. . . . But this is the conclusion reached by each and every rational herdsman sharing a commons. Therein is the tragedy. . . . Freedom in a commons brings ruin to all. . . . To couple the concept of freedom to breed with the belief that everyone born has an equal right to the commons is to lock the world into a tragic course of action (pp. 1244–46).

Hardin has been condemned repeatedly for suggesting mutual coercion, agreed upon by the majority of the people affected, in order to escape the horror and ruin of the commons—our earth.

If, as the evidence overwhelmingly indicates, individuals want many children, then family planning will only help them achieve that goal.

There is no evidence that people will voluntarily limit family size for the good of the nation. It takes a fairly high level of education and responsibility to control reproduction for the "common" good. Since that kind of social responsibility has not become uniform throughout the world, family planning may be promoted while stalling for time, or nations may move beyond family planning.

The goals of the family planning movement have always been stated in terms of a reduction in the birth rate. National boards talk of reductions from 50 to 40 births per thousand (in Pakistan), from 40 to 25 births per thousand (in India), or of cutting population growth from 2.9 to 1.2 percent (in Korea). But, as Kingsley Davis (1967) points out, "under conditions of modern mortality, a crude birth rate of 25 to 30 per thousand will represent such a multiplication of people as to make use of the term 'population control' ironic. A rate of increase of 1.2 percent per year would allow South Korea's already dense population to double in less than 60 years. . . . A start must be made somewhere [but] the *next* steps are not considered" (p. 731). Zero population growth does not appear to be a popular goal among most religious groups, ethic communities, or nations. Indeed, Davis notes that family planning is often promoted in an attempt to prevent induced abortion, one of the surest means of controlling reproduction.

Family planning is individualistic planning; as such, it is not necessarily related to national and international goals. Although it enables families (if they so choose) to restrict the number of children produced, it offers only those means that are considered "respectable," not necessarily those that are most effective. The expensive search for "ideal" new contraceptives continues in the belief that only if some new means is found, will birth control be complete. Couples may, however, continue to want more children than the world can ultimately support. The "greatest good for the greatest number" is a logical and physical impossibility. The greatest number can only be supported at a concentration camp level of existence. Adequate nutrition to provide the energy needed for work and play cannot be provided to the maximum number of persons. The questions are where and how the limitation of quantity will come about. Population policies have worked to increase the numbers of people alive by improving health and lowering mortality and, as a result, allowing more births. In fact, birth rates in backward countries are more likely to be rising than falling. In Ridley's study of 26 underdeveloped countries (1965), the trend was upward in twice as many nations as downward.

Davis (1967) suggests:

> The things that make family planning acceptable are the very things that make it ineffective for population control. By stressing the right of parents to have the number of children they want, it evades the basic question of population policy, which is how to give societies the number of children

they need. By offering only the means for *couples* to control fertility, it neglects the means for societies to do so (p. 738).

Proponents of family planning have objected to the Davis critique on the grounds that family planning has yet to be given an all-out commitment. Although some means of birth control have been available in advanced countries for more than 50 years, neither developed nor underdeveloped countries have made a complete commitment to family planning. Opponents of complete reliance on the family planning clinic maintain that an all-out effort would have to include more than the present-day approach.

Certainly there are limits to the means that would be acceptable to control human population. No one seriously suggests using atomic war or spreading disease and misery to reduce population. There have, however, been many proposals to people to lower their reproductive ideals and performance.

## *BEYOND FAMILY PLANNING*

What can be done to produce a more rapid decline in population growth than is presently being achieved or than is in prospect, especially in the developing countries? Bernard Berelson (1969) has collated 29 proposals, some of which are very recent and others of which have been mentioned often in the literature.[2]

### *Extensions of Voluntary Fertility Control*

1. Maternal care centers in rural areas of developing countries could provide, as a central component of the program, family planning education and services aimed particularly at women with few children.

2. Induced abortion could be legalized. Abortions, under the direction of medical doctors, are cheaper and safer than childbirth. To this should be added possibility of legalized voluntary sterilization, already a popular means of fertility control in some countries (see Presser, 1970).

### *Establishment of Involuntary Fertility Control*

3. It might be possible for governments to regulate births through the use of some as yet unknown fertility control agent. A related suggestion

[2] See Berelson (1969) for the 79 original sources.

involves the addition of temporary sterilants to water supplies or staple foods.

4. National governments might issue licenses to have children, which could be bought and sold or passed around within families.

5. All girls could be temporarily sterilized by means of time-capsule contraceptives with reversability allowed only by specific approval. Popular vote might be used to determine desired population growth.

6. Compulsory sterilization of men with two or three living children could be combined with a requirement of induced abortion for all illegitimate pregnancies.

### *Intensified Educational Campaigns*

7. Various types of educational materials on population could be included in primary and secondary school systems.

8. National satellite television programs specifically for the purposes of spreading information on population and family planning and for promoting modern attitudes of planning in general could be promoted.

### *Incentive Programs*

9. Money or some other reward, for example a transistor radio, could be given for accepting sterilization or for the effective practice of contraception.

10. Governments might pay a bonus for child spacing or nonpregnancy during specific years, among certain age groups, or after a specific number of births.

### *Tax and Welfare Benefits and Penalties*

11. Maternity benefits could be withdrawn, perhaps after the birth of a specific number (*N*) of children.

12. Child or family allowances could be eliminated, either altogether or after the birth of N children.

13. A tax could be levied on all births after the Nth child.

14. Governmental provision of medical treatment, housing, scholarships, loans, subsidies, and so on could be limited to families with fewer than *N* children.

15. Tax benefits could be reversed to favor the unmarried and the parents of few rather than many children.

16. The state could provide to each family a specific limited number of years of free schooling at all levels to be allocated among the children within the family as desired.

17. Pensions could be initiated in the underdeveloped countries for poor parents with zero, one, or two children, as social security for their old age.

*Shifts in Social and Economic Institutions*

18. The minimum age at marriage could be raised by legislation, positive rewards for late marriage, or specific fines for early marriage.

19. The promotion or requirement of female participation in the labor force would make motherhood an additional burden and at the same time provide alternative interests for women.

20. The family's socializing function and its hold on members could be reduced.

21. Governments could license two types of marriage: one childless and easily dissolved, the other more stable with children permitted.

22. Social changes leading toward lower fertility—such as improved education, communication, and transportation—could be encouraged.

23. The further lowering of infant and child mortality may help parents realize that fewer children need be produced in order for some to survive.

*Political Channels and Organizations*

24. U.S. or international aid could be allocated on the basis of a nation's willingness to promote population limitation.

25. Certain national and international agencies could be reorganized to deal specifically with the problem of population growth.

26. Zero population growth could be promoted now as an ultimate goal, so current programs will move as quickly as possible in that direction.

*Augmented Research Efforts*

27. Research on the social means of achieving necessary fertility goals, that is, no more births than deaths, might be increased.

28. Research might be focused on predetermination of the sex of children. If parents want one boy and one girl, rather than simply two children, the odds are now that three children will be required to satisfy

that goal. The desire for two male offspring, common within the less developed nations, similarly inflates the average number of births.

29. Research on contraceptive technology could be increased. The production of a morning-after pill is much in demand (though technically it would be an abortifact rather than a contraceptive).[3]

These proposals vary in terms of their scientific, medical and technological viability; their political, administrative, and economic feasibility; their moral, ethical, and philosophical acceptability; and their presumed effectiveness. Some of the methods are already being used in various nations, where their effectiveness may be measured. Others would require new organizational approaches and new attitudes. Berelson (p. 539) concludes that "there is no easy way to achieve population control." Nevertheless, with so many possibilities to choose from, it must surely be possible to test the effectiveness of various approaches. Only a few of the proposals listed involve coercion. Most offer increased motivations to restrict family size. The suggestions are not mutually exclusive; many could be promoted simultaneously. Most of these proposals would simply facilitate and encourage the use of presently known methods of limiting procreation.

## *SUMMARY*

Each major theoretical perspective relating to population makes assumptions about individual and social group behavior. Malthusian theory implies that without positive motivation, the manipulation of rewards and punishments, families are likely to reproduce up to the limit of the food supply. Optimum theories disagree on the criteria by which the most advantageous level of population may be judged, but, like the Malthusian view, imply the necessity of positive national population policy. The theory of demographic transition, on the other hand, suggests that as economic development occurs, the birth rate will follow the death rate downward. Proponents of this view have understandably focused on economic development rather than on direct attempts to retard population growth.

Current national and international population policies are based on recognized or unrecognized theoretical or ideological perspectives. Although theories are by definition open to questioning and testing, ideologies are sets of beliefs to be accepted in toto. The two are not dichotomous cate-

[3] A thirtieth proposal appeared as Berelson was completing his article. Professor Chandrasekhar suggested that in honor of Gandhi's 100th anniversary "every married couple in India deny themselves sexual intercourse for a year. . . . Abstinence for a year would do enormous good to the individual and the country" (*The New York Times,* October 21, 1968; Berelson, p. 1969 n. 541).

gories, however, theories may in time come to be treated as ideologies and accepted without question. Conversely, ideologies may be weakened by overwhelming factual disproof.

Most of the world's great religions have little to say directly on the subject of population. The Roman Catholic Church, however, has taken a definite stand. Despite recognizing the problems created by world population growth, it has opposed national and international policies that would go beyond the rhythm method of birth control. Catholic nations had in effect formed an alliance with the communist bloc nations to prevent the United Nations from taking action in the area of family planning. In spite of Marxist dogma, the communist group has followed the Russian lead in reversing its position, apparently recognizing that population growth has impeded economic development.

United Nations agencies now will be able to continue gathering population data, but they will also be able to help those nations that ask for advice and help in family planning. The next question is whether each family's right to decide the number and spacing of children will lead to population limitation. Donald Bogue concludes that the world will achieve zero or near-zero growth by the year 2000, while Garrett Hardin and Kingsley Davis argue that family planning alone is unlikely to reach that goal.

It is not necessary to think in categorical terms of voluntary action versus coercion. Such a division can only obscure the many possible means of fertility reduction. In various aspects of life, human beings are encouraged to do what is best for themselves and for human group life. There are many different ways of motivating individuals and families to control reproduction.

In the matter of limiting population growth, the sooner the better. In only 20 years, while the United States avoided "offending the sensibilities" of some of its citizens and the United Nations discussions of the subject were blocked by Catholic-Communist opposition, world population grew by one billion persons. The number of hungry, sick, and illiterate people increased in spite of tremendous worldwide increases in food production, medical services, and educational programs. If our concern for improving the *quality* of human life is genuine, attention to the *quantity* of human beings can no longer be avoided.

## *REFERENCES*

AVERY, ROGER, AND RONALD FREEDMAN. 1970. Taiwan: Implications of fertility at replacement levels. *Studies in family planning*, no. 59 (November), 1–4. New York: The Population Council.

Berelson, Bernard. 1969. Beyond family planning. *Science,* 163 (February), 533–42.

Bogue, Donald J. 1963. Population growth in the United States. In *The population dilemma,* ed. Philip M. Hauser, pp. 70–93. Englewood Cliffs: Prentice-Hall.

———. 1967. The end of the population explosion. *The Public Interest,* No. 7 (Spring), pp. 11–20.

———. 1969. *Principles of demography.* New York: John Wiley & Sons.

Bouvier, Leon F. 1971. Let's not overdo not overdoing Z. P. G. In *Concerned Demography,* II, 5 (April), 37–42.

Brackett, James W. 1968. The evolution of Marxist theories of population: Marxism recognized the population problem. *Demography,* 5, no. 1, 158–73.

Chandrasekhar, Sripati. 1967. Communist China's demographic dilemma. In *Asia's population problems,* ed. S. Chandrasekhar, pp. 48-71. London: George Allen & Unwin.

Cole, William Graham. 1955. *Sex in Christianity and psychoanalysis.* New York: Oxford University Press.

Concepcion, Mercedes B., and Edmund M. Murphy. 1967. Wanted: A theory of the demographic transition. pp. 5–7. In *International union for the scientific study of population, contributed papers,* Sydney Conference, Australia (August 21–25).

Davis, Kingsley. 1955. Malthus and the theory of population. In *The language of social research,* ed. Paul F. Lazarsfeld and Morris Rosenberg, pp. 540–53. New York: Free Press.

———. 1963. The theory of change and response in modern demographic history, *Population Index* 29, no. 4 (October), 345–66.

———. 1967. Population policy: Will current programs succeed? *Science,* 158 (November 10), 730–39.

Durkheim, Emile. 1933. *The division of labor in society.* Trans. by George Simpson. New York: Macmillan, 1933. Originally written in 1898.

Enke, Stephen, and Richard G. Zind. 1969. Effect of fewer births on average income. *Journal of Biosocial Science,* I, 41–55.

Eversley, D. E. C. 1959. *Social theories of fertility and the Malthusian debate.* Oxford: Clarendon Press.

Fagley, Richard M. 1960. *The population explosion and Christian responsibility.* New York: Oxford University Press.

Freedman, Ronald, J. Y. Peng, Y. Takeshita, and T. H. Sun. 1963. Fertility trends in Taiwan: Tradition and change. *Population Studies,* 16, no. 3 (March), 219–36.

Frejka, Tomas. 1970. United States: The implications of zero population growth. *Studies in Family Planning* no. 60 (December), 1–4.

Guzevaty, A. 1966. Population problems in developing countries. *International Affairs* (September), pp. 52–58.

Hardin, Garrett. 1968. The tragedy of the commons. *Science,* 163 (December 13), pp. 1243–48.

Kirk, Dudley. 1966. Factors affecting Moslem natality. In B. Berelson *et al.,*

*Family Planning and Population Programs*. Chicago and London: The University of Chicago Press, pp. 561–79.

LORIMER, FRANK. 1969. Issues of population policy, In *The population dilemma*, ed. Philip M. Hauser, pp. 168–206. Englewood Cliffs, N.J.: Prentice-Hall.

MALTHUS, THOMAS ROBERT. 1960. *On population*. Reproduction of 7th edition, 1872, ed. and introduced by Gertrude Himmelfarb. New York: The Modern Library. (Originally published in 1798.)

MARX, KARL. 1933. *Critique of the Gotha Programme*. New York: International Publishers.

———. and F. Engels. 1939. *The German Ideology*, ed. R. Pascal. New York: International Publishers.

*Message from the President of the United States relative to population growth*, House of Representatives Document No. 91–39, 91st Congress, 1st Session, July 21, 1969. Washington, D.C.: Government Printing Office.

NORTH, ROBERT C. 1965. Communist China and the population problem. In *The population crises*, eds. Larry K. Y. Ng and Stuart Mudd, pp. 89–99. Bloomington, Ind.: Indiana University Press.

NORTMAN, DOROTHY. 1970. Population and family planning programs: A factbook. *Population Council Reports on Population/Family Planning* (July).

PETERSEN, WILLIAM. 1964. *The politics of population*. New York: Doubleday.

———. 1969. *Population*. New York: Macmillan.

POPULATION REFERENCE BUREAU. 1967. The United Nations on population—1966. *Population Bulletin*, 23 (February).

———. 1967b. Soviet population theory from Marx to Kosygin. *Population Bulletin*, 23, 4.

———. 1968. Do Roman Catholic countries have the highest birth rates? *Population Profile* (July), pp. 1–7.

PRESSER, HARRIET B. 1970. Voluntary sterilization: A world view. *Population Council Report on Population/Family Planning* no. 5 (July).

RIDLEY, JEANNE, 1965. Recent natality trends in underdeveloped societies. In *Public health and population change*, ed. Ships and Ridley, pp. 143–73. Pittsburgh: University of Pittsburgh Press.

SNOW, EDGAR. 1965. Population control in China: An interview with Chou Enlai. In the population crisis, eds. Larry K. Y. Ng and Stuart Mudd, pp 99–103, Bloomington, Ind.: Indiana University Press.

UNITED NATIONS, Department of Economic and Social Affairs. 1953. Determinants and consequences of population trends. *United Nations Population Studies* No. 17, ST/SUA/SerA/17.

UNITED NATIONS. 1966. Official Records of the Economic and Social Council, *Thirty-ninth Session* 9, Supplement No. 9 (E/4019). (December). New York: United Nations.

UNITED STATES Bureau of the Census. 1970. *Statistical Abstract of the United States, 1970*. Washington, D.C.: U.S. Department of Commerce.

UNITED STATES Commission on Population Growth and the American Future. 1971. An interim report to the president and the congress. Washington D.C.: Government Printing Office.

# Suggestions for Further Reading

*CURRENT POPULATION PROBLEMS:*

BERELSON, BERNARD, *et al.*, eds., *Family Planning and Population Programs.* Chicago: University of Chicago Press, 1966, 839 pp. Reports the progress and problems of programs in specific countries.

DAY, LINCOLN AND ALICE DAY, *Too Many Americans.* New York: Dell Publishing Co., Inc., 1965. A brief examination of the problems of population growth in the U.S.

The Editors of *The Progressive, The Crisis of Survival.* New York: William Morrow and Company, 1970, 256 pp. Overpopulation is examined as one of the major threats to the survival of mankind.

EHRLICH, PAUL AND ANNE EHRLICH, *Population, Resources, Environment: Issues in Human Ecology.* San Francisco: W. H. Freeman and Company, 1970. Population biologists present a strong case for population control.

FAGLEY, RICHARD M., *The Population Explosion and Christian Responsibility.* New York: Oxford University Press, 1960, 234 pp. Presents the historical and recently revised positions of Christian churches.

FREEDMAN, RONALD, ed., *Population: The Vital Revolution.* Garden City, N. Y.: Doubleday and Company, 1964, 274 pp. Brief articles by a number of experts cover recent trends for the world and for specific areas and nations of the world.

HARDIN, GARRETT, *Population, Evolution, and Birth Control: A Collage of Controversial Ideas*. San Francisco: W. H. Freeman and Company, 1964, 380 pp. 123 essays likely to increase the controversy in the subject areas.

HAUSER, PHILIP M., ed., for The American Assembly, *The Population Dilemma*, Englewood Cliffs, N. J.: Prentice-Hall, Inc., 1969, 1963, 206 pp. A review of the facts of population growth, problems for economic development, resource adequacy and population control, presented by a panel of experts.

MALTHUS, THOMAS, JULIAN HUXLEY, AND FREDERICK OSBORN, *Three Essays on Population*. New York: New American Library, 1960, 144 pp. A short version of Malthus's classic is combined with recent essays on the subject with a focus on the underdeveloped nations.

National Academy of Sciences, Study Committee of the Office of the Foreign Secretary, *Rapid Population Growth: Consequences and Policy Implications*. Baltimore: The Johns Hopkins Press, 1971, 680 pp. Research papers by scholars representing diverse disciplines describe the problems and implications of increasing human numbers. The summary and recommendations brought together under the direction of Dr. Roger Revelle comprise Vol. I, with the research papers and details in Vol. II.

OSBORN, FAIRFIELD, ed., *Our Crowded Planet: Essays on the Pressures of Population*. Garden City, N. Y.: Doubleday and Company, Inc., 1962, 240 pp. Essays on the relationship between population and economics, humanities, mores, peace, biological principles, and religion.

POHLMAN, EDWARD, *The Psychology of Birth Planning*. Cambridge, Mass: Schenkman Publishing Company, Inc., 1969, 444 pp. Discusses the general desire for children, the effects of unwanted conceptions, and psychological aspects of overpopulation.

PRICE, DANIEL O., ed., *The 99th Hour: The Population Crisis in the United States*. Chapel Hill: The University of North Carolina Press, 1967, 130 pp. Examines the challenge to quality of life posed by population growth in the U. S.

SZABADY, EGON, ed., *World View of Population Problems*. Budapest: Demographic Committee of the Hungarian Academy of Sciences and Demographic Research Institute, 1968, 447 pp. Leading demographers from many nations discuss current research and issues in the field.

UDALL, STEWART L., 1976: *Agenda for Tomorrow*. New York: Harcourt Brace Jovanovich, 1968, 157 pp. The former U.S. Secretary of the Interior suggests that the size of the human population is the key to the quality of the environment.

WRONG, DENNIS H., *Population and Society*, 3rd ed. New York: Random House, Inc., 1967, 134 pp. A brief introduction to the main components of population study.

YOUNG, LOUISE B., ed., *Population in Perspective*. New York: Oxford University Press, 1968, 560 pp. An anthology of views on population from writers of many disciplines.

*STANDARD POPULATION AND DEMOGRAPHY TEXTS:*

BOGUE, DONALD J., *Principles of Demography*. New York: John Wiley and Sons, 1969, 917 pp. Demography and its subfields are presented in a systematic fashion, utilizing comparative data.

Heer, David M., *Society and Population.* Englewood Cliffs, N. J: Prentice-Hall, Inc., 1968, 118 pp. A brief text indicating the importance of the study of population to other subject areas of sociology.

Petersen, William, *Population.* New York: Macmillan Co., 1969, 697 pp. An intellectually stimulating, detailed text.

Thomlinson, Ralph, *Population Dynamics: Causes and Consequences of World Demographic Change.* New York: Random House, Inc., 1965, 576 pp. A standard text for the study of population.

Thompson, Warren S., and David T. Lewis, *Population Problems,* 5th ed. New York: McGraw-Hill Book Co., 1965, 594 pp. A very readable undergraduate text.

*READERS FOR THE GENERAL STUDY OF POPULATION:*

Ford, Thomas R. and Gordon F. DeJong, eds., *Social Demography.* Englewood Cliffs, N.J.: Prentice-Hall, Inc. 1970, 690 pp. These readings demonstrate the relationship between population variables and social institutions, attitudes and class and ethnic differences.

Hauser, Philip M. and Otis Dudley Duncan, eds., *The Study of Population: An Inventory and Appraisal.* Chicago: University of Chicago Press, 1959. A collection of articles by eminent authors on the nature of demography as a science and its development and curent status in various nations of the world. The book also includes a look at the areas of specialization within demography and its relationship to other social sciences.

Heer, David M., ed., *Readings on Population.* Englewood Cliffs, N. J.: Prentice-Hall, Inc. 1968. A selection of articles on urbanization, fertility, mortality, and migration to accompany his text.

Nam, Charles B., ed., *Population and Society: A Textbook of Selected Readings.* Boston: Houghton Mifflin Co., 1968. A broad selection of papers dealing with the elements of population analysis and the interrelationships between population and selected areas of social life.

Spengler, Joseph J. and Otis Dudley Duncan, eds., *Demographic Analysis: Selected Readings.* New York: The Free Press, 1956. A massive collection of articles dealing with empirical rather than theoretical studies of population.

*METHODS OF POPULATION ANALYSIS:*

Barclay, George W., *Techniques of Population Analysis.* New York: John Wiley and Sons, 1958, 311 pp. A clearly written introduction to the measurements used in demographic research. Persons without advanced mathematical background or experience in analyzing demographic statistics will find this a useful reference book.

Benjamin, Bernard, *Demographic Analysis.* New York: Frederick Praeger, 1969, 160 pp. A short presentation of demographic methods.

Keyfitz, Nathan, *Introduction to Mathematics of Population.* Reading, Mass: Addison-Wesley, 1968, 450 pp. An advanced and systematic presentation of quantitative methods used in population analysis.

*HISTORICAL DEMOGRAPHY:*

CARR-SAUNDERS, ALEXANDER M., *World Population: Past Growth and Present Trends.* London: Frank Cass & Co., 1964, 336 pp. Population history during the modern era up to the early 1930's.

GLASS, DAVID V. AND D. E. C. EVERSLEY, eds., *Population in History—Essays in Historical Demography.* Chicago: Aldine Publishing Co., 1965, 692 pp. Twenty-seven essays on the history of population of Europe and the U. S.

HIMES, NORMAN E., *Medical History of Contraception.* New York: Gamut Press, 1964, 521 pp. The history of contraception with medical, social and economic implications.

WRIGLEY, E. A., *Population and History.* New York: McGraw-Hill Book Co., 1969, 234 pp. An easy introduction to the special methods and contribution of historical demography to our understanding of the past and the process of social change by one of the world's foremost historical demographers.

*PERIODICALS AND BIBLIOGRAPHIES:*

*Demography.* Population Association of America, P. O. Box 14182, Benjamin Franklin Station, Washington, D. C. 20044. Quarterly. Of primary interest to professional demographers, its manuscripts represent a wide range of topics.

ELDRIDGE, HOPE T., *The Materials of Demography: A Selected and Annotated Bibliography.* New York: International Union for the Scientific Study of Population and the Population Association of America, 1959, 222 pp. Significant works prior to publication are listed under categories of general population analysis, population problems and theories, regional studies, demographic methods, fertility, mortality, migration, programs and policies.

*Journal of Biosocial Science.* The Galton Foundation, Blackwell Scientific Publications, Ltd., 5 Alfred Street, Oxford, England. Quarterly. Articles and book reviews focus on the relationship between biological and social factors and eugenic considerations.

*Journal of Marriage and the Family.* National Council on Family Relations, 1219 University Avenue, S. E. Minneapolis, Minn. Quarterly. Articles on family size, birth rates, child spacing and attitudes toward fertility are relevant to population study.

*Milbank Memorial Fund Quarterly.* Milbank Memorial Fund, 40 Wall St. New York, N. Y. Quarterly. Scholarly papers analyzing demographic trends and family planning programs.

*Population Bulletin.* Population Reference Bureau, 1755 Massachusetts Ave. N. W., Washington, D. C. Published six times a year covering topics of current interest to students and teachers.

*Population Chronicle.* Population Council and International Institute for the Study of Human Reproduction, Columbia University. Population Council, 245 Park Ave. N. Y., N. Y. Monthly. A free newsletter aimed at the general public.

*Population Index*. Office of Population Research, Princeton University and Population Association of America, Inc. Office of Population Research, Princeton University, Princeton, N. J. Quarterly. Provides both in-depth articles and a comprehensive listing of the latest literature in all phases of population study.

*Population Studies*. Population Investigation Committee, London School of Economics, Houghton St., Aldwych, London W. C. 2, England. Published three times a year, the articles are contributed by professional demographers from all over the world.

*Social Biology* (formerly Eugenics Quarterly). American Eugenics Society, University of Chicago Press, 5750 Ellis Ave., Chicago, Ill. Quarterly. Articles report biological and socio-cultural factors affecting human populations.

# Index